A COMPANION TO YOUR STUDY OF THE DOCTRINE AND COVENANTS

VOL. 2 APPENDIXES

Daniel H. Ludlow

Deseret Book Company
Salt Lake City, Utah
1978

© 1978 by Daniel H. Ludlow
All rights reserved
Printed in the United States of America
ISBN 0-87747-729-9
Library of Congress Catalog Card No. 78-64752

CONTENTS

APPENDIX A
DEFINITIONS AND EXPLANATIONS OF KEY WORDS AND TERMS

DEFINITIONS AND EXPLANATIONS OF KEY WORDS AND TERMS

Aaronic Priesthood (*see also* Priesthood)

There is only one priesthood of God, and it has two major divisions: the Melchizedek and the Aaronic. The Aaronic Priesthood is the "lesser priesthood" in the sense that the members of this priesthood do not have the same keys or directing power as do those who hold the Melchizedek Priesthood. The keys of the Aaronic Priesthood pertain to the preparatory gospel of preaching faith, repentance, and baptism of water for the remission of sins. This division of the priesthood receives its name from Aaron, the brother of Moses.

Selected Quotations

"The Aaronic Priesthood holds the keys of the preparatory Gospel. . . . These keys were conferred upon Aaron and have descended through his posterity from generation to generation until John the Baptist, who held the keys by divine right and through blessing as well as lineage. Had the Church of Jesus Christ been fully organized and properly organized with the Jews in John's day, that is, when he was preaching in the wilderness, instead of the Jews being in a dreadful state of apostasy, John the Baptist would have taken his place by right as the presiding priest of the Aaronic order. But the Jews recognized him not, and failed to understand the nature of his authority, even as they failed to comprehend the authority of our Lord. By right of his authority, John laid the foundation for the overthrow of their power and kingdom, which was based on a false foundation. (D&C 84:28.) Had they accepted John, then also would they have accepted the Savior. There is perfect order in the Kingdom of God, and he recognizes the authority of his servants. It was for this reason John, who acted under the direction of Peter, James and John, came to Joseph Smith and Oliver Cowdery and restored the Aaronic Priesthood, which John held in the dispensation of the Meridian of Time. (*HC* 1:40.)" (Joseph Fielding Smith, *CHMR* 1:64.)

"After the children of Israel came out of Egypt and while they were sojourning in the wilderness, Moses received a commandment from the Lord to take Aaron and his sons and ordain them and consecrate them as priests for the people. (Ex. 28.) At that time the males of the entire tribe of Levi were chosen to be the priests instead of the first-born of all the tribes, and Aaron and his sons were given the presidency over the Priesthood thus conferred. Since that time it has been known as the Priesthood of Aaron, including the Levitical Priesthood. The males of the tribe of Levi . . . were to be invested with authority from that time forth in Israel. It should be remembered that the Melchizedek Priesthood was withdrawn from the people when Moses was taken away, so that the Aaronic Priesthood remained with the carnal law, or the law of Moses, until the coming of Jesus Christ. In the calling of Aaron and his sons, the Lord made it known that this presiding authority over this Priesthood should be handed down from father to son. This was true also of the Levitical, which is a division of the Aaronic. All who were of the tribe of Levi were entitled to be priests and to officiate in some capacity in this authority. In making the change and choosing the Levites instead of the first-born of all the tribes, the Lord said: [Num. 3:6, 12-13, 45-58 quoted.]

"The Lord had promised to make Israel a nation of priests, but because of their rebellion and failure to hearken to his word, in his anger, he took the Melchizedek Priesthood away with Moses, and left the people subject to the ministrations of the tribe of Levi. The prophets in Israel, however, received special ordination and were from the several tribes. . . .

"The Levitical Priesthood conferred on the men of the tribe of Levi was subject to the authority of Aaron and was part of the Aaronic Priesthood. It was the duty of the Levites to assist the priests of Aaron. Their duties are stated in the book of Numbers. [Num. 3:5-9 quoted.]" (Joseph Fielding Smith, *CHMR* 1:64-65.)

"We should all realize that there is nothing in the world more powerful than the priesthood of God. However, I fear that too often some seem to take it for granted as a *right* and not a *privilege.* Many seem to feel that *age* should determine when they are entitled to receive the priesthood or advance in it.

"Let us just stop and think for a moment of the great importance the Lord placed on the Aaronic Priesthood when it was restored. John the Baptist, who baptized the Savior, was sent to restore the Aaronic Priesthood. Placing his hands upon the heads of Joseph Smith and Oliver Cowdery, he said: [D&C 13 quoted.]

"We should all realize that great works of righteousness can be and are performed by the Aaronic Priesthood. President Wilford Woodruff said: 'I desire to impress upon you the fact that it does not make any difference whether a man is a Priest or an Apostle, if he magnifies his calling. A Priest holds the keys of the ministering of angels. Never in my life, as an Apostle, as a Seventy, or as an Elder, have I ever had more of the protection of the Lord than while holding the office of a Priest.' (*MS* 53:629.)" (N. Eldon Tanner, *Ensign,* May 1976, pp. 41-42.)

Scriptural References: D&C 13:1; 107:1, 6, 13, 20, 87; JS-H 1:66-72.

Adam; Michael; Michael the Archangel; the Ancient of Days

Adam is the earthly name of the personage of spirit in the pre-earthly existence who was known as Michael. He is also known by the title Michael the Archangel and the Ancient of Days.

Adam was a member of the Council of the Gods in the pre-earthly existence. He was chosen and foreordained to be the first physical man upon this earth, and thus became the father of all mankind in the sense that all others since Adam and Eve are their descendants.

Adam is one of the greatest men who has ever lived on the earth; because of his faithfulness, he will rule as a god in the hereafter. This Latter-day Saint belief is in sharp contrast to the creeds of many churches, which state that Adam is depraved and "next to the devil."

Adam has appeared on the earth in this dispensation (D&C 128:20) and will appear again at Adam-ondi-Ahman when all the keys of the priesthood that have ever been placed upon the earth will be returned to him so he can return them to Jesus Christ, whose right it is to rule upon the earth. This great event will take place shortly before the second coming of Jesus Christ.

Selected Quotations

"Michael, who is Adam, holds the keys of salvation for the human family, under the direction and counsel of Jesus Christ, who is the Holy One of Zion. [See 78:15-16.] Adam will, when the earth is cleansed and purified and becomes a celestial globe, preside over the children of men, who are of his posterity. He is Adam, 'the prince, the arch-angel.' In the eternities before this earth was formed he was the arch-angel. He became Adam when he came to this earth to be the father of the human family. (D&C 107:54-57.)

"The Prophet Joseph Smith said of Adam: 'Commencing with Adam, who was the first man, who is spoken of in Daniel as the "Ancient of Days," or in the other words, the first and oldest of all, the great progenitor of whom it is said in another place is Michael. . . . Adam holds the keys of all the dispensations of the fulness of times, i.e. the dispensations of all times have been and will be revealed through him from the beginning.' (*TPJS,* pp. 167-68.)" (Joseph Fielding Smith, *CHMR* 1:310.)

"In the 107th Section, the Lord speaks of Adam as 'Michael, the Prince, the Archangel,' and says that he shall be a prince over the nations forever. We may with perfect propriety call him prince, the ancient of days, or even God in the meaning of the words of Christ, which I have just quoted: [D&C 78:16] but we do not worship him, we worship the same God that he worshipped." (Anthon H. Lund, *CR,* Oct. 1902, p. 81.)

"Adam, at this meeting, was sustained as Michael, the Prince, the Archangel. *Michael* means, 'Who is as God.' Adam was created in the image, after the likeness of God, and the name expresses this wonderful fact. *Prince* is a title. Jesus, the Son of God, is the *Prince of Peace.* Adam, Son of God, is also a prince. That title was, later, given to each of the twelve heads of the tribes of Israel (Num. 1:16), who were to the people of the Old Covenant what the Twelve Apostles were, and are, to the Church of Christ. The Apostles are princes in the kingdom of God, and Adam was sustained as Michael, the Prince.

"*Archangel* . . . denotes an office. As one of the arch-angels, or chief messengers, of God, Adam has a special work to perform in connection with the divine plan of salvation. In Daniel 10:13-21 he is represented as having special charge of the Hebrew nation, and in Dan. 12:1 it is said that he will 'stand up' for that nation, for its deliverance, at the time of the end. In Jude 9 he is said to have disputed with Satan about the body of Moses, and in Rev. 12 he is represented as being at war with the adversary." (Smith and Sjodahl, *DCC,* p. 706.)

"It is held by some that Adam was not the first man upon this earth, and that the original human being was a development from lower orders of the animal creation. These, however, are the theories of men. The word of the Lord declares that Adam was 'the first man of all men' [Moses 1:34], and we are therefore in duty bound to regard him as the primal parent of our race." (First Presidency, *IE,* November 1909, pp. 75-81.)

Scriptural References: D&C 27:11; 107:41-56; 116:1; 128:18-21; Dan. 7:9-13; 10:13-21; 12:1.

Adam-ondi-Ahman

This term is unique in this dispensation to Latter-day Saints and is a remnant of the Adamic language (the original language taught to Adam by God). In this valley, declared by the Prophet Joseph Smith to be located at Spring Hill, Daviess County, Missouri, Adam called together his children and blessed them three years before his death, and here Adam shall again come to visit his people.

Selected Quotations

"We have then an understanding that [Adam ondi Ahman] was the place where Adam dwelt. . . . 'Ondi-Ahman' . . . means the place where Adam dwelt. 'Ahman' signifies God. The whole term means Valley of God where Adam dwelt. It is the original language spoken by Adam, as revealed to the Prophet Joseph." (Orson Pratt, *JD* 18:342.)

"The valley of Adam-ondi-Ahman . . . was located on the western hemisphere of our globe . . . about fifty miles north of Jackson County, in the State of Missouri. The Lord has revealed to us that Adam dwelt there towards the latter period of his probation. Whether he had lived in that region of country from the earliest period of his existence on the earth, we know not. He might have lived thousands of miles distant in his early days." (Orson Pratt, *JD* 16:48.)

"I saw Adam in the valley of Adam-ondi-Ahman. He

called together his children and blessed them with a patriarchal blessing. The Lord appeared in their midst, and he (Adam) blessed them all and foretold what should befall them to the latest generation." (Joseph Smith, *HC* 3:388.)

"Wednesday, Oct. 3rd, the camp traveled to Ambrosial Creek where they were visited by the Prophet, his counselors Sidney Rigdon and Hyrum Smith, and Elder Brigham Young. That evening one of the brethren said, by the Spirit of the Lord:

" 'Brethren, your long and tedious journey is now ended; you are now on the public square of Adam-ondi-Ahman. This is the place where Adam blessed his posterity, when they rose up and called him Michael, the Prince, the Archangel, and he being full of the Holy Ghost predicted what should befall his posterity to the latest generations.' (See D&C 107:53-55.)" (Joseph Fielding Smith, *CHMR* 2:106.)

Scriptural References: D&C 78:15, 20; 95:17; 107:53; 116:1; 117:8, 11; Dan. 7:9-14.

Adultery; adulterous (*see also* Sex Sins; Ten Commandments)

The power to procreate or to have children is one of the greatest gifts of God to man in this physical, earthly existence. The Lord through his prophets has given clear and definite instructions concerning the purposes and the conditions for the exercise of this power. Inasmuch as the righteous exercise of these powers has the potential for a great blessing, according to the eternal law of justice that indicates that every law has equal and opposite consequences, the unrighteous use of these powers has the possibility of serious punishment or suffering. Adultery is one of the most serious unrighteous uses of the powers of procreation; it is so serious a sin that, if not repented of, it becomes unforgivable.

Selected Quotations

"A case of adultery is different. That sin is one of impurity where one or both offenders are married. Anciently this wickedness was punished by death so the Lord commanded. (Lev. 20:10.) 'Sexual union is lawful in wedlock, and if participated in with right intent is honorable and sanctifying. But without the bonds of marriage, sexual indulgence is a debasing sin, abominable in the sight of Deity.' (President Joseph F. Smith, *Gospel Doctrine,* pp. 386-7.)

" 'We accept without reservation or qualification the affirmation of Deity, through an ancient Nephite prophet: "For I the Lord God, delight in the chastity of women. And whoredoms are an abomination before me; thus saith the Lord of Hosts." (Jacob 2:28.) . . . We hold that sexual sin is second only to the shedding of innocent blood in the category of personal crimes; and that the adulterer shall have no part in the exaltation of the blessed.' (President Joseph F. Smith, *Gospel Doctrine,* p. 388.)" (Smith and Sjodahl, *DCC,* pp. 236-37.)

"How severe is the judgment on the man who has committed adultery, even though he apparently is repentant? In the Doctrine and Covenants, 42:24-26, the Lord has given us a key to this situation. If a person commits adultery and then repents with all his heart, he may be forgiven. If he repeats the offense, he is not to be forgiven, but is to be cast out. As I read it, the Lord has not provided that, under those circumstances, he can come back again.

"Now this revelation was given *before the endowment* was made known. Since that time when a man is married in the temple, he takes a solemn covenant before God, angels, and witnesses that he will keep the law of chastity. Then if he violates that covenant it is not easy to receive forgiveness. I call your attention to this statement by the Prophet Joseph Smith: 'If a man commit adultery, he cannot receive the celestial kingdom of God. Even if he is saved in any kingdom, it cannot be the celestial kingdom.' (*HC* 6:81.)

"Of course, a man may, according to the Doctrine and Covenants, 132:26, receive forgiveness, if he is willing to pay the penalty for such a crime: that is he 'shall be destroyed in the flesh, and shall be delivered unto the buffetings of Satan unto the day of redemption,' which is the time of the resurrection.

"We have been taught that adultery is a crime second only to the shedding of innocent blood. We cannot treat it lightly." (Joseph Fielding Smith, *DS* 2:93-94, 99.)

"The Lord in His time and in ours has put adultery and fornication side by side. Both are cardinal sins.

"The Church has from the beginning demanded of its youth—male and female—one standard only, absolute continence until proper marriage has legalized and hallowed the sexual relations.

"Yet there is forgiveness for the sinner who truly repents. God's mercy is just as boundless as his justice. To the woman taken in adultery, condemned to death by the Mosaic law, Jesus said: 'Go, and sin no more.' (John 8:11.) But the heart must be ripened in repentance before forgiveness can come, and sorrow alone is not repentance. A new and righteous life must be led.

"Church members, young and old, the Lord demands that you be chaste; the Church requires chastity from you under penalty of disfellowshiping and excommunication. If any have already sinned, your brethren and sisters stand ready and anxious to forgive if you shall come with a repentant heart and contrite spirit." (J. Reuben Clark, *CR*, October 1938, pp. 136-38.)

Scriptural References: D&C 42:24-25; Matt. 5:27-28, 32; 12:39; 16:4; 19:9, 18; Alma 23:3; 30:10.

Adversity; chastening; conflicts; opposition; tribulations; trials

One of the purposes of a physical mortal existence is to learn the differences between opposites—good and evil, pleasure and pain, bitter and sweet, sorrow and joy, disappointment and success, sickness and health, adversity and serenity. The possibility of opposites, then, is part of the plan of progression of our loving merciful Father in heaven for his children.

Selected Quotations

"Just as Jesus had to endure affliction to prove himself, so must all men endure affliction to prove themselves.

" 'Abel was slain for his righteousness. . . . Abraham . . . was laid upon the iron bedstead for slaughter; and . . . cast into the fire. . . . Moses . . . was driven from his country and kindred. Elijah had to flee his country. . . . Daniel was cast into a den of lions: Micah was fed on the bread of affliction; and Jeremiah was cast into the filthy hole under the Temple. . . . All the Saints . . . prophets and apostles, have had to come up through great tribulation. . . .' (*TPJS*, pp. 260-61.)

"From his own experiences, the Prophet Joseph was eminently qualified to talk about affliction, and this he most eloquently did.

"President Brigham Young is quoted as observing that the Prophet was more perfect in 38 years, with the severe tribulation through which he passed, than he would have been in a thousand years without it. . . .

"If we can bear our afflictions with the understanding, faith, and courage, and in the spirit in which they bore theirs, we shall be strengthened and comforted in many ways. We shall be spared the torment which accompanies the mistaken idea that all suffering comes as chastisement for transgression. We shall be comforted by the knowledge that we are not enduring, nor will we be required to endure, the suffering of the wicked who are to 'be cast out into outer darkness [where] there shall be weeping, and wailing, and gnashing of teeth.' (Alma 40:13.)

"We can draw assurance from the Lord's promise that 'he that is faithful in tribulation, the reward of the same is greater in the kingdom of heaven.' " (Marion G. Romney, *IE,* December 1969, pp. 67-68.)

"The diamond is enhanced and made more valuable with polishing. Steel is made harder and more valuable through tempering. So also opposition builds the character of man. All progress is made by overcoming an opposing force. Lehi said to his son Jacob: 'For it must needs be, that there is an opposition in all things. . . .' (2 Ne. 2:11.) Opposition, then, is good for us as long as we don't seek it for opposition's sake." (Eldred G. Smith, *Ensign,* January 1974, p. 63.)

"Strength comes by courageously adjusting our lives to our trials, and by so doing we are brought closer to God.

"We cannot afford to meet adversities with impatience or bitterness. President Brigham Young taught that 'if the Saints could realize things as they are when they are called to pass through trials, and to suffer what they call sacrifices, they would acknowledge them to be the greatest blessings that could be bestowed upon them. . . .

" '. . . without the opposite and they could not know enjoyment; they could not realize happiness. . . . If they should not taste the bitter, how could they realize the sweet? They could not!' (*JD* 2:301-2.)

"If our existence terminated with death, adversities might tend to overwhelm us. But with the gospel as a foundation and with faith in a just God who watches over all, each one may receive the comfort and acquire the fortitude to meet the vicissitudes of life." (ElRay L. Christiansen, *IE,* June 1969, p. 66.)

"Now, we find many people critical when a righteous person is killed, a young father or mother is taken from a family, or when violent deaths occur. Some become bitter when oft-repeated prayers seem unanswered. Some lose faith and turn sour when solemn administrations by holy men seem to be ignored and no restoration seems to come from repeated prayer circles. But if all the sick were healed, if all the righteous were protected and the wicked destroyed, the whole program of the Father would be annulled and the basic principle of the Gospel, free agency, would be ended.

"If pain and sorrow and total punishment immediately followed the doing of evil, no soul would repeat a misdeed. If joy and peace and rewards were instantaneously given the doer of good, there could be no evil—all would do good and not because of the rightness of doing good. There would be no test of strength, no development of character, no growth of powers, no free agency, only satanic controls. . . .

"It is evident that even the righteous will not always be healed and even those of great faith will die when it is according to the purpose of God. Joseph Smith died in his thirties as did the Savior. Solemn prayers were answered negatively." (Spencer W. Kimball, *BYUSY,* Dec. 6, 1955.)

"I don't know all the reasons the Lord tries us in this life, but there are two or three that come to mind. First, I think he wants to know whom he can trust.

"Secondly, the Lord tells us in the Doctrine and Covenants section 122 that adversity came to Joseph Smith to give him experience.

"Thirdly, I believe that only through such experiences can a person develop true charity. And I mean by *charity* the pure love of Christ." (Loren C. Dunn, *Ensign,* May 1974, p. 28.)

"As we contemplate these devastating conditions rampant in the world today—the wars, death, suffering, poverty, and disease—and while many question why God permits such troublous conditions to plague us, let us remember that man himself is responsible. Even though the innocent suffer with the wicked in many instances, all the strife and contention and wickedness abroad in the land today is because man has chosen to follow Satan instead of accepting and living according to the teachings of Jesus Christ. From the beginning we have been told that there must be opposition in all things in order that we might progress according to God's plan for us." (N. Eldon Tanner, *Ensign,* July 1973, p. 10.)

"After some of the persecutions and the evidence of the

power of evil over our first missionaries in London, these missionaries returned to the Prophet to seek an answer as to why these experiences with evil spirits had come to them. Had they done some things wrong that the evil had thus tried to overthrow them? And the Prophet replied, 'I rejoiced when I heard of your experiences because I have passed through similar experiences, and I want to say this to you: the nearer a person approaches the Lord, a greater power will be manifested by the adversary to prevent the accomplishment of his purposes.'

"That is what the Master meant when he said: 'Blessed are ye, when men shall revile you, and persecute you, and shall say all manner of evil against you falsely, for my sake. Rejoice, and be exceeding glad: for great is your reward in heaven: for so persecuted they the prophets which were before you.' [Matt. 5:11-12.]" (Harold B. Lee, *CR,* October 1955, pp. 56-57.)

Scriptural References: D&C 103:13; 121:7; 128:21.

Advocate; Jesus Christ as the Advocate (*see also* Jesus Christ)

The basic meaning of *advocate* is "to represent, plead for, or defend another." Jesus Christ is our Advocate with the Father in all these senses. We not only chose Jesus Christ as our Advocate in the pre-earth councils (he was chosen from before the foundations of the earth), but he also earned the right and assumed the responsibility of being the Advocate of all mankind through his atonement.

Selected Quotations

"Adam was banished because of his transgression from the presence of the Father. The scriptures say he became spiritually dead—that is, he was shut out from the presence of God. From that time on Jesus Christ comes on the scene as our advocate, pleading for us as our mediator through his ministry and labors to reconcile us, to bring us into agreement with God, his Father." (Joseph Fielding Smith, *AGQ* 1:16.)

"Jesus is the advocate before God for mankind—the Mediator standing to plead the cause of the children of men, 'who wrought out this perfect atonement through the shedding of his own blood.' (D&C 76:69.) This has been his mission since the fall of man." (Joseph Fielding Smith, *CHMR* 1:194-95.)

Scriptural References: D&C 29:5; 32:3; 45:3; 62:1, 110:4; 1 Jn. 2:1.

Agent of the Lord; agent of the Church

The noun *agent* has as its basic meanings "to act, to do, to lead—one who acts or exerts power; one who acts for or in the place of another by authority from him; a representative." Thus, an agent of the Lord is one who represents the Lord and acts for and in behalf of the Lord by virtue of the authority given to him by the Lord. In a similar manner, an agent of the Church is authorized by the presiding officials of the Church to act in its behalf and to serve as its representative.

Selected Quotations

"We are the Lord's agents; we represent him; he has given us authority which empowers us to do all that is necessary to save and exalt ourselves as well as his other children in the world.

"We are ambassadors of the Lord Jesus Christ. Our commission is to represent him. We are directed to preach his gospel, to perform the ordinances of salvation, to bless mankind, to heal the sick and perhaps perform miracles, to do what he would do if he were personally present—and all this because we hold the holy priesthood.

"As the Lord's agents we are bound by his law to do what he wants us to do regardless of personal feelings or worldly enticements. Of ourselves we have no message of salvation, no doctrine that must be accepted, no power to baptize or ordain or marry for eternity. All these things come from the Lord, and anything we do with reference to them is the result of delegated authority.

"When we join the Church and receive the priesthood, we are expected to forsake many of the ways of the world and live as becometh saints. We are no longer to dress or speak or act or even think as others too often do. Many in the world use tea, coffee, tobacco, and liquor, and are involved in the use of drugs. Many profane and are vulgar and indecent, immoral and unclean in their lives, but all these things should be foreign to us. We are the saints of the Most High. We hold the holy priesthood." (Joseph Fielding Smith, *Ensign,* June 1971, p. 49.)

Scriptural References: D&C 53:4; 57:6; 70:11.

Alpha and Omega; Alphus (*see also* Jesus Christ)

The words *alpha* and *omega* are the first and last letters of the Greek alphabet; when used together, these terms mean "the first and last." The phrase may also be of Semitic origin, and Bible scholars have noted the similarity of *alpha* to *aleph,* which is the first letter in the Hebrew alphabet.

When used in reference to Jesus Christ, the term *Alpha and Omega* indicates the timeless nature of the Lord's existence.

Alphus is derived from *Alpha* and is used in D&C 95:17 as a name-title for Jesus Christ. Again, its use indicates that Jesus Christ had high status in the pre-earthly existence and will continue to have high status in the hereafter.

Selected Quotations

"The Lord introduced himself [75:1] as 'Alpha and Omega, your Lord, and your God.' These Greek letters mean the beginning and the end. Jesus Christ is just that. He is our Lord and our God. He was in the beginning, by him this world was created. He held authority and power as the Son of God in the eternities before this earth was formed. He holds the keys of salvation for all time, and he shall reign as Lord of lords with full power and dominion, under his Father, throughout all eternity." (Joseph Fielding Smith, *CHMR* 1:275.)

Scriptural References: D&C 19:1; 35:1; 68:35; 81:7; Rev. 1:8, 11; 21:6; 22:13.

Apostasy; apostates

The basic meaning of *apostasy* is "to stand elsewhere," and the word is derived from the two Greek roots that comprise the word.

In a religious sense, apostasy could either refer to an individual or to the religious organization. A person apostatizes from the religious organization when his beliefs differ from the beliefs of the group. A religious organization could apostatize if it changes its beliefs from its original position. The term *apostasy from the church* refers to an individual or group of individuals leaving the church, whereas *apostasy of the church* indicates the church itself has changed its position.

Selected Quotations

"How does apostasy come about? By neglect of duty, failing to keep in our souls the spirit of prayer, of obedience to the principles of the Gospel; by failure to pay an honest tithing, or to observe the word of wisdom, and to absent one's self from sacrament meetings where we have been commanded to go and renew our covenants. Apostasy comes through the sins of omission as well as through the sins of commission. Immorality is a deadly sin and those who are guilty, if they do not repent, will lose the spirit and deny the faith. Apostasy does not come upon an individual suddenly, but it is a gradual growth in which darkness through sin crowds out the spirit of light from the soul. When a man who was once enlightened loses the Spirit of truth, the darkness which takes its place is overwhelming. Alma gives us a good example of this. (Alma 12:9-11.)

"How true it is that when the light goes out of a man's soul and darkness takes its place it becomes intense; there is no darkness equal to it." (Joseph Fielding Smith, *CHMR* 2:125, 385.)

"Strange as it may appear at first thought, yet it is no less strange than true, that notwithstanding all the professed determination to live godly, apostates after turning from the faith of Christ, unless they have speedily repented, have sooner or later fallen into the snares of the wicked one, and have been left destitute of the Spirit of God, to manifest their wickedness in the eyes of multitudes. From apostates the faithful have received the severest persecutions. Judas was rebuked and immediately betrayed his Lord into the hands of his enemies, because Satan entered into him. There is a superior intelligence bestowed upon such as obey the Gospel with full purpose of heart, which, if sinned against, the apostate is left naked and destitute of the Spirit of God. . . . When once that light which was in them is taken from them, they become as much darkened as they were previously enlightened." (Joseph Smith, *TPJS*, p. 67.)

"I will give you a key which Brother Joseph Smith used to give in Nauvoo. He said that the very step of apostasy commenced with losing confidence in the leaders of this Church and kingdom, and that whenever you discerned that spirit, you might know that it would lead the possessor of it on the road to apostasy. . . .

"No man or woman can have the spirit of prophecy and at the same time do evil and speak against their brethren." (Heber C. Kimball, *LHCK*, p. 465.)

"One word and one word alone describes the dismal state that prevailed: apostasy. Generations before, Isaiah had prophesied: 'Darkness shall cover the earth, and gross darkness the people.' (Isa. 60:2.) Amos had foretold of a famine in the land: 'Not a famine of bread, nor a thirst for water, but of hearing the words of the Lord.' (Amos 8:11.) Had not Peter warned of false teachers bringing damnable heresies, and Paul predicted that the time would come when sound doctrine would not be endured?" (Thomas S. Monson, *Ensign,* May 1975, p. 15.)

Scriptural References: D&C 85:2, 11; 86:3.

Arm of the Lord

The term *arm of the Lord* suggests "the power, might, strength, or authority of God." Thus, the use of the longer term *arm of the Lord to be revealed* in both the introductory and closing sections of the Doctrine and Covenants suggests that in this dispensation the power and authority of the Lord will again be clearly manifested on the earth.

The statement that the arm of the Lord will not be shortened (D&C 35:8; 133:67) suggests that the Lord will do everything that needs to be done in order for His righteous purposes to be accomplished.

References from the Doctrine and Covenants include the following references on this topic:

Arm of the Lord to be revealed—1:14; 45:45, 47; 56:1; 109:51; 123:17; 133:3.

Arm of God over all the earth—15:2; 16:2; 29:1.

Power, might, and strength of the outstretched arm of the Lord—3:8; 103:17; 123:6; 136:22.

Arm of the Lord not to be shortened—35:8; 133:67.

Other Scriptural References: D&C 35:8; 103:17; Isa. 52:10; John 12:38; 3 Ne. 9:14; 16:20; 20:35.

Armor of the Lord; "take to you the whole armor of God"

The term *armor of the Lord* was used in biblical times (Eph. 6:10-18) as well as in modern scripture. The Bible lists several offensive and defensive weapons that comprise the armor (or arms) for war, including the following:

1. *Offensive weapons:* sword, spear, bow and arrow, sling, and rod—a staff cut from a tree that might be used as a weapon by a shepherd (Ps. 23:4) or a soldier (Ps. 2:9).

2. *Defensive weapons:* breastplate, helmet, greave (foot and shin guard), and shield.

The Roman armor in the days of Paul consisted of essentially the same items. Thus, Paul used these elements in urging the former-day saints to put on the "whole armour" of God. (Eph. 6:10-13.)

The Lord uses most of these same terms in urging Latter-day Saints to be valiant in their testimonies:

Armor—27:15.

Breastplate of righteousness—27:16.

Feet *shod* with preparation of the gospel—27:16; 112:7.

Shield of faith—27:17.

Helmet of salvation—27:18.

Sword of the Lord's spirit—27:18.

The term *gird up your loins* (27:15; 35:14; 36:8; 38:9; 43:19; 61:38; 73:6; 75:22; 106:5; 112:7, 14) is also used by the Lord in connection with being prepared to defend his work.

Selected Quotations

"We have the four parts of the body that . . . [are] the most vulnerable to the powers of darkness. The loins, typifying virtue, chastity. The heart, typifying our conduct; our feet, our goals or objectives in life; and finally, our head, our thoughts. . . .

"We should have our loins girt about with truth. What is truth? Truth, the Lord said, is knowledge of things as they are, things as they were, and things as they are to come. [D&C 93:24.] . . . 'Our loins shall be girt about with truth,' the prophet said.

"And the heart, what kind of breastplate shall protect our conduct in life? We shall have over our hearts a breastplate of righteousness. Well, having learned truth we have a measure by which we can judge between right and wrong, and so our conduct will always be gauged by that thing which we know to be true. Our breastplate to cover our conduct shall be the breastplate of righteousness.

"By what shall we protect our feet, or by what shall we gauge our objectives or our goals in life? . . . 'Your feet shall be shod with the preparation of the gospel of peace.' [Eph. 6:15.] How fortunate are you if in your childhood in the home of your father and mother you were taught the doctrine of repentance, faith in Christ, the Son of the living God, the meaning of baptism and what you gain by the laying on of hands for the gift of the Holy Ghost. Fortunate is the child who has been taught to pray and who has been given those steps to take on through life. Feet shod with the preparation of the gospel of peace! . . .

"And then finally, the helmet of salvation. . . . What is salvation? Salvation is to be saved. Saved from what? Saved from death and saved from sin.

"[The] armoured man holds in his hand a shield and in his other hand a sword, which were the weapons of those days. The shield was the shield of faith and the sword was the sword of the spirit, which is the Word of God. I can't think of any more powerful weapons than faith and a knowledge of the scriptures, in which are contained the Word of God. One so armoured and one so prepared with those weapons is prepared to go out against the enemy that is more to be feared than the enemies that strike in the darkness of the night, that we can't see with our eyes." (Harold B. Lee, *BYUSY,* 1954.)

" 'Above all, taking the shield of faith, wherewith ye shall be able to quench all the fiery darts of the wicked.' (Eph. 6:10-11, 14-16.)

"We were dressed in our home each morning, not only with hats and raincoats and boots to protect us from physical storm, but even more carefully our parents dressed us each day in the armor of God. As we would kneel in family prayer and listen to our father, a bearer of the priesthood, pour out his soul to the Lord for the protection of his family against the fiery darts of the wicked, one more layer was added to our shield of faith. While our shield was being made strong, theirs was always available, for they were available and we knew it." (L. Tom Perry, *Ensign,* May 1974, p. 98.)

Scriptural References: D&C 27:15-18; Eph. 6:11, 13; 2 Ne. 1:23.

Atonement; Atonement of Jesus Christ (*see also* Advocate; Jesus Christ)

The atonement (at-one-ment) of Jesus Christ is the most basic and fundamental principle of the gospel of Jesus Christ. In the final analysis, nearly everything else in the gospel is based on or derives its validity from the atonement. As Elder Bruce R. McConkie has indicated, the atonement "is the most important single thing that has ever occurred in the entire history of created things; it is the rock foundation upon which the gospel and all other things rest." (*MD,* p. 60.)

The atonement includes the activities and the accomplishments both of the Garden of Gethsemane and of Calvary and the empty tomb. It provides redemption unconditionally from the original transgression of Adam and Eve and conditionally from our individual sins if we repent. It includes unconditionally the resurrection from the dead for all mankind and opens the doors to eternal degrees of glory based on our degree of obedience to eternal law.

Selected Quotations

"The atonement of the Master is the central point of world history. Without it, the whole purpose for the creation of earth and our living upon it would fail. . . . Without it, no man or woman would ever be resurrected. . . . And so all the world, believers and non-believers, are indebted to the Redeemer for their certain resurrection, because the resurrection will be as wide as was the fall, which brought death to every man.

There is another phase of the atonement which makes me love the Savior even more and fills my soul with gratitude beyond expression. It is that in addition to atoning for Adam's transgression, thereby bringing about the resurrection, the Savior by his suffering paid the debt for my personal sins. He paid the debt for your personal sins and for the personal sins of every living soul that ever dwelt upon the earth or that ever will dwell in mortality upon the earth. But this He did conditionally. The benefits of this suffering for our individual transgressions will not come to us unconditionally in the same sense that the resurrection will come regardless of what we do. If we partake of the blessings of the atonement as far as our individual transgressions are concerned, we must obey the law." (Marion G. Romney, *CR,* October 1953, pp. 34-36.)

"The errand of Jesus to earth was to bring his brethren and sisters back into the presence of the Father; he has done his part of the work, and it remains for us to do ours. There is not one thing that the Lord could do for the salvation of the human family that he has neglected to do; and it remains for the children of men to receive the truth or reject it; all that can be accomplished for their salvation, independent of them, has been accomplished in and by the Savior. . . . Jesus paid the debt; he atoned for the original sin; he came and suffered and died on the cross." (Brigham Young, *JD* 13:59.)

Scriptural References: D&C 19:16-19; 20:21-29; 29:42-47; 74:7; 76:40-42, 69; 88:14-16; John 1:29-36; 3:14-18; 10:17-18; 11:25-26; 12:32-33; Alma 9:27; 34:8-16; 42; 3 Ne. 8-10; 11:1-17; 27:13-32.

Babylon

In Old Testament times, the title *Babylon* referred to the name of both city and country, but by the New Testament period the title was used symbolically to represent wickedness and corruptness as the opposite of the heavenly Jerusalem. (Rev. 17:5.) The word appears in five sections of the Doctrine and Covenants, each time as a symbol of worldliness and evil.

Selected Quotations

"We are all commanded to labor 'while it is called today.' None shall be spared from this burning who 'remain in Babylon.' Babylon is the world, those who remain in Babylon are those who follow the practices of the world, and who do not accept in their hearts the word of the Lord. He has said that he will send his angels in that day and they 'shall gather out of his kingdom all things that offend, and them which do iniquity.' (Matt. 13:41.)" (Joseph Fielding Smith, *CHMR* 1:239.)

" 'Babylon' is the name the Prophets give to the capital of the domain of antichrist, because ancient Babylon represented the power under which the Hebrews suffered oppression for many years. The preaching of the everlasting gospel shakes the foundations of antichrist in the world. . . . The greatness of the papal Babylon will not prevent her fall, but will make it more dreadful and remarkable' (Henry and Scott, Rev. 14:8)." (Smith and Sjodahl, *DCC*, p. 186.)

Scriptural References: D&C 1:16; 35:11; 64:24; 86:3; 133:5, 7, 14; Jer. 51:1-64; Rev. 14:8; 18:2, 10, 21.

Banners; "terrible as an army with banners"

A banner is a standard, an ensign, or a flag; the word is used in both ancient and modern scriptures as a means of identification or of rallying support. (Num. 2:2; Ps. 74:4; Isa. 5:26.)

The term *terrible as an army with banners* is found in only one book of the Bible. (Song of Solomon 6:4, 10.) It appears three times in the Doctrine and Covenants (5:14; 105:31;

109:73), where it is used in conjunction with the terms *fair as the sun* and *clear as the moon,* symbols of the great power and glory that will be associated with the true church when it becomes sanctified.

Selected Quotations

"We believe in the sanctification that comes by continued obedience to the law of heaven. I do not know of any other sanctification that the Scriptures tell about, of any other sanctification that is worth the consideration of rational beings. If we would be sanctified then, we must begin to-day, or whenever the Lord points out, to obey his laws just as far as we possibly can; and by obedience to these laws we continually gain more and more favor from heaven, more and more of the Spirit of God, and thus will be fulfilled a revelation given in 1834, which says that before Zion is redeemed, let the armies of Israel become very great, let them become sanctified before me; that they may be as fair as the sun, clear as the moon, and that their banners may be terrible unto all the nations of the earth—not terrible by reason of numbers, but terrible because of the sanctification they will receive through obedience to the law of God. Why was Enoch, and why were the inhabitants of the Zion built up before the flood terrible to all the nations around about? It was because, through a long number of years, they observed the law of God, and when their enemies came up to fight against them, Enoch, being filled with the power of the Holy Ghost, and speaking the word of God in power and in faith, the very heavens trembled and shook, and the earth quaked, and mountains were thrown down, rivers of water were turned out of their course, and all nations feared greatly because of the power of God, and the terror of his might that were upon his people. [Moses 7:12-17.]

"We have this account of ancient Zion in one of the revelations that God has given. What was it that made their banners terrible to the nations? It was not their numbers. If, then Zion must become great it will be because of her sanctification." (Orson Pratt, *JD* 17:112.)

Scriptural References: D&C 5:15; 105:31; 109:73.

Baptism: baptism for the dead; baptism of the Spirit; baptism of water

Baptism is the third principle (following faith in the Lord

Jesus Christ and repentance) and the first essential ordinance
of the gospel of Jesus Christ. It has been the required
doorway to the church and kingdom of God in both ancient
and modern times.

As an ordinance, baptism must be performed by one who
is ordained according to a prescribed pattern. This pattern
was established on this earth in the days of Adam (Moses
6:64-67) and has been followed wherever the true church has
existed upon the earth (D&C 20:23-28; 84:26-28).

Baptism of water is for the remission of sins and is to be
performed by immersion by one holding the proper authority in the Aaronic Priesthood. Immersion represents the
death, burial, and resurrection of Jesus Christ (Rom. 6:1-12),
and is also symbolic of the death of the old life of sin and the
birth of a new life of righteousness on the part of the person
being baptized.

Baptism of the Spirit (of the Holy Ghost, or of fire) is for
the sanctification of the person and is to be performed by
one holding the Melchizedek Priesthood.

Baptism of the water and of the Spirit is required to be
performed for every person who has lived on earth and committed sin before that person can enter the celestial kingdom
regardless of when the person may have lived upon the
earth. Thus, baptisms for the dead are performed by proxy
as a means whereby the worthy dead of all ages can become
heirs of the celestial kingdom. This vicarious baptismal
work for the dead was performed in the days of Paul and
used in a discussion by him to prove the resurrection of Jesus
Christ. (1 Cor. 15:29.)

Selected Quotations

"Baptism is a sign to God, to angels, and to heaven that
we do the will of God, and there is no other way beneath the
heavens whereby God hath ordained for man to come to
him to be saved, and enter into the Kingdom of God, except
faith in Jesus Christ, repentance, and baptism for the remission of sins, and any other course is in vain; then you
have the promise of the gift of the Holy Ghost." (Joseph
Smith, *HC* 4:444.)

"Baptism by immersion symbolizes the death and burial
of the man of sin; and the coming forth out of the water, the
resurrection to a newness of spiritual life. After baptism,
hands are laid upon the head of the baptized believer, and

he is blessed to receive the Holy Ghost. Thus does the one baptized receive the promise or gift of the Holy Ghost . . . by obedience to whom one so blessed might receive the guidance and direction of the Holy Ghost in its daily walks and talks. . . . To receive such guidance and such direction from the Holy Ghost is to be spiritually reborn." (Harold B. Lee, *CR,* October 1947, p. 64.)

"Every child born into this world comes by the water; the blood and the Spirit. The unborn babe is cradled in water, the blood enters its body and by blood it is born and the spirit which the Lord created enters its body, thus there are three witnesses in birth, the water, the blood and the spirit of the child. So likewise we must be born again, by a burial in water, 'for by the water ye keep the commandment; by the Spirit ye are justified and by the blood ye are sanctified.' (Moses 6:60.) John the Beloved understood this principle thoroughly and he said: 'For there are three that bear record in heaven, the Father, the Word, and the Holy Ghost; and these three are one. And there are three that bear witness in earth, the spirit, and the water, and the blood: and these three agree in one.' (1 John 5:7-8.) . . .

"In relation to the false doctrine of 'baptizing' infants, the Prophet said: 'The doctrine of baptizing children, or sprinkling them, or they must welter in hell, is a doctrine not true, nor supported in Holy Writ, and is not consistent with the character of God. All children are redeemed by the blood of Jesus Christ, and the moment that children leave this world, they are taken to the bosom of Abraham.' (*HC* 4:554.)" (Joseph Fielding Smith, *CHMR* 2:211, 298.)

"That immersion was the form of ordinance introduced by John the Baptist, submitted to by the Savior, and perpetuated by his Apostles, is a plain and reasonable inference from the teachings of the New Testament. Jesus, when about to be baptized, must have gone down into the water; for after baptism, he 'went up straightway out of the water.' (Matt. 3:16.) When Philip baptized the Eunuch, 'they went down both into the water.' (Acts 8:38.) John baptized in Aenon, near to Salim, because there was much water there (John 3:23)—another proof presumptive of immersion, the only mode requiring 'much water' for its performance.

"If this had not been the proper form, Paul would not have compared baptism to burial and resurrection (Rom. 6:3-5; Col. 2:12) nor would he have recognized as baptism the passage of the Israelites through the Red Sea. (1 Cor. 10:1, 2.) Note also his words to the Corinthians relative to vicarious baptism and in support of resurrection, a doctrine that some of them denied: 'Else what shall they do which are baptized for the dead, if the dead rise not at all? Why are they then baptized for the dead?' (1 Cor. 15:29.) In other words, why use the symbol of the resurrection if there be no resurrection—if the symbol does not symbolize?" (Orson F. Whitney, *SNT*, pp. 251-53.)

Scriptural References: D&C 13:1; 33:11; 127:5, 10; 128:1-18; 2 Ne. 9:23-24; 31:5-9; 31:17.

Bishop; Presiding Bishop (*see also* Priesthood offices; Church offices and presiding quorums)

The office of bishop is an office in the Aaronic Priesthood and, as is true with all other such offices, a person is *ordained* to that office; he may then be *set apart* to function as the bishop of a particular ward. The Presiding Bishop of the Church is considered to be a General Authority.

Selected Quotations

"The first bishops were called at an early day in the Church. The presiding bishop, if he is a literal descendant of Aaron, has a legal right to the office. He must be the firstborn among the sons of Aaron. 'For the firstborn holds the right of the presidency over this priesthood, and the keys of authority of the same.' (D&C 86:16-18.) If a man could prove by lineage or revelation that he is the firstborn to Aaron, he could claim his anointing, but he would have to be worthy, and his anointing, or ordination, would have to be done under the hands of the Presidency of the Church. Since high priests may officiate in all the ordinances of the Gospel, they can officiate as bishops, when they are called and ordained by proper authority to that office.

"The bishop is a common judge in Israel, and members are amenable to his jurisdiction." (Joseph Fielding Smith, *CHMR* 2:21.)

"A bishop is the presiding officer of his ward, and where the bishop is in the ward, his counselors and those who are members of his ward are subject to his presidency. . . .

"The presiding officer is the head, should be regarded in his place, and his place should be held sacred in the minds of his associates. . . .

"The work of the bishop is both temporal and spiritual. The average bishop gives all his time and efforts for the betterment of the people over whom he presides." (Joseph F. Smith, *GD,* pp. 185, 188.)

"The laws defining the duties of the Bishopric were not yet fully revealed, but in a general way it was understood that the gathering of the Saints was commanded for their temporary salvation, and that the office was instituted with this end in view. The Revelation concerning gathering (Sec. 38) also contained more than an intimation of the United Order (vv. 24-27). Orson F. Whitney well remarks:

" 'An order of unity and equality, a system of consecration and stewardships, the abolition of fraud and monopoly in all their phases, a sinking of individual into and for the purpose of the common good, the sacrifice of self at the shrine of principle—of pure religion, whose incense—call it charity, philanthropy, or what we will, is the pure love of God and humanity. It was to the establishment of such an order,—one object of which, in the arcana of the faith, was to pave the way for the Zion of Enoch, which the Saints believe will yet descend to Earth, the planet whence it was taken,—that Joseph Smith, as early as February, 1831, more than fifty years before Edward Bellamy and his ingenious book "Looking Backward" were heard of, directed his thoughts and labors. A movement to that end was the organization of the Bishopric, representing the temporal wing of the Mormon Church government. The Apostleship, which pertains to the Priesthood of Melchizedek, through possessing general powers, has a special calling to minister in spiritual things; while the Bishopric, which is the presidency of the Priesthood of Aaron, administers, under the direction of the higher authority, in things temporal' (*History of Utah* 1:85). See also Secs. 42:30-32; 51:3-6 and 13-17.

"The controversy over the meaning of 'Bishop' has never been settled satisfactorily in the world. The New Testament has no office into which the Bishops of the various churches fit, and therefore they are at a loss to explain their duties. They notice that the Bishops in the Bible are sometimes called Elders and sometimes Bishops, and they are confused because they cannot understand how a Bishop can be an Elder. In Eph. 4:11, the Bishops are 'Pastors,' or Shepherds, and are placed next to the teachers. This is another puzzle.

The fact is, that the Apostles appointed some to superintend the spiritual, and others to have charge of the temporal wants of the churches. The latter were called 'Bishops,' which means 'overseers.' To the Latter-day Saints, the controversy, in the light of modern revelation, is meaningless." (Smith and Sjodahl, *DCC*, p. 217.)

"There is no position in the Church that will bring a greater blessing to any man than the office of a bishop if he will honor that office and be a real father to the flock over whom he is called to preside. Do not forget that. . . . I want to say to you that there is no bishop, nor has there been a bishop in the Church, who has given the time that the Lord expected him to give in looking after the flock and teaching his people and preparing them to do the work, that has not received one hundred percent of the blessings that he labored for, and they will extend to him throughout the ages of eternity.

"He may not have had wealth, may not have had distinction. He may not have had the honor of presiding over clubs and things of that kind, but if he has done his duty as a bishop, he has been hand in hand with the Father of us all, and everything that he has done to bless his kind is laid up as a treasure in heaven and nobody can take the blessing from him." (George Albert Smith, *CR*, October 1948, pp. 186-87.)

"He [bishop] was to be a common judge among the inhabitants of Zion, or in a Stake of Zion, or in a branch of the Church, *when he shall be set apart unto his ministry.* His Bishopric is sufficient for any of these places when set apart: and he can only fill those offices for which he is set apart. But a literal descendant of Aaron has a legal right to the Presidency of this Priesthood, to *the keys* of this ministry, to act in the office of Bishop, without Counselors. . . . The Bishopric is the Presidency of the Aaronic Priesthood, which is 'an *appendage* to the greater or Melchizedek Priesthood,' and that no man has a legal right to hold the KEYS of the Aaronic Priesthood, which presides over all Bishops and all the lesser Priesthood, except he be a literal descendant of Aaron. But, that 'as a High Priest of the Melchizedek Priesthood has authority to officiate in all the lesser offices, he may officiate in the office of Bishop,' . . . if *called, set apart, and ordained unto this* power 'by the hands of the Presidency of the Melchizedek Priesthood.' [D&C 107:17.] The power and right of selecting and calling of the Presiding Bishop and general Bishops is vested in the First Presidency, who also must try those appointed by them in case of transgression.

"That the Presiding Bishop, who presides over all Bishops, and all of the lesser Priesthood, should consult the First Presidency in all important matters pertaining to the Bishopric." (John Taylor, *Items on Priesthood*, pp. 29, 31-32.)

"The Lord has so organized His Church that there is accessible to every member—man, woman, and child—a spiritual advisor, and a temporal counselor as well, who knows them intimately and who knows the circumstances and conditions out of which their problems come, and who, by reason of his ordination, is entitled to an endowment from our Heavenly Father of the necessary discernment and inspiration of the Lord to enable him to give the advice which the one in trouble so much needs. We refer to the Bishop or Branch President. If the Bishop or Branch President needs assistance, he may go to the Stake or Mission President. These brethren may in turn seek counsel from one of the General Authorities, should such be necessary." (First Presidency, letter to members, Jan. 29, 1973.)

Scriptural References: D&C 20:67; 72:2-25; 107:17-88; 1 Tim. 3:1-2; Tit. 1:7; 1 Pet. 2:25.

Book of life; book of the law of God; the Lamb's book of life

The book of life is a record kept in heaven which contains the names of the righteous and an account of their covenants with the Lord and their righteous deeds. It is also referred to in the scriptures as the Lamb's book of life and the book of the names of the sanctified. It is possible for the names of righteous saints yet living to be included in the book of life (see *TPJS*, p. 9), but such names will be blotted out if such a person reverts to wickedness.

Selected Quotations

"The Lord knew that there would be some who would falter; some who would come to Zion not willing to enroll themselves and their property to the welfare of Zion, and therefore could not be given stewardships in the covenant which the Lord had made with the saints. . . . The Lord said 'Their names shall not be found, neither the names of the fathers, nor the names of the children written in the book of the law of God, saith the Lord of Hosts.' The book of the law of God was the book to be kept by the Lord's clerk. There is also another book which is kept in heaven, and the one kept by the Lord's clerk should be accurately kept so that it would agree with the Lamb's Book of Life. In the Lamb's Book of Life only the names are received of those who have washed their garments white 'in the blood of the Lamb.' This is in harmony with the word of the Lord to John: 'And there shall in no wise enter into it anything that defileth, neither whatsoever worketh abomination, or maketh a lie: but they which are written in the Lamb's Book of Life.' (Rev. 21:27.)" (Joseph Fielding Smith, *CHMR* 1:349.)

"We are not going to be saved in the kingdom of God just because our names are on the records of the Church. It will require more than that. We will have to have our names written in the Lamb's Book of Life, and if they are written in the Lamb's Book of Life then it is an evidence we have kept the commandments. Every soul who will not keep the commandments shall have his name blotted out of that book." (Joseph Fielding Smith, *CR*, September 1950, p. 10.)

"There is a special record which is called the 'Book of God,' or the 'Book of Life,' which contains the names of those who shall rise from the dead in the first resurrection. Moses, on one occasion, asked the Lord to forgive; 'and if not,' he said, 'blot me, I pray thee, out of the book which thou hast written.' The Lord's reply was, 'Whosoever hath sinned against me, him will I blot out of my book' (Ex. 32:32-3). The disciples of our Lord, after their first missionary journey, returned to their Master full of enthusiasm, and reported that even demons were subject to them in His name. Jesus replied, 'Notwithstanding in this rejoice not . . . but rather rejoice, because your names are written in heaven' (Luke 10:20). In the Revelation by John it is stated that all who dwell on Earth, 'whose names are not written in the Book of Life of the Lamb' shall worship the 'beast' with seven heads and ten horns. (Rev. 13:8.)" (Smith and Sjodahl, *DCC*, p. 459.)

Scriptural References: D&C 76:68; 85:5, 7; 88:2; 128:6, 7; 132:19; Ps. 69:28; 2 Chr. 17:9; Philip. 4:3; Rev. 3:5; 13:8; 17:8; 20:12-15; Alma 5:58.

Book of Mormon
The Book of Mormon is accepted by Latter-day Saints as

sacred scripture and as one of the standard works of the Church. Faithful Saints accept wholeheartedly the testimony of Joseph Smith regarding this book, including his statement that "the Book of Mormon [is] the most correct of any book on earth, and the keystone of our religion, and a man would get nearer to God by abiding by its precepts than by any other book." (*HC* 4:461.)

According to Latter-day Saints, the Book of Mormon has many credentials, including the following, some of which are unique.

1. The book was translated by a prophet of God by the gift and power of God and through means of a divine instrument, the Urim and Thummim.

2. Three special witnesses were shown, by an angel of God, the plates from which the record was taken, and the voice of the Lord declared that the translation of the book was correct.

3. Eight other witnesses were allowed to handle the plates from which the record was taken. None of the eight or the three special witnesses ever denied their testimony.

4. The book contains precious truths of the gospel of Jesus Christ, written in plainness and simplicity.

5. It is a witness of the Bible, and in no way nor at any time does it contradict the Bible or its essential teachings. The Bible (stick of Judah) and Book of Mormon (abridged stick of Joseph) thus form two separate and distinct witnesses to the divinity of Jesus Christ, inasmuch as both of them contain proof of his resurrection.

Selected Quotations

"The authenticity of the Book of Mormon and the restoration of the gospel rest upon the same two fundamentals: first, the reality of modern revelation, and second, the fact that Joseph Smith was a prophet of God. These two verities are inseparably connected in their relationship to the Book of Mormon and the restored gospel. To accept one of them is to accept the other." (Marion G. Romney, *CR*, October 1971, p. 27.)

"Robert B. Downs wrote a book entitled *Books That Changed America.* He listed the Book of Mormon as one of twenty-five such books. In his comments he said, 'Throughout the history of Mormonism, the Church's most powerful and effective weapon has been the Book of

Mormon.' (Robert B. Downs, *Books That Changed America,*
New York: Macmillan Co., 1970, p. 35.)

"*It is a powerful book!*

"Many individuals have read it. It has caused them to
leave their churches in which they have been active
members. It has caused them to give up their fathers,
mothers, and families. Their faith in the book and the truths
it teaches was so strong they still believed even though they
were told they would be disowned if they joined the Church.
. . . There is a special power about the Book of Mormon. It
bears a strong, silent witness of its truth as one reads it.

"Parley P. Pratt stated, 'The Spirit of the Lord came upon
me, while I read [The Book of Mormon], and enlightened
my mind, convinced my judgment, and rivetted the truth
upon my understanding, so that I knew that the book was
true, just as well as a man knows the daylight from the dark
night.' (*JD* 5:194.)

"Brigham Young said as he read the book, 'I knew it was
true, as well as I knew that I could see with my eyes, or feel
by the touch of my fingers, or be sensible of the demonstra-
tion of any sense.' (*JD* 3:91.)" (James A. Cullimore, *Ensign,*
May 1976, pp. 84-86.)

Bridegroom; Jesus Christ as the bridegroom (*see also* Second
Coming; Jesus Christ; Virgins)

The Old Testament prophets often compared the spiritual
relation between God and his people to a betrothal or marriage; apostasy, through idolatry or other sin, was likened to
unfaithfulness on the part of the marriage partner. (Isa. 1:21;
Jer. 3:1-20; Ezek. 16, 23; Hosea 2.)

The New Testament writers also occasionally referred to
Christ as "the bridegroom in the supper of the Lamb,"
which has been identified by prophets in this dispensation to
refer to his second coming. It is usually in this setting that the
word *bridegroom* is used in the Doctrine and Covenants to
refer to Jesus Christ. In section 33 the world is urged to "be
ready at the coming of the Bridegroom" (verse 17); in section 65 the people are to "prepare . . . the supper of the
Lamb, make ready for the Bridegroom" (verse 3); and later
sections indicate that the "Bridegroom cometh; go ye out to
meet him" (88:92; see also 133:10, 19).

Selected Quotations

"Let the Church, therefore, prepare as a bride to receive

her bridegroom; let the Saints have on their wedding garments, and have their lamps well supplied with oil, trimmed and burning; let all things be made ready for the reception of our Savior and Redeemer, even our Lord the Christ. Let all the Saints throughout the world live their religion, that they may be worthy to enjoy his presence and have converse with the angels of our God; let them gird up their loins and step forth in the power and might of Elijah's God to do battle in this great cause, and armed with high heaven's panoply, even the armour of salvation and the helmet of righteousness, go forth conquering and to conquer, until the gospel shall be sounded to every nation, kindred, tongue and people, and the pure in heart, the meek of the earth, the Israel of our God, be gathered out from the wicked nations and brought to inherit and worship under their own vines and fig trees, and learn of him whose glory will rest upon his temple as a cloud by day and a pillar of fire by night." (First Presidency, *MS* 18:4.)

Scriptural References: D&C 33:17; 65:3; 88:92; 133:10, 19; Matt. 9:15; John 3:29; Rev. 18:23.

Burned; earth to be burned; wicked to be burned at second coming (*see also* Second coming)

In the time of Noah, the wicked were destroyed by a flood; at the second coming of the Messiah, the wicked will be destroyed by fire through burning. (Mal. 3:2, 4; D&C 64:23-25). Prophets of this dispensation have indicated that the fire which destroys the wicked at the second coming will be as literal as the water which destroyed the wicked in ancient times. During this time of great burning, the elements shall melt and all things shall become new; the earth will also be renewed then and receive its paradisiacal glory. (D&C 101:23-31.)

Selected Quotations

"It is not a figure of speech that is meaningless, or one not to be taken literally when the Lord speaks of the burning. All through the scriptures we have the word of the Lord that at his coming the wicked and the rebellious will be as stubble and will be consumed. Isaiah has so prophesied. . . . Surely the words of the Lord are not to be received lightly or considered meaningless." (Joseph Fielding Smith, *CHMR* 1:238.)

"The scriptures abound in declarations and reiterations, in repeated and solemn affirmations of the great fact that the day of the Lord's coming will be a day of glory and a day of terror—of glory and recompense unto those who are living righteously, and a day of terror unto the proud and unto all who do wickedly. Now, many have asked, do we interpret that scripture as meaning that in the new day of the Lord's coming, all who are not members of the Church shall be burned, or otherwise destroyed, and only this little body of men and women, very small compared with the uncounted hosts of men now living, shall be spared the burning and shall escape destruction? I think not so. I do not think we are justified in putting that interpretation upon the Lord's word, for He recognizes every man according to the integrity of his heart, and men who have not been able to understand the Gospel or who have not had opportunity of learning it and knowing of it will not be counted as the wilfully sinful who are fit only to be burned as stubble; but the proud, who lift themselves in the pride of their hearts and rise above the word of God and become a law unto themselves and who wilfully rise above the word of God, and with knowledge deny the saving virtues of the atonement of Christ, and who are seeking to lead others away from the truth will be dealt with by Him according to both justice and mercy." (James E. Talmage, *CR*, April 1916, p. 128.)

Scriptural References: D&C 31:4; 38:12; 64:23; 86:7; 88:94; 101:66; 1 Ne. 22:15; Jacob 5:77; 6:3.

Calamities before Second Coming (*see also* Second coming)

The prophets have prophesied of many calamities that will come upon the earth before the coming of the "great and dreadful day of the Lord." One purpose of these calamities is to encourage the people to repent so they will not be destroyed at his coming.

Following are a few of the calamities mentioned in the Doctrine and Covenants:

Desolating scourge or sickness—5:19; 45:31.

Desolations—5:19; 29:8; 35:11; 45:19, 21, 31, 33; 84:114, 117; 88:85; 112:24.

Sun shall be darkened—29:14; 34:9; 45:42; 88:87; 133:49.

Moon shall be turned into blood—29:14, 34:9; 45:42; 88:87; 133:49.

Stars shall fall from heaven—29:14; 34:9; 45:42; 88:87; 133:49.

Flies and maggots to come upon the people—29:18.

Hailstorms will destroy the crops of the earth—29:16; 43:25; 109:30.

Lightning, thunderings, and earthquakes will be very destructive—43:25; 45:33; 87:6; 88:89-90.

Sea to heave itself beyond the bounds—88:90.

Great and abominable church destroyed—29:21; 88:94.

Wars in this country and foreign lands—45:26, 63; 63:33; 87.

Devastating whirlwind will cause much destruction—112:24.

Selected Quotations

"I will prophesy that the signs of the coming of the son of Man are already commenced. One pestilence will desolate after another. We shall soon have war and bloodshed. The moon will be turned to blood. I testify of these things, and that the coming of the Son of Man is nigh, even at your doors." (Joseph Smith, *HC* 3:390.)

"And now I am prepared to say by the authority of Jesus Christ, that not many years shall pass away before the United States shall present such a scene of bloodshed as has not a parallel in the history of our nation; pestilence, hail, famine, and earthquake will sweep the wicked of this generation from off the face of the land, to open and prepare the way for the return of the lost tribes of Israel from the north country." (Joseph Smith, *HC* 1:315.)

"Calamitous phenomena, before which the wicked shall fall, are definitely predicted as accompaniments of the second advent of our Lord. This is the prediction made through the prophet Joseph Smith in these days; and the fulfillment is nigh: [Sec. 88:87-91, quoted.]

"It may be argued that the storms, earthquakes, and other destructive occurrences . . . are not natural but supernatural phenomena, specially inflicted by Divine intent. Say rather that these happenings are supernaturally directed, following naturally and inevitably the sins of mankind and the unregenerate state of the race.

" 'The earth also is defiled under the inhabitants thereof; because they have transgressed the laws, changed the ordi-

nance, broken the everlasting covenant.' [Isa. 24:5.] " (James
E. Talmage, *IE,* July 1919, 22:801-2.)

"As was foreseen, aye, and foretold, by the Christ
Himself, and by His prophets who lived before His mortal
birth and by those who lived after, in the earlier ages, and by
the prophets of the present dispensation, great destruction
has come and shall come upon the earth because of the sins
of the human race. . . .

"It is beyond the wisdom of men to correctly deduce
results by applying the general laws or causes to individual
cases; and whenever the judgments of the Lord are permitted to fall upon the earth and upon its inhabitants, there are
many of the innocent who suffer with the guilty. Many go
down who are not personally culpable and who are not
directly responsible for that which has come.

"We know the Lord does permit these calamities to come
upon those who, according to our means of judgment and
powers of analysis, may not have deserved the fate, but
death, remember, is not finality. It is that which follows
death with which we should have concern. Many are allowed
to die in tempest and earthquake, whose death is but a
passage into the blessed realms because they are deserving of
blessings; while unto others death does come as a judgment; and the Lord knows who falls because of their sins
and who are permitted to fall because of their righteousness.
. . . The Lord deals with individuals: and salvation is an individual affair; but, nevertheless, he deals also with nations,
for he is the God of nations, which are set up or put down,
are preserved or destroyed, according to their fitness; and all
this is done in the Lord's due time and way. [Sec. 63:2-6.]"
(James E. Talmage, *CR,* October 1923, pp. 51-53.)

"You will find it recorded in one of the revelations to the
Prophet Joseph Smith and the elders of this church, that
after the testimony of the elders should come the testimony
of lightnings, of thunder, of earthquakes, of the sea heaving
itself beyond its bounds, and of destruction, the elements being engaged in bearing testimony—the thunder would cry
repentance. And yet in that same revelation the Lord said
they would not heed that warning voice any more than they
had heeded the warning voice of the servants of the Lord.
[Sec. 45:26-33.] Oh, that men would hear the voice of the elements proclaiming repentance, and if they shall not hear it

they shall be visited with dire calamity, for this is the day of settlement, the day of reckoning, the hour of God's judgment has come. I rejoice not in the prospects of the chastisement that awaits the nations of the earth, I would that they would save themselves. The means is yet at hand. By repentance and by turning to the Lord Jesus Christ they may find that salvation, but without it there is no salvation for this world." (Melvin J. Ballard, *CR*, October 1923, pp. 31-32.)

"It will not be long until calamities will overtake the human family unless there is speedy repentance. It will not be long before those who are scattered over the face of the earth by millions will die like flies because of what will come." (George Albert Smith, *CR*, April 1950, p. 169.)

"God has revealed that in the last days he would warn the people through the voice of tempests, earthquakes, and seas heaving themselves beyond their bounds. Do we hear his voice now and recognize it?

"When an estimated half million people are stricken in one hurricane in Pakistan, when one hundred thousand are left homeless in a single quake in Chile, and when these two disasters come within a few weeks of each other, can we ignore the warnings which they give?

"When two devastating hurricanes wipe out entire communities in Mississippi within a few months of each other, when oft-repeated earthquakes strike Los Angeles with death and a half-billion-dollar devastation, do we hear in them the voice of God as a fair warning to the rest of us? Can we relax and feel at ease because we take out insurance against earthquakes, fire, and storm damage? Can an insurance policy prevent a hurricane or stay an earthquake? Who can control such awesome forces? Who is the God of nature? Who stood in a storm-tossed boat with a group of frightened fishermen and rebuked the storm by simply saying 'Peace be still,' and the wind abated and there came a great calm? The extinct civilizations of the past now speak to us out of the dust of the ages, giving warning against the same conditions which brought them down to oblivion.

"Listen to what they say!" (Mark E. Petersen, *Ensign*, June 1971, p. 48.)

Scriptural References: D&C 1:17; 45:50; 109:46; 136:35; Mormon 2:27; 5:11; Ether 11:6.

Carnal; sensual; devilish

A standard dictionary definition of *carnal* is "relating to or given to crude bodily pleasures and appetites," while *sensual* is defined as "relating to or consisting in the gratification of the senses or the indulgence of appetite." Both words connote an inclination to gratify the flesh, and both words indicate a physical rather than a spiritual orientation. The word *devilish,* of course, refers to the characteristics of the devil.

Both ancient and modern scriptures indicate that since the fall of Adam and Eve, men have become carnal, sensual, and devilish. (Moses 5:13; 6:49; Alma 42:10; Mosiah 16:1-4.) The words also appear in the following sections of the D&C:

Carnal—3:4; 29:35; 67:10, 12; 84:27.

Sensual—20:20; 29:35.

Devilish—20:20.

The scriptures also indicate how mankind can forsake carnality and become spiritually minded through the rebirth of baptism of the water and of the Spirit. (Mosiah 4:2; 16:1-4, 12; 26:4; 27:25; Alma 22:13; 41:10-15.)

Selected Quotations

"An ancient prophet on this continent said, ". . . the natural man is an enemy to God.' [Mosiah 3:19.] The world today has become carnal, as much so now as in the beginning when Adam attempted to teach his children the principles of eternal truth, and Satan came along and commanded them to believe it not.

"Surely we see these indications prevalent in our own land and in foreign lands. Men have become carnal. They have become enemies to God. [Moses 6:49-50.]" (Joseph Fielding Smith, *CR*, April 1952, p. 27.)

"When Adam, by command of the Lord, taught his children the Gospel plan, we read: 'And Satan came among them saying: I am also a son of God, and he commanded them saying: Believe it not; and they believed it not, and they loved Satan more than God. And men began from that time forth to be carnal, sensual and devilish. [Moses 5:13.]' In a revelation to the Church at the time of its organization, the Lord reiterated this statement and said:

" '. . . But by the transgression of these holy laws, man became sensual and devilish, and became fallen man.' (D&C 20:20.) That this is true is clearly taught in the pages of history. Seldom has the divine truth of the Gospel been accepted by the people, and when it has, it has been by a very small number among the multitudes upon the face of the earth." (Joseph Fielding Smith, *CHMR* 1:11.)

Scriptural References: Rom. 7:14; 8:7; 15:27; 1 Cor. 8:1-4.

Celestial (*see also* Degrees of glory)

The celestial glory is the highest of the three degrees of glory. It has within it three heavens or degrees. (D&C 131.) Those persons who receive exaltation are in the highest degree of the celestial glory.

Selected Quotations

"Those who partake of the fulness of the celestial kingdom are those who have received the testimony of Jesus and were baptized in his name and, after receiving baptism and the gift of the Holy Ghost, continue to 'be washed and cleansed from all their sins,' through obedience to the Gospel to the end." (Joseph Fielding Smith, *CHMR* 1:286.)

"The heavens were opened upon us, and I beheld the celestial kingdom of God, and the glory thereof, whether in the body or out I cannot tell. I saw the transcendent beauty of the gate through which the heirs of the kingdom will enter, which was like unto circling flames of fire; also the blazing throne of God, whereon was seated the Father and the Son. I saw the beautiful streets of that kingdom, which had the appearance of being paved with gold. . . .

"Thus came the voice of the Lord unto me, saying—

" 'All who have died without a knowledge of this Gospel, who would have received it if they had been permitted to tarry, shall be heirs of the celestial kingdom of God; also all that shall die henceforth without a knowledge of it, who would have received it with all their hearts, shall be heirs of that kingdom, for I, the Lord, will judge all men according to their works, according to the desire of their hearts.'

"And I also beheld that all children who die before they arrive at the years of accountability, are saved in the celestial kingdom of heaven." (Joseph Smith, *HC* 2:380-81.)

"That law by obedience to which men gain an inheritance in the kingdom of God in eternity is called *celestial law.* It is the law of the gospel, the law of Christ, and it qualifies men for admission to the celestial kingdom because in and through it men are 'sanctified by the reception of the Holy Ghost,' thus becoming clean, pure, and spotless. (3 Ne. 27:19-21.)" (Bruce R. McConkie, *MD*, pp. 117-18.)

Scriptural References: D&C 76; 88; 1 Cor. 15:40-42; 2 Cor. 12:2.

Children; salvation of children; redemption of children (*note:* for information on the responsibility of parents to teach children, see also material listed after 68:25)

It is the clear and definite teaching of The Church of Jesus Christ of Latter-day Saints and its scriptures that little children are saved through the atonement of Jesus Christ. In one of the latest revelations accepted by the Church as official canon and scripture, the Prophet Joseph Smith recorded in his vision of the celestial kingdom: "And I also beheld that all children who die before they arrive at the years of accountability, are saved in the celestial kingdom of heaven." (JS-V 1:10.)

The Inspired Version of the Bible includes the teachings of Jesus that little children "shall be saved" (Matt. 19:13), and modern scriptures contain many references to this effect (see Mosiah 15:25; Moroni 8:8; D&C 29:46-47; 45:58; 93:38).

The Church and its prophets also teach that little children who die in infancy or childhood come forth in the resurrection in the same physical form they possessed at the time of death. Righteous parents of such children will have the privilege in the resurrection of rearing these children to the full state of the spirits.

Selected Quotations

"Little children too young to have sinned, and therefore without need of repentance, are exempt from baptism, and it is a sin to baptize them, involving as it does the vain use of a sacred ordinance. (Moroni 8:8-10, 19, 22.) Redeemed by the blood of Christ from the foundation of the world, their innocence and purity are typical of the saved condition of men and women, who must become like them before entering the kingdom of heaven. [D&C 29:46-47; 74:6.] As children advance in years, however, they become accountable, and then must yield obedience to the requirements of the Gospel. (Moses 6:55.) Eight years is the recognized age of ac-

countability in the Church of Christ. [D&C 68:25-27.]"
(Orson F. Whitney, *SNT,* pp. 245-46.)

"Joseph Smith declared that the mother who laid down
her little child, being deprived of the privilege, the joy, and
the satisfaction of bringing it up to manhood or womanhood
in this world, would, after the resurrection, have all the joy,
satisfaction and pleasure, and even more than it would have
been possible to have had in mortality, in seeing her child
grow to the full measure of the stature of its spirit." (Joseph
F. Smith, *MS* 57:388-39.)

"I lost a son six years of age, and I saw him a man in the
spirit world after his death, and I saw how he had exercised
his own freedom of choice and would obtain of his own will
and volition a companionship, and in due time to him, and
all those who are worthy of it, shall come all of the blessings
and sealing privileges of the house of the Lord. Do not worry
over it. They are safe; they are all right. [D&C 74:7.]"
(Melvin J. Ballard, *SMJB,* p. 260.)

"Little children . . . born during the millennium, when
Satan is bound and cannot tempt them, 'shall grow without
sin unto salvation.' " (Joseph Fielding Smith, *DS* 2:56-57.)

Scriptural References: D&C 29:46-47; JS-V 1:10; Matt.
18:3-14; 3 Ne. 17:11-24; Moro. 8:11.

Church; "Church of the living God"

In the early days of this dispensation, the Church was
referred to by the Lord and others by such titles as his
Church, the Church of Christ, or the Church of the living
God. In section 115, the Lord revealed that the exact name
of his church in this dispensation should be The Church of
Jesus Christ of Latter-day Saints.

Even then, however, the Lord continued to refer to the
Church as "the only true and living church" (1:30) and as
"the church of the living God" (70:10; 82:18). Concerning
this usage, Elder Gordon B. Hinckley has written:

In the latter-day scriptures the Lord speaks of "the only true and
living church upon the face of the whole earth, with which I, the
Lord, am well pleased." (D&C 1:30.) There is much difference
between a dead and living church. While one may have the form
and shape, the ritual and dimension, the living church has life. A
living prophet leads the Church today. There is a vibrant, living
movement to it, a captivating spirit about it, a glory to it that lifts
and builds and helps and blesses the lives of all it touches. The

Church will move forward to its divine destiny. (*Ensign,* May 1975, p. 92.)

Selected Quotations

"The true Church must be established by authority of God, and there must be the life of the Holy Spirit in it. The Holy Ghost must be conferred upon the members by the ordinance ordained for its bestowal [D&C 20:41], and when the Spirit is received it will testify unto the recipients that they have obeyed the demands of the true Gospel." (Anthon H. Lund, *CR,* October 1915, p. 10.)

"We require a living tree—a living fountain—living intelligence, proceeding from the living priesthood in heaven, through the living priesthood on earth." (John Taylor, *GK,* p. 34.)

Scriptural References: Matt. 16:18-19; 3 Ne. 27:8; 4 Ne. 1:26-27.

Church of the Firstborn

Members of the Church of the Firstborn are those saints who are heirs of exaltation in the celestial kingdom and who will be joint-heirs with Christ in receiving of the fulness of the Father. In this dispensation only worthy and righteous members of The Church of Jesus Christ of Latter-day Saints could become members of the Church of the Firstborn, a title reflecting the fact that Jesus Christ was and is the Firstborn Son of God in the spirit and is also the leader of those who receive of the fulness of the Father.

Selected Quotations

"Members of The Church of Jesus Christ of Latter-day Saints who so devote themselves to righteousness that they receive the higher ordinances of exaltation become members of the Church of the Firstborn. Baptism is the gate to the Church itself, but celestial marriage is the gate to membership in the Church of the Firstborn, the inner circle of faithful saints who are heirs of exaltation and the fulness of the Father's kingdom. (D&C 76:54, 67, 71, 94, 102; 77:11; 78:21; 88:1-5; Heb. 12:23.)

"The Church of the Firstborn is made up of the sons of God, those who have been adopted into the family of the Lord, those who are destined to be joint-heirs with Christ in receiving all that the Father hath." (Bruce R. McConkie, *MD,* p. 139.)

Scriptural Reference: Heb. 19:23.

Church offices and presiding quorums (*see also* First Presidency; Council of the Twelve; First Quorum of Seventy; Presiding Bishopric)

The Lord has revealed the organization of the various presiding offices and quorums of his church "line upon line, precept upon precept, here a little and there a little" according to the needs of the members of his church and their willingness to receive these truths. Undoubtedly, additional changes and enlargements will continue to be made in church organization as the Church continues to fulfill its divine destiny as a worldwide institution.

At the present time, the Church is governed by three major presiding quorums:

1. The Quorum of the First Presidency, consisting of the President of the Church and his counselors.

2. The Quorum (or Council) of Twelve Apostles, consisting of 12 special witnesses of Jesus Christ who have been called, ordained apostles, and set apart as members of the quorum.

3. The First Quorum of the Seventy, presided over by seven presidents and consisting of men who have been called and set apart to serve as members of the quorum. The Lord has already provided for the establishment of additional quorums of seventy as "the labor in the vineyard of necessity requires it." (107:96.)

The Patriarch to the Church and the members of the Presiding Bishopric are also considered to be general officers (General Authorities), but they do not form quorums in the same sense as the three quorums mentioned earlier.

Each of these major positions, quorums, and groups is discussed in this appendix under the title of the group and occasionally in the appropriate places where they are mentioned in the sections of the Doctrine and Covenants. Particular attention might be given to the materials for sections 20, 84, and 107.

Selected Quotations

"I believe that when the Presidency of this Church nominates a person for an office, it is not a personal nomination. I have that confidence in the Presidency and that testimony of the divinity of this Church. I believe that the Lord

Jesus Christ reveals to them through the Spirit of the Holy Ghost the men they should name to office, and I believe that same Spirit will inspire and direct the presidents of stakes and the bishops of wards and the heads of other organizations in this Church, if they will live for such inspiration, so that when they name people for office they will name them under the inspiration of the Holy Ghost." (Marion G. Romney, *CR,* October 1947, pp. 39-40.)

"I will inform you that it is contrary to the economy of God for any member of the Church, or anyone, to receive instructions for those in authority, higher than themselves; therefore, you will see the impropriety of giving heed to them; but if any person have a vision or a visitation from a heavenly messenger, it must be for his own benefit and instruction, for the fundamental principles, government, and doctrine of the Church are vested in the keys of the kingdom." (Joseph Smith, *HC* 1:388.)

Scriptural References: D&C 84; 102; 107; 112.

Common consent; "all things to be done by common consent" (*see also* Sustain)

Two guiding principles of administration in The Church of Jesus Christ of Latter-day Saints are (1) that officers are to be selected by the spirit of revelation by those who are in authority and (2) that people over whom those officers are to preside have the right and privilege to sustain them in their positions. Briefly, this law of common consent ultimately provides that the Lord counsels what should be done in his church and earthly kingdom, but then he allows the members to exercise their free agency in either accepting or rejecting the proposed officers. Through thus exercising their free agency, members can learn to operate on righteous principles and prepare themselves for the type of government that prevails in the celestial kingdom where righteous followers fully support and sustain their Righteous King.

Although the law of common consent prevails in regard to officers, where individual personalities are involved, the same principle does not apply to the validity of revelations or other basic, fundamental laws or truths. God is a God of truth, and he reveals only that which is true. Thus, it is not the prerogative of the people to vote whether or not a particular truth or revelation is valid. Opportunity may be given to the members, however, to indicate whether or not they favor the publication of a particular revelation with the official canon (scriptures) of the Church; they may also be given the opportunity to bind themselves by covenant to follow the instructions contained in the revelation.

The law of common consent is based upon the principle of free agency and is designed to enhance the spiritual growth and development of the saints.

Selected Quotations

"Administrative affairs of the Church are handled in accordance with the law of *common consent*. This law is that in God's earthly kingdom, the King counsels what should be done, but then he allows his subjects to accept or reject his proposals. Unless the principle of free agency is operated in righteousness men do not progress to ultimate salvation in the heavenly kingdom hereafter. Accordingly, church officers are selected by the spirit of revelation in those appointed to choose them, but before the officers may serve in their positions, they must receive a formal sustaining vote of the people over whom they are to preside. (D&C 20:60-67; 26:2; 28; 38:34, 35; 41:9-11; 42:11; 102:9; 124:124-145.)" (Bruce R. McConkie, *MD,* pp. 149-50.)

"It was designed by the Almighty in the organization of this Church, that the voice of the people should respond to the voice of the Lord. It is the voice of the Lord and the voice of the people together in this Church that sanctions all things therein. [Sec. 20:63-66.] In the rise of the Church the Lord gave a revelation which said that 'all things shall be done by common consent.' And the Lord designs that every individual member shall take an interest therein, shall bear a part of the responsibility, and shall take upon him or her the spirit of the Church, and be an active living member of the body." (Charles W. Penrose, *JD* 21:45-46.)

Scriptural References: D&C 26:2; 28:13; 104:21, 71-72, 85.

Confess; confessed; confession

Confession is an integral part of the law of forgiveness: "I, the Lord, forgive sins unto those who confess their sins before me and ask forgiveness, who have not sinned unto death." (D&C 64:7.) The sin should always be confessed to the Lord and to any aggrieved person or persons. Also, if the sin is serious enough, it should be confessed to the person's bishop or branch president. Recognition of guilt is one of the first steps of repentance and thus forgiveness. Confession of sin is another logical and necessary step in the process.

Selected Quotations

"I would assume that we are to confess all our sins unto the Lord. For transgressions which are wholly personal, affecting none but ourselves and the Lord, such confession would seem to be sufficient.

"For misconduct which offends another, confession should also be made to the offended one, and his forgiveness sought.

"Finally, where one's transgressions are of such a nature as would, unrepented of, put in jeopardy his right to membership or fellowship in the Church of Jesus Christ, full and effective confession would, in my judgment, require confession by the repentant sinner to his bishop or other proper presiding Church officer—not that the Church officer could forgive the sin (this power rests in the Lord himself and those only to whom he specifically delegates it) but rather that the Church, acting through its duly appointed officers, might with full knowledge of the facts take such action with respect to Church discipline as the circumstances merit.

"One having forsaken his sins and, by proper confession, cleared his conduct with the Lord, with the people he has offended, and with the Church of Jesus Christ, where necessary, may with full confidence seek the Lord's forgiveness and go forth in newness of life, relying upon the merits of Christ." (Marion G. Romney, *CR,* October 1955, p. 125.)

"Perhaps confession is one of the hardest of all the obstacles for the repenting sinner to negotiate. His shame often restrains him from making known his guilt and acknowledging his error. . . .

"The ideal confession is voluntary, not forced. It is induced from within the offender's soul, not sparked by being found out in the sin. Such confession, like the voluntary humility of which Alma spoke (Alma 32:13-16), is a sign of growing repentance. It indicates the sinner's conviction of sin and his desire to abandon the evil practices. The voluntary confession is infinitely more acceptable in the sight of the Lord than is forced admission, lacking humility, wrung from an individual by questioning when guilt is evident. Such forced admission is not evidence of the humble heart which calls forth the Lord's mercy: ". . . For I, the Lord, forgive sins, and am merciful unto those *who confess their sins* with humble hearts.' (D&C 61:2. Italics added.) . . .

"Generally it is unwise and quite unnecessary to confess the same sin over and over again. If a major transgression has been fully confessed to and cleared by the proper authority, the person may usually clear himself in any future interview by explaining that this is so and giving the authority's name. Providing there has been no repetition of the offense, nor a commission of any other serious transgression, usually the matter may be considered settled." (Spencer W. Kimball, *MF,* pp. 178-79, 181, 187.)

Scriptural References: D&C 19:20; 42:88-92; Lev. 5:5; Matt. 10:32; Luke 12:8; Mosiah 16:1; 26:29, 35-36; 27:31, 35.

Consecration; law of consecration (*see also* United Order)

The law of consecration is one of the highest laws of God given to man on the earth because it requires complete and total dedication to God and to his divine purposes. Obedience to this great law also brings great blessings, because the blessings that come from obedience to a law are commensurate with the nature of that particular law.

Unfortunately, so far in this dispensation, the Latter-day Saints have not been able to live the high standards of the law of consecration. The Lord has indicated, however, that this law must be observed by at least a righteous portion of the Saints before Jesus Christ will inaugurate his millennial reign of peace and righteousness upon the earth.

Selected Quotations

"It is written: 'He who is not able to abide the law of a celestial kingdom cannot abide a celestial glory.' (D&C 88:22.) The law of sacrifice is a celestial law; so also is the law of consecration. Thus to gain that celestial reward which we so devoutly desire, we must be *able* to live these two laws.

"Sacrifice and consecration are inseparably intertwined. The law of consecration is that we consecrate our time, our talents, and our money and property to the cause of the Church; such are to be available to the extent they are needed to further the Lord's interests on earth. . . .

"We are not always called upon to live the whole law of consecration and give all of our time, talents, and means to the building up of the Lord's earthly kingdom. . . .

"But what the scriptural account means is that to gain celestial salvation we must be *able* to live these laws to the full if we are called upon to do so. Implicit in this is the reality that we must in fact live them to the extent we are called upon so to do." (Bruce R. McConkie, *Ensign,* May 1975, p. 50.)

"It is a strange thing that there are members of the Church who cannot distinguish the difference between the law of consecration and communism. Consecration and communism have nothing in common. Communism as it is practiced relieves the individual of all his inherent rights bestowed upon him by divine agency. It makes of him a pawn of the state and removes from him his freedom. He is denied the right of independent action. Even his home life is disturbed and is controlled by the state. All freedom of expression is gone and fear takes the place of love; obedience is forced, not voluntarily given. In the Lord's plan, the inalienable rights of the individual are strictly and jealously protected. What he does he does voluntarily, not by force. His stewardship is given into his own hands and is of his own choice. His wants are carefully guarded and he is at liberty to surround himself with such comforts and conveniences as suit his fancy. His work is entirely voluntary and what he does is based on love of his fellowman. Such a plan naturally is for the salvation, temporally and spiritually, of man, and to the glory of God." (Joseph Fielding Smith, *CHMR* 1:306-7.)

Scriptural References: D&C 42:32-33; 83:6; 85:3; 105:29; 124:21; Acts 2:44; 4:32.

Constitution; Constitution of the United States

The leaders of the Church in this dispensation have clearly taught that the Constitution of the United States is a divine document and was prepared by wise men who were raised up by the Lord for the exact purpose of bringing forth principles of freedom and truth. The Prophet Joseph Smith placed the Constitution in an important context when he taught: "We say that God is true; that the Constitution of the United States is true; that the Bible is true; that the Book of Mormon is true; that the Book of Covenants is true; that Christ is true." (*HC* 3:304.)

The value and place of the Constitution, as compared with other principles and types of government, have been explained and extolled by Church leaders as indicated in the following selected quotations and other materials listed in connection with sections 98 (verses 5, 6), 101 (verses 77, 80), 109 (verse 54), and 124 (verse 63).

Selected Quotations

"The Constitution of the United States is a glorious standard; it is founded in the wisdom of God. It is a heavenly banner; it is to all those who are privileged with the sweets of its liberty, like the cooling shades and refreshing waters of a great rock in a thirsty and weary land. It is like a great tree under whose branches men from every clime can be shielded from the burning rays of the sun. . . ." (Joseph Smith, *HC* 3:304.)

"The constitution of this government was written by men who accepted Jesus Christ as the Savior of mankind. Let men and women in these United States then continue to keep their eyes centered upon him who ever shines as a Light to all the world. Men and women who live in America, 'the land of Zion,' have a responsibility greater than that yet borne by any other people. Theirs the duty, the obligation to preserve not only the Constitution of the land but also the Christian principles from which sprang that immortal document." (David O. McKay, *CR,* October 1942, p. 70.)

"Every Latter-day Saint should love the inspired Constitution of the United States—a nation with a spiritual foundation and a prophetic history—which nation the Lord has declared to be his base of operations in these latter days.

"Following the drafting of the Constitution, it awaited ratification by the states. In 1787 three states ratified the Constitution. In the next year eight more followed: and on April 6, 1789, the Constitution of the United States went into operation as the basic law of the United States when the electoral college unanimously elected George Washington as the first president of the nation. This date, I believe, was not accidental.

"In 1973 the First Presidency of the Church made public this statement: 'We urge members of the Church and all Americans to begin now to reflect more intently on the meaning and importance of the Constitution, and of adherence to its principles.' (*Ensign,* November 1973, p. 90.)

"I reverence the Constitution of the United States as a sacred document. To me its words are akin to the revelations of God. For God has placed his stamp of approval on the Constitution of this land. I testify that the God of heaven selected and sent some of his choicest spirits to lay the foundation of this government as a prologue to the restoration of the gospel and the second coming of our Savior." (Ezra Taft Benson, *Ensign*, May 1976, pp. 91-93.)

"The Constitution, as approved by the Lord, is still the same great vanguard of liberty and freedom in human government that it was the day it was written. No other human system of government, affording equal protection for human life, liberty, and the pursuit of happiness, has yet been devised or vouchsafed to man. Its great principles are as applicable, efficient and sufficient to bring today the greatest good to the greatest number, as they were the day the Constitution was signed. Our Constitution and our Government under it, were designed by God as an instrumentality for righteousness through peace, not war." (J. Reuben Clark, Jr., *CR*, April 1957, pp. 50-52.)

"The statement has been made that the Prophet said the time would come when this Constitution would hang as by a thread, and this is true. There has been some confusion, however, as to just what he said following this. I think that Elder Orson Hyde has given us a correct interpretation wherein he says that the Prophet said the Constitution would be in danger. Said Orson Hyde:

" 'I believe he said something like this—that the time would come when the Constitution and the country would be in danger of an overthrow; and said he: "If the Constitution be saved at all, it will be by the Elders of the Church." I believe this is about the language, as nearly as I can recollect it.' (*JD* 6:152.)" (Joseph Fielding Smith, *CR*, April 1950, p. 159.)

Scriptural References: D&C 89:10; 98:5-6; 101:77, 80; 109:54; 124:63.

Conversion; convert; converted

Conversion to the gospel of Jesus Christ involves much more than the changing of one's beliefs or ideas; it involves a complete change in one's manner of thinking and living. The change is so complete and real in true conversion that the scriptures refer to it as rebirth or as being born again. (Mosiah 27:24-29.)

Unfortunately, some people have confused *conviction* with *conversion,* and there is actually a world of difference between the two. A person can be convinced of something or can have a testimony of a particular thing and yet not do anything about it. However, if a person is truly converted to a principle or thing, then his actions are 100 percent consistent with what he knows to be right.

Selected Quotations

"Webster says the verb *convert* means 'to turn from one belief or course to another,' that *conversion* is 'a spiritual and moral *change* attending a *change* of belief with conviction.' As used in the scriptures, *converted* generally implies not merely mental acceptance of Jesus and his teachings, but also a motivating faith in him and in his gospel, a faith which works a transformation, an actual *change* in one's understanding of life's meaning and in one's allegiance to God—in interest, in thought, and in conduct. While *conversion* may be accomplished in stages, one is not really converted in the full sense of the term unless and until he is at heart a new person. *Born again* is the scriptural term." (Marion G. Romney, *Ensign,* November 1975, p. 71.)

"Some may ask the question as to how we convert others to the truth. The answer is, we do not. Conversion comes from above. Our part in this work is to plant the seeds of truth. These seeds are born of our conviction when we testify of the divine mission of Jesus Christ, the Son of the Living God, who offered himself as a sacrifice for the sins of the world. We rely upon the gift and power of the Holy Ghost to carry our message into the hearts of our listeners and witness unto them the truthfulness of our stated conviction." (Henry D. Moyle, *CR,* April 1961, pp. 101-2.)

"Somebody recently asked how one could know when he is converted. The answer is simple. He may be assured of it when by the power of the Holy Spirit his soul is healed. When this occurs, he will recognize it by the way he feels, for he will feel as the people of Benjamin felt when they received remission of sins. The record says, '. . . the Spirit of the Lord came upon them, and they were filled with joy, having received a remission of their sins, and having peace of conscience. . . .' (Mosiah 4:3.)" (Marion G. Romney, *CR,* October 1963, pp. 23-25.)

Scriptural References: D&C 42:64; 44:4; 109:65, 70; 112:13; Matt. 13:15; 18:3; Acts 3:19; 15:3; 28:27; Alma 19:16-31; 23:3-16.

Council of the Twelve; Twelve Apostles (*see also* Church offices and presiding quorums)

The Council of the Twelve Apostles is the second highest of the presiding quorums of the Church. The twelve apostles who comprise this quorum are special witnesses of the divinity of Jesus Christ.

Selected Quotations

"What importance is there attached to the calling of these Twelve Apostles, different from the other callings or officers of the Church? . . . They are the Twelve Apostles, who are called to the office of the Traveling High Council, who are to preside over the churches of the Saints, among the Gentiles, where there is a presidency established; and they are to travel and preach among the Gentiles, until the Lord shall command them to go to the Jews. They are to hold the keys of this ministry, to unlock the door of the Kingdom of heaven unto all nations, and to preach the Gospel to every creature. This is the power, authority, and virtue of their apostleship." (Joseph Smith, *HC* 2:200.)

"Though an Apostle is thus seen to be essentially an envoy or ambassador, his authority is great, as is also the responsibility associated therewith, for he speaks in the name of a power greater than his own—the name of Him whose special witness he is. When one of the Twelve is sent to minister in any stake, mission or other division of the Church or to labor in regions where no Church organization has been effected, he acts as the representative of the First Presidency, and has the right to use his authority in doing whatever is requisite for the furtherance of the work of God." (James E. Talmage, *Liahona, or Elders' Journal* 11:581.)

"On March 27, 1836, the Prophet Joseph Smith called upon the 'quorums and congregation of Saints to acknowledge the Twelve Apostles who were present as Prophets, Seers and Revelators' (*HC* 2:417) and they were thus sustained." (George Q. Cannon, *JI* 26:27-28.)

Scriptural References: D&C 1:14; 18:27; 20:2, 38; 21:1; 27:12; 29:12; 52:9; 64:39; 84:63; 102:30; 107:23, 33, 35, 58;

112:30; 124:128; 136:3; Mark 3:14; 6:7; Eph. 2:20, 4:11; 1 Ne. 1:10; 12:9; 3 Ne. 12:1; 13:25.

Covenant; covenants; "the new and everlasting covenant"

A covenant has been defined as a "two-edged promise." The dictionary suggests that a covenant is an agreement or promise, usually between two or more parties, for the performance of some action.

In the gospel sense, a covenant is a promise by the Lord that he will do certain things for us if we, in turn, promise to do certain things. Thus, a covenant of the gospel might be defined as a promise with blessing.

All principles and ordinances of the gospel are based on the principle of covenant. *"The* new and everlasting covenant" in its fulness is identical to the fulness of the gospel; both embrace all of the principles, ordinances, terms, conditions, and agreements inherent in the dealings of God with man here and in eternity. Sometimes a particular principle or ordinance might be referred to as *"a* new and everlasting covenant," but such usage does not rule out the possibility that other principles and ordinances might be referred to in the same words.

Selected Quotations

"We discover in this expression the thought that the covenants of the Lord, although they are from the beginning, are always new. Truth does not grow old. The same ordinances which are given us for our salvation are the ordinances required in all ages of the world. Not only that, but since our Father in heaven is unchangeable, and from everlasting to everlasting, that is from eternity to eternity, therefore his laws must be like him, also unchangeable. We may know, therefore, that the plan of salvation which has been given to us, was the same that was given to Adam. (Moses 7:64-68.) We can go still farther back and declare that these ordinances which are given us by which we seek salvation, have been the ordinances for salvation on other earths undergoing similar conditions, and so it will be through the countless ages of eternity. A divine law cannot be changed. The law of faith is eternal and is applied throughout the universe. The same is true of the law of repentance, of baptism, and every other principle of eternal truth." (Joseph Fielding Smith, *CHMR* 1:110.)

"There are some members of the Church who seem to think that the new and everlasting covenant is the covenant of celestial marriage, or marriage for eternity, but this is not so. Marriage for eternity is an everlasting covenant, and like the Lord said of baptism, we may say of marriage, it is a new as well as an everlasting covenant because it was from the beginning. It will be, if properly performed according to the law of the Lord, eternal. In the opening verses of Section 132, the Lord draws a distinction between *a* new and everlasting covenant and *the* new and everlasting covenant. While the definition is given in the negative form, it is plainly discernible that the new and everlasting covenant is the fulness of the Gospel." (Joseph Fielding Smith, *CHMR* 2:356.)

"When one joins the Church, he pledges certain things as he goes into the waters of baptism. When accepting the priesthood, we make a very definite covenant with the Lord. When partaking of the sacrament, we renew our covenants. I am using covenants, promises, and pledges interchangeably.

"When partaking of the sacrament, we renew those covenants. When accepting office in the Church, we agree to do certain things. We take upon ourselves certain covenants; we make certain pledges. You who have been to the temple know the covenants you make and the obligations you take upon yourselves.

"In home teaching, or any assignment that is given to us, if we accept that assignment, we certainly covenant with the Lord and the one who is giving the assignment that we will perform that duty. . . . It is important . . . that we keep our pledges and our covenants and keep our name good." (N. Eldon Tanner, *CR,* October 1966, pp. 98-100.)

Scriptural References: D&C 1:15, 22; 22:1, 3; 45:9; 82:11-21; 84:39-41; 88:131-35; 132:4-6, 15-19; 133:57.

Covet; covetousness (*see also* Ten Commandments)

The basic meaning of the word *covet* is to desire; thus, the word has both good and bad connotations. Using the term in a good and righteous sense, Paul encourages us to "covet earnestly the best gifts" (1 Cor. 12:31), including prophecy (1 Cor. 14:39). The denotation of *covet* is basically negative; the dictionary states that to covet is "to wish for enviously," "to desire what belongs to another inordinately or culpably."

Covetousness would be "marked by inordinate desire for wealth or for another's possessions."

Covetousness is contrary to the spirit of love and concern for others that is inherent in the gospel. The Lord condemned it in the Ten Commandments (Ex. 20:17; Mosiah 13:24) and has specifically stated that a person should not covet his "neighbor's wife" nor "thine own property" (D&C 19:25-26; 88:123; 136:20).

Selected Quotations

"To covet is to have an eager, extreme, and ungodly desire for something. The presence of *covetousness* in a human soul shows that such person has not overcome the world and is not living by gospel standards of conduct. Coveting is such a serious offense, and it is so imperative that man overcome all tendencies thereto, that the Lord condemned it in the Ten Commandments. (Ex. 20:17; Mosiah 13:24.)" (Bruce R. McConkie, *MD*, p. 156.)

Scriptural references: D&C 19:25-26; Ex. 18:21; 20:17; Luke 12:15; 16:14; 1 Cor. 5:10-11; 6:10; Mosiah 4:25; 13:24.

Creator; Jesus Christ as the Creator (*see also* Jesus Christ)

Shortly after Jesus Christ was crucified and even before his resurrection, he introduced himself to the people of the Book of Mormon in these words: "Behold, I am Jesus Christ the Son of God. I created the heavens and the earth, and all things that in them are." (3 Nephi 9:15.) Earlier in the Book of Mormon, Jesus Christ is identified as "the Creator of all things from the beginning" (Mosiah 3:8) and as the creator of "heaven and earth, and all things" (Mosiah 4:2).

This truth is also taught in the Doctrine and Covenants when the Lord introduced himself to David Whitmer through a revelation to Joseph Smith as "Jesus Christ, the Son of the living God, who created the heavens and the earth." (D&C 14:9.)

The leaders of the Church in this dispensation have explained that the plan of creation was proposed by God the Father but that it was carried out under the direction of His Son, Jesus Christ. Joseph Smith taught that the word *create* meant "to organize." Thus, the word *Creator* in referring to Jesus Christ could also mean the *Organizer*.

Selected Quotations

"John commences his record of the ministry of Jesus Christ with the following words:

" 'In the beginning was the Word, and the Word was with God, and the Word was God.

" 'The same was in the beginning with God.

" 'All things were made by him; and without him was not anything made that was made.' (John 1:1-3.)

"In modern revelation, and in the revelation given to the ancients which has been revealed to us in this dispensation, we have received the definite information that Jesus Christ was the Creator of this earth. Not only of this earth, but of many other earths. The Book of Moses (see Chap. 1) is very explicit on this matter and we are taught this doctrine in the Book of Mormon as well. [1 Ne. 19:7-10; Mosiah 16:15; Alma 11:39 quoted.] . . .

"Scriptures that refer to God in any way as the Father of the heavens and in the earth are to be understood as signifying that God is the Maker, the Organizer, the Creator of the heavens and the earth.

"With this meaning, as the context shows in every case, Jehovah, who is Jesus Christ, the Son of Elohim, is called 'the Father,' and even 'the very eternal Father of heaven and earth.' (See Mosiah 16:15.) With analogous meaning, Jesus Christ is called 'The Everlasting Father.' (Isa. 9:6; compare 2 Ne. 19:6.) The descriptive titles 'Everlasting' and 'eternal' in the foregoing texts are synonymous.

"That Jesus Christ, who we also know as Jehovah, was the executive of the Father, Elohim, in the work of creation is set forth in the book *Jesus the Christ,* Chap. 4. Jesus Christ, being the Creator, is constantly called the Father of heaven and earth in the sense explained above; and since his creations are of eternal quality, he is very properly called the Eternal Father of heaven and earth." (Joseph Fielding Smith, *CHMR* 1:167.)

"It has been usual to refer to the Father of our Lord as the Creator, and this is true in the sense that He is the originator of the plan. But the worlds were created through the Son. He was the great Architect, the Executive of the Great Council in heaven, through whom the plan of creation was made a reality, as well as the plan of redemption (Comp. Heb. 1:2).

"Note that the worlds were 'created,' which means, 'formed,' 'organized.' They were not 'made' out of 'nothing,' or *ex nihilo,* as the learned express that impossible proposition. Nor are they without beginning, in their present form. The world, as we know it, has a beginning; it will have an end. Matter itself has neither beginning nor end, as far as mortals can know.

"John, the beloved, in his visions on Patmos, saw the Lord in the midst of the seven candlesticks, or the seven principal churches in Asia Minor, among which the Apostle had been laboring for some years. He describes His appearance (Rev. 1:13-16). John had known the Master intimately in the flesh, but in His glory He inspired even John with terror (v. 17). In this vision of Joseph and Sidney, the element of terror was absent. The Lord had opened their eyes and quickened them beforehand, so that they could gaze on His glory though its radiance surpassed that of the sun." (Smith and Sjodahl, *DCC,* p. 449.)

Scriptural References: Moses 1:33; 2:1, 27; 7:48; Isa. 40:28; 43:15; 2 Ne. 9:5-6; 29:7; 3 Ne. 9:15.

Cross; "take up your cross"

Inasmuch as the cross was one of the instruments of crucifixion employed by the Romans in the death of Jesus, the symbol of the cross has become a symbol of Jesus Christ in the minds of many people. Some have even sculptured representations of Christ on the cross.

Members of The Church of Jesus Christ of Latter-day Saints, however, emphasize the resurrected and living Jesus Christ; the symbol of the cross or of the crucifix, which depicts the dead or dying Christ, is therefore not part of our worship.

The term *take up your cross* is found in both ancient and modern scripture, including at least three references in the Doctrine and Covenants (23:6; 56:2; 112:12). In Matthew 16:24 the Savior says, "If any man will come after me, let him deny himself, and take up his cross, and follow me." The Inspired Version of the Bible provides the meaning of this term as given by Jesus Christ himself: "And now for a man to take up his cross, is to deny himself all ungodliness, and every worldly lust, and keep my commandments." (Matt. 16:25-26.)

The meaning of this term is also clarified in other scriptures. For example, the Lord in 3 Nephi 12:30 states: "It is better that ye should deny yourself of these things, wherein ye will take up your cross, than that ye should be cast into hell."

Each person has areas of weakness where he or she must strive diligently to overcome that weakness and turn it into a strength. The term "take up your cross" has to do with this strengthening process by denying yourself "all ungodliness" and by keeping the commandments of God.

Selected Quotations

"The cross to be taken up may be heavy, perhaps to be dragged because too burdensome to be borne. We are apt to assume that self-denial is the sole material of our cross; but this is true only as we regard self-denial in its broadest sense, comprising both positive and negative aspects. One man's cross may consist mostly in refraining from doings to which he is inclined, another's in doing what he would fain escape. One's besetting sin is evil indulgence; his neighbor's a lazy inattention to the activities required by the Gospel of Jesus Christ, coupled perchance with puritanical rigor in other observances." (James E. Talmage, *VM*, p. 353.)

"We recently held an open house in the Arizona Temple. Following a complete renovation of that building, nearly a quarter of a million people saw its beautiful interior. On the first day of the opening, clergymen of other religions were invited as special guests, and hundreds responded. It was my privilege to speak to them and to answer their questions at the conclusion of their tours. I told them that we would be pleased to answer any queries they might have. Many were asked. Among these was one which came from a Protestant minister.

"Said he: 'I've been all through this building, this temple which carries on its face the name of Jesus Christ, but nowhere have I seen any representation of the cross, the symbol of Christianity. I have noted your buildings elsewhere and likewise find an absence of the cross. Why is this when you say you believe in Jesus Christ?'

"I responded: 'I do not wish to give offense to any of my Christian brethren who use the cross on the steeples of their cathedrals and at the altars of their chapels, who wear it on their vestments, and imprint it on their books and other literature. But for us, the cross is the symbol of the dying Christ, while our message is a declaration of the living Christ.'

"He then asked: 'If you do not use the cross, what is the symbol of your religion?'

"I replied that the lives of our people must become the only meaningful expression of our faith and, in fact, therefore, the symbol of our worship." (Gordon B. Hinckley, *Ensign,* May 1975, p. 92.)

Scriptural References: D&C 23:6; 56:2; 112:14; Matt. 10:38; 16:24; Mark 8:34; 10:21; Luke 9:23; 14:27; 3 Ne. 12:30.

Damned; damnation

The basic meaning of the word *damned* is "to condemn to a punishment or fate"; another meaning is "to be constricted in or prevented from growth and progress." A person is damned whenever he is prevented from reaching his potential as a son or daughter of God. This damnation may result from the poor choices of the individual, from his unwillingness to obey those laws upon which certain blessings are predicated, or from his lack of valiancy. Therefore, even a person in the lower degrees of the celestial glory might be considered as damned in that he does not have the power of eternal increase and cannot enjoy eternal life nor reach his potential as a son of God.

Usually the words *damned* and *damnation* are used in connection with the lower degrees of glory (terrestrial and telestial), and they are particularly relevant to those who are not worthy to inherit any of the degrees of glory.

Selected Quotations

"We believe that all will be damned who do not receive the gospel of Jesus Christ; but we do not believe that they will go into a lake which burns with brimstone and fire, and suffer unnamed and unheard-of torments, inflicted by cruel and malicious devils to all eternity.

"The sectarian doctrine of final rewards and punishments is as strange to me as their bodiless, partless, and passionless God. Every man will receive according to the deeds done in the body, whether they be good or bad. [D&C 76:110-11.] All men, excepting those who sin against the Holy Ghost, who shed innocent blood or who consent thereto, will be saved in some kingdom [D&C 76:40-45; 88:29-32]; for in my father's house, says Jesus, are many mansions. [John 14:2.]" (Brigham Young, *JD,* 11:125-26.)

"What is it to be damned? Does it mean that all who come under that sentence shall be cast into hell, there to dwell forever and forever? The light of the century, given by the Lord, declares the falsity of that construction.

"Salvation is graded ever upward until it culminates in the glorious conditions of exaltation. Though the term salvation is used in scripture in a general way, and we must learn to discriminate between salvation and exaltation as we read, so damnation is graded; else what did the Lord mean as recorded in the twelfth chapter of Mark, when he spoke of those who used their power and position to oppress and to work evil; when he said of such: 'These shall receive greater damnation'? Well, if there be a greater damnation there are lesser degrees of damnation and the term is used in the same sense of deprivation and forfeiture. That man enters into a degree of damnation who has forfeited his opportunities and therefore has rendered himself incapable of the advancement that would otherwise be possible." (James E. Talmage, *CR,* April 1930, pp. 95-96.)

Scriptural References: D&C 19:7; 132:4, 6, 27; Matt. 23:14, 33; 3 Ne. 11:34; 18:29; 26:5.

Darkness; chains of darkness; chains of hell; outer darkness; power of darkness; veil of darkness (*see also* Light *for "light which shineth in darkness"*)

A symbol of God is light, and a sacred descriptive name-title applied to him is that he is the God of light. The symbol of light to represent God is found in many scriptural references, ancient and modern. (See, for example, John 8:12; 12:35, 46; 1 Pet. 2:9; 1 Thes. 5:4; 1 Jn. 2:9.)

The opposite of light is darkness. In the gospel sense darkness represents evil, iniquity, and apostasy. As light is from God, darkness is of the devil. Thus, the term *chains of darkness* means the same as *chains of the devil* or *chains of hell.* The term *veil of darkness* is descriptive of unbelief and apostasy, while *powers of darkness* are also powers of the evil one or of Satan.

In Latter-day Saint terminology, *outer darkness* refers to

that state or condition where people no longer respond to the light or influence of God. Certainly sons of perdition would be in outer darkness.

Selected Quotations

"The expression 'the light and life of the world' is explained by John when writing his Gospel. Jesus Christ is the light which shineth in darkness and the darkness comprehendeth it not. In other words, because of the wickedness of the world, men fail to discern between light and darkness, their deeds being evil. Having eyes they see not, and having ears they hear not, but the Lord through an ancient prophet pronounced a woe on all such. (2 Ne. 9:28-38.)" (Joseph Fielding Smith, *CHMR* 1:155.)

"There is no saying of greater truth than 'that which doth not edify is not of God.' And that which is not of God is darkness, it matters not whether it comes in the guise of religion, ethics, philosophy or revelation." (Joseph Fielding Smith, *CHMR* 1:201-2.)

"When Adam, our first parent, partook of the forbidden fruit, transgressed the law of God, and became subject unto Satan, he was banished from the presence of God, and was thrust out into outer spiritual darkness. This was the first death. Yet living, he was dead—dead to God, dead to light and truth, dead spiritually; cast out from the presence of God; communication between the Father and the Son was cut off. He was absolutely thrust out from the presence of God as was Satan and the hosts that followed him. That was spiritual death. But the Lord said that he would not suffer Adam nor his posterity to come to the temporal death until they should have the means by which they might be redeemed from the first death, which is spiritual. Therefore angels were sent unto Adam, who taught him the gospel, and revealed to him the principle by which he could be redeemed from the first death, and be brought back from banishment and outer darkness into the marvelous light of the gospel." (Joseph F. Smith, *CR,* October 1899, p. 72.)

Scriptural References: D&C 1:30; 6:21; 10:21, 58; 21:6; 38:5, 8, 11; 50:23, 25; 95:6, 12; JS-H 2:13, 15, 20; Isa. 9:2; 29:18; 42:7; 49:9; 50:10; 58:10; 60:2; Matt. 6:23; 8:12; 22:13; 25:30; 27:45; 1 Ne. 12:17; 21:9; 22:12; 3 Ne. 13:23.

Dead; salvation of the dead, including baptism for the dead

There is no dead in the eyes of the Lord. Those who are dead to us (separated from us) are alive with God. God is not God of the dead, but is God of the living, for we are all alive to him.

God is also no respecter of persons; he is a God of law and also a God of justice and mercy. If a person is going to receive a particular blessing, he must obey the law upon which that blessing is predicated; this eternal law applies to those who have already departed from this life as well as to those who are now living or who will yet live upon the earth.

Many people have lived upon the earth during periods when the saving principles and ordinances of the gospel have not been available to them. Inasmuch as God is fair and is no respecter of persons, every person must have an opportunity to receive the gospel—if not in this life, then in the life to come. However, those who hear and receive the gospel in their spiritual post-earthly condition are not able to observe some of the gospel ordinances that require the use of physical matter: immersion in physical water for the remission of sins; laying on of physical hands for the reception of the Holy Ghost, etc. These ordinances are performed "for and in behalf of" these people by worthy members of the Church who qualify as their vicarious representatives on the earth.

The great principles of salvation for the dead open up the possibility of eternal gospel blessings to billions of the children of our Heavenly Father who did not have opportunity to hear and receive the gospel on the earth.

Selected Quotations

"I first mentioned the doctrine [baptism for the dead] in public when preaching the funeral sermon of Brother Seymour Brunson; and have since then given general instructions in the Church on the subject. The Saints have the privilege of being baptized for those of their relatives who are dead, whom they believe would have embraced the Gospel, if they had been privileged with hearing it, and who have received the Gospel in the spirit, through the instrumentality of those who have been commissioned to preach to them while in prison.

"Without enlarging on the subject, you will undoubtedly

see its consistency and reasonableness; and it presents the Gospel of Christ in probably a more enlarged scale than some have imagined it." (Joseph Smith, *HC* 4:231.)

" 'Else what shall they do which are baptized for the dead, if the dead rise not at all? why are they then baptized for the dead?' (1 Cor. 15:29.)

"This is a challenging question. Why are you performing vicarious baptisms for those who are dead if there is no resurrection? History bears out the facts of the practice of baptizing for those who had died without the benefit of this ordinance. It would seem certain, from the question that was asked by Paul, that this vicarious practice was followed in the branch of the church in Corinth. His query is well taken. There would be no sense in such ordinances except there be a resurrection." (Howard W. Hunter, *IE,* June 1969, p. 107.)

"We have been authorized to perform baptisms vicariously so that when they [the dead] hear the gospel preached and desire to accept it, that essential ordinance will have been performed. They need not ask for any exemption from that essential ordinance. Indeed, the Lord Himself was not exempted from it.

"And so the question may be asked, 'You mean you are out to provide baptism for all who have ever lived?'

"And the answer is simply, 'Yes.' For we have been commanded to do so.

" 'You mean for the entire human family? Why, that is impossible. If the preaching of the gospel to all who are living is a formidable challenge, then the vicarious work for all who have ever lived is impossible indeed.'

"To that we say, 'Perhaps, but we shall do it anyway.' . . .

"I say that no point of doctrine sets this church apart from the other claimants as this one does. Save for it, we would, with all of the others, have to accept the clarity with which the New Testament declares baptism to be essential and then admit that most of the human family could never have it.

"But we have the revelations. We have those sacred ordinances." (Boyd K. Packer, *Ensign,* November 1975, p. 99.)

"Before the Church was officially established, when the so-called 'constitution' of the Church was laid down by revelation in Section 20 of the Doctrine and Covenants, a statement of the universality of the mission of Jesus Christ was given which included the dead as well as the living:

" 'Not only those who believed after he came in the meridian of time, in the flesh, *but all those from the beginning, even as many as were before he came,* . . . should have eternal life.' (D&C 20:26. Italics added.)

"Much of the work we do in the Church is preparatory work for us to qualify ourselves so that we can be of service not only to our fellowmen now living on the earth, but to those who lived before us. These good men and women are our ancestors, our fathers and our mothers through whose blood we receive our bodies and our life. What a debt we owe them to see that they too receive eternal life in Jesus Christ through the work and sacrifices we make in their behalf.

"This work of salvation for the dead is so important that Paul stated that they who are dead cannot be made perfect without our help. (Heb. 11:40.) Joseph Smith added that neither can we be made perfect without doing proxy ordinance work for our deceased ancestors. (D&C 128:18.)" (Theodore M. Burton, *IE,* December 1970, pp. 58-59.)

"The Lord has placed the baptismal font in our temples below the foundation, or the surface of the earth. This is symbolical, since the dead are in their graves, and we are working for the dead when we are baptized for them. Moreover, baptism is also symbolical of death and the resurrection, in fact, is virtually a resurrection from the life of sin, or from spiritual death, to the life of spiritual life. (See D&C 29:41-45.) Therefore when the dead have had this ordinance performed in their behalf they are considered to have been brought back into the presence of God, just as this doctrine is applied to the living. Other ordinances of the endowment and sealings therefore do not have to be performed below the surface of the earth as in the case of baptism." (Joseph Fielding Smith, *CHMR* 4:137-38.)

"It matters not what else we have been called to do, or what position we may occupy, or how faithfully in other ways we have labored in the Church, none is exempt from this great obligation [of helping to save those who have died]. It is required of the apostle as well as the humblest elder. Place, or distinction, or long service in the Church, in the mission field, the stakes of Zion, or where or how else it may have been, will not entitle one to disregard the salvation of one's dead.

"Some may feel that if they pay their tithing, attend their regular meetings and other duties, give of their substance to the poor, perchance spend one, two, or more years preaching in the world, that they are absolved from further duty. But the greatest and grandest duty of all is to labor for the dead." (Joseph Fielding Smith, *DS* 2:148-49.)

Scriptural References: D&C 124:29, 32-39; 127:5-6, 10; 128:1-18.

Death; "second death" (*for information on the term* "shall not taste of death" *see material listed after* 42:46)

Death is a separation of the spirit from the physical body. The physical death is usually described in the scriptures as "temporal death," since it is temporary and will eventually be overcome through the resurrection. As Paul wrote anciently: "As in Adam all die, even so in Christ shall all be made alive." (1 Cor. 15:22.)

Death can also be used to refer to a separation from God or from the teachings of God (the gospel). The scriptures sometimes refer to "spiritual death," which is death (or separation) from things pertaining to righteousness, or spiritual alienation from God.

"Second death" is a spiritual death and is much more serious in its consequences than physical death. The Savior taught, "Fear not them which kill the body, . . . but rather fear him which is able to destroy both soul and body in hell." (Matt. 10:28.)

The "second spiritual death" is the most serious death of all; it consists of permanent separation from God and comes upon sons of perdition who are cast into outer darkness and are thus permanently dead (or separated) from God.

Selected Quotations

"Every man that is born into the world will die. It matters not who he is, nor where he is, whether his birth be among the rich and the noble, or among the lowly and poor in the world, his days are numbered with the Lord, and in due time he will reach the end. . . . All fear of this death has been removed from the Latter-day Saints. They have no dread of the temporal death, because they know that as death came upon them by the transgression of Adam, so by the righteousness of Jesus Christ shall life come unto them, and though they die they shall live again. Possessing this knowledge, they have joy even in death, for they know that they shall rise again and shall meet again beyond the grave. They know that the Spirit dies not at all; that it passes through no change, except the change from imprisonment in this mortal clay to freedom and to the sphere in which it acted before it came to this death." (Joseph F. Smith, *CR,* October 1899, pp. 70-71.)

"Pretend, my little friends, that my hand represents your spirit. It is alive. It can move by itself. Suppose that this glove represents your mortal body. It cannot move. When the spirit enters into your mortal body, then it can move and act and live. Now you are a person—a spirit with a body, living on the earth.

"Someday, because of old age, or perhaps a disease, or an accident, the spirit and the body will be separated. We then say a person has died. Death is a separation. All of this was according to a plan.

"Remember my hand represents your spirit and the glove represents your body. While you are alive the spirit inside the body can cause it to work and to act and to live.

"When I separate them, the glove, which represents your body, is taken away from your spirit; it cannot move anymore. It just falls down and is dead. But your spirit is still alive.

" 'A spirit born of God is an immortal thing. When the body dies, the spirit does not die.' (First Presidency, *IE,* March 1912, p. 463.)

"It is important that you get in your mind what death is. Death is a separation.

"The part of you that looks out through your eyes and allows you to think and smile and act and to know and to be, that is your spirit and that is eternal. It cannot die." (Boyd K. Packer, *Ensign,* July 1973, pp. 51, 53.)

"In this natural body are the seeds of weakness and decay, which, when fully ripened or untimely plucked up, in the language of scripture, is called 'the temporal death.' The spirit is also subject to what is termed in the scriptures and revelation from God, 'spiritual death.' The same as that which befell our first parents, when through disobedience and transgression they became subject to the will of Satan, and were thrust out from the presence of the Lord and became spiritually dead. . . .

"The 'temporal death' is one thing, and the 'spiritual death' is another thing. The body may be dissolved and become extinct as an organism, although the elements of which it is composed are indestructible or eternal, but I hold it as self-evident that the spiritual organism is an eternal, immortal being, destined to enjoy eternal happiness and a fullness of joy, or suffer the wrath of God, and misery—a just condemnation, eternally. Adam became spiritually dead, yet he lived to endure it until freed therefrom by the power of the atonement, through repentance, etc. Those upon whom the second death shall fall, will live to suffer and endure it, but without hope of redemption. The death of the body or natural death is but a temporary circumstance to which all were subjected through the fall and from which all will be restored or resurrected by the power of God, through the atonement of Christ." (Joseph F. Smith, *JD* 23:169-70.)

Scriptural References: D&C 63:17; 76:37; Alma 12:16, 32; 13:30.

Degrees of glory (*see also* Celestial; Terrestrial; Telestial)

Every person will be judged according to the degree to which he (or she) has been obedient and faithful to the laws given to him. The degree of faithfulness differs almost from person to person; thus, logic and reason would both suggest that there must be many degrees of judgment.

The Doctrine and Covenants contains the most complete account of the present scriptures on the eventual destiny of man. The revelations in this scripture (particularly sections 76, 88, and 131) indicate that there are three major heavens or degrees of glory:

1. Celestial—the highest, of which the sun is a symbol, for those who are righteous and "valiant in the testimony of Jesus."

2. Terrestrial—the middle, of which the moon is a symbol, for the less valiant but still "honorable men of the earth" who do not keep all of the "thou shalt" commandments.

3. Telestial—the lowest, of which the stars are symbols, for those who break the "thou shalt not" commandments of God (murderers, liars, adulterers, etc.).

Section 131 indicates there are "three heavens or degrees" within the celestial glory, which would indicate that both the terrestrial glory and the telestial glory might also have different "heavens or degrees." In addition to the three major degrees of glory, there is at least one degree that is not a degree of *glory;* the sons of perdition are cast out to this degree of *"un*glory."

Selected Quotations

"Paul informs us of three glories and three heavens. He knew a man that was caught up to the third heaven. [2 Cor. 12:1-5.] Now, if the doctrine of the sectarian world, that there is but one heaven, is true, Paul, what do you tell that lie for, and say there are three? Jesus said unto His disciples, 'In my Father's house are many mansions, if it were not so, I would have told you. I go to prepare a place for you, and I will come and receive you to myself, that where I am ye may be also.' [John 14:2-3.]" (Joseph Smith, *HC* 5:425-26.)

"The Lord has shown to us that there are differences of rewards. Some of his children will attain to what is called celestial glory. Other of his children will not have faith enough nor exercise their agency in this direction to gain that glory; but they will gain terrestrial glory. There are others that will not progress that far; they will feel reluctant to obey the laws that pertain to the terrestrial, and they will obtain telestial glory. There are still others, that will not attain even to the telestial glory. Why is it that there are these differences? Is it because God has chosen some of us for the telestial glory, some of us for the terrestrial glory, and some of us for the celestial glory? No, there is no such predestination as this. We are all born with our free agency; with the power within ourselves, aided by the blessings of God, to attain unto the highest glory. How shall we attain unto the highest glory? There is only one way, and that is by observing the highest laws. The highest laws, when obeyed, bring as a reward the highest glory; and the man or woman who expects to attain to the highest glory without obeying these laws, deceives himself or herself. It cannot be done. If I rise above the telestial glory, I must obey a law that will lift me above that. If I rise to the terrestrial glory, it will be by obeying terrestrial law. If I do not obey laws higher than that, I cannot attain to a higher glory." (George Q. Cannon, *CR,* April 1900, p. 54.)

"The three different degrees of glory are made very plain and clear [in Section 76], I think, to all people who will read with a prayerful heart. The celestial glory is likened to the sun, because the sun is the biggest luminary that we know much about; the sun in our firmament is to us the brightest orb that revolves, and the glory of the terrestrial kingdom is likened to the moon, because the moon is second in our sight in glory; and the third degree, telestial, is called the glory of the stars, and as one star differs from another star in its magnitude and glory, according to what we know of astronomy, so it is called the telestial kingdom." (Charles W. Penrose, *CR,* April 1922, p. 29.)

Scriptural References: D&C 76; 78:7, 14; 88; 1 Cor. 15:41-43; 2 Cor. 15:2.

Discernment (*see also* Gifts of the Spirit)

The power of discernment has been given to all men in varying degrees and is a manifestation of the light of Christ, which is given to all, as explained in Moroni 7:12-18. However, faithful Latter-day Saints are also promised the spirit or gift of discernment, which can be received through revelation from the Holy Ghost. (D&C 63:41.) This gift can be used not only to discern good from evil (Moroni 7:12-18), the righteous from the wicked (D&C 101:95; Malachi 3:18; 3 Ne. 24:18), and false spirits from spirits sent from God (D&C 46:23; 1 Cor. 12:10), but its perfect operation can also make known even "the thoughts and the intents of the heart" (D&C 33:1; Alma 12:1-3; Hebrews 4:12).

Selected Quotations

"The gift of discernment is essential to the leadership of the Church. I never ordain a bishop or set apart a president of a stake without invoking upon him this divine blessing, that he may read the lives and hearts of his people and call forth the best within them. The gift and power of discernment in this world of contention between the forces of good and the power of evil is essential equipment for every son and daughter of God." (Stephen L Richards, *CR,* April 1950, p. 163.)

"The Saints should be guided by the Spirit of God and subject to those who preside in the meetings. If the Bishop, who is a common judge in Israel, tells a person to restrain this gift, or any other gift it is the duty of that person to do it. The Bishop has a right to the gift of discernment, whereby he may tell whether these spirits are of God or not, and if they are not they should not have place in the congregations of the Saints. No man or woman has a right to find fault with the Bishop for restraining him or her in any of these matters. The Bishop is the responsible party and it is his privilege to say what shall be done." (Abraham O. Woodruff, *CR,* April 1901, p. 12.)

Scriptural References: D&C 33:1; 46:23, 27; 63:41; 101:95; 131:7; Moses 1:27-28; Matt. 16:3; Heb. 4:12; 5:14; Alma 18:18; 24:30; 32:35; 3 Ne. 24:18.

Dispensation; "dispensation of the fulness of times"

The basic meanings of *dispense* are "to weigh out," "to deal out in portions," "to prepare and distribute." In a sense, a dispensation of the gospel is when there has been a special "giving out" or dispensing of gospel truths.

The earliest dispensation on this earth was in the days of Adam (the Adamic dispensation). But due to subsequent apostasy, it was necessary to restore some of the gospel truths at varying times in the days of Enoch, Noah, Abraham, Moses, the meridian of time, and Joseph Smith. The Book of Mormon indicates other periods of time when truths of the gospel were either restored or given to a greater extent; for example, reference is sometimes made to the Jaredite dispensation, the Nephite dispensation, etc.

However, the ancient prophets foretold of a time when there would be a restitution or restoration of all the gospel truths (principles and ordinances) that had ever been revealed on the earth, during the "dispensation of the fulness of times."

The teachings of the Lord in the Doctrine and Covenants indicate that the present dispensation is indeed the long-awaited dispensation of the fulness of times.

Selected Quotations

"The dispensation of the fulness of times will bring to light the things that have been revealed in all former dispensations; also other things that have not been before revealed. [D&C 124:41.]" (Joseph Smith, *HC* 4:426.)

"We are living the dispensation of the fulness of times, and in this dispensation . . . not only are the people to be gathered together, but the glorious truths which have been made manifest in the ages that are past will all be brought forth in the dispensation in which we are living, and things kept hid from the foundation of the world will be made manifest; for the Lord has promised it; and His promises never fail of fulfillment." (Charles W. Penrose, *CR,* October 1911, pp. 48-49.)

Scriptural References: D&C 27:13; 110:12, 16; 112:30-32; 121:31; 124:41; 128:9, 18, 20-21; 1 Cor. 9:17; Eph. 1:10; Col. 1:25.

Divorce (*see also* Marriage)

Marriage is intended to be eternal. Divorce (the "legal dissolution of a marriage" or, in biblical times "writing of divorcement") is not encouraged by the Church except under extreme circumstances, although it is permitted and the divorced persons can remarry if worthy.

Selected Quotations

"We continue to be concerned with the rising divorce rate. Every divorce means saddened lives, broken vows, neglected and deprived children, and broken homes. We decry divorce and feel that there are relatively few divorces which are justifiable. Great care should be taken in forming marriage alliances; then both parties should do their utmost to keep these marriages happy ones. This can be done. . . . Family stability is fairly well measured by the divorce rate in the community." (Spencer W. Kimball, *Ensign,* November 1975, p. 6.)

"Analyze the divorces of which you know, and you will find so often selfishness is in them. Most divorces are unwarranted and come of weakness and selfishness and often result in great unhappiness for the divorced persons and also almost irreparable damage and frustration to the unfavored children, who are torn and disturbed.

"Certainly, selfishness is near its greatest peak when innocent children must suffer for the sins of their parents. Almost like a broken record come from divorcees that it is better to have them grow up in a single-parent home than a fighting home. The answer to that specious argument is: there need be no battling parents in fighting homes.

"Someone checked a long list of divorces and found that almost all of them came about through selfishness, where people were determined to *get* as much as they could and *give* as little as possible. It was found in this survey that about 90 percent gave as the reason for the breakup immorality on the part of one or both of the participants.

"Immorality is totally selfish. Can you think of a single unselfish element in that sin? Accordingly, if two good people will discard selfishness, generally they can be compatible." (Spencer W. Kimball, *Ensign,* May 1974, p. 7.)

Scriptural References: Matt. 5:31-32; 19:7; 3 Ne. 12:31-32.

Earth; the earth abides its law; earth to be transfigured; "ends of the earth"; "face of the earth"; "four quarters of the earth"

The earth was created as a living thing to provide a place wherein man could gain a physical body and live out his mortal probation. As a living entity, the earth itself is subject to laws, obedience to which will gain for the earth a celestial glory. The earth was baptized of water at the time of the flood; will be baptized of fire and the spirit; will die, be resurrected, and attain a physical celestial status as a fit dwelling place eternally for the celestial beings. The meek will then inherit the earth, as has been promised in both ancient and modern times.

Several terms are used in the scriptures as idioms signifying everyone or everywhere on the earth, including such expressions as "ends of the earth" (meaning every conceivable place on the earth), "face of the earth" (meaning everywhere on the earth), and "four quarters of the earth" (meaning from every direction and covering or including the entire earth).

Selected Quotations

"The materials out of which this earth was formed, are just as eternal as the materials of the glorious personage of the Lord himself. . . . This Being, when he formed the earth, did not form it out of something that had no existence, but he formed it of materials that had an existence from all eternity: they never had a beginning, neither will one particle of substance now in existence ever have an end. There are just as many particles now as there were at any previous period of duration, and will be while eternity lasts. Substance had no beginning; . . . the earth was formed out of eternal materials, and it was made to be inhabited and God peopled it with creatures of his own formation." (Orson Pratt, *JD* 19:286.)

"Associated with matter-energy was the implication in Joseph Smith's teachings that the energy in the universe is a form of intelligence; that is, in a manner not fully understood by man, some form of life resides in all matter, though of an order wholly different from the organized intelligence of men or higher living things. Hence, everything in the universe is alive. The differences among rock, plant, beast, and man are due to the amount and organization of life element. Confirming this view, the Prophet in a revelation said: [D&C 88:26, quoted.] That implies clearly that the earth is a living organism. . . . We live then in a living universe which in all its component parts is intelligent." (John A. Widtsoe, *JS,* pp. 149-50.)

"And this world, so benighted at present, and so lightly esteemed by infidels, when it becomes celestialized, it will be like the sun, and be prepared for the habitation of the Saints, and be brought back into the presence of the Father and the Son. It will not then be an opaque body as it now is, but it will be like the stars of the firmament, full of light and glory; it will be a body of light. John compared it, in its celestialized state, to a sea of glass." (Brigham Young, *JD* 10:175.)

"Are the wicked to receive the earth as an inheritance? No; for Jesus did not say, Blessed are the wicked, for they shall inherit the earth; this promise was made only to the meek. Who are the meek? None but those who receive the ordinances of the Gospel, and live according to them. . . . And after they have died as the earth will die, they will have to be resurrected as this earth will be resurrected, and then receive their inheritances upon it." (Orson Pratt, *JD* 1:293.)

"The opinion that this globe is to be annihilated finds no support in the Word of God. Here, the important truth is revealed that our globe will be sanctified from all unrighteousness, and prepared for celestial glory, so that it will be fit for the presence of God, the Father. It will die (v. 26), but it will be quickened again. It will not remain a dead planet, whirling about aimlessly in space; nor will it be distributed in the form of cosmic dust, throughout the universe. It will be glorified, by celestial glory, and become an abode for resurrected beings (v. 20)." (Smith and Sjodahl, *DCC,* p. 543.)

Scriptural References: D&C 14:9; 29:9-26; 38:5-39; 49:6-23; 59:2-18; 63:20-37; 65:1-6; 101:23-46; 109:38-74.

Elect; elect of God; "mine elect"

In order to further and promote his purposes on the earth, God has "elected" or chosen certain people or groups of people to represent him or further his cause upon the earth. Several terms are used in the scriptures to refer to these people—"chosen people," "holy nation," "peculiar people," "royal priesthood," "mine elect," etc.

It was foreordained and prophesied that Jesus Christ would be born upon the earth through the lineage of one of these groups of chosen people—the Jews, who are one of the major branches of the house of Israel. The Savior frequently referred to this people as the elect of God or as "mine elect." After the Jewish people as a nation rejected Jesus Christ as the Messiah, he said, "I came unto my own, and my own received me not." (3 Ne. 9:16.)

In the Doctrine and Covenants, the Savior promised that in the last days he would gather his "elect from the four quarters of the earth, even as many as will believe in me, and hearken unto my voice." (D&C 33:6.) Included among these elect ones will be some of the seed of Judah as prophesied by Isaiah: "I will bring forth a seed out of Jacob, and out of Judah an inheritor of my mountains: and mine elect shall inherit it, and my servants shall dwell there." (Isa. 65:9.)

Scriptural References: D&C 25:3; 29:7; 33:6; 35:20; 84:24; 124:3; Moses 7:62; JS-M 1:22, 27, 37, 39.

Election; calling and election

The term *calling and election* appears in 53:1 and *election of grace* in 84:99. In both places, the election is made by God and involves worthiness and faithfulness to the end.

Selected Quotations

"St. Paul exhorts us to make our calling and election sure. This is the sealing power spoken of by Paul in other places: 'In whom ye also trusted, that after ye heard the word of truth, the gospel of your salvation; in whom also after that ye believed, ye were sealed with that holy Spirit of promise, Which is the earnest of our inheritance until the redemption of the purchased possession, unto the praise of his glory.' (Eph. 1:13-14.)

"For some reason many members of the Church are troubled over the expression 'sealed by the Holy Spirit of promise.' They have wondered if this is a separate Spirit other than the Holy Ghost, and if the sealing by the Holy Spirit of promise has reference only to marriage for eternity. The Holy Spirit of promise is the Holy Ghost. Not only is he a Spirit of promise in marriage, but in every other ordinance—baptism, confirmation, ordination, etc. The promise is that the Holy Spirit places the stamp of approval on each ordinance and there it will remain if the recipient is just and true. Every blessing is based upon this promise of faithfulness. If the covenanting person or persons break their covenant, the Holy Spirit removes the seal and the promised blessing is not received.

"In quoting the words of Paul (Eph. 1:14) the Prophet added these words to the Bible text: 'that we may be sealed up unto the day of redemption.' This evidently was said by Paul, but was not included in the translation as it has come down to us." (Joseph Fielding Smith, *CHMR* 2:215.)

Scriptural References: D&C 53:1; 84:99; Rom. 11:5; 1 Thes. 1:4; 1 Pet. 1:10.

Elias

Biblical scholars have assumed that Elias and Elijah are the same person, claiming that *Elias* is simply the Greek form of the Hebrew name *Elijah.* The visions in section 110 of the Doctrine and Covenants clearly indicate that there were at least two ancient prophets who were known by the titles or names of Elias and Elijah.

Selected Quotations

"After the departure of Moses, Elias who held the keys of the gospel in the days of Abraham appeared and conferred the keys of his dispensation, saying 'that in us and our seed all generations after us should be blessed.' By this expression, reference is not made to the 'seed' of Joseph Smith and Oliver Cowdery but to the 'seed' of all faithful members of the Church. We know that the Lord called Abraham and made some very important promises to him and his posterity. His descendants through Isaac and Jacob, constitute the house of Israel, the people to whom the Lord intrusted the covenants and delivered his word through prophets for the guidance of the whole world. What prophet this Elias is that was sent to restore these keys is not definitely known. The title 'Elias' has been given to several prophets who have been appointed to important work in different dispensations. The work of an 'Elias' is the work of a forerunner, or one who goes before a greater to prepare the way. John the Baptist was an Elias, Noah was an Elias. (D&C 27:7.) The Lord has declared that Elias shall restore all things spoken of by all the holy prophets. (D&C 27:6.) This may have reference to all the prophets who were sent with keys of authority to Joseph Smith and Oliver Cowdery." (Joseph Fielding Smith, *CHMR* 2:49.)

Scriptural References: D&C 27:6-7; 76:100; 77:9, 14; 110:12.

Elijah; calling of Elijah; mission of Elijah (see also *Elias*)

The life and ministry of Elijah the prophet are primarily documented in the books of 1 and 2 Kings of the Old Testament. He was translated or assumed into heaven by being taken up in a chariot of fire (2 Kings 2:1-11); thereafter he disappeared from the Old Testament record except for the prophecy of Malachi that he would return to the earth "before the coming of the great and dreadful day of the Lord." (Mal. 4:5.)

Three of the New Testament writers record the appearance of Elijah and Moses to Peter, James, and John on the Mount of Transfiguration. (Matt. 17:3; Mark 9:4; Luke 9:30.)

The Book of Mormon indicates that the resurrected Jesus Christ quoted Malachi's prophecy concerning Elijah to the surviving Lehites. (3 Ne. 25:5.)

The Pearl of Great Price includes the words of the angel Moroni when he appeared to Joseph Smith on September 21, 1823, and quoted the prophecy concerning Elijah. (JS-H 1:38.)

The Doctrine and Covenants includes both the prophecy of the coming of Elijah (Sec. 2) and also an account of his appearance in the Kirtland Temple. (Sec. 110.)

Thus, Elijah is mentioned in all the standard works of The Church of Jesus Christ of Latter-day Saints. It is also interesting to note that the title "the prophet" is consistently used in connection with this great man. Malachi's prophecy indicated that it was necessary for Elijah to return to the earth before the second coming of Jesus Christ (before the "great and dreadful day of the Lord"); otherwise, the earth would be utterly wasted at his coming. The following references indicate why the calling, mission, and latter-day appearance of Elijah are so important to all mankind.

Selected Quotations

"Elijah was the last prophet that held the keys of the Priesthood, and who will, before the last dispensation, restore the authority and deliver the keys of the Priesthood, in order that all the ordinances may be attended to in righteousness. It is true that the Savior had authority and power to bestow this blessing; but the sons of Levi were too prejudiced. 'And I will send Elijah the prophet before the great and terrible day of the Lord,' etc. etc. [Mal. 4:5-6.] Why send Elijah? Because he holds the keys of the authority to administer in all the ordinances of the Priesthood; and without the authority is given, the ordinances could not be administered in righteousness." (Joseph Smith, *HC* 4:211.)

"Joseph Smith was ordained under the hands of Peter, James and John, receiving the Melchizedek Priesthood, and he went forth and built the Church in this dispensation. All that he did was valid; all those ordinances were valid; but in order that the binding power should come which is recognized in the heavens, and by which we pass by the angels and the Gods to exaltation, it had to come from Elijah, who held that power upon the face of the earth, for the Lord had given it to him, and so he came to Joseph Smith and Oliver Cowdery on the 3rd day of April, and bestowed upon them the keys of his priesthood." (Joseph Fielding Smith, *Elijah the Prophet and His Mission,* pp. 36-37.)

"Through the power of this priesthood which Elijah bestowed, husband and wife may be sealed, or married for eternity; children may be sealed to their parents for eternity; thus the family is made eternal, and death does not separate the members. This is the great principle that will save the world from utter destruction.

"In like manner, the children who are living may have the same ordinances performed for their ancestors who are dead. . . .

"The sealing power of Elijah makes it possible for this joining of the families, generation to generation, back to the beginning. Now, if these units of authority were not here, then the work of sealing, by which the family units are preserved, could not be performed; then the binding power by which all blessings are sealed in heaven, as well as on earth, would be lacking. If this were so, the earth would be smitten with a curse, for all work which had been done, without these binding or sealing ordinances, would fall to the ground unfulfilled.

"If Elijah had not come, we are led to believe that all the work of past ages would have been of little avail, for the Lord said the whole earth, under such conditions, would be utterly wasted at his coming. Therefore his mission was of vast importance to the world. It is not the question of baptism for the dead alone, but also the sealing of parents and children to parents, so that there should be a 'whole and complete and perfect union, and welding together of dispensations, and keys, and powers, and glories,' from the beginning down to the end of time. . . .

"Why would the earth be wasted? Simply because if there is not a welding link between the fathers and the children— which is the work for the dead—then we will all stand rejected; the whole work of God will fail and be utterly wasted. Such a condition, of course, shall not be." (Joseph Fielding Smith, *DS* 2:118, 120-22.)

"Edersheim in his work, *The Temple,* says: 'To this day, in every Jewish home, at a certain part of the Paschal service [i.e. when they drink the "third cup"]—the door is opened to admit Elijah the prophet as forerunner of the Messiah, while appropriate passages are at the same time read which foretell the destruction of all heathen nations. It is a remarkable coincidence that, in instituting his own Supper, the Lord Jesus connected the symbol, not of judgment, but of his dying love, with his "third cup." '

"It was, I am informed on the third day of April, 1836, that the Jews, in their homes at the Paschal feast, opened their doors for Elijah to enter. On that very day Elijah did enter—not in the home of the Jews to partake of the Passover with them—but he appeared in the house of the Lord, erected to his name and received by the Lord in Kirtland, and there bestowed his keys to bring to pass the very things for which these Jews, assembled in their homes, were seeking." (Joseph Fielding Smith, *DS* 2:100-101.)

Scriptural References: D&C 2:1-2; 27:9; 35:4; 98:16; 110:13-15; 128:17; 133:55; JS-H 2:38-39; Mal. 4:5; 3 Ne. 25:5.

Endowment; the endowment

The word *endow* means "to furnish, provide, equip, or give." In a general sense the word *endowment* could refer to the act or the process of endowing or to the thing that is being endowed (given). Among Latter-day Saints the word *endowment* has special meaning, as it refers to a special gift of knowledge or understanding of the eternal purposes of life that is given in the temple. As indicated in some of the following quotations, the "endowment" received by the Saints in the Kirtland Temple is not the same or as complete as the endowment given in temples today.

Selected Quotations

"As early as January, 1831, the Lord said he had called the members of the Church out of New York to the Ohio, and he would give them his law; and there they would be 'endowed with power from on high.' (D&C 38:32.) In this same month he said he had kept in store a blessing such as is not known among the children of men, and it shall be poured forth upon their heads. And from thence men shall go forth into all nations. They were to go forth with greater power because of the endowment. In February, 1831, he further said that the elders should be taught from on high. 'Sanctify yourselves and ye shall be endowed with power that ye may give even as I have spoken.' (43:16.) In June, 1833, the Lord commanded that his house in Kirtland be built. 'Yea, verily I say unto you, I gave unto you a commandment that you should build a house, in the which house, I design to endow those whom I have chosen with power from on high.' (D&C 95:8.) The elders were commanded to tarry until they could receive this endowment.

"In Kirtland, November 12, 1835, in a council meeting with the apostles, the Prophet said: 'You need an endowment, brethren, in order that you may be prepared and able to overcome all things; and those that reject your testimony will be damned.' (*HC* 2:309.) January 20, 1836, a council meeting was held in the Kirtland Temple in which the endowment was given, consisting of washing, anointing with oil, washing of feet and other ordinances. It was on this occasion that the Prophet had the heavens opened to his view in which he saw the glory of the celestial kingdom, and the redemption of little children in the kingdom of God. (*HC* 2:379-381.)" (Joseph Fielding Smith, *CHMR* 2:304.)

"The endowment promised and received in the Kirtland Temple was not the same as today's temple endowment ceremony, though priesthood members did participate in a 'partial endowment, the full ordinance being reserved for a future performance when a temple designed for ordinance work itself should be built [at Nauvoo].' " (Bruce R. McConkie, *Ensign,* August 1976, p. 10.)

"The first complete endowments in this dispensation were given in Nauvoo, May 4, 1842. These, of course, could not be given in the temple, and were given elsewhere. In the time of poverty and when necessity requires the giving of blessings which belong to the House of the Lord, and there is no such house, they may be given in the wilderness, on a mountain or some other spot, consecrated to that purpose. The Savior had to give an endowment to Peter, James and John, on the Mount of Transfiguration. The saints of that dispensation had to be baptized for the dead and give other ordinances for the dead in the wilderness, for the temple in Jerusalem was closed to them and had been desecrated, therefore the wilderness, mountain tops and rivers, had to be utilized for the temple work for their dead in that dispensation." (Joseph Fielding Smith, *CHMR* 2:333.)

Scriptural References: D&C 38:32, 38; 43:16; 95:8; 105:11-12, 18, 33; 110:9; 124:39; 132:59.

Endure to the end

Many people start out on a venture full of hope and enthusiasm but soon fall by the wayside and abandon the enterprise. The Lord rightfully expects his Saints to be faithful at all times, under all conditions, and in all seasons. Both ancient and modern scriptures urge the faithful to "endure to the end" because only then will the promised blessings be received.

Selected Quotations

"Why endure to the end? Why is it so important to our salvation? Can we not be faithful part of the time and stray a bit, and yet get our salvation? Why does he limit the application to 'whosoever is of my church, and endureth of my church to the end'? To answer these questions we must ask and answer one more: What is the purpose of our existence?

"We are the children of God, actually his offspring. He is our Father. We are not mere creatures of the Almighty, but rather we are his sons and daughters. We are of the divine race. We are in this life to prove ourselves, and develop within us Godlike traits of character. We must become Christlike in our souls in order to come into his presence. . . .

"The Gospel is the plan. The commandments are the detailed instructions. By living them we achieve our goal. But where does 'enduring to the end' come in? Steadfastness is part of good character. If we are not steadfast, we are not strong. If we are not steadfast, we waver, we are undecided, unpredictable; we stumble and fall; . . . we never overcome.

"There is nothing Christlike in weakness, neither in disobedience. We are commanded to 'overcome.' What is it that we are to overcome? Weakness, indecision, turning back, failure, sin. We are to fight a battle and win. The victory and all the effort leading up to it, build character. Do we build character in being wishy-washy? Do we build character in only partial performance?

"To become like him we must be strong. We must not bow to temptation. We must not be idle. Only in labor is there true excellence. But we must follow the right road to perfection. We must adopt the correct instructions. That is why he emphasized that he is the door to the sheepfold, that the way to life is straight and narrow. There is only one way.

"Hence he taught: [D&C 10:69, quoted.] In his Church, and only in his Church, is the way of salvation. By following that path—to the very end—we gain salvation. [D&C 53:7; 66:12; 76:5.]" (Mark E. Petersen, *YFY,* pp. 288-89.)

"It is he who endureth to the end that shall be saved, he who, in the midst of all the afflictions and trials to which he may be subjected, keeps his integrity unsullied and never swerves from his rectitude in the severest trials and temptations. Men and women of this description are rare. We may know this by reading the words of Jesus . . . that few there be that find that strait and narrow way which leadeth unto eternal lives." (George Q. Cannon, *MS* 25:88-89.)

"Lest we lull ourselves into thinking that only the gross sins of life cause us to falter, consider the experience of the rich young man who came running to the Savior and asked the question: [Matt. 19:16-22 quoted.]

"He preferred the comforts of earth to the treasures of heaven. He would not purchase the things of eternity by abandoning those of time. He faltered. He failed to finish.

"So it was with Judas Iscariot. He commenced his ministry as an apostle of the Lord. He ended it a traitor.

"Lust for power, greed of gold, and disdain for honor have ever appeared as faces of failure in the panorama of life. Captivated by their artificial attraction, many noble souls have stumbled and fallen, thus losing the crown of victory reserved for the finisher of life's great race.

"Concerning those who fall short, John Greenleaf Whittier's words seem particularly fitting:

" 'For of all sad words of tongue or pen, The saddest are these: "It might have been!" ' ('Maude Muller.')" (Thomas S. Monson, *Ensign,* July 1972, pp. 68-69.)

Scriptural References: D&C 14:7; 18:22; 20:25, 29; 53:7; 63:47; Matt. 10:22; 24:13; 3 Ne. 15:9; 27:6, 16, 17.

Enoch; city of Enoch; the Zion of Enoch (*for further information on the* "order of Enoch," *see* United Order)

Very little is known by the world concerning the great prophet Enoch, who is mentioned in the Bible only in Genesis 4 and 5 of the Old Testament and Luke 3:37, Hebrews 11:5, and Jude 1:14 of the New Testament. However, the writers of both the Old Testament and New Testament indicate that Enoch was so righteous that he was translated (transfigured).

Modern scriptures and revelations provide much additional information on this great man, including some of his writings. His life and teachings are of particular importance to Latter-day Saints, because Enoch was able to prepare a people who became so righteous they were actually taken off the telestial earth so they could live a terrestrial order. In a somewhat similar manner, a people must be prepared in these latter days to be worthy to live at least a terrestrial order so they will be able to live with Jesus Christ when he comes on the earth to rule in power and great glory.

Selected Quotations

"We learn amongst other truths, all based upon Enoch's faith in the atoning blood of the Lamb slain from before the foundation of the world, the following:

"That Enoch was clothed with glory and saw the Lord who talked with him as one man talks with another, even face to face.

"That the Lord commanded Enoch to preach repentance; and to baptize in the name of the Father, and the Son, which is full of grace and truth, and the Holy Spirit, which bears record of the Father and the Son.

"That so great was the faith of Enoch that he led the people of God, overthrew their enemies, and at his word the earth trembled, whilst the mountains, rivers, and seas obeyed his command.

"That through his faith Enoch saw the days of the coming of the Son of Man in the flesh, and by it he obtained a covenant from the Lord that after Noah's day He would never again cover the earth by a flood, and obtained an unalterable decree that a remnant of his seed should always be found among all nations while the earth should stand.

"That the Lord showed Enoch the world and its future history for the space of many generations, even unto the end of the world.

"That so great was the faith and righteousness of Enoch and his people, that the Lord came down and dwelt with them, and in process of time Enoch's city, Zion, was taken up into heaven, and many, through the testimony of the Father and the Son, were afterwards caught up by the powers of Heaven into Zion.

"And, further, that Enoch, through the favor of the Almighty, . . . obtained a promise that the future peopling of the earth should come through his seed; thus making him one of the great agencies to administer salvation in the heavens and upon the earth. [Moses ch. 7.]" (John Taylor, *MA*, pp. 79-80.)

"In this day of wickedness it is difficult to understand how an entire people could become so righteous that it was no longer expedient that they should remain on the earth, and, therefore, were translated and taken away to await the time when righteousness should come. The people of the city of Enoch, because of their integrity and faithfulness, were as pilgrims and strangers on the earth. This is due to the fact that they were living the celestial law in a telestial world, and all were of one mind, perfectly obedient to all commandments of the Lord. When Christ comes, these people will be returned to the earth again, for this is their eternal abode." (Joseph Fielding Smith, *CHMR* 1:195.)

Scriptural References: D&C 38:4; 45:11; 76:57, 67, 100; 78:1, 4, 9; 84:15-16; 107:48, 53, 57; 133:54; Moses 5:42-8:19; Gen. 4:17-18; 5:18-24; Luke 3:37; Heb. 11:5; Jude 1:14.

Eternal life

Eternal life is distinct from and much more than immortality. It is the power to have eternal increase ("eternal lives") after the resurrection; it is exaltation in the highest degree of the celestial kingdom; it is the type of life lived by God, our Heavenly Father. The possibility of eternal life is God's greatest gift to man. As the Lord has said: "For behold, this is my work and my glory—to bring to pass the immortality and eternal life of man." (Moses 1:39.) Eternal life is mentioned or discussed in at least thirty sections of the Doctrine and Covenants.

Selected Quotations

"*Immortality* denotes length of life—deathless. *Eternal life* denotes quality of life—the quality of life God enjoys." (Marion G. Romney, *Ensign,* May 1975, p. 85.)

"Eternal life means more than merely continuing to exist. Its qualitative value will be determined by what we believe and do while in mortality and by our conformity to eternal law in the life to come. Eternal existence would be most undesirable if that existence became fixed and static upon arrival there. . . . We cannot imagine nor would we desire an eternity without opportunity for growth and development. We believe in eternal progression." (Hugh B. Brown, *IE,* December 1969, p. 32.)

"God's greatest gift is eternal life, but that pertains to Eternity. The greatest blessing that our Heavenly Father can bestow upon us in time, or while we are here, is the power to lay hold upon eternal life. The Everlasting Gospel, through obedience to its every requirement, and the gift of the Holy Ghost, gives this power. It not only saves—it exalts men to where God and Christ dwell in the fulness of Celestial Glory." (Orson F. Whitney, *CR,* October 1929, p. 30.)

"Conversion and baptism alone are not sufficient to one's assurance of eternal life. To receive exaltation in the kingdom of God, a person must abide the fulness of celestial law. (See D&C 76:50-70.) Some people erroneously think if they receive all the ordinances of the gospel, regardless of their transgressions, they will inherit the celestial mansions of our God. What a rude awakening awaits such false-thinking individuals, '. . . for the Lord cannot look upon sin with the least degree of allowance.' (Alma 45:16.) The gift of eternal life cannot be obtained outside of the Church established by the Father and the Son." (Delbert L. Stapley, *Ensign,* January 1974, pp. 44-45.)

Scriptural References: D&C 5:22; 6:7; 20:14, 26; 88:4; 98:13, 20; 124:55; 128:12, 23; 131:5; 132:24, 55, 63; Moses 1:39; 5:11; 6:59; 7:45; Abr. 2:11; Mosiah 5:15; 15:23-25; 18:9, 13; 26:20; 28:7; 3 Ne. 9:14; 15:9.

Eternity to eternity

The term *eternity to eternity* (39:1; 76:4) essentially means from the pre-earthly existence to the post-earthly existence.

Selected Quotations

"The thing that seems so puzzling is that God is 'the same yesterday, today, and forever'; that he is 'from all eternity to all eternity.' Well, is not this true, and is there any conflict with the thought that he has passed through the same states that we are destined to do? *From eternity to eternity means from the spirit existence through the probation which we are in, and then back again to the eternal existence which will follow.* Surely this is everlasting, for when we receive the resurrection, we will never die. We all existed in the first eternity. I think I can say of myself and others, we are *from* eternity; and *we will be to eternity everlasting if we receive the exaltation.* The intelligent part of man was never created but always existed. That is true of us as well as it is part of God, yet we are born sons and daughters of God in the spirit and are destined to exist forever. *Those who become like God will also be from eternity to eternity.* " (Joseph Fielding Smith, *DS* 1:12.)

" 'Everlasting to everlasting' means from the eternity past to the eternity future as far as man's understanding is concerned, from the pre-existence through the temporal (mortal) life unto the eternity following the resurrection." (Joseph Fielding Smith, *AGQ* 2:127.)

Scriptural References: D&C 39:1; 76:4; Moses 6:67; 7:29, 31; Mosiah 3:5; Alma 13:7; Moro. 8:18.

Everlasting fire (*see also* material for 19:6-12)

The term *everlasting fire* is used in somewhat the same sense as the terms *everlasting torment, everlasting hell, everlasting punishment,* and *everlasting damnation.* The word *everlasting* indicates that it is endless or eternal; the word *fire* refers to the type of torment and anguish experienced by the wicked as they attempt to satisfy the demands of the laws of justice for their sins. As explained in D&C 19, such punishment is referred to as "eternal" or "endless" in the sense that the law of justice is always operating, and thus the possibility of suffering or payment of broken law is always present. It does not necessarily mean that the punishment of any one person will be endless, eternal, or everlasting in its duration.

Scriptural References: D&C 29:28; 43:33; 63:17, 34, 54; 76:36, 44, 105; 101:66; 2 Ne. 9:16; Mosiah 26:27.

Exaltation

Exaltation is a synonym for eternal life. Exaltation comes only to those who inherit the highest degree within the celestial kingdom. It is the power to have eternal increase after the resurrection; it consists in the continuation of the family unit throughout eternity; it is the type of life that is lived by our Heavenly Father.

The possibility of exaltation, or of eternal life, is God's greatest gift to man. The word *exaltation* appears in at least eleven verses of section 132 and is discussed in further detail in the supplementary readings of that section.

Selected Quotations

"The perfection upon which exaltation hangs is an individual matter. It is conditioned upon the observance of celestial laws as they apply to earth life. The Word of Wisdom is one of them, so also are chastity, tithing, observance of the Sabbath day, prayer, honesty, industry, love of God and fellow men, patience, kindness, charity, and all the rest of the principles and ordinances of the gospel of Jesus Christ. Each individual who observes one or more of these laws shall receive the blessings predicated thereon, and each Church member who will, with all the energy of his soul, diligently strive to live them all, shall receive the blessings predicated upon such striving. Eternal life, the greatest gift of God, is that blessing, and it will follow the living of the gospel as the night the day, regardless of statistics or averages, or of what others think or say or do." (Marion G. Romney, *CR,* October 1956, pp. 15-16.)

"It is not necessary for a man to be a president of a stake, or a member of the Quorum of the Twelve, in order to attain a high place in the celestial kingdom. The humblest member of the Church, if he keeps the commandments of God, will obtain an exaltation just as much as any other man in the celestial kingdom. . . . In as far as we observe to keep the laws of the Church we have equal opportunities for exaltation." (George Albert Smith, *CR,* October 1933, p. 25.)

Scriptural References: D&C 109:69; 124:9; 132:17-63.

Excommunication

Excommunication is the most severe form of discipline or penalty that can presently be imposed by a Church court. It consists in severing the person from his Church ties so that he can no longer be considered a member of the Church. If the excommunicant subsequently repents, proves to be faithful, and is found qualified and worthy by the appropriate Church authorities, he may be readmitted to the Church through baptism. Following further testing and proven faithfulness, the former blessings of the readmitted member may also be restored. Excommunication differs from disfellowshipment in its severity and in the steps that must be followed before the person can again become a member of the Church in good standing.

Selected Quotations

"The Church applies only two kinds of punishment. The first and lightest is that of being disfellowshipped, which means that the hand of fellowship is withdrawn from the accused, who cannot then officiate in the activities of the Church, though he may be present and partake of the spirit of all Church gatherings. In the course of time, if his conduct justifies it, he is again admitted into full fellowship by the tribunal that found him guilty. Re-baptism is not necessary.

"The second punishment is that of excommunication. This means loss of membership in the Church. An excommunicated member can re-enter the Church only after showing full faith, and sincere repentance, by being again baptized." (John A. Widtsoe, *PC,* p, 175.)

"There are some who claim that even though they are excommunicated from the Church, their priesthood and temple blessings are not taken away. Let us remind those persons that the power to seal is also the power to loose, for the Lord has said of his true servants that 'whatsoever thou shalt bind on earth shall be bound in heaven: and whatsoever thou shalt loose on earth shall be loosed in heaven.' (Matt. 16:19; D&C 132:46.) Excommunication takes away all rights, privileges, and blessings of the Church." (Mark E. Petersen, *Ensign,* July 1973, pp. 110-11.)

Scriptural References: D&C 41:1; 64:12-13; 76:29-37; 82:1-7; 104:8-9; 121:13-25; 134:10; Matt. 18:15-19; 1 Cor. 5:1-5; 1 Tim. 1:20.

Faith (*see also* Gifts of the Spirit)

Faith in the Lord Jesus Christ has been identified by the Prophet Joseph Smith as the first principle of the gospel, the foundation of all righteousness, and the moving cause of all action in intelligent beings. Without faith, the Prophet said, "there is no power, and without power there could be no creation nor existence." (Lectures on Faith, end of Lecture 1.) Faith is more than belief, as faith impels to action whenever action is required. As James stated, "Faith, if it hath not works, is dead, being alone." (James 2:17.)

Selected Quotations

"We cannot know what faith is if we have never had it, and we cannot obtain it as long as we deny it. Faith and doubt cannot exist in the same time, for one will dispel the other." (Thomas S. Monson, *IE,* June 1964, 67:509.)

"I admit that difficulties are to be encountered because a man cannot really know what faith is until he has experienced it, nor can he really experience it without recognizing it for what it is. It is rather confusing to say to one who denies the reality of spiritual things, 'You, sir, cannot know what faith is because you have never had it and you cannot get it as long as you deny it.' This sounds paradoxical, but in reality, it is not so absurd as it sounds, for this reason—faith is a divine gift open to all men to receive, if only their attitude and life will permit its reception. It is true only the faithful know this, but their knowledge of it is so certain that they never despair of bringing the knowledge to others. In this absolute certitude of the faithful lies the hope and promise of universal conversion." (Stephen L Richards, *CR*, October 1937, p. 36.)

"Whether seeking for knowledge of scientific truths or to discover God, one must have faith. This becomes the starting point. Faith has been defined in many ways, but the most classic definition was given by the author of the letter to the Hebrews in these meaningful words: 'Now faith is the substance of things hoped for, the evidence of things not seen.' (Heb. 11:1.) In other words, faith makes us confident of what we hope for and convinced of what we do not see. The scientist does not see molecules, atoms, or electrons, yet he knows they exist. He does not see electricity, radiation, or magnetism, but he knows these are unseen realities. In like manner, those who earnestly seek for God do not see him, but they know of his reality by faith. It is more than hope. Faith makes it a conviction—an evidence of things not seen.

"The author of the letter to the Hebrews continues: 'Through faith we understand that the worlds were framed by the word of God, so that things which are seen were not made of things which do appear.' (Heb. 11:3.) Faith is here described as believing or having the conviction that the world was created by the word of God. Witnesses cannot be produced to prove this fact, but faith gives the knowledge that what we see in the wonders of the earth and in all nature was created by God. It is just as reasonable to believe in an unseen God, in a literal resurrection, or in the miracles of the things pertaining to the spiritual as it is to believe in some of the discoveries in the field of the physical sciences. Faith is the primary tool in the realm of religion, and it is also the tool of the scientist." (Howard W. Hunter, *Ensign*, November 1974, p. 97.)

Scriptural References: James 1:5-6; 5:14-15; Alma 32:26-43.

Fasting; fast offering; fast day; fast meeting

The law of the fast was taught in Old Testament times, preached by the righteous in the Book of Mormon, and instituted in the Church in this dispensation directly by the Lord. When combined with prayer, fasting increases spirituality, faith, devotion, love, and humility in the person fasting, increases his understanding and appreciation of his dependence upon God, and subjects his physical body to higher spiritual laws. Fasting in the right spirit should be observed because it is a commandment of God; it might also properly be observed with a specific goal or objective in mind.

Fasting has been defined by Church leaders as complete abstinence from food and drink from "even to even." The money saved by not consuming the food should be donated for the benefit and blessing of the poor. These fast offerings should be administered by the proper authorities in the Church, who should be aware of the needs of others.

Fasting, when properly observed, is conducive to spiritual growth, and the Lord has provided a special testimony meeting to be held in connection with the fasting of the Saints where they can "meet together . . . to speak one with another concerning the welfare of their souls." (Moro. 6:5.) In recent times this fast and testimony meeting has been combined with a sacrament meeting, usually the first sacrament meeting of each month.

Selected Quotations

"Now, while the law requires the Saints in all the world to fast from 'even to even' and to abstain both from food and drink, it can easily be seen from the scriptures and especially from the words of Jesus, that it is more important to obtain the true spirit of love for God and man, 'purity of heart and simplicity of intention,' than it is to carry out the cold letter of the law. The Lord has instituted the fast on a reasonable and intelligent basis, and none of his works are vain or unwise. His law is perfect in this as in other things. Hence, those who can are required to comply thereto; it is a duty from which they cannot escape; but let it be remembered that the observance of the fast day by abstaining twenty-four hours from food and drink is not an absolute rule, it is no iron-clad law to us, but it is left with the people as a matter of conscience, to exercise wisdom and discretion.

"But those should fast who can, and all classes among us should be taught to save the meals which they would eat, or their equivalent, for the poor. None are exempt from this; it is required of the Saints, old and young, in every part of the Church." (Joseph F. Smith, *GD*, pp. 243-44.)

"It is generally conceded that most people usually consume more food than the body requires. Overeating clogs the system with deleterious waste products. When such a condition exists a short fast is useful as a means of restoring the body to its normal active state.

"But besides this there is the spiritual strength derived from the subjecting of the physical appetite to the will of the individual. 'He who reigns within himself and rules passions, desires and fears is more than a king.' If there were no other virtues in fasting but gaining strength of character, that alone would be sufficient justification for its universal acceptance." (David O. McKay, *CR,* April 1932, pp. 64-65.)

"To keep the Sabbath in this manner is fasting and prayer; or, in other words, rejoicing and prayer.

"Fasting should be rejoicing.

"Fasting, as an expression of sorrow, is natural, for in deep affliction man does not crave nourishment to the same extent as under normal conditions. In the Law of Moses one annual fast day was provided—the day of atonement (Lev. 23:27-29). But on solemn occasions other fast days were observed. Joshua and the leading Elders of Israel were prostrate before the Ark one entire day after the defeat in the battle of Ai (Josh. 7:6). David fasted when his child was sick (2 Sam. 12:16). Moses fasted forty days on Mount Horeb. Elijah fasted a similar period, as did our Lord before entering upon His ministry. The children of God, in all ages, have found comfort and strength in fasting and prayer. In answer to prayer with fasting, extending over a period of two days and nights, Alma was healed (Mosiah 27:22, 23). Alma fasted and prayed many days, in order to receive a testimony of the truth (Alma 5:46). There are many instances of fasting recorded in the Book of Mormon. Paul reminded the Saints that he and his companions had proved themselves to be ministers of God in 'fastings' as well as in all other circumstances (2 Cor. 6:5). Our Lord warns His disciples not to fast as hypocrites who look sad and distort their countenances in order to be seen by men, but to appear as if going to a social function in order that God, "who seeth in secret" may reward them openly (Matt. 6:16-18). This is in harmony with what God revealed through Joseph the Prophet, that fasting should be rejoicing. It is also in harmony with the view taken by Isaiah (58:3-8). The Latter-day Saints have a Fast Sunday every month, on which they bear testimony to the goodness of the Lord to them, and remember the poor by donations. If they understand the gospel, they will make every Sunday a fast-Sunday, by abstaining from work, partaking of simple food, and devoting the day to spiritual matters." (Smith and Sjodahl, *DCC,* pp. 352-53.)

Scriptural References: D&C 59:13-14; 88:76, 119: 95:7, 16; 109:8, 16; Isa. 58:3-6; Matt. 4:2; 6:16-18; 9:14-15; 3 Ne. 13:16, 18; 27:1.

Feet; cleansing of feet; "shake off the dust of thy feet"

The custom of having missionaries cleanse their feet, either by washing or wiping off the dust, as a testimony against the wicked who refused to accept the gospel, was practiced in New Testament times and was reinstituted by the Lord in this dispensation. Because of the serious obligation associated with this act, Church leaders have counseled that it should only be done under the direction of the Spirit. The act appears to be associated with the commandment that the missionaries (and members) are to make certain they are clean from the sins of the wicked.

Selected Quotations

"The elders were to seek out from among the people the honest in heart and leave their warning testimony with all others, thus they would become clean from their blood. The cleansing of their feet, either by washing or wiping off the dust, would be recorded in heaven as a testimony against the wicked. This act, however, was not to be performed in the presence of the offenders, 'lest thou provoke them, but in secret, and wash thy feet, as a testimony against them in the day of judgment.' The missionaries of the Church who faithfully perform their duty are under the obligation of leaving their testimony with all with whom they come in contact in their work. This testimony will stand as a witness against those who reject the message, at the judgment." (Joseph Fielding Smith, *CHMR* 1:206.)

"Our Lord instructed His first Apostles to shake the dust off their feet, when they departed from a house or a city in which their message had been rejected. Paul and Barnabas did so, when they were forced to leave Antioch in Pisidia (Acts 13:50-1). Paul, at Corinth, when the Jews opposed him and blasphemed, shook his raiment and said, 'Your blood be upon your own heads; I am clean' (Acts 18:6). The significance of this solemn act is made clear in Nehemiah 5:13. This prophet, after having taken a promise of the priests, shook his lap and said, 'God shake out every man from his house, and from his labor, that performeth not this promise, even thus be he shaken out and empty.' To shake the dust of the feet signified the same thing. The Elders of the Church were to perform this act in secret, as a testimony against scoffers and persecutors on the day of judgment, and only when prompted by the Spirit, lest they should make a serious mistake." (Smith and Sjodahl, *DCC,* p. 360.)

Scriptural References: D&C 24:15; 60:15; 75:26; 84:92; 88:139-40; 99:4; John 11:2; 12:3; 13:5-14.

First Presidency (*see also* Church offices and presiding quorums)

The quorum of the First Presidency consists of the President of the Church and his counselors and is the presiding quorum in the Church today.

Selected Quotations

"The First Presidency of the Church was organized March 18, 1833, with Joseph Smith, president, and Sidney Rigdon and Frederick G. Williams as counselors. This was in fulfillment of the commandment given in a revelation the eighth of that month (Sec. 90). . . .

"One year before, in March 1832, the Lord had called Frederick G. Williams to this position as a counselor and to hold the 'keys of the kingdom, which belongeth always unto the Presidency of the High Priesthood.' Sidney Rigdon was also called and these men had acted in this calling for one full year before they were set apart. The Prophet laid his hands on the head of each in turn and conferred upon each the authority to take part with him in the First Presidency of the Church. In this manner the presiding council of the Church was organized for the first time in this dispensation." (Joseph Fielding Smith, *CHMR* 1:392-93.)

"The Lord in the beginning of this work revealed that there should be three High Priests to preside over the High Priesthood of His Church and over the whole Church. (D&C 107:22, 64, 65, 66, 67, 91, and 92.) He conferred upon them all the authority to preside over all the affairs of the Church.

They hold the keys of the house of God, and of the ordinances of the Gospel, and of every blessing which has been restored to the earth in this dispensation. This authority is vested in a Presidency of three High Priests. They are three Presidents. The Lord himself so calls them. (D&C 107:29.) But there is one presiding President, and his counselors are Presidents also. . . . I have always held . . . that it is wrong for one man to exercise all the authority and power of presidency in The Church of Jesus Christ of Latter-day Saints." (Joseph F. Smith, *CR,* November 1901, p. 82.)

"The question as to whether the Counselors held the same power as the President was soon debated among the people. What could the counselors do without direct appointment from the President? These questions were answered in a meeting on January 26, 1836. The prophet there said, 'The Twelve are not subject to any other than the First Presidency . . . and where I am not, there is no First Presidency over the Twelve.' In other words, were the President taken, the Counselors would have no authority. The Counselors do not possess the power of the President and cannot act in Church matters without direction and consent of the President." (John A. Widtsoe, *JS,* p. 303.)

"There are certain ordinances which belong to the Priesthood, from which flow certain results; and the Presidents or Presidency are over the Church; and revelations of the mind and will of God to the Church are to come through the Presidency. This is the order of heaven, and the power and privilege of this Priesthood." (Joseph Smith, *HC* 2:477.)

"It does not follow and never has followed that the members of the first presidency of the Church are necessarily to be ordained apostles. They hold by virtue of their rights as presidents of the Church all the keys and all the authority that pertains to the Melchizedek Priesthood, which comprehends and comprises all of the appendages to that priesthood, the lesser priesthood and all the offices in the priesthood from first to last, and from least to greatest." (Joseph F. Smith, *CR,* April 1913, p. 4.)

Scriptural References: D&C 68:15, 19, 22; 102:26-27, 33; 112:20, 30; 117:13; 120:1; 124:126.

First Quorum of the Seventy (*see also* Seventy; Church offices and presiding quorums)

The First Quorum of the Seventy is the third highest of

the presiding quorums of the Church. The members of this quorum serve under the direction of the First Presidency and the Council of the Twelve.

Selected Quotations

"On the 28th of February, the Church in council assembled, commenced selecting certain individuals to be Seventies, from the number of those who went up to Zion with me in the camp . . . to begin the organization of the first quorum of Seventies, according to the visions and revelations which I have received. The Seventies are to constitute traveling quorums, to go into all the earth, whithersoever the Twelve Apostles shall call them." (Joseph Smith, *HC* 2:201-2.)

"Next to the Twelve Apostles are the First Seven Presidents of the Seventies. These Seven Presidents are called to look after the interests of this great body of Seventies, to counsel, to direct, to warn them against the spirit of neglect and indifference, or commend them for their good works.

"The seven presidents of Seventies labor under the direction of the Twelve Apostles, and hold themselves in constant readiness to respond to every call." (Rudger Clawson, *CR*, October 1903, p. 59.)

"If the first Seventy are all employed and there is a call for more laborers, it will be the duty of the seven presidents of the first Seventy to call and ordain other Seventy and send them forth to labor in the vineyard, until, if needs be, they set apart seven times seventy, and even until there are one hundred and forty-four thousand thus set apart for the ministry." (Joseph Smith, *HC* 2:221.)

"The First Quorum of the Seventy will be gradually organized, eventually with seventy members, the presidency of which will be made up of the seven members. . . .

"Today we shall present . . . additional members of the First Quorum of the Seventy to you for your votes. . . . These changes bring to thirty-nine the total number in the First Quorum of the Seventy, thus providing a quorum to do business.

"With this move, the three governing quorums of the Church defined by the revelations—the First Presidency, the Quorum of the Twelve, and the First Quorum of the Seventy—have been set in their places as revealed by the

Lord. This will make it possible to handle efficiently the present heavy workload and to prepare for the increasing expansion and acceleration of the work, anticipating the day when the Lord will return to take direct charge of His church and kingdom." (Spencer W. Kimball, *CR*, October 1976, p. 10.)

Scriptural References: D&C 107:25-26, 36.

First Vision

The term *first vision* is used in the Church to refer to the vision of Joseph Smith in the spring of 1820 when he beheld and talked with the Father and the Son. This was the "first" vision of this dispensation and in a sense inaugurated the great dispensation of the fulness of times.

Selected Quotations

"It came about in a regular, normal process. An inspired, fourteen-year-old boy had difficulty learning from the scriptures alone what the future was. In a dense grove of trees he sought the Lord and prayed for wisdom.

"The time had come, and though the adversary, Satan, recognizing all the powers of eternity which would be revealed with the gospel, did everything in his power to destroy the lad and destroy the prospects of the Restoration—in spite of him there came the splendid and magnificent vision to this pure, inquiring lad. Exerting all his powers, and with the strength of the Lord, the darkness was dispelled. Satan yielded and the vision proceeded, with a pillar of light coming exactly over the boy's head—a light above the brightness of the sun, which gradually descended until it fell upon him. The young Joseph continues:

" 'It no sooner appeared than I found myself delivered from the enemy which held me bound. When the light rested upon me I saw two Personages, whose brightness and glory defy all description, standing above me in the air. One of them spake unto me, calling me by name and said, pointing to the other—This is My Beloved Son. Hear Him!' (JS-H 1:17.)

"This formal introduction by the Father to the Son was most important, for this would be the world of Jesus Christ and the Church of Jesus Christ and the kingdom of Jesus Christ.

"Questions were asked and answered, and eternal truths were given." (Spencer W. Kimball, *Ensign*, May 1976, p. 9.)

"The occurrence which ranks in importance alongside the greatest verities of revealed religion, is one that took place in a grove of trees near Palmyra, New York, on a beautiful, clear day early in the spring of 1820. Was it on the sixth of April? Perhaps—such at least is the tradition. But be that as it may, what transpired at that time was destined to affect the salvation of the billions of our Father's children who should live on earth from that day to the great winding up scene when the Son shall deliver up the kingdom, spotless, to his Father.

"Once or twice in a thousand years a new door is opened through which all men must enter if they are to gain peace in this life and be inheritors of eternal life in the realms ahead.

"Once or twice in a score of generations a new era dawns: the light from the east begins to drive the darkness of the earth from the hearts of men.

"Now and then in a peaceful grove, apart from the gaze of men, heaven and earth share a moment of intimacy, and neither are ever thereafter the same. Such a moment occurred on that beautiful, clear morning in the spring of 1820 in a grove of trees near Palmyra, New York. Man asked and God answered. Joseph Smith saw the Father and the Son." (Bruce R. McConkie, *Ensign,* November 1975, pp. 15, 18.)

"When Joseph Smith went out to the grove to pray, he had no idea that the Father and the Son were separate Personages. His religious training had been solely along the lines of the sectarian Protestant and Catholic world. This doctrine proclaimed with apparent assurance that the Father and the Son were *one;* that God was a Spirit in some mysterious form that could not be understood, and definitely not an anthropomorphic being. The current doctrine was that God was invisible to mortal eyes.

"We may well believe that when the youthful prophet knelt and prayed he never expected such a visitation, which was contrary to the universal religious views in his day. Evidently his mind was not clear as to how an answer would be received. Possibly he could have thought he might hear a voice or even that an angel might appear to him, as angels once appeared in ancient times. That he would receive a visitation from both Father and Son absolutely could not have entered his mind. Their presence, therefore, must have been just as great a shock to him as his repeating it to certain ministers must have been to them. For telling it he was severely rebuked and accused of blasphemy.

"Without doubt, one of the chief reasons for the coming of both Father and Son was to establish the great truth which was lost to the world, that the declaration of the scriptures is true, and that once again there was to be witness in the flesh to bear testimony to the world. Through the mixture of the gospel with pagan philosophy, the true nature of God had been lost. It was necessary that it be restored again through the presence of a living witness. There were other reasons, of course, why the Lord should have living witnesses on the earth. The time had come for the light of the gospel to break through the dark clouds of superstition and false philosophy." (Joseph Fielding Smith, *AGQ* 1:20-21.)

Scriptural Reference: JS-H 1:2.

Firstborn; Jesus Christ as the Firstborn (*see also* Jesus Christ; Church of the Firstborn)

God the Father is the Father of the spiritual bodies of every person who has ever lived on this earth, who is now living on this earth, or who will ever live on this earth. We are all sons and daughters unto God so far as our spiritual bodies are concerned, and we are brothers and sisters to each other. Jehovah (I AM; Jesus Christ) was the Firstborn Son of God in the spirit; he is also our Elder Brother.

Selected Quotations

"The Lord Jesus, whose witnesses we are, is the Firstborn of the Father, the Firstborn of every creature. He was the Beloved and Chosen One from the beginning." (Bruce R. McConkie, *Ensign,* May 1977, pp. 12-13.)

"Now, who is Jesus? He is our brother, the firstborn. What, the firstborn in the flesh? O no, there were millions and millions born in the flesh before he was. Then how is he the firstborn? Because he is the eldest—the first one born of the whole family of spirits and therefore he is our elder brother." (Orson Pratt, *JD* 14:241.)

"There is no impropriety . . . in speaking of Jesus Christ as the Elder Brother of the rest of human kind. That He is by spiritual birth Brother to the rest of us is indicated in Hebrews: 'Wherefore in all things it behooved him to be made like unto his brethren, that he might be a merciful and faithful high priest in things pertaining to God, to make reconciliation for the sins of the people.' (Heb. 2:17.) Let it not be forgotten, however, that He is essentially greater than any and all others, by reason (1) of His seniority as the oldest or firstborn; (2) of His unique status in the flesh as the offspring of a mortal mother and of an immortal, or resurrected and glorified Father; (3) of his selection and foreordination as the one and only Redeemer and Savior of the race; and (4) of his transcendent sinlessness.

"Jesus Christ is not the Father of the spirits who have taken or yet shall take bodies upon this earth, for He is one of them." (First Presidency, *AF,* pp. 472-73.)

Scriptural References: D&C 76:54, 67, 71, 94, 102; 77:11; 78:21; 88:5; 93:21-22; 107:19; Col. 1:15-19; Heb. 1:6; 2:17; 19:23.

Foreordination (*see also* Pre-earthly existence)

The principle of foreordination is that certain people were preselected or "ordained before" their birth upon the earth to certain positions or responsibilities while in their physical, mortal condition. Such selection would be possible because of the knowledge of God concerning the individual's strengths, inclinations, and predispositions in the pre-earthly existence. Foreordination in no sense violates the principle of free agency, as the individual is still free to decide whether or not he will do those things to which he has been foreordained.

Selected Quotations

"There is no chance in the call of these brethren to direct the Lord's work on earth. His hand is in it. He knows the end from the beginning. He ordained and established the plan of salvation and decreed that his everlasting gospel should be revealed to man in a series of dispensations commencing with Adam and continuing to Joseph Smith. And he—the Almighty—chooses the prophets and apostles who minister in his name and present his message to the world in every age and dispensation. He selects and foreordains his ministers; he sends them to earth at the times before appointed; he guides and directs their continuing mortal preparations; and he then calls them to those positions they were foreordained to receive from before the foundations of the earth.

"Joseph Smith said, 'Every man who has a calling to minister to the inhabitants of the world was ordained to that very purpose in the grand council of heaven before this world was.' Then the Prophet said of himself, 'I suppose that I was ordained to this very office in that grand council.' (*TPJS*, p. 365.)

"All those who receive the Melchizedek Priesthood in this life were, as Alma teaches, 'called and prepared from the foundation of the world according to the foreknowledge of God,' because they were among the noble and great in that premortal sphere. (Alma 13:3.)

"And Paul says that through this law of foreordination, which he calls the doctrine of election, there came to the whole house of Israel 'the adoption, and the glory, and the covenants, and the giving of the law, and the service of God, and the promises.' (Rom. 9:4.) He says that the faithful members of the Church, those 'that love God' and 'are called according to his purpose,' are foreordained 'to be conformed to the image of his Son,' to be 'joint-heirs with Christ,' and to have eternal life in our Father's kingdom. (Rom. 8:17, 28.)

"He says also of members of the Church that God 'hath chosen us in him before the foundation of the world, that we should be holy and without blame before him in love,' and that we were foreordained to become the children of Jesus Christ by adoption, thus gaining a 'forgiveness of sins' in this life and an inheritance of eternal glory in the life to come. (Eph. 1:7.)

"True, a curtain has been drawn so we do not recall our associations there. But we do know that our Eternal Father has all power, all might, all dominion, and all truth and that he lives in the family unit. We do know that we are his children, created in his image, endowed with power and ability to become like him. We know he gave us our agency and ordained the laws by obedience to which we can obtain eternal life. We know we had friends and associates there. We know we were schooled and trained and taught in the most perfect educational system ever devised, and that by obedience to his eternal laws we developed infinite varieties and degrees of talents.

"And hence comes the doctrine of foreordination. When we come into mortality, we bring the talents, capacities, and abilities acquired by obedience to law in our prior existence.

Mozart composed and published sonatas when but eight years of age because he was born with musical talent. Melchizedek came into this world with such faith and spiritual capacity that 'when a child he feared God, and stopped the mouths of lions, and quenched the violence of fire.' (Gen. 14:26, JST.) Cain, on the other hand, like Lucifer, was a liar from the beginning and was told in this life: '. . . thou shalt be called Perdition; for thou wast also before the world.' (Moses 5:24.)

"Now this is the doctrine of foreordination; this is the doctrine of election." (Bruce R. McConkie, *Ensign,* May 1974, pp. 72-73.)

Scriptural References: Abr. 3:24-26; Jer. 1:5; Acts. 17:26-27: 1 Pet. 1:20; Alma 13:2-4.

Forgiveness

Forgiveness means to be "given before" and is conditioned upon repentance, which in turn is made possible because of the law of mercy. The eternal law of justice requires that there must be a payment (or suffering) made for every law that is broken in the moral realm. The law of mercy makes possible the vicarious payment of broken law; that is, the law of mercy makes it possible for a person other than the person who broke the law to pay (or suffer) for the broken law.

Because Jesus Christ was the Son of God in the flesh as well as in the spirit, and because he lived a sinless life upon the earth, he was able to atone (or pay or suffer) for our sins upon the condition of our repentance. He was willing to do this for us because of his great love for us.

Whenever any of us break a law (commit sin) in the moral realm, a payment must be made in order for the law to be brought back into a state of balance (order) and so that the law will no longer have claim upon us. The basic question then is, Will we pay or suffer for the broken law ourselves, or will we stop breaking the law (repent) so then Jesus Christ can and does pay for us, and we are "given before" (forgiven) the punishment that would naturally have devolved upon us?

When understood in its true light, forgiveness is one of the most meaningful and beautiful principles of the gospel. It is made active in our lives through repentance, and in repenting we can either stop doing those things that we have been doing that are wrong or we can start doing those things that we have not been doing that are right. Repentance and the forgiveness associated with it are vital, important, and necessary principles that must be utilized by man in order for him to achieve eternal life and exaltation.

No wonder President Kimball has referred to forgiveness as a miracle, and like other miracles of God it results in great blessings.

Selected Quotations

"One of the wonderful things about the restored gospel is that it provides a way whereby mankind may gain forgiveness of their sins. True repentance followed by baptism is the gate which initially puts men on the path of salvation, but even after going through the gate and getting on the path, all men sin to some extent, and some grievously. What is the law of repentance for such Church members? What must they do to cleanse themselves? [D&C 58:42-43.]

"The formula of forgiveness is plainly set forth in the scriptures. First men must forsake their sins. Then they must confess to the Lord and also to those against whom they have sinned, asking for forgiveness. Grievous sins which affect the standing in the Church should be made known to the bishop of the ward. One of the important factors in our escape from sin is the matter of making restitution to those against whom we have sinned. This we should do so far as it is within our power—the Lord expects it. We must also be willing to forgive other people who have offended us and finally we must press forward in doing the works of righteousness for the rest of our lives." (Mark E. Petersen, *YFY*, pp. 92-93.)

"Forgiveness is as wide as repentance. Every person will be forgiven for all the transgression of which he truly repents. If he repents of all his sins, he shall stand spotless before God because of the atonement of our Master and Savior, Jesus Christ, while he that exercises no faith unto repentance remains '. . . as though there had been no redemption made, except it be the loosing of the bands of death.' (Alma 11:41.) Such is the gift of God's merciful plan of redemption." (Marion G. Romney, *CR*, October 1955, pp. 123-25.)

"There are many people who seem to rely solely on the Lord's mercy rather than on accomplishing their own repentance. One woman rather flippantly said, 'The Lord knows my intents and that I'd like to give up my bad habits. He will understand and forgive me.' But the scriptures will not bear this out. The Lord may temper justice with mercy, but he will never supplant it. Mercy can never replace justice. God is *merciful,* but he is also *just.* The Savior's atonement represents the mercy extended. Because of this atonement, all men can be saved. Most men can be exalted.

"Many have greatly misunderstood the place of mercy in the forgiveness program. Its role is not to give great blessings without effort. Were it not for the atonement of Christ, the shedding of his blood, the assumption by proxy of our sins, man could never be forgiven and cleansed. Justice and mercy work hand in hand. Having offered mercy to us in the overall redemption, the Lord must now let justice rule for he cannot save us in our sins, as Amulek explained. (Alma 11:37.) . . .

" 'There should be no license for sin,' said the Prophet, 'but mercy should go hand in hand with reproof.' And again, 'God does not look on sin with allowance, but when men have sinned, there must be allowance made for them." (Spencer W. Kimball, *MF,* pp. 358-59.)

"If the time comes when you have done all that you can to repent of your sins, whoever you are, wherever you are, and have made amends and restitution to the best of your ability; if it be something that will affect your standing in the Church and you have gone to the proper authorities, then you will want that confirming answer as to whether or not the Lord has accepted of you. In your soul-searching, if you seek for and you find that peace of conscience, by that token you may know that the Lord has accepted of your repentance. [Mosiah 4:2-3.] Satan would have you think otherwise and sometimes persuade you that now having made one mistake, you might go on and on with no turning back. That is one of the great falsehoods. The miracle of forgiveness is available to all of those who turn from their evil doings and return no more, because the Lord has said in a revelation to us in our day: '. . . go your ways and sin no more; but unto that soul who sinneth [meaning again] shall the former sins return, saith the Lord your God.' (D&C 82:7.)" (Harold B. Lee, *CR,* April 1973, pp. 177-78.)

Scriptural References: D&C 42:25; 64:7-13; 76:34; 95:1; Moses 6:53; Lev. 4:20; 19:22; Matt. 6:12, 14-15; 9:6; 12:32; 18:35; Mosiah 4:2; 26:29; 3 Ne. 13:14.

Free agency; agency of man

Free agency has been described as the most far-reaching gift of God to man because without the opportunity of choice and the freedom of choice all other gifts or blessings of God would be virtually meaningless. All of the basic principles of growth, development, and progression are based on the premise that God will give us law (the opportunity of choice) and free agency (the freedom of choice).

The scriptures teach that righteousness is obedience to law. The scriptures also teach that every blessing is predicated upon obedience to law. Thus, righteousness results in blessings. However, righteousness (obedience to law) would not be possible unless unrighteousness (disobedience to law) were also a possibility. Our Heavenly Father gave to man the opportunity of choice by giving him law. He also gave the freedom of choice to man from the very beginning in the days of Adam. Free agency *on this earth* is a gift from God and, when used in righteousness, can help man achieve blessings, including eternal life, which is the greatest blessing of all.

Selected Quotations

"There is no compulsion in any part of the gospel. The Lord said in 1833, 'Behold, here is the agency of man, and here is the condemnation of man; because that which was from the beginning is plainly manifest unto them, and they receive not the light.' (D&C 93:31.)

"This means that since Adam the Lord has taught us correct doctrines and we may accept or reject them, but the responsibility is ours. It means that, having the Holy Ghost which we received at baptism time, we all know good from evil. The conscience whispers to us what is right and what is wrong. We cannot blame others or circumstances. We know what is right.

"Every person has his free agency. He may steal or curse or drink; he may defile himself with pornographic material; he may laze away his life, fail to do his duty, commit sexual sins, or even take life. There is no force, but he must know that sin brings its proper punishment, sooner or later and in total, so that one is stupid indeed to choose to do the wrong things.

"Every person can fail to attend his meetings, fail to pay his tithing, fail to fill a mission, ignore his temple obligations and privileges, but if he is smart, he must know that he is the deprived one." (Spencer W. Kimball, *Ensign,* May 1974, p. 87.)

"One of God's greatest gifts to man is freedom of choice.

"At an early period in the journey through life, man finds himself at a crossroad where he must choose one of two great highways—the right, leading to progress and happiness; and the wrong, leading to retardation and sorrow. There exists this eternal law that each human soul, through the choices he makes, will shape his own destiny. Our success or failure, peace or discontent, happiness or misery, depend on the choices we make each day." (N. Eldon Tanner, *Ensign,* July 1973, p. 7.)

"The agency of man is not interfered with by Divine Providence. If men were not left free to choose the good and refuse the evil, or vice versa, there would be no righteousness or even reason in bringing them to judgment. In consequence of the power of volition they become responsible beings, and therefore will receive the results of their own doings. They will be rewarded or punished according to their works, when the books are opened and they are judged out of the things written therein.

"God, doubtless, could avert war, prevent crime, destroy poverty, chase away darkness, overcome error, and make all things bright, beautiful and joyful. But this would involve the destruction of a vital and fundamental attribute in man, the right of agency. It is for the benefit of His sons and daughters that they become acquainted with evil as well as good, with darkness as well as light, with error as well as truth, and with the results of the infraction of eternal laws. Therefore He has permitted the evils which have been brought about by the acts of His creatures, but will control their ultimate results for His own glory and the progress and exaltation of His sons and daughters when they have learned obedience by the things they suffer. The contrasts experienced in this world of mingled sorrow and joy are educational in their nature, and will be the means of raising humanity to a full appreciation of all that is right and true and good. The foreknowledge of God does not imply His action in bringing about that which man does or refuses to do. The comprehension of this principle makes clear many questions that puzzle the uninformed as to the power and works of Deity." (Joseph Fielding Smith, *Deseret News,* December 1914.)

Scriptural References: D&C 29:35-39; 58:27; 88:86; 93:31; 98:8; 101:78; 134:2, 7; Alma 12:31; 29:4-5; 41:3-7.

Garments; "clean garments"; "spotted garments"

The Lord has indicated that "it becometh every man who hath been warned to warn his neighbor." (D&C 88:81.) Those who have been blessed in receiving the gospel have the responsibility to teach the gospel to others. In a similar way, if a person is aware that another person is committing sin, and he does not warn that person of his evil acts, then in some way he assumes part of the responsibility for the evil deed.

The counsel of the Lord to keep our garments clean from the blood of the wicked generation in which we live is a descriptive reminder of our responsibility to warn and teach others. For example, if we teach others the gospel and they do not accept the teachings, then the responsibility has been shifted from us to them ("their blood shall be upon their own heads"); however, if we do not teach them the gospel and they do not even have the opportunity to accept, then the responsibility remains with us ("our garments shall be spotted with their blood").

Selected Quotations

" 'Save yourselves from this untoward generation, and come forth out of the fire, hating even the garments spotted with the flesh.' [36:6] This expression is found in Jude (23), and the Lord said to John (Rev. 3): 'Thou hast a few names even in Sardis which have not defiled their garments; and they shall walk with me in white; for they are worthy.' This is symbolic language, yet is plain to understand. This is an untoward generation, walking in spiritual darkness, and the punishment for sin is spoken of as punishment in fire. Garments spotted with flesh are garments defiled by the practices of carnal desires and disobedience to the commandments of the Lord. We are commanded to keep our garments unspotted from all sin, from every practice that defiles. We are therefore commanded to come out of the world of wickedness and forsake the things of this world." (Joseph Fielding Smith, *CHMR* 1:162-63.)

"Can we fold our arms in peace and cry 'all is peace in Zion,' when, so far as we have the power of the priesthood resting upon us, we can see the condition of the world? Can we imagine that our garments will be clean without lifting our voices before our fellow men and warning them of the things that are at their doors? No, we cannot. There never was a set of men since God made the world under a stronger responsibility to warn this generation, to lift up our voices long and loud, day and night so far as we have the opportunity and declare the words of God unto this generation. We are required to do this. This is our calling. It is our duty." (Wilford Woodruff, *JD* 21:122.)

"*Garments spotted with the flesh:* This expression is also found in Jude 23. The garment, a tunic worn next to the body, was thought of as polluted by indulgence in carnal sins, or defiled by the stains of diseases caused by transgression. The Elders of the Church were to cry repentance as the only means of salvation from the burning fires of the lusts of the flesh." (Smith and Sjodahl, *DCC,* p. 192.)

Scriptural References: D&C 20:6; 36:6; 61:34; 88:85; 109:76; 112:33; 135:5; 2 Ne. 8:24; 9:44; 19:5; 3 Ne. 20:36; 27:19.

Gathering; gathering of Israel

From the days of Joshua until approximately 722 B.C. a group of people called Israel lived in a land known today as Israel. The Israelites were descendants of Jacob (Israel) and were divided into the twelve tribes of Israel; collectively they were known as the house of Israel.

For about 350 years (approximately 1450-1095 B.C.) the Israelites were governed by at least thirteen judges, with Samuel being the last judge. Then they formed the United Kingdom, which lasted for approximately 120 years (about 1095-975 B.C.). Upon the death of Solomon, the people divided into two kingdoms: the kingdom of Israel (northern kingdom) and kingdom of Judah (southern kingdom).

About 722 B.C. the kingdom of Israel was conquered by Assyria, and many of the people in the ten tribes comprising that kingdom were taken into captivity. The next year (721 B.C.) they fled north from Assyria and disappeared from the pages of the Bible and from history. Even today they are known as the ten lost tribes of Israel. Thus, the blood descendants of Israel started to be separated from the land of Israel.

In approximately 587 B.C. the southern kingdom was conquered by Babylonia. The Lord warned some of the people of that kingdom to flee into the wilderness to escape that destruction. The progenitors of one of the major groups in the Book of Mormon—Lehi and his family, Ishmael and his family, and Zoram—were dispersed from Israel and eventually arrived in the promised land, the Americas. Therefore, another major group of blood Israel was separated from the land of Israel.

Other people of the kingdom of Judah were taken captive into Babylonia; but when that country was conquered by Persia, the Israelites were allowed to return to their own country.

When the Savior was born among these people in that land, what was previously the kingdom of Judah was a province in the Roman Empire. The Savior prophesied that soon even these people (primarily Jews—descendants of Judah and/or citizens of the previous Kingdom of Judah) would be scattered. Under the Roman emperors Nero and Vespasian, the city of Jerusalem and its temple were destroyed, many of the people killed, and most of the remaining Israelites were scattered throughout the Roman Empire.

Thus, nearly all of the blood of Israel was scattered from the land of Israel in three major scatterings: (1) the lost tribes, (2) the dispersed of Israel, and (3) the descendants of Judah.

Throughout the centuries, however, the Lord told his prophets that Israel would be gathered together again in the last days. These prophecies are recorded in many of the books of the Old Testament and the New Testament, as well as in the Book of Mormon.

In the Doctrine and Covenants, the Lord has revealed many things associated with three aspects of the gathering of Israel in the last days.

1. The gathering of the dispersed of Israel to Zion. The great missionary program of the Church is an important part of this aspect of the gathering.

2. The gathering of the descendants of Judah to the land of Jerusalem. This aspect of the gathering has been emphasized for about one hundred years, but has greatly accelerated since May 15, 1948, when the modern country of Israel was established.

3. The return of the lost tribes. This aspect of the gathering is apparently still largely in the future.

Selected Quotations

"Six years after the Church was organized, the keys of gathering were committed to Joseph Smith and Oliver Cowdery in the Kirtland Temple. The record of that marvelous restoration is given in these words: [D&C 110:11, quoted.] The spirit of gathering has been with the Church from the days of that restoration. Those who are of the blood of Israel, have a righteous desire after they are baptized, to gather together with the body of the Saints at the designated place. This, we have come to recognize, is but the breath of God upon those who are converted, turning them to the promises made to their fathers.

"But the designation of gathering places is qualified in another revelation by the Lord to which I would desire to call your attention. After designating certain places in that day where the Saints were to gather, the Lord said this: [D&C 101:21, quoted.]

"Thus, clearly, the Lord has placed the responsibility for directing the work of gathering in the hands of the leaders of the Church to whom he will reveal his will where and when such gathering would take place in the future." (Harold B. Lee, *CR*, April 1948, pp. 54-56.)

"What was the object of gathering the Jews, or the people of God in any age of the world? . . .

"The main object was to build unto the Lord a house whereby He could reveal unto His people the ordinances of His house and the glories of His kingdom, and teach the people the way of salvation; for there are certain ordinances and principles that, when they are taught and practiced, must be done in a place or house built for that purpose.

"It is for the same purpose that God gathers together His people in the last days, to build unto the Lord a house to prepare them for the ordinances and endowments, washings and anointings, etc." (Joseph Smith, *HC* 5:423-24.)

Gathering to Zion

"By it [Book of Mormon] we learn that our western tribes of Indians are descendants from that Joseph which was sold into Egypt, and that the land of America is a promised land unto them, and unto it all the tribes of Israel will come, with as many of the Gentiles as shall comply with the requisitions of the new covenant. But the tribe of Judah will return to old Jerusalem." (Joseph Smith, *HC* 1:315.)

"I received, by a heavenly vision, a commandment in June following [1831], to take my journey to the western boundaries of the State of Missouri, and there designate the very spot which was to be the central place for the commencement of the gathering together of those who embrace the fullness of the everlasting gospel. Accordingly I undertook the journey, with certain ones of my brethren, and after a long and tedious journey, suffering many privations and hardships, arrived in Jackson County, Missouri, and after viewing the country, seeking diligently at the hand of God, He manifested Himself unto us, and designated, to me and others, the very spot upon which He designed to commence the work of the gathering, and the upbuilding of an 'holy city,' which should be called Zion—Zion, because it is a place of righteousness, and all who build thereon are to worship the true and living God, and all believe in one doctrine, even the doctrine of our Lord and Savior Jesus Christ." (Joseph Smith, *HC* 2:254.)

Gathering of Judah

"The promise is . . . made to the Jews that they shall be gathered again, after their pain and suffering. They will gather as predicted by Zechariah and by the Lord in . . . revelation (D&C 45) in their unbelief. They will begin to believe in Christ but will not be ready to accept him in his full right as their Deliverer and as the Son of God. (See 2 Nephi 30:5-8.) In this state they shall gather to Jerusalem and its vicinity. When their enemies come upon them and part of the city is taken, there shall come a great earthquake and the mount of Olives shall cleave in twain forming a valley into which the Jews shall flee for safety. At that time, Christ will appear to them and show them his hands and his feet, and they shall fall down and acknowledge him as their King and Redeemer." (Joseph Fielding Smith, *CHMR* 1:265.)

"In our day, in that first visit of Moroni to the Prophet Joseph Smith, mention was made that the 'dispersed of Judah would be gathered from the four corners of the earth.' Thirteen years later, when Moses delivered the keys for the gathering of Israel and the Kirtland Temple was dedicated, the Prophet Joseph made further reference to the promises made to Judah and appealed to the Lord that the time may soon come when the children of Judah would return to the land promised to their father, Abraham. [D&C 109:61-64.]" (Ezra Taft Benson, *CR,* Apr. 1950, pp. 72, 74-77.)

Gathering of the Lamanites

"Zion is bound to rise and flourish. The Lamanites will blossom as the rose on the mountains. . . . Every word that God has ever said of them will have its fulfillment, and they, by and by, will receive the Gospel." (Wilford Woodruff, *JD* 15:282.)

"The Lamanites must rise in majesty and power." (Spencer W. Kimball, *CR,* October 1947, p. 22.)

"This prophetic statement was made on October 3, 1947, when in Central America we had fewer than 100 members and in that great land of Mexico fewer than 5,000, half of whom were in the Mormon colonies. 'The Lamanites must rise in majesty,' I repeat. The fewer than 100 in Central America when these prophetic words were uttered has blossomed into more than 40,000 as of today. From the fewer than 5,000 in Mexico at that time, a rich harvest of over 150,000 stand tall in the field white already to harvest; the total membership of 1947 but represents harvest of a pair of months today." (J. Thomas Fyans, *Ensign,* May 1976, pp. 12-13.)

"The day of the Lamanite is surely here and we are God's instrument in helping to bring to pass the prophecies of renewed vitality, acceptance of the gospel, and resumption of a favored place as part of God's chosen people. The promises of the Lord will all come to pass; we could not thwart them if we would. But we do have it in our power to hasten or delay the process by our energetic or neglectful fulfillment of our responsibilities." (Spencer W. Kimball, *FPM,* pp. 348-49.)

Gathering of Lost Tribes

"All that God has said with regard to the ten tribes of Israel, strange as it may appear, will come to pass. They will, as has been said concerning them, smite the rock, and the mountains of ice will flow before them, and a great highway will be cast up, and their enemies will become a prey to them to Zion. These things are as true as God lives." (Wilford Woodruff, *JD* 21:300-301.)

"Notwithstanding all that has been written, there are

many members of the Church who think that these 'lost tribes' were scattered among the nations and are now being gathered out and are found through all the stakes and branches of the Church. They reach this conclusion because the general opinion is that these tribes went into the North, and it is the northern countries from whence most of gathered Israel has been found. . . .

"Speaking of this, Elder Orson F. Whitney has said:

" 'It is maintained by some that the lost tribes of Israel—those carried into captivity about 725 B.C.—are no longer a distinct people; that they exist only in a scattered condition, mixed with the nations among which they were taken by their captors, the conquering Assyrians. If this be true, and those tribes were not intact at the time Joseph and Oliver received the keys of the gathering why did they make so pointed a reference to "the leading of the ten tribes from the land of the north"? . . . What need to particularize as to the Ten Tribes, if they were no longer a distinct people? And why do our Articles of Faith give these tribes a special mention?' (See *SNT,* p. 174.)

"Another striking statement pointing to the fact that these people are now in a body in preparation for their return is the statement by the Prophet Joseph Smith at the conference held in Kirtland, June 3 to 6, 1831. At this conference the Prophet said: 'John the Revelator was then among the ten tribes of Israel who had been led away by Shalmaneser, King of Assyria, to prepare them for their return from their long dispersion.' The Savior also bore witness that these tribes were in a body like the Nephites and he would visit them. [3 Ne. 15:20 and 16:1-4.]" (Joseph Fielding Smith, *Signs of the Times,* pp. 158-60.)

"We live in the age of restoration. Peter calls it 'the times of restitution,' meaning the period or time in the earth's history when that which once was shall be restored in all its original glory and perfection. He says the things to be restored include 'all things, which God hath spoken by the mouth of all his holy prophets since the world began.' (Acts 3:21.) . . .

"As is clear from the inspired account, Zion shall be built up—she shall obtain that perfection and glory which is hers—when the Lord appears in his glory. . . . This will be during the Millennium when the restoration of all things is completed. Zion shall be perfected after the second coming of Christ. . . .

"We have been commissioned to prepare a people for the second coming of the Son of Man. We have been called to preach the gospel to every nation and kindred and tongue and people. We have been commanded to lay the foundations of Zion and to get all things ready for the return of Him who shall again crown the Holy City with his presence and glory. . . .

"Now, what is Zion, and where shall she be established? On what ground shall we build her walls? Where shall we place her gates and strong towers? Who shall dwell within her portals? And what blessings shall rest upon her inhabitants? . . .

"Truly the scripture saith, 'The Lord loveth the gates of Zion more than all the dwellings of Jacob. Glorious things are spoken of thee, O city of God. . . . And of Zion it shall be said, This and that man was born in her: and the highest himself shall establish her.' (Ps. 87:2-3, 5.) Zion has been established many times among men. From the day of Adam to the present moment—whenever the Lord has had a people of his own; whenever there have been those who have hearkened to his voice and kept his commandments; whenever his saints have served him with full purpose of heart—there has been Zion.

"Our first scriptural account relative to Zion concerns Enoch and his city. That prophet of transcendent faith and power lived while father Adam yet dwelt in mortality. It was a day of wickedness and evil, a day of darkness and rebellion, a day of war and desolation, a day leading up to the cleansing of the earth by water. Enoch, however, was faithful. He 'saw the Lord,' and talked with him 'face to face' as one man speaks with another. (Moses 7:4.) The Lord sent him to cry repentance to the world, and commissioned him to 'baptize in the name of the Father and of the Son, which is full of grace and truth, and of the Holy Ghost, which beareth record of the Father and the Son.' (Moses 7:11.) Enoch made converts and assembled a congregation of true believers, all of whom became so faithful that 'the Lord came and dwelt with his people, and they dwelt in righteousness,' and were blessed from on high. 'And the Lord called his people Zion, because they were of one heart and one mind, and dwelt in righteousness; and there was no poor among them.' (Moses 7:18.)

"Please note: Zion is people; Zion is the saints of God; Zion is those who have been baptized; Zion is those who have received the Holy Ghost; Zion is those who keep the commandments; Zion is the righteous; or in other words, as our revelation recites: 'This is Zion—the pure in heart.' (D&C 97:21.)

"As is well known, ancient Israel was scattered among all the nations of the earth because they forsook the Lord and worshipped false gods. As is also well known, the gathering of Israel consists of receiving the truth, gaining again a true knowledge of the Redeemer, and coming back into the true fold of the Good Shepherd. In the language of the Book of Mormon, it consists of being 'restored to the true church and fold of God,' and then being 'gathered' and 'established' in various 'lands of promise.' (2 Ne. 9:2.) 'When they shall come to the knowledge of their Redeemer, they shall be gathered together again to the lands of their inheritance.' (2 Ne. 6:11.)

"Two things are accomplished by the gathering of Israel: First, those who have thus chosen Christ as their Shepherd; those who have taken upon themselves his name in the waters of baptism; those who are seeking to enjoy his Spirit here and now and to be inheritors of eternal life hereafter— such people need to be gathered together to strengthen each other and to help one another perfect their lives.

"And second, those who are seeking the highest rewards in eternity need to be where they can receive the blessings of the house of the Lord, both for themselves and for their ancestors in Israel who died without a knowledge of the gospel, but who would have received it with all their heart had opportunity afforded. . . .

"You cannot create a stake of Zion without creating a part of Zion. Zion is the pure in heart; we gain purity of heart by baptism and by obedience. A stake has geographical boundaries. To create a stake is like founding a City of Holiness. Every stake on earth is the gathering place for the lost sheep of Israel who live in its area. The gathering place for Peruvians is in the stakes of Zion in Peru, or in the places which soon will become stakes. The gathering place for Chileans is in Chile; for Bolivians it is in Bolivia; for Koreans it is in Korea; and so it goes through all the length and breadth of the earth. Scattered Israel in every nation is called to gather to the fold of Christ, to the stakes of Zion, as such are established in their nations.

"Each one of us can build up Zion in our own lives by being pure in heart. And the promise is, 'Blessed are the pure in heart: for they shall see God.' (Matt. 5:8.) Each one of us can extend the borders of Zion by gathering our friends and neighbors into the fold of Israel. . . .

"God grant us the zeal and good sense to go forth on his errand living the gospel ourselves and saving our own souls, and offering these glorious principles of salvation to his other children. This is the Lord's work." (Bruce R. McConkie, *Ensign,* May 1977, pp. 115-18.)

Scriptural References: D&C 10:65; 29:7; 42:9; 45:25; 77:14; 110:11; A of F 1:10; Jer. 3:17; 23:3; 29:14; 31:10; 32:37; Matt. 23:37; John 11:52; Eph. 1:10; 3 Ne. 5:24; 16:5; 20:13, 29; 21:24.

Generation

The word *generation* may refer to a state or condition as well as to a time period. The dictionary lists several accepted definitions of the word in addition to the commonly accepted "average span of time between the birth of parents and that of their offspring."

The scriptures refer to an "unbelieving and stiffnecked generation" (D&C 5:8), a "crooked and perverse generation" (D&C 33:2), this "untoward generation" (D&C 36:6), an "evil and adulterous generation" (Matt. 12:39). All of these uses of the word suggest a state or condition rather than a specific period of time. Thus, when the Lord states that a certain thing will occur in "this generation," he may be referring to the conditions which are then existing, to a general period of time similar to "this dispensation," or to the more specific period of time pertaining to the lifetimes of the people then living.

Selected Quotations

"There have been various interpretations of the meaning of a generation. It is held by some that a generation is one hundred years; by others that it is one hundred and twenty years; by others that a generation as expressed in this and other scriptures has reference to a period of time which is

indefinite. The Savior said: 'An evil and adulterous generation seeketh after a sign.' This did not have reference to a period of years, but to a period of wickedness. A generation
may mean the time of the present dispensation. . . ." (Joseph
Fielding Smith, *CHMR* 2:102.)

Scriptural References: D&C 6:8-9; 45:19-31; 84:4-5; 88:75,
85.

Gentile: gentiles; fulness of the gentiles; nations of the gentiles;
times of the gentiles

The basic meaning of the word *gentile* is a stranger or
foreigner. To a member of a particular group, a gentile is
any person who does not belong to that group. To a Hebrew
(a descendant of Abraham), a gentile is a person who is not a
Hebrew. To an Israelite (a descendant of Jacob or Israel), a
gentile is a person who is not an Israelite. To a Jew (a
descendant of Judah; a citizen of the Kingdom of Judah or a
descendant of such a citizen), a gentile is a non-Jew.

Thus, it is consistent that a Latter-day Saint should refer
to those who are not Latter-day Saints as gentiles. However,
this usage is very difficult for many nonmembers to understand inasmuch as the word *gentile* as used by Latter-day
Saints could includes people who are Jews, Israelites, and
Hebrews.

The word *Hebrew* is first used in the Bible in Genesis 14,
the word *Israel* in Genesis 32, and the word *Jews* in 2 Kings
16. Most of the Bible was written after these terms were in
rather common usage. The word *gentile*, then, refers either to
non-Hebrew, non-Israelite, or non-Jew, depending on the
time and the situation of the usage.

The major story in the Book of Mormon begins during the
days of the kingdom of Judah. Lehi, Ishmael, Mulek, and
those associated with them were evidently citizens of the
Kingdom of Judah, and Mulek himself was a descendant of
Judah through his father, Zedekiah. The peoples of the Book
of Mormon are sometimes referred to as Jews, and in keeping with such usage the peoples who are not descendants of
the Jews or of one of the Book of Mormon groups are referred to as gentiles.

The specialized term *times of the gentiles* refers to the period of time when the gospel will be taken primarily to the
peoples who are not considered to be Israelites even though

many of them may actually be descendants of Jacob (Israel). When the gospel is taken primarily to those who are recognized by the world as Israelites (the Jews), in a sense the "times of the gentiles will be fulfilled."

Selected Quotations

"The name Gentile is not with us a term of reproach. It comes from Gentiles, meaning of a nation, a family or a people not of Israel—that is all. 'Mormon' is a nickname for Latter-day Saints, but 'gentile' is not a nickname. It simply means, with us, one who does not belong to the Church." (Orson F. Whitney, *CR*, April 1928, pp. 59-60.)

"Let us also remember that we are of the Gentiles! By this I mean that the Latter-day Saints have come to their blessings through the Gentile nations. President Brigham Young . . . said that Joseph Smith was a pure Ephraimite. This is true; yet Joseph Smith came also of a Gentile lineage. So do most members of the Church. We may boast of our lineage and rejoice in the fact that Patriarchs have declared us to be of Ephraim, but at the same time let us not despise the Gentiles, for we are also of them. If it were not so the scriptures would not be fulfilled. [1 Nephi 15:13-14, Ether 12:22.]" (Joseph Fielding Smith, *WP*, p. 140.)

" 'Gentiles' means 'nations,' as distinct from the Jews. It is the *goyim* of the Hebrews—a term applied to all outside the Mosaic faith. In the Church literature 'Gentile' is not a term of disrespect, but merely one of convenience. It is not used frequently in our day." (Smith and Sjodahl, *DCC*, p. 185.)

Scriptural References: D&C 18:6, 26; 19:27; 35:7; 45:28; 57:4; 90:9; Isa. 11:10; 49:6; 60:3; 66:19; Rom. 3:29; 11:25; 3 Ne. 15:22; 16:10; 20:27; 21:14; 22:3.

Gifts of the Spirit

Some of the gifts of the Spirit are listed in the scriptures (1 Cor. 12:8-11; Moroni 10:8-17); section 46 of the Doctrine and Covenants enumerates fourteen of these gifts. However, Elder Bruce R. McConkie has indicated: "These are by no means all of the gifts. In the fullest sense, they are infinite in number and endless in their manifestations." (*MD*, p. 315.)

Selected Quotations

"We believe in the gift of the Holy Ghost being enjoyed now, as much as it was in the Apostles' days; we believe that

it (the gift of the Holy Ghost) is necessary to make and to organize the Priesthood, that no man can be called to fill any
office in the ministry without it; we also believe in prophecy,
in tongues, in visions, and in revelations, in gifts, and in
healings; and that these things cannot be enjoyed without
the gift of the Holy Ghost. . . . We believe in it (this gift of
the Holy Ghost) in all its fullness, and power, and greatness,
and glory." (Joseph Smith, *HC* 5:27-30.)

"The gifts named in the seventh Article of Faith are gifts
of the Holy Ghost. The enjoyment of them has always been
a distinctive characteristic of the Church of Jesus Christ. As a
matter of fact, without the gift of revelation, which is one of
the gifts of the Holy Ghost, there could be no Church of
Jesus Christ. This is apparent from the obvious fact that in
order for his Church to exist, there must be a society of
people who individually have testimonies that Jesus is the
Christ. According to Paul, such testimonies are revealed only
by the Holy Ghost, for said he, '. . . no man can say [know]
that Jesus is the Lord, but by the Holy Ghost.' (See 1 Cor.
12:3.) In the 46th section of the Doctrine and Covenants, the
Lord specifically lists such knowledge as one of the gifts of
the Holy Ghost, as follows: 'To some it is given by the Holy
Ghost to know that Jesus Christ is the Son of God. . . .'
(D&C 46:13.) Everyone who has a testimony of Jesus has received it by revelation from the Holy Ghost. The Holy Ghost
is a revelator, and everyone who receives him receives
revelation.

"Wherever and whenever revelation is operative, manifestations of other gifts of the Holy Ghost are prevalent.
This has been so in all dispensations. . . . Yes, all the gifts of
the Holy Spirit are in the Church today." (Marion G.
Romney, *CR*, April 1956, p. 68.)

"Believing as we do in all the gifts named in the 46th Section of the Doctrine and Covenants, and knowing that there
are counterfeits to them, how are we to distinguish between
the truth and the false, the genuine and the counterfeit? . . .

"Without attempting an exhaustive discussion of this
question, I shall take the liberty to suggest three simple tests
which, if applied, will prove of great value in making the distinction.

"First, determine whether the alleged supernatural
manifestation is edifying. If it is not, then it is not of God be-

cause spiritual gifts are given for the edification of God's people. . . .

"Second—this pertains particularly to purported supernatural healings—find out whether the purported healer follows the divinely established procedure, that is, does he do as Jesus did, when he laid his hands upon the sick and healed them. (See Mark 6:5.) . . .

"Third, find out whether the worker of the purported miracle has himself received the gift of the Holy Ghost through the prescribed ordinances. If he has not, then his works, whatever they may be, are not the manifestations of the Holy Spirit. This is a key test because, as we have already pointed out, the gifts of the spirit are given by the power of the Holy Ghost. Without the gift of the Holy Ghost, the manifestations of his gifts may not be enjoyed." (Marion G. Romney, *CR*, April 1956, pp. 68-73.)

Scriptural References: D&C 8:2-3; 39:6; 46:13-29; 68:3-4; Acts 19:6; 21:10-12; 1 Cor. 12:3-14; Gal. 5:22-23; 2 Pet. 1:20-21; Moro. 8:25-26; 10:4-19.

God; attributes and characteristics of God; God is the same yesterday, today, and forever; God knoweth all things; living God (*see also* Knowledge of God)

The word *God* is a title; it is not a name. The title *God* could refer to several personages; as Paul stated, "there be gods many." (1 Cor. 8:5.)

Three of the Gods form the Godhead—the Father, the Son, and the Holy Ghost. These three are separate and distinct from each other in person, personality, and substance, but they form a unity in witness, testimony, purpose, and plan. Usually when the scriptures use the word *God*, the term refers to one of these three persons, most often either to the Father or to the Son.

The God who is the Father of the spirits of all mankind and who resides in heaven (and is rightfully referred to as our Father in heaven or as our Heavenly Father) has been given a name-title by Latter-day Saints: Elohim. The name-title Elohim does not appear in any English scripture; it is a transliteration of the Hebrew word for *Gods*.

One purpose of the scriptures is to tell us something about the nature, person, personality, attributes, and characteristics of God. Jesus taught: "This is life eternal, that they might know thee the only true God, and Jesus Christ whom thou hast sent." (John 17:3.)

The scriptures teach that God the Father is loving, kind, merciful, gracious, just, and true. He is a God of truth, and cannot lie. He is a God of justice, and is unchanging in his obedience to all law. He is the all-knowing (omniscient) and all-powerful (omnipotent) Creator of all good things. Although as a person with a physical body he can be in only one place at one time, yet his influence can be felt everywhere in the universe (he is omnipresent).

God the Father is infinite and eternal, from eternity to eternity, the same yesterday, today, and forever. These attributes and characteristics enable us to have absolute faith in God, for we know we can trust him completely.

Selected Quotations

"It is the first principle of the Gospel to know for a certainty the character of God, and to know that we may converse with him as one man converses with another." (Joseph Smith, *TPJS*, p. 345.)

"There is a God in heaven who is infinite and eternal. He has all power, all might, and all dominion. There is no power he does not possess and no truth he does not know. Every good thing dwells in him independently in its eternal fulness. He is the Creator, Upholder, and Preserver of all things. His name is Elohim, and he is our Father in heaven, the literal Father of the spirits of all men. He has a body of flesh and bones as tangible as man's, and is in fact a resurrected and glorified Person. The name of the kind of life he lives is eternal life; and eternal life, by definition and in its nature, consists of life in an eternal family unit and of the possession of the fulness of the glory and power of the Father." (Bruce R. McConkie, *Ensign*, May 1977, p. 12.)

"There are a few statements in the Bible which have been misunderstood and have led to a misconception of the personality and form of God and of his Son, Jesus Christ. Brief consideration might be given to some of them:

" 'No man hath seen God at any time; the only begotten Son, which is in the bosom of the Father, he hath declared him.' (John 1:18.)

" 'No man hath seen God at any time. If we love one another, God dwelleth in us, and his love is perfected in us.' (1 John 4:12.)

"In the Inspired Version of the Bible, as rendered by the Prophet Joseph Smith, he gives us the following: 'And no man hath seen God at any time, except he hath borne record of the Son; for except it is through him no man can be saved.' (John 1:19.)

"He also gives us the rendition of 1 John 4:12 as follows: 'No man hath seen God at any time, except them who believe. If we love one another, God dwelleth in us, and his love is perfected in us.' " (LeGrand Richards, *MWW*, pp. 18-19.)

"The doctrine that man is created in the image of God was lost in the apostasy. The vision given to Joseph Smith restored the true doctrine in relation to this question. It is just as strange that man, in his spiritual darkness, would change this glorious doctrine and in these later times substitute for it the abominable doctrine that man has ascended through countless ages from lower forms of life, as it is that they could make of the Father and the Son and the Holy Ghost a God to be worshipped that is without substance, immaterial and therefore non-existent. Here are a few references showing the error of the teaching of the so-called Christian world, all creeds and denominations, on this point, and proving that God has both body, parts and passions: Gen. 1:26, 5:1 and 9:6; James 3:8-9; Ex. 33:9-23; Num. 12:7-8; Ex. 20:5; Deut. 4:24." (Joseph Fielding Smith, *CHMR* 1:12.)

Scriptural References: D&C 19:4; 20:17; 50:15-34; 59:5; 75:1; 76; 77:2-12; 85:3-8; 93:14-38; JS-H 1:14-19.

Godhead; oneness of the Godhead (*see also* God)

Three of the Gods of heaven—the Father of the spirits of all mankind; the Firstborn Son of God in the spirit, who is also the Only Begotten Son of God in the flesh; and the Holy Ghost—combine to comprise the Godhead. Although they are separate and distinct from each other in person and substance, yet they are united in purpose, plan, witness, testimony, and in many other ways. The gospel plan of eternal progression was conceived by and is carried out under the direction of the three great Gods who comprise the Godhead.

Selected Quotations

"There is much said about God and the Godhead. The scriptures say there are Gods many and Lords many, but to us there is but one living and true God, and the heaven of heavens could not contain him [1 Cor. 8:5-6]; for he took the liberty to go into other heavens. The teachers of the day say that the Father is God, the Son is God, and the Holy Ghost is God, and they are all in one body and one God. Jesus prayed that they were one; (one in spirit, in mind, in purpose). [John 17:22.] If I were to testify that the Christian world were wrong on this point, my testimony would be true.

"Peter and Stephen testify that they saw the Son of Man standing on the right hand of God. [Acts 3:22; 1 Pet. 3:22; Acts 7:55-56.] Any person that had seen the heavens opened knows that there are three personages in the heavens who hold the keys of power, and one presides over all." (Joseph Smith, *HC* 5:426.)

"There is the oneness of Deity, the three in one; not as some preachers try to expound it, in the doctrines of the outside world, in the Article of Faith that they have, making them one immaterial spirit, no body, no real personage, no substance. On the contrary, they are three individuals, one in spirit, one in mind, one in intelligence united in all things that they do, and it takes the Father, and the Son, and the Holy Ghost, to make the perfect Trinity in one, three persons and one God or Deity, one Godhead." (Charles W. Penrose, *CR,* April 1928, pp. 13-14.)

"It is perfectly true, as recorded in the Pearl of Great Price and in the Bible, that to us there is but one God. [Moses 1:6; Mark 12:32.] Correctly interpreted, God in this sense means Godhead, for it is composed of Father, Son, and the Holy Spirit. This Godhead presides over us, and to us, the inhabitants of this world, they constitute the only God, or Godhead. There is none other besides them. [1 Cor. 8:5-6.] To them we are amenable and subject to their authority, and there is no other Godhead unto whom we are subject. However, as the Prophet has shown, there can be, and are, other Gods." (Joseph Fielding Smith, *AGQ* 2:142.)

Scriptural References: D&C 20:28; 76:22-24; A of F 1:1; John 8:17-18; 10:30; 12:28-29; 14:7-9; 17:11, 20-23; 20:17; Acts 7:55-56; Eph. 3:14; 4:4-6; 1 Ne. 11:9-11.

Godhood

One of the definite and distinctive teachings of The Church of Jesus Christ of Latter-day Saints is the principle of eternal progression. Carried to its ultimate conclusion, this principle indicates that through obedience to divine commandments, and by virtue of an eternal law that "like begets after its own kind," it is possible for sons and daughters of God to become as he is. This doctrine of the potential godhood of mankind was clearly understood in biblical times but was lost to the world during the period of the great apostasy.

Selected Quotations

"Every man who reigns in celestial glory is a God to his dominions. . . .

"They who obtain a glorious resurrection from the dead are exalted far above principalities, powers, thrones, dominions, and angels, and are expressly declared to be heirs of God and joint-heirs with Jesus Christ, all having eternal power." (Joseph Smith, *TPJS*, p. 374.)

"The Church of Jesus Christ of Latter-day Saints, basing its belief on divine revelation, ancient and modern, proclaims man to be the direct and lineal offspring of Deity. God Himself is an exalted man, perfected, enthroned, and supreme. . . .

"Man is the child of God, formed in the divine image and endowed with divine attributes, and even as the infant son of an earthly father and mother is capable in due time of becoming a man, so the undeveloped offspring of celestial parentage is capable, by experience through ages and aeons, of evolving into a God. [D&C 76:58, 132:20-24.]" (Joseph Fielding Smith, *IE*, November 1909, pp. 75-81.)

"As man now is, our God once was; /As now God is, so man may be." (Lorenzo Snow, *IE*, June 1919, 22:660.)

"As our Father and God begat us, sons and daughters, so will we rise immortal, males and females, and beget children to inherit these worlds, the same as we were sent here, and thus will the works of God continue, and not only God himself, and His Son Jesus Christ have the power of endless lives, but all of His redeemed offspring. They grow up like the parents; that is a law of nature so far as this world is concerned. Every kind of being begets its own like, and when fully matured and grown up the offspring become like the parent. So the offspring of the Almighty, who begot us, will grow up and become literally God, or the sons of God.

[D&C 132:17-24.]" (Orson Pratt, *JD* 14:242.)
Scriptural References: D&C 132:20, 37.

Gospel: fulness of the gospel
The basic meaning of the word *gospel* has traditionally been given as "good news"; modern dictionaries also indicate that it means "something accepted as infallible truth or as a guiding principle."

The gospel of Jesus Christ includes the good news that he is indeed the Son of God; that he broke the bands of death through his resurrection, thus enabling us all to achieve immortality; that through his atonement he made it possible for us to become sinless (sanctified) again; and that through his life and teachings he showed us what we must do to regain the presence of our Heavenly Father.

The fulness of the gospel, therefore, would include those principles and ordinances which would enable us to sanctify ourselves so that we can live again with our heavenly Father. Sometimes this has been referred to as the gospel of salvation in the presence of God, and the Book of Mormon contains these aspects of the gospel.

Additional principles and ordinances not listed in our present Book of Mormon are required in order for a person to be exalted in the presence of God, such as the temple endowment and marriage for time and eternity. Many of these are found in the revelations of the Doctrine and Covenants.

Selected Quotations
"I will proceed to tell you what the Lord requires of all people, high and low, rich and poor, male and female, ministers and people, professors of religion and nonprofessors, in order that they may enjoy the Holy Spirit of God to a fulness, and escape the judgments of God, which are almost ready to burst upon the nations of the earth. Repent of all your sins, and be baptized in water for the remission of them, in the name of the Father, and of the Son, and of the Holy Ghost, and receive the ordinance of the laying on of the hands of him who is ordained and sealed unto this power, that ye may receive the Holy Spirit of God; and this is according to the Holy Scriptures [Acts 2:37-39], and the Book of Mormon [2 Ne. 31:17-18; Moro. 2:1-2]; and the only way that man can enter into the celestial kingdom. These are the requirements of the covenant, or first prin-

ciples of the Gospel of Christ." (Joseph Smith, *HC* 1:314-15.)

"I was brought up in scientific laboratories, where I was taught to test things, never to be satisfied unless a thing was tested. We have the right to test the Gospel of the Lord Jesus Christ. By testing it I mean living it, trying it out. Do you question the Word of Wisdom? Try it. Do you question the law of tithing? Practice it. Do you doubt the virtue of attending meetings? Attend them. Only then shall we be able to speak of these things intelligently and in such a way as to be respected by those who listen to us. Those who live the Gospel of Jesus Christ gain this higher knowledge, this greater testimony, this ultimate assurance that this is the truth." (John A. Widtsoe, *CR*, October 1938, p. 129.)

"The gospel might be likened to the keyboard of a piano—a full keyboard with a selection of keys on which one who is trained to play a variety without limits; a ballad to express love, a march to rally, a melody to soothe, and a hymn to inspire; an endless variety to suit every mood and satisfy every need.

"How shortsighted it is, then, to choose a single key and endlessly tap out the monotony of a single note, or even two or three notes, when the full keyboard of limitless harmony can be played.

"It is not unusual to find people who take an interest in The Church of Jesus Christ of Latter-day Saints but give only casual attention to the ideal that the fulness of the gospel is here.

"They become attracted by a single key, a doctrine, often one to which they take immediate exception and object to. They investigate it by itself alone. They want to know all there is about it without reference, in fact, with specific objection and rejection, to anything else.

"They want to hear that key played over and over again. It will give them little knowledge unless they see that there is a fullness—other complementary ideals and doctrines that present a warmth and a harmony, and a fullness, that draw at the right moment upon each key, which if played alone might seem discordant.

"Now that danger is not limited to investigators alone. Some members of the Church who should know better pick out a hobby key or two and tap them incessantly, to the irritation of those around them. They can dull their own spiritual sensitivities. They lose track that there is a fullness of the gospel and become as individuals, like many churches have become. They may reject the fullness in preference to a favorite note. This becomes exaggerated and distorted, leading them away into apostasy." (Boyd K. Packer, *Ensign,* December 1971, p. 41.)

Scriptural References: D&C 33:10-12; 76:40-42; 133:57; Rom. 1:16-17; Gal. 1:6-9; 1 Ne. 8.

Great and dreadful day of the Lord (*See also* Calamities before second coming; Second coming)

This term is used consistently in the Doctrine and Covenants to refer to the period associated with the second coming of Jesus Christ in great power and glory. This period will be a great day for the righteous upon the earth, for the day of their deliverance will have come; it will be a dreadful day for the wicked upon the earth, for they will be destroyed while still in their unrepented condition.

Selected Quotations

"What 'great and deadful day of the Lord' is meant in the words of our text? [Mal. 4:5-6.] . . . Surely this coming of our Lord has relation to the great and terrible day, the day of burning, the day in which wickedness should be entirely swept from the earth, and no remnants of the wicked left, when every branch of them and every root of them should become as stubble, and be consumed from the face of the earth. [D&C 101:23-24; Mal. 4:1.]" (Orson Pratt, *JD* 7:76-77.)

"A characteristic of present-day revelation is the reiteration of the fact that the event [second coming] is nigh at hand, 'even at the doors.' The fateful time is repeatedly designated in scripture, 'the great and dreadful day of the Lord.' [D&C 110:14, 16; Joel 2:31, Mal. 4:5.] Fearful indeed will it be to individuals, families, and nations, who have sunk so far into sin as to have forfeited their claim to mercy. The time is not that of the final judgment—when the whole race of mankind shall stand in the resurrected state before the bar of God—nevertheless it shall be a time of unprecedented blessing unto the righteous and of condemnation and vengeance upon the wicked." (James E. Talmage, *JC,* pp. 786-87.)

"A dreadful day; a day of pestilence, of famine, of earthquake, of tempests, and a day of burning, designated . . . in very impressive language as 'the great and dreadful day of the Lord! When that day comes, the power of the Priesthood must be upon the earth to protect and deliver the people of God from destruction; for the righteous and those who keep the commandments of God, including those who are tithed, shall not be burned. [D&C 64:23-24.]" (Rudger Clawson, *CR*, April 1902, p. 28.)

Scriptural References: D&C 2:1; 110:14, 16; 128:17; JS-H 1:38; 3 Ne. 25:5.

Great and marvelous work

In one of its widest applications, the term *great and marvelous work* refers to all of the principles, powers, keys, ordinances, and events associated with the dispensation of the fulness of times, which would include the restitution and restoration of all things since the beginning of time upon the earth.

In some of its narrower applications, the term might be used to refer to one or another aspect of this dispensation. In such limited usage, for example, the events associated with the coming forth of the Book of Mormon might be referred to as a "great and marvelous work."

Selected Quotations

"Not only in numbers have we become a 'marvelous work and a wonder' but in a greater and a larger sense have we become a marvelous people, for we have impressed our thought upon the whole world. The world does not believe today as it did ninety years ago. A few days ago I picked up a recent number of a great magazine, and my feelings were roused within me and my testimony increased when I found one of the writers declaring to the readers of the magazine that 'God cannot look upon sin with the least degree of tolerance,' borrowed almost word for word from section one of the Doctrine and Covenants [v. 31]. In such a way have the doctrines taught by the despised Latter-day Saints been appropriated by the nations of the earth; and whether the people of the earth accept the inspiration of Joseph Smith, nevertheless, in fact the whole current of human thought has been changed by the doctrines of this people. That is perhaps the greatest achievement of 'Mormonism.' . . . Who cares if we are few? We are as yeast in the dough, and will yet ferment the whole earth." (John A. Widtsoe, *CR*, October 1921, p. 109.)

Scriptural References: D&C 6:1; 76:114; 3 Ne. 21:9; 28:31.

Harvest symbols (*See also* material after 4:4)

Frequently the Savior in his teachings would use examples and symbols with which the people could easily and readily identify. Inasmuch as all of us on the earth must rely for sustenance upon the agricultural products that come directly or indirectly from the soil, most of us are acquainted with terms having to do with harvesting. It should not be surprising, therefore, that the Master Teacher frequently used symbols pertaining to the harvest.

The major symbols of the harvest, possible definitions, and selected references where they may be found in the Doctrine and Covenants are as follows:

Vineyard or field—the world, or that part of the world ("area of the vineyard"), in which the activity was being carried forth; 4:4; 6:3; 11:3; 12:3; 14:3; 31:4; 33:3, 7.

Harvest—the precious souls of mankind in the world; sometimes the word also has reference to the actual process of teaching the gospel or carrying out the activity indicated; 4:4; 6:3; 11:3; 12:3; 14:3; 33:3, 7; 45:2; 56:16; 86:7; 101:64.

Laborers—the missionaries or others who have the responsibility to teach the gospel or carry out the activity indicated; 33:3; 39:17; 88:70, 74.

Reap with a sickle or scythe—the process of harvesting or of teaching the gospel; the sickle is an important implement used in cutting the grain or crop so it can be harvested; 4:4; 6:3, 4; 11:3, 4, 27; 12:3, 4; 14:3, 4; 31:5; 33:7.

Sheaves—the people of the world who are converted to the true gospel; 31:5; 75:5; 79:3.

The Savior also noted these symbols in New Testament times. Luke records that when the Lord organized his missionary forces he "appointed other seventy also, and sent them two and two" and said to them, "The harvest truly is great, but the labourers are few: pray ye therefore the Lord of the harvest, that he would send forth labourers into his harvest." (Luke 10:1-2.) He also counseled his disciples, "Lift up your eyes, and look on the fields; for they are white already to harvest. And he that reapeth receiveth wages, and gathereth fruit unto life eternal." (John 4:35-36.)

As indicated earlier, the symbol of the "white field already to harvest" denotes the people of the earth who are ready to receive the gospel. The "Lord of the harvest" is, of course, Jesus Christ whose gospel it is. (See Matt. 9:37-38; Rev. 14:14; Alma 17:13; 26:5-7.)

Scriptural References: Matt. 9:37-38; 13:30, 39; 2 Ne. 19:3; Alma 17:13; 26:7.

Healing; the gift of healing (*see also* Gifts of the Spirit)

Healings of the sick may be the result of faith and manifestations of one of the gifts of the Spirit. Such healings have been performed by faithful men in all ages by virtue of the priesthood power and authority bestowed upon them.

During the Savior's mortal ministry, he went "forth amongst men, working mighty miracles, such as healing the sick, raising the dead, causing the lame to walk, the blind to receive their sight, and the deaf to hear, and curing all manner of diseases." (Mosiah 3:5.)

Later he gave this authority to his apostles in the meridian of time, and this gift has also been restored in this dispensation of the fulness of times.

Selected Quotations

"The healing spiritual power of the Lord is sought in cases of sickness, by the formal administration to the sick. This is in full harmony with the practice of the Christian Church from the beginning. (James 5:14, 15; Mark 6:13; Luke 4:40; Acts 28:8; D&C 42:43, 44.) Such administrations should be made at the request of the sufferer, so that it may be done in answer to faith. One of the two elders called in applies oil, consecrated for the purpose, to the head of the sick person, and the other elder is mouth in sealing the anointing and in praying to the Lord for the restoration of the health of the sick brother or sister. Tens of thousands of healings have followed such administrations." (John A. Widtsoe, *PC*, p. 111.)

"Though the authority to administer to the sick belongs to the elders of the Church in general, some possess this power in an unusual degree, having received it as an especial endowment of the Spirit. Another gift, allied to this, is that of having faith to be healed, which is manifested in varying degrees. Not always are the administrations of the elders followed by immediate healings; the afflicted may be permitted to suffer in body, perhaps for the accomplishment of good purposes (see instances of Job), and in the time appointed all must experience bodily death." (James E. Talmage, *AF*, p. 226.)

" 'Is it proper for an elder to take with him a brother holding the Aaronic Priesthood to assist in administering to the sick?' This question has been answered by the First Presidency and Council of the Twelve as follows:

" '. . . it was the sense of the Council . . . that the practice (of administering) be confined to the elders; but in the case of absolute necessity, that is where an elder finds himself in the situation that he cannot avail himself of the company of another elder, he may, if opportunity affords, avail himself of the company of a member of the Aaronic Priesthood, or even a lay member, but for the purpose only of being supported by the faith of such member or members, the elder alone to officiate in the ordinance of administration; or the elder may administer alone without such assistance of a lay member or one holding the Aaronic Priesthood.' (*Journal History,* Feb. 18, 1903.)

" 'If a man and his wife were alone with a sick person, could he anoint with the oil and then seal the anointing with his wife assisting, using the priesthood she holds jointly with her husband?'

"President Joseph F. Smith, in *The Improvement Era,* Vol. 10, page 308, answered this question as follows:

" 'Does a wife hold the priesthood with her husband, and may she lay hands on the sick with him, with authority?

" 'A wife does not hold the priesthood with her husband, but she enjoys the benefits thereof with him; and if she is requested to lay hands on the sick with him, or with any other officer holding the Melchizedek Priesthood, she may do so with perfect propriety. It is no uncommon thing for a man and wife unitedly to administer to their children. . . .'

"*The wife would lay on hands just as would a member of the Aaronic Priesthood, or a faithful brother without the priesthood, thus giving support by faith to the ordinance.* The Prophet Joseph Smith said, 'Respecting females administering for the healing of the sick, there could be no evil in it, if God gave his sanction by healing; that there could be no more sin in any female laying hands on and praying for the sick, than in wetting the face with water; it is no sin for anybody to administer that has faith; or if the sick have faith to be healed by their administration.' (*Teachings of the Prophet Joseph Smith,* pp. 224-225.) Such an administration would not be by virtue of the priesthood, but a manifestation of faith." (Joseph Fielding Smith, *IE*, Aug. 1955, 58:558-59.)

"There are two kinds of healing. One is mental; the other we may call spiritual. Mental healing is as old as the race. It is done through 'suggestion,'" or even 'auto-suggestion.' The spirit within is an intelligent being and is greatly helped, in its efforts to repair tissue or withstand the attacks of adverse agencies, by the suggestion of others who have great will-power; or even by auto-suggestion. The disciples of the Pharisees cast out demons by that power, and many modern 'healers' operate under the law of suggestion. This is mental healing. Spiritual healing is by the Spirit of God, through the Priesthood. It is healing effected by the Holy Spirit imparting the strength necessary to overcome the causes of diseases, and it often operates instantaneously. Its power is circumscribed, for all men must die; but those who live so that they are receptive to the healing influences of the Holy Spirit should live to a ripe age, and then fall 'asleep' in sweet slumber, conscious of the beginning of a new life in the morning of the resurrection. Spiritual healing is divine healing. It is part of the gospel. Mental healing is human. It is good in its place, but it is not part of the gospel any more than common therapeutics, or surgery." (Smith and Sjodahl, *DCC*, p. 403.)

Scriptural References: D&C 35:9; 42:43; 52:40; 66:9; 84:63; 124:98; Matt. 4:23; 8:17; 10:1; 14:14; James 5:14; Mosiah 3:5; 3 Ne. 17:7; 4 Ne. 1:5; Morm. 9:24.

Hell; chains of darkness; chains of hell; gates of hell (*see also* Darkness)

Hell is both a place and a condition. As a place, hell is that part of the post-earthly spirit world where the spirits of the wicked are in fear, trembling, and anguish while awaiting their eventual resurrection from the dead. In this "outer darkness," the wicked suffer the torments of the damned.

Hell as a condition pertains to those feelings of the wicked (fear, trembling, anguish, anxiety, torment of conscience) which they take with them wherever they go until they repent and obey the laws of God. Hell will eventually have an end for all those who are worthy of being resurrected to a degree of glory; celestial, terrestrial, or telestial. However, so far as the scriptures indicate, for the sons of perdition there is no relief from the torment of conscience and other conditions of hell.

Selected Quotations

"That part of the spirit world inhabited by wicked spirits who are awaiting the eventual day of their resurrection is called hell. Between their death and resurrection, these souls of the wicked are cast out into outer darkness, into the gloomy depression of sheol, into the hades of waiting wicked spirits, into hell. There they suffer the torments of the damned; there they welter in the vengeance of eternal fire; there is found weeping and wailing and gnashing of teeth; there the fiery indignation of the wrath of God is poured out upon the wicked." (Bruce R. McConkie, *MD*, p. 349.)

"A man is his own tormentor and his own condemner. Hence the saying, they shall go into the lake that burns with fire and brimstone. The torment of disappointment in the mind of man is as exquisite as a lake burning with fire and brimstone. I say, so is the torment of man." (Joseph Smith, *HC* 6:314.)

"The great misery of departed spirits in the world of spirits, where they go after death, is to know that they come short of the glory that others enjoy and that they might have enjoyed themselves, and they are their own accusers." (Joseph Smith, *HC* 5:425.)

"Even to hell there is an exit as well as an entrance; and when sentence has been served, commuted perhaps by repentance and its attendant works, the prison doors shall open and the penitent captive be afforded opportunity to comply with the law, which he aforetime violated. . . .

"The inhabitants of the telestial world—the lowest of the kingdoms of glory prepared for resurrected souls, shall include those 'who are thrust down to hell' and 'who shall not be redeemed from the devil unto the last resurrection.' [D&C 76:82-85.] And though these may be delivered from hell and attain to a measure of glory with possibilities of progression, yet their lot shall be that of 'servants of the Most

High, but where God and Christ dwell they cannot come, worlds without end.' [V. 112.] Deliverance from hell is not admittance to heaven." (James E. Talmage, *VM*, pp. 254-56.)

Scriptural References: D&C 10:26; 76:84, 106; 104:18; 122:1; 123:8; Moses 1:20; 6:29; JFS-V 1:23; Isa. 14:9, 15; Matt. 5:22; 10:28; 11:23; 16:18; Alma 5:7; 12:11; 13:30; 26:13; 30:60; 54:7; 3 Ne. 11:40; 27:11.

Holy Ghost: the Comforter; Holy Spirit; "Holy Spirit of Promise"

Holy Ghost is the title given to the personage of spirit who is a God and who serves with the Father and the Son in the Godhead. He serves many functions and carries out many responsibilities in relationship to man upon the earth. He is a Comforter, Testator (Testifier), Revelator, and Sanctifier. Sometimes in the scriptures the Holy Ghost is referred to by such titles as the Holy Spirit of Promise (meaning that He is the Holy Spirit *promised* to the Saints).

Sometimes the term *Holy Ghost* is used to refer to the *power* or *gift* of that member of the Godhead, rather than to refer to his actual personage. In the ordinance of confirmation, newly baptized persons are instructed to "receive the Holy Ghost," meaning his power or gift.

Selected Quotations

"The question is often asked, Is there any difference between the Spirit of the Lord and the Holy Ghost? The terms are frequently used synonymously. We often say the Spirit of God when we mean the Holy Ghost; we likewise say the Holy Ghost when we mean the Spirit of God. The Holy Ghost is a personage in the Godhead [D&C 130:22], and is not that which lighteth every man that cometh into the world. [John 1:9.] It is the Spirit of God which proceeds through Christ to the world, that enlightens every man that comes into the world, and that strives with the children of men, and will continue to strive with them, until it brings them to a knowledge of the truth and the possession of the greater light and testimony of the Holy Ghost. [D&C 84:44-48.] If, however, he receives that greater light, and then sins against it, the Spirit of God will cease to strive with him, and the Holy Ghost will wholly depart from him." (Joseph F. Smith, *GD*, pp. 67-68.)

"The Prophet explained the difference between the Holy Ghost and the gift of the Holy Ghost. 'Cornelius received the Holy Ghost before he was baptized, which was the convincing power of God unto him of the truth of the Gospel, but he could not receive the gift of the Holy Ghost until after he was baptized. Had he not taken this sign or ordinance upon him, the Holy Ghost which convinced him of the truth of God would have left him. Until he obeyed these ordinances and received the gift of the Holy Ghost, by the laying on of hands, according to the order of God, he could not have healed the sick or commanded an evil spirit to come out of a man, and it obey him; for the spirits might say unto him, as they did to the sons of Sceva: "Paul we know and Jesus we know, but who are ye?" ' (*HC* 4:555.)

"The Holy Ghost is the third member of the Godhead. The gift of the Holy Ghost, is the bestowal of the power by which one becomes the companion of the Holy Ghost. One who receives the gift has the right, through faithfulness, to the guidance of the Holy Ghost in all things. While a man who sincerely seeks the truth may have manifestation of the Holy Ghost, he has no claim to a continued guidance by that Holy Spirit, unless he is baptized and has the gift bestowed upon him by the laying on of hands. None but members of the Church can obtain this gift, for the Lord has said that the world cannot receive it. (John 14:17.)" (Joseph Fielding Smith, *CHMR* 2:300.)

"*The Holy Spirit of Promise* is the Holy Spirit *promised* the saints, or in other words the Holy Ghost. This name-title is used in connection with the sealing and ratifying power of the Holy Ghost, that is, the power given him to ratify and approve the righteous acts of men so that those acts will be binding on earth and in heaven. 'All convenants, contracts, bonds, obligations, oaths, vows, performances, connections, associations, or expectations,' must be sealed by the Holy Spirit of Promise, if they are to have 'efficacy, virtue, or force in and after the resurrection from the dead; for all contracts that are not made unto this end have an end when men are dead.' (D&C 132:7.)

"To seal is to *ratify*, to *justify*, or to *approve*. Thus an act which is sealed by the Holy Spirit of Promise is one which is ratified by the Holy Ghost; it is one which is approved by the Lord; and the person who has taken the obligation upon himself is justified by the Spirit in the thing he has done. The ratifying seal of approval is put upon an act only if those entering the contract are worthy as a result of personal righteousness to receive the divine approbation. They 'are sealed by the Holy Spirit of promise, which the Father sheds forth upon all those who are *just* and *true.*' (D&C 76:53.) If they are not just and true and worthy the ratifying seal is withheld.

"When any ordinance or contract is sealed by the Spirit, it is approved with a promise of reward, provided unrighteousness does not thereafter break the seal, remove the ratifying approval, and cause loss of the promised blessing." (Joseph Fielding Smith, *DS* 1:55; 2:94-99.)

Scriptural References: D&C 20:28, 73; 33:15; 121:26; 130:22-23; Moses 5:9-14; Matt. 3:16; Acts 1:5-8; 2:1-4, 38; 7:51-55; 3 Ne. 9:20; 11:27-36; Moro. 2:2-3; 6:4-9.

Honesty

If a person were completely honest, he would obey all of the commandments of the Lord, including the Ten Commandments, for he would be dependable and trustworthy in all his dealings with God and with his fellowmen. As pride has been called the mother of all sins, so honesty might be called the mother, or at least the companion, of all virtues.

Selected Quotations

On Mount Sinai the finger of the Lord wrote the law on tablets of stone: 'Thou shalt not steal.' (Ex. 20:15.) There was neither enlargement nor rationalization. And then that declaration was accompanied by three other commandments, the violation of each of which involves dishonesty: 'Thou shalt not commit adultery.' 'Thou shalt not bear false witness.' 'Thou shalt not covet.' (Ex. 20:14, 16-17.)

Was there ever adultery without dishonesty? In the vernacular, the evil is described as 'cheating.' And cheating it is, for it robs virtue, it robs loyalty, it robs sacred promises, it robs self-respect, it robs truth. It involves deception. It is personal dishonesty of the worst kind, for it becomes a betrayal of the most sacred of human relationships, and a denial of covenants and promises entered into before God and man. It is the sordid violation of a trust. It is a selfish casting aside of the law of God, and like other forms of dishonesty its fruits are sorrow, bitterness, heart-broken companions, and betrayed children.

'Thou shalt not bear false witness.' Dishonesty again.

'Thou shalt not covet.' Is not covetousness—that dishonest, cankering evil—the root of most of the world's sorrows? For what a tawdry price men of avarice barter their lives! . . .

"Wrote the author of Proverbs: 'These six things doth the Lord hate: yea, seven are an abomination unto him: A proud look, a lying tongue, and hands that shed innocent blood, An heart that deviseth wicked imaginations, feet that be swift in running to mischief, A false witness that speaketh lies, and he that soweth discord among brethren.' (Prov. 6:16-19.)

"The appraisal spoken long ago by an English poet is true yet today: 'An honest man's the noblest work of God.' (Alexander Pope, *An Essay on Man. Epistle III,* line 248.) Where there is honesty, other virtues will follow.

"The final Article of Faith of The Church of Jesus Christ of Latter-day Saints affirms that, 'We believe in being honest, true, chaste, benevolent, virtuous, and in doing good to all men.'

"We cannot be less than honest, we cannot be less than true, we cannot be less than virtuous if we are to keep sacred the trust given us. Once it was said among our people that a man's word was as good as his bond. Shall any of us be less reliable, less honest than our forebears?" (Gordon B. Hinckley, *Ensign,* May 1976, pp. 60-62.)

"Dishonesty is directly related to selfishness, which is its origin and source. Selfishness is at the root of nearly all the disorders that afflict us, and man's inhumanity to man continues to make countless thousands mourn. If all mankind were honest, we could have heaven here on earth. We would have no need for armies or navies, nor even a policeman in the smallest community, for there would be no crime, no invasion of other people's rights, no violence of one person against another." (Mark E. Petersen, *Ensign,* December 1971, p. 72.)

"In public office and private lives, the word of the Lord thunders: 'Thou shalt not steal: . . . nor do anything like unto it.' (D&C 59:6.)

"We find ourselves rationalizing in all forms of dishonesty, including shoplifting, which is a mean, low act indulged in by millions who claim to be honorable, decent people.

"Dishonesty comes in many other forms: in hijacking, in playing upon private love and emotions for filthy lucre; in robbing money tills or stealing commodities of employers; in falsifying accounts; in taking advantage of other taxpaying people by misuse of food stamps and false claims; in taking unreal exemptions; in taking out government or private loans without intent to repay; in declaring unjust, improper bankruptcies to avoid repayment of loans, in robbing on the street or in the home money and other precious possessions; in stealing *time,* giving less than a full day of honest labor for a full day's compensation; in riding public transportation without paying the fare; and all forms of dishonesty in all places and in all conditions.

"To all thieveries and dishonest acts, the Lord says, 'Thou shalt not steal.' Four short common words He used. Perhaps He wearied of the long list He could have made of ways to steal, misrepresent, and take advantage, and He covered all methods of taking that which does not properly belong to one by saying, 'Thou shalt not steal.' " (Spencer W. Kimball, *Ensign,* Nov. 1976, p. 6.)

Scriptural References: D&C 51:9; 98:10.

Hosanna

Hosanna is a transliteration of a Hebrew (or Semitic) word that literally means "save now" and that could be translated "grant us salvation." Most of the prayers said by the Jews at the Feast of Tabernacles begin with this word, and it was also used by the multitude as they greeted Jesus Christ when he came into Jerusalem during the last week of His life upon the earth. (Matt. 21:9, 15.) This term appears in five sections of the D&C—19:37; 36:3; 39:19; 109:79; 124:101.

Scriptural References: Matt. 21:9, 15; Mark 11:9-10; John 12-13.

I AM; the great I AM (*see also* Jesus Christ)

I AM is a divine descriptive title that refers to the pre-earthly Jehovah, who was known on the earth as Jesus Christ. This name-title emphasizes the eternal nature of the power, authority, might, mission, and calling of Jesus Christ. Unfortunately, the translators of the Bible have not understood the nature and significance of these words. The King James Version of the Bible punctuates John 8:58 as follows:

"Before Abraham was, I am." This is confusing in syntax as well as in meaning. The verse would more correctly be punctuated: "Before Abraham, was I AM," indicating that Jesus Christ was the great Jehovah, the preexistent One, who was a God before Abraham was even born on the earth.

Selected Quotations

"Christ revealed Himself in the Old Testament as 'I am,' —Hebrew, *'Ehyeh 'asher 'Ehyeh* (Ex. 3:14), which implies that, while He *is*, or exists, and is therefore different from all non-existing deities of merely human imagination, He is not an abstract existence without form or substance, but He is a real Being, manifesting Himself in history ever anew; He is always with His people, active for their welfare." (Smith and Sjodahl, *DCC*, p. 86.)

"When Moses was tending the flocks of his father-in-law, Jethro, at Horeb, the mountain of God, the Lord appeared to him in a flaming bush and gave him commandment to go to Egypt and lead Israel from bondage. Moses said to the Lord: 'Behold, when I come unto the children of Israel, and shall say unto them, The God of our Fathers hath sent me unto you; and they shall say to me, What is his name? what shall I say unto them? And God said unto Moses, I am that I am; and he said, Thus shalt thou say unto the children of Israel, I Am hath sent me unto you.'

"When Jesus was contending with the Jews, and they were boasting of their descent from Abraham, he said to them: 'Your father Abraham rejoiced to see my day: and he saw it and was glad. Then said the Jews unto him, Thou art not yet fifty years old, and hast thou seen Abraham? Jesus said unto them, Verily, verily, I say unto you, Before Abraham was, I am.' (John 8:56-58.) Observe, he did not say, 'Before Abraham was, I was.'

"The name given to Moses is the same as given by Jesus Christ to the Jews, and the meaning of it is expressed in the saying that God is 'omnipotent, omnipresent, and omniscient; without beginning of days or end of life; and that in him every good gift and every good principle dwell.' (Lecture on Faith, No. 2.) Jesus declared to the Jews that which they were incapable of understanding, which is that the great I Am who appeared to Moses, was himself, and that he was God and gave commandments to Abraham.

"In [Sec. 38] we again have our Lord declaring himself as 'the great I Am, Alpha and Omega, the beginning and the end.' " (Joseph Fielding Smith, *CHMR* 1:165-66.)

Scriptural References: D&C 39:1; Ex. 3:14; John 8:58.

Idolatry

The basic meaning of *idolatry* is "idol worship," and in Old Testament times it referred to the pagan practices of worshiping idols of stone, wood, or metal. However, in a sense any type of worship (such as worship of money or power) that is not directed toward God is a form of idolatry.

Selected Quotations

"The great trouble with the world today is that it has become idolatrous. We read of idolatry and think of it as a practice or series of practices in the past. This is an idolatrous generation, defying the commandment written by the finger of God—'Thou shalt have no other Gods before me.' [Ex. 20:3.] ... Men are praising the gods of silver and of gold and of all the other valuable commodities that make up wealth, and the God in whose hand their breath is and whose are all their ways they will not recognize. . . .

"The Israelites were distinguished in the first place as worshipers of a living God, a personal God, in whose image they had been created and made. [Gen. 1:26-27; Ex. 33:21-23.] No other nation on the face of the earth recognized the living God. That was a sign by which the covenant people, descendants of Abraham, through Isaac and Jacob, were known. . . . Are we worshipping the true and living God, or are we going idolatrously after the gods of gold and silver, of iron and wood, and brass, diamonds, and other idols of wealth? Are we worshipping our farms, our cattle and sheep? Who is our God?" (James E. Talmage, *CR*, October 1930, pp. 71, 73.)

Scriptural References: D&C 52:39; Ex. 20:3; 32:4; Acts 17:6; 1 Cor. 10:14; Col. 3:5; 1 Pet. 4:3; Mosiah 9:12; 11:7; 27:8.

Inspired Version of the Bible

In the First Vision, Joseph Smith was informed that the creeds then prevalent in Christianity were an abomination before the Lord. Later the Lord and his servants (the Angel Moroni and others) indicated that some of the plain and precious truths of the gospel had been taken out of the Old Testament and New Testament. The Prophet was instructed by the Lord to go through the Bible and revise it as he would be inspired to do so. This revision is sometimes referred to as the New Translation of the scriptures. However, because the changes were made under inspiration from God, the term Inspired Version of the Bible is frequently used. It is also known as the Joseph Smith Translation (abbreviated JST).

The Inspired Version has never been used as the official Bible of The Church of Jesus Christ of Latter-day Saints as it is felt that the Prophet never completed the revision chapter by chapter. The following statements substantiate this position:

Emma Smith Bidamon in a letter to her son, Joseph Smith III, dated February 10, 1867: "My heart is made glad by your report of your progress in the New Translation as you know something of my fears with regard to its publication, on account of what your Father said about the unfinished condition of the work." (Robert J. Matthews, *Joseph Smith's Translation of the Bible: A History and Commentary,* p. 208.)

We have heard President Brigham Young state that the Prophet before his death had spoken to him about going through the translation of the scriptures again and perfecting it upon points of doctrine which the Lord had restrained him from giving in plainness and fulness at the time of which we write. (George Q. Cannon, *Life of Joseph Smith the Prophet,* p. 148, footnote.)

George Reynolds to Mr. C. J. Hunt:

Dear Sir: I am directed by President Wilford Woodruff . . . to say, that the Church of Jesus Christ of Latter-day Saints does not use the revision of the Scriptures made by the Prophet Joseph Smith, for the reason that he never completed the work. It was his intention to have gone all through the Bible again and make further corrections, but he did not have the opportunity of doing so. Consequently it is deemed an injustice both to the dead prophet and to the reader to place this unfinished work in the hands of the public. Though we may rest assured that the changes that he has made are correct, we have no assurance that he would not have made many other corrections in his second revision. (Matthews, *Joseph Smith's Translation of the Bible,* p. 209.)

In course of time the Prophet went through the Bible, topic by topic, revising as he was led by revelation. The work was never fully completed, for he had intended, while at Nauvoo, a number of years later, to finish the work, but was cut off by his enemies. Nevertheless, many plain and precious things were revealed which throw great light upon many subjects. (Joseph Fielding Smith, *ECH,* pp. 139-40.)

One of the latest official statements of the Church on the use of the Inspired Version is this editorial of December 1974:

The Inspired Version does not supplant the King James Version as the official church version of the Bible, but the explanations and changes made by the Prophet Joseph Smith provide enlightenment and useful commentary on many biblical passages.

Part of the explanations and changes made by the Prophet Joseph Smith were finally approved before his death; and some of these have been cited in current church instructional materials or may be cited in future church instructional materials.

Accordingly, these cited portions of the Inspired Version may be used by church writers and teachers, along with the Book of Mormon, Doctrine and Covenants, and Pearl of Great Price, in connection with Biblical interpretations, applying always the divine injunction that whoso is enlightened by the Spirit shall obtain benefit therefrom. (D&C 91:5.)

When the Book of Mormon, Doctrine and Covenants, and Pearl of Great Price offer information relative to biblical interpretation, these should be given preference in writing and teaching. But when these sources of latter-day revelation do not provide significant information which is available in the Inspired Version, then this version may be used.

The King James Version will, of course, constitute the basic English-speaking Bible text of the church. (*Church News,* December 7, 1974, p. 16.)

Selected Quotations

"All of the changes made by Joseph Smith in the King James Version of the Bible . . . are the voice of truth and revelation to the Latter-day Saints and carry the same verity as any of his revelations or inspired narration." (Bruce R. McConkie, *Ensign,* August 1976, p. 8.)

"The eighth Article of Faith declares that 'We believe the Bible to be the word of God as far as it is translated correctly.' This implies that there are mistranslations in the Bible. Moreover, the Prophet Joseph Smith, from the beginning of his ministry, gave some time to revising passages in the Bible which had been translated incorrectly or so rendered as to make the meaning obscure. . . .

"Latter-day Saints believe that the protecting hand of the Lord has been over the Bible, whether in the ancient manuscripts or in copies of the earliest documents. Modern scholarship and modern revelation have clarified erroneous and difficult passages." (John A. Widtsoe, *ER* 1:100-101.)

"The teachings of the Book of Mormon, and the revelations he had received, convinced Joseph that in the Bible were many errors, such as unauthorized additions, incomplete statements, and faulty translations. This seemed to him, a lover and expounder of truth, out of keeping with the sacred nature of the volume.

"Therefore, after placing the matter before the Lord he began the so-called 'inspired translation' of the Bible. In June, 1830, less than three months after the Church was organized, there was revealed to him the 'Visions of Moses,' which gave a more complete account of the events mentioned in the book of Genesis, and set forth many lost doctrines; for example, the meaning of the fall of Adam and Eve, long misunderstood because of the imperfections of existing translations of the Bible, was cleared, and shown to be a necessary act in the development of the Lord's plan of salvation. [Moses, chapters 2-8.]

"Towards the end of the year 1830, with Sidney Rigdon as assistant, he began a somewhat full 'explanation and review' of the Old and New Testaments. The work then done is a convincing evidence of Joseph's inspiration.

"Thousands of the changes were made, all conforming to common sense, and many in full harmony with later modern scholarship. Disputed meanings were made clear, and new doctrines expounded. . . .

"Joseph Smith may well be accounted one of the early students who sought to restore the Bible to its original form and simplicity. All this which came as helps to the missionaries in the field was opposed by the ministers whose Bible teaching left the people confused and in a state of uncertainty." (John A. Widtsoe, *JS*, pp. 138-40.)

"Before the close of this year, the first of the existence of the Church, the Prophet Joseph commenced preparing a new English version of the Bible. It is referred to as an inspired 'translation,' although that term, in its generally accepted meaning of rendition of the spoken, or written, word from one language into another, hardly gives a correct idea of the character of that work. But if by 'translate' we mean, to render sentences which are obscure and difficult to understand, into language more easy of comprehension, and free from ambiguity and contradiction, then the attempted revision is a translation. For that is what the Prophet aimed at, by the guidance of the Holy Spirit. Sidney Rigdon aided him as secretary. On the 2nd of February, 1833, the New Testament was completed, and on the 2nd of July, the same year, the Old Testament was completed, as far as the Prophet was directed to revise these records up to that time. This work of revision was never completed fully, and the Prophet intended to take up this work in Nauvoo, but persecution and difficulties prevented him from finishing this work.

"Regarding the publication of this work, the Prophet, in a letter to W. W. Phelps, dated June 25th, 1833, wrote: 'In regard to the printing of the New Translation: It cannot be done until we can attend to it ourselves, and this we will do, as soon as the Lord permits' (*HC* 1:365). From this it is clear that the publication of this version is not authorized. 'It cannot be done *until we can attend to it ourselves.*'

"The prophet expected some indication from the Lord that the time for publication had come. But, during the later years of his life, events crowded upon him so fast that it became a physical impossibility for him to give his personal attention to everything that seemed to be necessary. The publication of the New Translation would, no doubt, have involved a final revision by himself; that no one else could do; and he did not do it; the Lord did not command him to put the finishing touch to the work, and, therefore, it remained in manuscript, unpublished.

"But we must not suppose that the patient labor spent on the study of the Old and New Testament was lost. It was while Joseph Smith and Sidney Rigdon were engaged in this work that they received the wonderful Revelation on the resurrection, recorded in Section 76; also the Key to John's revelation, recorded in Section 77. It was during the same time that the Prophet received the Revelation explaining 1 Cor. 7:14. There can be no doubt that the close study of the Scriptures, such as that in which the Prophet engaged during these years particularly—for he was always a Bible student—was one of the means by which the Holy Spirit revealed to him the grand and glorious truths concerning the salvation of the children of men, before he sealed his testimony with his blood." (Smith and Sjodahl, *DCC*, pp. 193-94.)

Scriptural References: D&C 35:20; 42:56-60; 45:60-61; 73:3-4; 93:53; 94:10; 104:58; 124:89.

Intelligence; intelligences

The word *intelligence* is usually used in the Doctrine and

Covenants in the regular sense pertaining to the general areas of knowledge, wisdom, understanding, etc. (See D&C 130:18-19.)

However, the word *intelligences* is frequently used in a specialized sense by Latter-day Saints to refer to a part of the pre-earthly existence. The Pearl of Great Price records that the Lord showed unto Abraham "the intelligences that were organized before the world was." (Abr. 3:22.)

Selected Quotations

"The word *intelligence* as used by Latter-day Saints has two chief meanings, both found in the dictionary but of secondary use. First, a man who gathers knowledge and uses it in harmony with the plan of salvation is intelligent. He has intelligence. . . . Second, the word when preceded by the article *an,* or used in the plural as *intelligences,* means a person, or persons, usually in the spiritual estate. Just as we speak of a person or persons, we speak of *an intelligence,* or *intelligences.*

"This second use of the word has come into being among Latter-day Saints because of a statement made by the Lord to the Patriarch Abraham: [Abr. 3:22-23 quoted.]

"These remarkable statements use the words *intelligences, souls, spirits,* and *Abraham* (a man not yet on the earth) interchangeably. Thus has come the frequent use in the Church of the term *an intelligence,* meaning usually a personage in the spirit world, who may come on earth.

"Implied in the use of this term is the doctrine of pre-existence. It is a basic belief of the Church that man lived as a personal being before he came on earth. He was a spirit child of God, begotten by God. His life as a spirit in the heavenly domain is often spoken of as the first estate of man. In this estate most of the spirit children of God grew toward perfection. They possessed the right of all the children of God to act for themselves, to accept or to reject any and every offering. When they had arrived at the proper degree of development, they were given the opportunity of further training through a mortal experience on earth. . . .

"Elder Joseph Fielding Smith, writing on this subject, adds: 'Some of our writers have endeavored to explain what an intelligence is, but to do so is futile, for we have never been given any insight into this matter beyond what the Lord has fragmentarily revealed. We know, however, that there is something called intelligence which has always existed. It is the real eternal part of man, which was not created or made. This intelligence combined with the spirit constitutes a spiritual identity or individual.' (Joseph Fielding Smith, *The Progress of Man,* p. 10.) . . .

"Under this concept, the eternal ego of man was, in some past age of the other world, dim to us, clothed with a spiritual body. That was man's spiritual birth and his entrance into the spiritual world. Then later, on earth, if permitted to go there, he will receive a material body. As a result, after the resurrection he will be master of the things of the spiritual and material universes, and in that manner approach the likeness of God.

"This view of the nature of man is a widespread belief among Latter-day Saints. The term an *intelligence* is then applied to the external ego existing even before the spiritual creation.

"In reading Latter-day Saint literature, the two-fold sense in which the terms *an intelligence* or *intelligences* are used— applied to spiritual personages or to pre-spiritual entities— must be carefully kept in mind." (John A. Widtsoe, *ER* 3:74-77.)

Scriptural References: D&C 88:40; 93:29, 30, 36; 130:18-19; Abr. 3:21-22; JS-H 2:54.

Israel; Israelites; house of Israel; tribes of Israel (*see also* Gathering)

The patriarch Abraham had a son named Isaac who had a son named Jacob who was also given the name Israel. Thus, the word *Israel* was first used in reference to a particular man—Jacob. Later this term was used to refer to the descendants of this man (Israelites; house of Israel) and even to the land or area in which they lived.

Collectively the Israelites may be called the "house of Israel," but sometimes they are designated by their tribal names and then become the "tribes of Israel." Some of these people entered into covenants with the Lord, and they are sometimes referred to as "covenant Israel."

The word *Israel* can mean many different things to different people. To some, it refers to the descendants of Jacob ("blood Israel"); to others, it refers to the place where these people lived ("land Israel"); to still others, the word refers to the things they believed in ("covenant Israel").

Selected Quotations

"Much confusion and misapplication exists in the minds of many with respect to the use of the name *Israel.* Many think of it, even today, as referring to the Jews or to the house of Judah, forgetting that Judah was only one of the twelve sons of Israel." (LeGrand Richards, *MWW,* pp. 61-62.)

"Israel—The combined name and title, *Israel,* in the original sense of the word, expressed the thought of one who had succeeded in his supplication before the Lord; 'soldier of God,' 'one who contends with God,' 'a prince of God,' are among the common English equivalents. The name first appears in sacred writ as a title conferred upon Jacob, when the latter prevailed in his determination to secure a blessing from his heavenly visitor in the wilderness, receiving the promise: 'Thy name shall be called no more Jacob, but Israel: for as a prince hast thou power with God and with men, and hast prevailed.' [Gen. 32:28.] We read further: 'And God appeared unto Jacob again, when he came out of Padanaram, and blessed him. And God said unto him, Thy name is Jacob: thy name shall not be called any more Jacob, but Israel shall be thy name: and he called his name Israel.' [Gen. 35:9.]

"But the name-title thus bestowed under conditions of solemn dignity acquired a wider application, and came to represent the posterity of Abraham, through Isaac and Jacob [1 Sam. 25:1; Isa. 48:1; Rom. 9:4; 11:1], with each of whom the Lord had covenanted that through his descendants should all nations of the earth be blessed. The name of the individual patriarch thus grew into the designation of a people, including the twelve tribes, who delighted in the title Israelites, or children of Israel." (James E. Talmage, *AF,* p. 313.)

Scriptural References: D&C 8:3; 29:12; 35:25; 36:1; 38:33; 39:11; 50:44; 86:11; 103:16-17; 136:22; Abr. 2:9-11; Gen. 32:24-30; 35:9-13; 49:28; Ex. 3:16; 19:5-6; Deut. 32:7-9; Rom. 9:6-8; 1 Pet. 2:9; 2 Ne. 6:5-15; 9:11-53; 3 Ne. 10:4-7; 16:5-15.

Jehovah (*see also* Jesus Christ)

Jehovah is the pre-earthly name of Jesus Christ. It was one of the major titles by which Jesus Christ was known on the earth before his birth and the bestowal of his earthly name

and title of Jesus the Christ. The God of the Old Testament
(Jehovah) and the God of the New Testament (Jesus Christ)
are one and the same.

Selected Quotations

"Jesus of Nazareth, who in solemn testimony to the Jews
declared himself the *I Am* or *Jehovah,* who was God before
Abraham lived on earth, was the same Being who is
repeatedly proclaimed as the God who made covenant with
Abraham, Isaac, and Jacob; the God who led Israel from the
bondage of Egypt to the freedom of the promised land, the
one and only God known by direct and personal revelation
to the Hebrew prophets in general.

"The identity of Jesus Christ with the Jehovah of the Israelites was well understood by the Nephite prophets, and
the truth of their teachings was confirmed by the risen Lord
who manifested himself unto them shortly after his ascen-
sion from the midst of the apostles at Jerusalem. [3 Ne.
11:13-14 quoted.]" (James E. Talmage, *JC,* p. 38.)

"Jesus Christ of the New Testament, is Jehovah of the Old
Testament, and he so proclaimed it when he came to the
Prophet Joseph and Oliver Cowdery in the temple of the
Lord, the account of which we read in the 110th section of
the Doctrine and Covenants. They speak of his appearance,
the glorious appearance and power, and his voice was like
the rush of many waters. It was the voice of Jehovah of the
Old Testament." (Charles W. Penrose, *CR,* April 1920, p.
30.)

Scriptural References: D&C 109:34, 42, 56, 68; 110:3;
128:9; Abr. 1:16; Gen. 22:14; Ex. 6:3; 17:15; Judg. 6:24; Ps.
83:18; Isa. 12:2; 26:4; 2 Ne. 22:2; Moro. 10:34.

Jesus Christ; positions and titles of Jesus Christ; "no other
name given whereby salvation cometh"

The following scriptural references and selected quotations from General Authorities provide important information and background on Jesus the Christ, who is the most important person who has or who will ever live on this earth.

As numerous scriptures testify, his name is the only name
under heaven whereby salvation comes. Because of his
atonement, all mankind, living or dead, are guaranteed
resurrection from physical death and given the opportunity

of eternal joy and happiness through obedience to the principles and ordinances of his gospel.

His divine mission has many different aspects; it started in the pre-earthly existence, continued in this life, and will extend throughout the eternities to come. Many names and titles have been used throughout the centuries to refer to his various roles. These titles are also found in the quotations and scriptural references that follow.

Selected Quotations

"None ever were perfect but Jesus; and why was He perfect? Because He was the Son of God, and had the fullness of the Spirit, and greater power than any man." (Joseph Smith, *HC* 4:358.)

" 'The hinge of history is on the door of a Bethlehem stable.' (Ralph Sockman.) The name Jesus Christ and what it represents has been plowed deep into the history of the world, never to be uprooted. Christ was born on the sixth of April. Being one of the sons of God and His Only Begotten, his birth is of supreme importance." (Spencer W. Kimball, *Ensign,* May 1975, p. 4.)

"It was He, Jesus Christ, who came forth from the tomb a resurrected being, and He, who 'though he were a Son, yet learned he obedience by the things which he suffered.' (Heb. 5:8.)

"It was this same Jesus Christ who gave revelations to his prophets and revealed to them also through John the Revelator: 'I am Alpha and Omega, the first and the last . . .

" 'I am he that liveth, and was dead: and, behold, I am alive for evermore, Amen; and have the keys of hell and of death.' (Rev. 1:11, 18.)

"It was He, Jesus Christ, in his glorified state who came to the ancestors of the Indians, who is variously known by them as the Great White Spirit, the Fair God and numerous other names.

"It was He, Jesus Christ, our Savior, who was introduced to surprised listeners at Jordan (see Matt. 3:13-17), at the holy Mount of Transfiguration (see Matt. 17:1-9), at the temple of the Nephites (see 3 Ne. 11-26), and in the grove at Palmyra, New York (see Joseph Smith 2:17-25); and the introducing person was none other than his actual Father, the holy Elohim, in whose image he was and whose will he carried out.

"Many people have grown up with the idea that it was the Father who was in charge through the Old Testament history days whenever the title God or Lord was used.

"It is noteworthy that the Father, God, Elohim came to the earth upon each necessary occasion to introduce the Son to a new dispensation, to a new people; then Jesus Christ, the Son, carried forward his work." (Spencer W. Kimball, *Ensign,* November 1977, pp. 73-74.)

"God the Father has given Jesus Christ a name above all others, so that eventually every knee will bow and every tongue confess that Jesus is the Christ. He is the way, the truth, and the light, and no one can come back into the presence of our Father in heaven except through him. Christ is God the Son and possesses every virtue in its perfection. Therefore, the only measure of true greatness is how close a man can become like Jesus. That man is greatest who is most like Christ, and those who love him most will be most like him." (Ezra Taft Benson, *Ensign,* January 1973, p. 57.)

"Joseph Smith was asked, 'What are the fundamental principles of your religion?' He answered: 'The fundamental principles of our religion are the testimony of the Apostles and Prophets, concerning Jesus Christ, that He died, was buried, and rose again the third day, and ascended into heaven; and all other things which pertain to our religion are only appendages to it.' (HC 3:30.)

"That is to say, the atoning sacrifice of the Lord is the center of all things, as far as we are concerned. God our Heavenly Father created us, without which we would have no existence. And Christ the Son has redeemed us, without which there would be neither immortality nor eternal life." (Bruce R. McConkie, *Ensign,* July 1972, p. 110.)

Jesus Christ as Father

"Father because of the Atonement. Our scriptures teach that Jesus Christ is both the Father and the Son. The simple truth is that he is the Son of God by birth, both in the spirit and in the flesh. He is the Father because of the work that he has performed. . . .

"The Savior becomes our Father, in the sense in which this term is used in the scriptures, because he offers us life, eternal life, through the atonement which he made for us. . . .

"So, we become the children, sons and daughters of Jesus Christ, through our covenants of obedience to him. Because of his divine authority and sacrifice on the cross, we become spiritually begotten sons and daughters, and he is our Father.

"Father by divine investiture of authority. Christ is also our Father because his Father has given him of his fulness; that is, he has received a fulness of the glory of the Father. This is taught in Doctrine and Covenants 93:1-5, 16-17, and also by Abinadi in the 15th chapter of Mosiah. Abinadi's statement that he is 'the Father, because he was conceived by the power of God,' harmonizes with the Lord's own words in section 93 that he is the Father because he has received of the fulness of the Father. Christ says he is the Son because, 'I was in the world and made flesh my tabernacle, and dwelt among the sons of men.' Abinadi expresses this truth by saying he is 'the Son because of the flesh.'

"The Father has honored Christ by placing his name upon him, so that he can minister in and through that name as though he were the Father; and thus, so far as power and authority are concerned, his words and acts become and are those of the Father.

"Father as Creator. Our Lord is also called the Father in the sense that he is the Father or Creator of the heavens and the earth and all things." (Joseph Fielding Smith, *DS* 1:28-30.)

Jesus Christ as the Only Begotten Son of God in the Flesh

"We should understand this, that Jesus the Christ came into the world, in the Meridian of Time, to be the Only Begotten Son of God in the flesh. That is a doctrine established in this Church, and we have received it by revelation so we can put aside any doubts or speculations or contentions in regard to it. Jesus as we call him, the Nazarene, the son of Mary, was the Son of God, who is the Father of his spirit. So, in the beginning he was with God and was the firstborn of this great family [D&C 93:21], and on the earth he was the Only Begotten of the Father in the flesh. [D&C 29:42.]" (Charles W. Penrose, *CR,* April 1921, pp. 10-11.)

Names and Titles of Jesus Christ

"In The Church of Jesus Christ of Latter-day Saints we

worship the living Christ. We know that he came forth from the tomb, that he is a resurrected being, that he is our advocate with the Father, that only through him and by obedience to the gospel he has given us can we return into his presence and that of the Father.

"Jesus Christ is our Redeemer and Savior. He was begotten of the Father in the spirit, the Firstborn of the Father, and is the Only Begotten of the Father in the flesh. He is our elder brother. He is the second member of the Godhead. He was the Creator of heaven and earth under the direction of the Father. He is the Jehovah of the Old Testament. He is Jesus of Nazareth.

"He is the Way, the Truth, and the Life. He is the Light of the world. He is the Author of our salvation. He was chosen before the foundation of the world to be the Lamb slain as an offering for our sins. Ultimately every knee must bow and every tongue confess that he is the Christ." (Joseph Anderson, *Ensign,* November 1974, p. 103.)

"His name shall be called 'Immanuel,' which being interpreted is, 'God with us.' Hence He is not only called the Son of God, the First Begotten of the Father, the Well Beloved, the Head, Ruler, and Dictator of all things, Jehovah, the I Am, the Alpha and Omega, but He is also called the very Eternal Father. Does not this mean that in Him were the attributes and power of the very Eternal Father?" (John Taylor, *MA,* p. 138.)

Jesus Christ the Only Name Given Whereby Salvation Comes

"We realize that there is no virtue for salvation and exaltation outside of the atoning blood of Jesus Christ, our Savior. There is no other name under heaven by which man may obtain salvation. [D&C 29:17; 38:4; 45:4; 76:69; Alma 34:8-17.] The whole plan of salvation is founded upon revelation and Jesus Christ; rejecting these there is no foundation left upon which to build nor to stand. The ordinances of the Gospel have virtue in them by reason of the atoning blood of Jesus Christ, and without it there would be no virtue in them for salvation. [Moses 6:57-63.]" (George F. Richards, *CR,* April 1916, pp. 53-54.)

Old Testament Prophecies Concerning Christ

"He was to be born of a virgin; he was to be named Immanuel, which means 'God with us.' (Isa. 7:14 and Matt. 1:23.) He was to come out of Egypt (Hosea 11:1 and Matt. 2:13-23), and yet be born in Bethlehem of Judea (Micah 5:2). His enemies would cause great mourning for children in Bethlehem. (Jer. 31:15 and Matt. 2:18.) And he would finally be called a Nazarene; the Nazarenes were despised, and so people could call him a Nazarene, meaning 'despised.' (Isa. 53:3 and Matt. 2:23.) He was to do many marvelous acts which their recipients were not to make known in the streets. (Isa. 42:2 and Matt. 12:19.) He would cast out devils and heal the sick. (Isa. 53:4 and Matt. 8:17.) He was to teach in parables. (Ps. 78:2 and Matt. 13:35.) When he was proclaimed king, he would come lowly, and riding upon an ass, and upon a colt, the foal of an ass. (Zech. 9:9 and Matt. 21:4-9.)

"He would make the temple a house of prayer, driving the moneychangers from it in the process. (Isa. 56:7 and Matt. 21:12.) He would suffer an ignominious death; his executioners would part his raiment among them and cast lots for his garment. (Ps. 22:18 and Matt. 27:35.) And from the death price of thirty pieces of silver, a potter's field would be purchased. (Zech. 11:12-13 and Matt. 27:6-9.) In the process of dying he would cry out, 'I thirst.' (Ps. 69:21 and John 19:28-29.)

"In spite of the Roman custom of breaking the bones of those they crucified, the prophets proclaimed that not one of his bones would be broken. (Ex. 12:46, Ps. 34:20, and John 19:33-36.) He was to make his grave with the rich. (Isa. 53:9.) And after all this he would be called by Isaiah, 'Wonderful, Counseller, The mighty God, The everlasting Father, The Prince of Peace.' (Isa. 9:6.)" (S. Dilworth Young, *Ensign*, May 1974, p. 59.)

Jews; "mine own received me not" (*see also* Israel; Gathering)

The word *Jew* has meant different things during various periods of history. As first used in the Bible, it referred to the descendants of Judah, the fourthborn son of Jacob (Israel). For a while the Jews were known as one of the twelve tribes of Israel.

After the dispersion of the ten tribes of Israel, which had comprised the northern kingdom (or the kingdom of Israel), the major group of Israelites that remained in the eastern promised land was comprised of the Jews, or tribe of Judah, and the remaining political organization was known as the kingdom of Judah. In time all the Israelites living in the kingdom of Judah were known as Jews whether or not they were lineal blood descendants of Judah. This was particularly true after the ten tribes comprising the Kingdom of Israel were taken into captivity by the Assyrians in about 722 B.C.

The patriarchs of the people comprising the major story in the Book of Mormon, Lehi and Ishmael, were living in the kingdom of Judah in 600 B.C., and were known politically as Jews even though they were lineal blood descendants of Joseph. (See Alma 10:3.) Nephi, one of the sons of Lehi, states: "I have charity for the Jew—I say Jew, because I mean them from whence I came." (2 Ne. 33:8.)

Essentially, the only Israelites the world has known anything about for 2,700 years (since 722 B.C.) are the Jews; thus, in the minds of many people today the words *Jew* and *Israel* are synonyms.

Selected Quotations

"We have a great desire for their [Jews] welfare, and are looking for the time soon to come when they will gather to Jerusalem, build up the city and the land of Palestine, and prepare for the coming of the Messiah. When he comes again, he will not come as he did when the Jews rejected him. . . .

"When the Savior visits Jerusalem, and the Jews look upon him, and see the wounds in his hands and in his side and in his feet, they will then know that they have persecuted and put to death the true Messiah, and then they will acknowledge him, but not till then. [45:47-53.] They have confounded his first and second coming, expecting his first coming to be as a mighty prince instead of as a servant. They will go back by and by to Jerusalem and own their Lord and Master. [D&C 109:62-64; 110:11.]" (Brigham Young, *JD* 11:279.)

"It is true that Lehi and his family were descendants of Joseph through the lineage of Manasseh (Alma 10:3), and Ishmael was a descendant of Ephraim, according to the statement of the Prophet Joseph Smith. That the Nephites were descendants of Joseph is in fulfilment of the blessings given to Joseph by his father Israel. The Nephites were of the Jews, not so much by descent as by citizenship, although in the long descent from Jacob, it would be possible of some mixing of the tribes by intermarriage. Lehi was a citizen of Jerusalem, in the kingdom of Judah. Presumably his family had lived there for several generations, and all the inhabitants of the kingdom of Judah, no matter which tribe they had descended through, were known as Jews. . . .

"Not only in the book of Mormon are the descendants of Lehi called Jews, but also in the Doctrine and Covenants. In section 19, verse 27, this is found: [19:27, quoted.] Again, in giving instructions to the Elders who had journeyed from Kirtland to Missouri, the Lord revealed the place for the building of the temple and gave instruction for the purchase of land 'lying westward, even unto the line running directly between Jew and Gentile.' (57:4.) This line westward was the dividing line between the whites and Indians." (Joseph Fielding Smith, *IE,* October 1955, p. 702.)

Scriptural References: D&C 3:16; 11:29; 18:26; 19:27; 20:9; 21:12; 39:3; 45:8, 21, 51; 57:4; 74:2, 6; 77:15; 84:28; 90:9; 98:17; 107:33-35, 97; 112:4; 133:8; JS-M 1:4, 18, 21; 1 Ne. 13:23-24; 14:23; 2 Ne. 33:8.

John the Baptist

John the Baptist baptized the Savior in New Testament times (Matt. 3:1-17) and restored the Aaronic Priesthood in this dispensation (section 13). He should not be confused with John the Beloved, the apostle who restored the Melchizedek Priesthood together with Peter and James.

Selected Quotations

"The question arose from the saying of Jesus—'Among those that are born of women there is not a greater prophet than John the Baptist; but he that is least in the kingdom of God is greater than he [John].' How is it that John was considered one of the greatest prophets? His miracles could not have constituted his greatness.

"First. He was entrusted with a divine mission of preparing the way before the face of the Lord. . . .

"Secondly. He was entrusted with the important mission, and it was required at his hands, to baptize the Son of Man. . . .

"Thirdly. John, at that time, was the only legal administrator in the affairs of the kingdom there was then on the earth, and holding the keys of power. The Jews had to obey his instructions or be damned, by their own law; and Christ himself fulfilled all righteousness in becoming obedient to the law which he had given to Moses on the mount, and thereby magnified it and made it honorable, instead of destroying it. The son of Zacharias wrested the keys, the kingdom, the power, the glory from the Jews, by the holy anointing and decree of heaven, and these three reasons constitute him the greatest prophet born of a woman.

"Second Question: 'How was the least in the kingdom of heaven greater than he?' [John] In reply I asked—Whom did Jesus have reference to as being the least? Jesus was looked upon as having the least claim in God's kingdom, and [seemingly] was least entitled to their credulity as a prophet; as though he had said: 'He that is considered the least among you is greater than John—that is I myself.' " (Joseph Smith, *HC* 5:261.)

Scriptural References: D&C 27:7-8; JS-H 2:72; Matt. 3:1; 11:11, 12; 14:2; 16:14; 17:13; Mark 6:14, 24-25; 8:28; Luke 7:20, 28, 33; 9:19.

John the Beloved

The beloved apostle John was promised by the Savior that he should tarry until the second coming of Jesus Christ. (John 21:20-24.) In this dispensation, John the Beloved appeared with Peter and James, restoring the Melchizedek Priesthood to Joseph Smith. He should not be confused with John the Baptist, who restored the Aaronic Priesthood. (Section 13.)

Scriptural References: D&C 7:1; 20:35; 27:12; 77:1-6, 14; 128:6, 20; JS-H 1:72; 1 Ne. 14:27; 3 Ne. 28:6; Ether 4:16.

Judgment; judges; "all to be judged"

One of the distinguishing characteristics of law is that every law has consequences or results. For example, in the moral realm the consequence for obedience to the law (righteousness) is a blessing, which results in joy and happiness; the consequence for disobedience to the law (wickedness) is a punishment, which results in misery and unhappiness. By the very nature of law we will be judged (either here or in the hereafter or both) according to the laws that we keep or do not keep. Inasmuch as there are many kinds of law, many kinds of people and many degrees of faithfulness in obeying laws, and many types of willfulness in disobeying laws, it is obvious that there will be many types and degrees of judgment.

Selected Quotations

"God judges men according to the use they make of the light which He gives them." (Joseph Smith, *HC* 5:401.)

"He holds the reins of judgment in His hands; He is a wise Lawgiver, and will judge all men, not according to the narrow, contracted notions of men, but, 'according to the deeds done in the body whether they be good or evil,' or whether these deeds were done in England, America, Spain, Turkey, or India. He will judge them, 'not according to what they have not, but according to what they have,' those who have lived without law, will be judged without law, and those who have law, will be judged by that law. He will award judgment or mercy to all nations according to their several deserts, their means of obtaining intelligence, the laws by which they are governed, the facilities afforded them of obtaining correct information, and His inscrutable designs in relation to the human family; and when the designs of God shall be made manifest, and the curtain of futurity be withdrawn, we shall all of us eventually have to confess that the Judge of all the earth has done right." (Joseph Smith, *HC* 4:595-96.)

"We know that every man will be judged according to the deeds done in the body; and whether our sin be against our own peace and happiness alone or whether it affects that of others, as the Lord lives we will have to make satisfaction or atonement; God requires it, and it is according to his providences, and we cannot escape it." (Joseph F. Smith, *JD* 21:13.)

"We are told that we shall reap as we sow. This is the law of the harvest. If we sow wheat on our farms here on earth, we grow wheat. If, in our character building, we sow the seeds of righteousness, we shall reap that kind of harvest. So as the Lord himself said: 'Whatsoever ye sow, that shall ye also reap; therefore, if ye sow good ye shall also reap good for your reward.' (D&C 6:33.)

"It works out like this, for example: The Lord said, 'If ye forgive men their trespasses, your heavenly Father will also forgive you.' (Matt. 6:14.) And he added: 'With what judgment ye judge, ye shall be judged: and with what measure ye mete, it shall be measured to you again.' (Matt. 7:2.)" (Mark E. Petersen, *Ensign,* November 1974, p. 51.)

Scriptural References: D&C 1:36; 88:35; 107:72, 74, 78; Moses 6:61; 7:66; JS-H 1:45; Isa. 30:18; 61:8; Matt. 27:2; John 5:22; 8:16; 1 Pet. 4:17; Ether 11:20.

Keys of priesthood (*see also* Priesthood)

The priesthood of God has been defined as the power and authority to act for or in behalf of God. "Keys" of priesthood are concerned with the right to direct the functioning of the priesthood. Some keys of the priesthood are inherent within the priesthood itself, while others are bestowed as a person is "set apart" to a particular position.

Selected Quotations

"What is the distinction between Priesthood in general, and the keys of the Priesthood?

"The Priesthood in general is the authority given to man to act for God. Every man that has been ordained to any degree of the Priesthood, has this authority dedicated to him.

"But it is necessary that every act performed under this authority, shall be done at the proper time and place, in the proper way, and after the proper order. The power of directing these labors constitutes the keys of the Priesthood. In their fulness, these keys are held by only one person at a time, the prophet and president of The Church. He may delegate any portion of this power to another, in which case that person holds the keys of that particular labor. Thus, the president of a temple, the president of a stake, the bishop of a ward, the president of a mission, the president of a quorum, each holds the keys of the labors performed in that particular body or locality. His Priesthood is not increased by this special appointment, for a seventy who presides over a mission has no more Priesthood than a seventy who labors under his direction; and the president of an elders' quorum, for example, has no more Priesthood than any member of that quorum. But he holds the power of directing the official labors performed in the mission or the quorum, or in other words, *the keys* of that division of that work. So it is throughout all the ramifications of the Priesthood—a distinction must be carefully made between the general authority, and the directing of the labors performed by that authority." (Joseph F. Smith, *IE,* January 1901, p. 230.)

"We hold the holy Melchizedek Priesthood, which is the power and authority of God delegated to man on earth to act in all things for the salvation of men.

"We also hold the keys of the kingdom of God on earth, which kingdom is The Church of Jesus Christ of Latter-day Saints.

"These keys are the right of presidency; they are the power and authority to govern and direct all of the Lord's affairs on earth. Those who hold them have power to govern and control the manner in which all others may serve in the priesthood. All of us may hold the priesthood, but we can only use it as authorized and directed so to do by those who hold the keys.

"This priesthood and these keys were conferred upon Joseph Smith and Oliver Cowdery by Peter, James, and John, and by Moses and Elijah and others of the ancient prophets. They have been given to each man who has been set apart as a member of the Council of the Twelve. But since they are the right of presidency, they can only be exercised in full by the senior apostle of God on earth, who is the president of the Church." (Joseph Fielding Smith, *Ensign,* July 1972, p. 87.)

Scriptural References: D&C 7:7; 13:1; 27:5-6, 9, 12-13; 28:7; 35:25; 65:2; 68:17-18; Matt. 16:19; Rev. 1:18.

Killing; murder (*see also* Ten Commandments)

The Lord has commanded "Thou shalt not kill," and in both ancient and modern scriptures he has indicated the seriousness of taking human life. The sin of murder (the willful, knowing, premeditated shedding of innocent blood) has been identified by the Lord as one of the most serious sins that can be committed in this life.

Selected Quotations

"We solemnly make the following declaration, viz:

"That this Church views the shedding of human blood with the utmost abhorrence. That we regard the killing of a human being, except in conformity with the civil law, as a capital crime which should be punished by shedding the blood of the criminal, after a public trial before a legally constituted court of the land. . . .

"The revelations of God to this Church make death the penalty for capital crime, and require that offenders against life and property shall be delivered up to and tried by the laws of the land." (Wilford Woodruff, *Deseret Weekly* 39:809.)

"Many people in the world do not seem to realize what a terrible crime it is to take human life. When they become angry, for justifiable reasons as they think, they do not hesitate to destroy human life. Sometimes a life is taken in order that money or property may be seized. And yet there is no crime that a human being can commit that will so far alienate him from the blessings of eternal life in the celestial kingdom as murder. No other crime is equal to it. I think that it is our privilege in this Church to teach our children while in their tender years and while they are growing up, the enormity of the crime of taking human life." (George Albert Smith, *CR*, October 1932, p. 24.)

"There is no sin that a nation can commit, which the Lord avenges so speedily and fearfully, as he does the shedding of innocent blood, or, in other words, the killing of his anointed and authorized servants. No nation which has been guilty of this dreadful crime has escaped his vengeance. The thunderbolts of his wrath have been always launched forth for the destruction of the perpetrators of such wickedness. It is a rank offence against the majesty of Heaven and the authority of the Creator, which he never suffers to pass unrebuked; for such men act in his stead, and are his representatives on the earth. [D&C 1:38; 84:35-38.]" (George Q. Cannon, *MS* 26:363.)

"Self-Murder Pronounced: There is another evil that is growing amongst the peoples of the world that is not unfelt amidst the Latter-day Saints. It is the crime of self-murder. Suicide should be made odious among the people of God; it should be emphasized as a deadly sin, and no undue feelings of tenderness towards the unfortunate dead, or of sympathy towards the living bereaved, should prevent us denouncing it as a crime against God and humanity, against the Creator and the creature.

"We do not think that the same laudations and panegyrics should be pronounced over the self-murderer as are so freely uttered over the faithful Saint who has gone to his eternal rest. There is a difference in their death, and that difference should be impressed upon the living, unless the deceased, at the time of the rash act, was in such a mental condition as not to be wholly responsible for his actions; but again, if this condition be the result of sin, of departure from God's laws, then the unfortunate one, like the inebriate, is not altogether free from the responsibility of the acts committed while in this state of mental derangement; if he is not censurable for the act itself, he is for the causes that induced it. In such cases the mantle of charity must not be stretched so widely, in our desire to protect our erring friends, as to reflect dishonor on the work of God, or contempt for the principles of the everlasting Gospel. There is an unfortunate tendency in the natures of many to palliate sins by which they are not personally injured, but we must not forget that such palliation frequently increases the original wrong, and brings discredit on the Church and dishonor to the name and work of our blessed Redeemer; in other words, to save the feelings of our friends we are willing to crucify afresh the Lord of life and glory." (John Taylor, Pamphlet, Church Historical Library, October 1886.)

Scriptural References: D&C 42:18-19, 79; 59:6; 132:36; Ex. 20:13; Matt. 5:21; 10:28; 3 Ne. 12:21.

Kingdom; kingdom of God; kingdom of heaven

Kingdom of God is another term for The Church of Jesus Christ of Latter-day Saints. The Kingdom of God on the earth is the official agency through which the Lord works to bless his children and to provide them with the saving ordinances of the gospel. The Lord also has an organization in heaven (the kingdom of heaven) through which he blesses his Saints there. Sometime in the future these two kingdoms will essentially be one, and the Lord will directly and personally supervise his work both in heaven and on the earth. At that time, he will rule as King of kings and Lord of lords. Thus, the Lord has taught us to pray, "Thy kingdom come, thy will be done, on earth as it is in heaven."

Selected Quotations

"The Church of Jesus Christ of Latter-day Saints was restored in 1830 after numerous revelations from the divine source; and this is the kingdom, set up by the God of heaven that would never be destroyed nor superseded, and the stone cut out of the mountain without hands that would become a great mountain and would fill the whole earth." (Spencer W. Kimball, *Ensign,* May 1976, p. 8.)

"We might then ask, what is the kingdom of God? And again we are not left without an answer, for the Lord replied, 'The keys of the kingdom of God are committed unto men on the earth. . . .' Where there are the keys of the kingdom, there is the Church of Jesus Christ.

"The Prophet Joseph Smith makes this definition of the kingdom of God: 'Some say that the kingdom of God was not set up upon the earth until the day of Pentecost, and that John did not preach the baptism of repentance for the remission of sins, but I say to you in the name of the Lord that the kingdom of God was set up upon the earth in the days of Adam to the present time. Whenever there has been a righteous man on earth unto whom God revealed His word and gave power and authority to administer in His name, and where there is a priest of God . . . to administer in the ordinances of the gospel, and officiate in the priesthood of God, there is the kingdom of God. . . . Where there is a prophet, a priest, or a righteous man unto whom God gives His oracles, there is the kingdom of God; and where the oracles of God are not, there the kingdom of God is not.' (*TPJS,* pp. 271-72.)

"Just as the Master said in his day, the kingdom of God cometh not by observation, meaning that there would be no outward signs or no political changes, so today, it is now among us, as it has been in every dispensation of the gospel since the days of Adam.

"Another statement was made by the prophets of the New Testament which to me has significance. They are quoted as having said that '. . . the kingdom of God is within you.' (Luke 17:21.) A more correct translation probably would have said, 'The kingdom of God is among you or in your midst. . . .' " (Harold B. Lee, *CR,* October 1953, p. 26.)

Scriptural References: D&C 6:13, 37; 10:55; 15:6; 56:18; 65:2-6; 84:19, 34-38; 106:3; 136:31, 41; Matt. 3:2; 4:17; 5:3; 1 Ne. 13:37; Alma 11:37.

Knee; "every knee shall bow"

The idea that every person must acknowledge that Jesus Christ is the Son of God at the time of his second coming is expressed in two places in the D&C—76:110 and 88:104. Similar ideas are found in both the Old Testament (Isaiah 45:23) and the New Testament (Romans 14:11; Philip. 2:10). As indicated in the quotations under *Millennium,* however, the term *every knee shall bow* does not mean that everyone will be a member of the true church at that time.

Selected Quotations

"In the Millennium men will have the privilege of being Presbyterians, Methodists, or Infidels, but they will not have the privilege of treating the name and character of Deity as they have done heretofore. No, but every knee shall bow and every tongue confess to the glory of God the Father that Jesus is the Christ." (*Brigham Young*, JD 12:274.)

"When the kingdom of God triumphs, every knee shall bow and every tongue confess that Jesus is the Christ, to the glory of the Father. Even the Jews will do it then; but will the Jews and Gentiles be obliged to belong to the Church of Jesus Christ of Latter-day Saints? No; not by any means. . . . They will cease their persecutions against the Church of Jesus Christ, and they will be willing to acknowledge that the Lord is God and that Jesus is the Savior of the world." (*Brigham Young*, JD 11:275.)

Scriptural References: D&C 76:110; 88:104; Isa. 45:23; Rom. 14:11; Philip. 2:10; Mosiah 27:31.

Knowledge of God; God knoweth all things (*see also* God)

One of the attributes or characteristics of God the Father is that he "knoweth all things, and there is not anything save he knows it." (2 Ne. 9:20.) Because the knowledge of God is absolute and all things past, present, and future are continually before his eyes (D&C 130:7), he knows what is going to happen in the future and can reveal this information to his prophets as needed.

Selected Quotations

"Without the knowledge of all things, God would not be able to save any portion of his creatures; for it is by reason of the knowledge which he has of all things, from the beginning to the end, that enables him to give that understanding to his creatures by which they are made partakers of eternal life; and if it were not for the idea existing in the minds of men that God has all knowledge it would be impossible for them to exercise faith in him." (Joseph Smith, *Lectures on Faith*, No. 4.)

"The great Jehovah contemplated the whole of the events connected with the earth, pertaining to the plan of salvation, before it rolled into existence, or ever 'the morning stars sang together' for joy; the past, the present, and the future were and are, with him, one eternal 'now'; he knew of the fall of Adam, the iniquities of the antediluvians, of the depth of iniquity that would be connected with the human family, their weakness and strength, their power and glory, apostasies, their crimes, their righteousness and iniquity; he comprehended the fall of man, and his redemption; he knew the plan of salvation and pointed it out; he was acquainted with the situation of all nations and with their destiny; he ordered all things according to the council of his own will; he knows the situation of both the living and the dead, and has made ample provision for their redemption, according to their several circumstances, and the laws of the kingdom of God, whether in this world, or in the world to come." (Joseph Smith, *HC* 4:597.)

"Divine revelation of what is to come is proof of foreknowledge. God, therefore, knows, and has known from the beginning, what shall be, even to the end of the world. . . .

"But who will venture to affirm that foreknowledge is a determining cause? God's omniscience concerning Adam cannot reasonably be considered the cause of the Fall. Adam was free to do as he chose to do. God did not force him to obey the divine command. Neither did God's knowledge compel false Judas to betray the Christ, nor the recreant Jews to crucify their Lord.

"Surely the omniscience of God does not operate to make of men automatons; nor does it warrant the superstition of fatalism. The chief purpose of earth life, as a stage in the course of the soul's progression, would be nullified if man's agency was after all but a pretense, and he a creature of circumstance compelled to do as he does. . . .

"The Father of our spirits has a full knowledge of the nature and disposition of each of his children, a knowledge gained by observation and experience in the long ages of our primeval childhood, when we existed as unembodied spirits, endowed with individuality and agency—a knowledge compared with which that gained by earthly parents through experience with their children in the flesh is infinitesimally small. In that surpassing knowledge God reads the future of child and children, of men individually and of men collectively. He knows what each will do under given conditions, and sees the end from the beginning. His foreknowledge is based on intelligence and reason. He foresees the future of men and nations as a state that naturally and surely will be; not as a state of things that must be because he has arbitrarily willed that it shall be." (James E. Talmage, *VM,* pp. 318-20.)

Scriptural References: D&C 42:61; 50:40; 84:19; 88:79; 89:19; 93:24, 53; 101:25; 107:71; 109:67; 121:33, 42; 128:14; 130:19; 1 Sam. 2:3; Prov. 14:18; Isa. 33:6; 1 Cor. 12:8; Hel. 15:13; Ether 4:13.

Lamb; Lamb of God (*see also* Jesus Christ)

Jesus Christ is the Lamb of God in the sense that he is the Son of God and he offered himself as the sacrifice for the sins of man by the shedding of his blood. From the days of Adam, the righteous saints were instructed to offer up the firstlings of the flocks (including lambs) as a sacrifice to God, to remind them that in the meridian of time the "lamb without blemish and without spot: who verily was foreordained before the foundation of the world" (1 Peter 1:19) would be offered up as the last, infinite, eternal sacrifice. That Lamb, of course, was the sinless Jesus Christ, who was and is also the Firstborn Son of God in the spirit.

Scriptural References: D&C 88:106, 115; 58:11; 65:3; 76:21, 39, 85, 119; 109:79; 133:18, 55, 56; Moses 7:47; Ex. 12:5; Isa. 53:7; John 1:29; Acts 8:32; 1 Pet. 1:19; Rev. 5:12; 7:14; 13:8; 19:7, 9; 21:23; 22:3; 1 Ne. 10:10; 11:21; 12:11; 13:40; 14:1; 2 Ne. 31:4; Alma 7:14; 13:11; Morm. 9:6; Ether 13:10.

Law; laws; law of justice; law of mercy

God is a God of law, which essentially means that he knows, understands, and obeys great eternal principles that have certain and definite consequences. Every blessing is predicated upon obedience to a law, and the blessings, joy, and happiness enjoyed by God are the result of his absolute obedience to law. Because God is a God of law, he is also a God of order. If laws did not have definite and definable consequences, then it would be impossible to predict or determine what would happen if the law were either obeyed or disobeyed. In such a situation, chaos would prevail. However, inasmuch as laws do have definite consequences that can and have been determined, these consequences can be predicted and order results.

Selected Quotations

"We believe that everything is ruled by law. We are thankful that it is so, for otherwise we would live in a world of chance, in a fearful uncertainty of what would happen next. I believe that the material laws that can be traced in the creation had an intelligent will behind them, that the laws themselves were never superior to the will of God. He made those laws, and by His power they became effective to accomplish His purposes. It is to Him that we pray, and we know he is almighty and does hear prayers, and though He uses material laws to carry out His plans, His will was never subjected to the laws, but the laws have ever been subservient to Him. Let no one think that God is impotent, that the laws He has made stand in the way of His hearing His children and answering their prayers." (Anthon H. Lund, *CR,* April 1916, p. 12.)

"The other day I was talking to a young man who said, in effect, 'I am fed up and tired of being told, "You *have* to do this," or "You *have* to do that." I want to be free to decide for *myself* what I want to do.'

"My response was: 'You *are* free to choose *exactly* what you want to do, as long as it does not restrict or impose on the rights or liberties of others, but you must be responsible for your acts and prepared to take the consequences.'

"I explained that the Lord's greatest gift to mortal man is threefold: first, the right to immortality and eternal life; second, the plan by which he can gain it; third, *his free agency to choose what he will do.* The Lord gave us the plan which will bring us the greatest joy and happiness while on this earth, and which will prepare us for eternal life. All we have to do to enjoy this is to obey the law and keep his commandments.

"All the laws of God and the laws of nature and the laws of the land are made for the benefit of man, for his comfort, enjoyment, safety, and well-being; and it is up to the individual to learn these laws and to determine whether or not he will enjoy these benefits by obeying the law and by keeping the commandments. . . . Part of the purpose of our existence, . . . is to rise above . . . animal instincts, and to reach the highest plane of human behavior in our social relations.

"In order that we may accomplish this, God, our Father

and our Creator, and his Son Jesus Christ, who want us to be happy and successful, have given us the laws which, if applied in our lives, will improve our social conditions and our relationship to one another. . . .

"Someone has wisely said: 'Woe unto those who consider the laws of God only as forces of convenience, to be ignored or employed at will. Woe unto those individuals, classes, and nations that believe in the might of their wealth, in the strength of their armor, in the invincibility of their positions.'

"No culture can last, no nation or union of nations can survive if they ignore God's laws." (N. Eldon Tanner, *IE,* June 1970, pp. 30-32.)

Scriptural References: D&C 29:32; 41:3; 42:2, 59; 88:13, 21, 38, 42; 93:53; 107:84; 130:21; 132:5, 21, 32; Ezra 7:25; Ps. 1:2; 19:7; Isa. 2:3; 51:4; Jer. 31:33; Gal. 5:14; Heb. 8:10; James 1:25; 2 Ne. 2:26; 8:4; 9:25, 27.

Laying on of hands

The hands of authorized priesthood bearers are placed upon the heads of the recipients of several ordinances and blessings and upon a person to be set apart to a position. However, the term *laying on of hands* is usually reserved to refer to the ordinance of confirmation, which is the conferring of the Holy Ghost.

Selected Quotations

"The gift of the Holy Ghost by the laying on of hands cannot be received through the medium of any other principle than the principle of righteousness, for if the proposals are not complied with, it is of no use, but withdraws." (Joseph Smith, *HC* 3:379.)

"In order that men may indeed become the children of God, He has introduced in the first principles of the gospel the means of their becoming possessed of His Spirit through baptism and laying on of hands by those having authority, being sent and ordained and authorized by Him that they may receive the Holy Ghost." (John Taylor, *JD* 11:22.)

"It is well understood in our Church that those holding the Aaronic Priesthood have authority to officiate only in outward ordinances. By virtue of this priesthood, faith and repentance may be preached and baptism by immersion (in the temporal element of water) administered. But it requires the imposition of hands by those holding the higher or Melchizedek Priesthood to bestow the Holy Ghost and induct the convert into the spiritual concern of the kingdom." (Joseph F. Smith, *MS* 67:628.)

Scriptural References: D&C 20:41, 58, 68, 70; 25:8; 33:15; 35:6; 36:2; 39:23; 42:44; 49:14; 52:10; 53:3; 55:1; 66:9; 68:21, 25; 76:52; 84:6; 107:44, 67; JS-H 1:68; A of F 1:4-5; Gen. 48:17; Ex. 29:10; Lev. 1:4; 16:21; Num. 27:23; Deut. 34:9; Matt. 9:18; 19:13; Mark 5:23; 6:5; 7:32; 8:23; 16:18; Luke 4:40; 13:13; Acts 6:6; 8:17; 9:17; 13:3; 28:8; 1 Tim. 4:14; 5:22; 2 Tim. 1:6; Heb. 6:2; Alma 6:1; 31:36; 3 Ne. 18:36; Morm. 9:24; Moro. 2:2; 3:2.

Lie; lying; bearing false witness (*see also* Honesty; Ten Commandments)

"Thou shalt not lie" has been one of the commandments of God from the beginning. God is a God of truth; God does not and cannot lie. To the degree to which a person lies or deceives, he is removing himself from the influence and presence of God.

Lucifer, or Satan, is the opposite of God. He is referred to as "the father of lies" and as "a liar from the beginning." When a person lies or deceives, he is following the pattern of the devil and is placing himself under the power of Satan. One of the characteristic attributes of followers of Lucifer is that they are liars and lovers of lies.

Selected Quotations

" 'Yea, lie a little, take the advantage of one because of his words.' (2 Ne. 28:8.)

"Think of what that means, the whispering of the adversary to lie a little. Whether it be a lie intended to affect a religious organization, a business organization, a political organization, or an individual, the lie will brand the one who tells it, and sooner or later he will have to account for the wrong he has committed.

" 'Yea, lie a little, take the advantage of one because of his words, dig a pit for thy neighbor; there is no harm in this; and do all these things, for tomorrow we die; and if it so be that we are guilty, God will beat us with a few stripes, and at last we shall be saved in the kingdom of God.' (2 Ne. 28:8.)

"That is what the adversary of righteousness is saying to the children of men. That is what Lucifer, who goes out defiling the people, is breathing in their souls. That is the kind of doctrine that is being disseminated in the world by some of those who ought to be the leaders of morality and also of righteousness." (George Albert Smith, *CR*, October 1932, pp. 28-29.)

Scriptural References: D&C 10:25; 42:21, 86; 62:6; 63:17; 76:103; Moses 4:4; 5:24; Prov. 14:5; Heb. 6:18; James 3:4; Alma 1:17; 5:17; 12:4.

Light; light and the life of the world; light of Christ; "light which shineth in darkness" (*see also* Jesus Christ)

The symbol of light is one of the symbols ascribed to God and to Jesus Christ. Also, light is one of the attributes of Deity and comes from God. John records: "God is light, and in him is no darkness at all." (1 John 1:5). God's truths are also referred to as light, and the light of the gospel (or gospel light) enables men to be spiritually enlightened and come to an understanding of God and his ways.

Both ancient and modern scriptures contain many references to light in relationship to God the Father, Jesus Christ the Son, and to their gospel. The expression "I am the light which shineth in darkness, and the darkness comprehendeth it not" is used by the Savior on several occasions in latter-day revelations. (See D&C 10:58; 11:11; 14:9; 34:2; 39:2; 45:7; 88:49-50.) The apostle John also used this term in referring to the Savior: "In him was life; and the life was the light of men. And the light shineth in darkness; and the darkness comprehendeth it not." (John 1:4-5.)

In other revelations the Lord explained to Joseph Smith how He is the light and life of the world and some reasons why the people of the world would not accept Him and His gospel. (See D&C 45:28, 36; 50:24-27; 84:45-46; 88:6-13, 49-50, 56-58, 67; 93:9; 103:9.)

In his inspired version of the New Testament, Joseph Smith recorded John 1:4-5 as follows: "In him was the gospel, and the gospel was the life, and the life was the light of men; And the light shineth in the world, and the world perceiveth it not." (John 1:4-5.)

Selected Quotations

"Every man born into this world receives the guidance of the light of Christ, which is also called the light of truth, and the Spirit of Jesus Christ. (D&C 84:45-48.) This light of truth is not in any sense to be confounded with the Holy Ghost. It is the light or Spirit which emanates from God and fills the immensity of space. It is by this power that men are guided to right from wrong, for it quickens their understanding. If they will heed this Spirit it will lead them to the Gospel and then they may receive the greater light, even the Holy Ghost. It is the light which shineth and the power by which worlds are made and governed throughout the universe. . . .

"President Joseph F. Smith has drawn a clear distinction between the light of truth, or Spirit of Christ, and the Holy Ghost in these words.

" 'The question is often asked, Is there any difference between the Spirit of the Lord and the Holy Ghost? . . . The Holy Ghost is a personage in the Godhead, and is not that which lighteth every man that cometh into the world. It is the Spirit of God which proceeds through Christ to the world, that enlightens every man that comes into the world, and that strives with the children of men, and will continue to strive with them until it brings them to a knowledge of the truth and the possession of the greater light and testimony of the Holy Ghost.' (*GD*, p. 82.)" (Joseph Fielding Smith, *CHMR* 1:339-40.)

"This Light of Christ is not a personage. It has no body. I do not know what it is as far as substance is concerned; but it fills the immensity of space and emanates from God. It is the light by which the worlds are controlled, by which they are made. It is the light of the sun and all other bodies. It is the light which gives life to vegetation. It quickens the understanding of men, and has these various functions as set forth in these verses.

"It is: 'The light which is in all things, which giveth life to all things, which is the law by which all things are governed, even the power of God who sitteth upon his throne, who is in the bosom of eternity, who is in the midst of all things.'

"This is our explanation in regard to the Spirit of Christ, or Light of Truth, which every man receives and is guided by. Unless a man has the blessings that come from this Spirit, his mind would not be quickened; there would be no vegetation grow; the worlds would not stay in their orbits; because it is through this Spirit of Truth, this Light of Truth, according to this revelation, that all these things are done." (Joseph Fielding Smith, *DS* 1:52.)

"We have the sweet influence of the Spirit of God pleading with us to do that which is right, pleading with every human being that does not drive it from him; for every human being has a portion of the Spirit of God given unto him. We sometimes call it conscience; we call it by one name and we call it by another; but it is the Spirit of God that every man and woman possesses that is born on the earth. God has given unto all his children this Spirit." (George Q. Cannon, *JD* 26:191.)

Scriptural References: D&C 6:21; 14:9; 45:28; 50:24-27; 82:3; 84:45, 54; 88:6-13, 67, 87; 93:9, 29, 36-37; 103:9; 106:8; 115:5; 124:9; 128:20; 133:49; Ps. 27:1; Isa. 5:20; 8:20; 9:20; 42:6; 45:7; 50:10-11; 58:8; 60:1, 3, 19; John 1:4; 3:19; 5:35; 8:12; 12:35; Alma 9:23; 19:6; 32:35.

Lineage

The term *lineage* refers to line of descent or genealogy and can refer either to a person or to power and authority (priesthood). It is used in all of these senses in the seven verses of the Doctrine and Covenants where it appears: 68:21; 84:14-15; 86:8, 10; 107:41; 113:8.

Additional Scriptural References: Abr. 1:27; Luke 2:4.

Living God (*see also* God)

God is a vital, active, living Personage of flesh and bones and spirit. He is not a God who lived a long time ago and has already accomplished all his work, nor is he a God who is dead and no longer has any power or force or interest in the world. At the time of the First Vision in 1820, many of the creeds of Christianity contained elements suggesting that God had either already accomplished his work or was no longer exercising his power in the earth. However, in his revelation to the Prophet Joseph Smith, as recorded in the Doctrine Covenants, God frequently reiterates that he is a "living God" and that his church is a "living church."

Scriptural References: D&C 14:9; 20:19, 32; 42:1; 50:1; 55:2; 61:28; 68:1, 6, 25; 70:10; 76:66; 77:9; 82:18; Moses 5:29; Matt. 16:16; 26:63; Jer. 10:10; 23:36; 1 Tim. 3:15; 4:10; 6:17; Heb. 3:12; 9:14; 10:31; 12:22; Alma 5:13; 7:6; 11:25-27; 43:10; 3 Ne. 30:1.

Love; God of love (*see also* God)

One definition of God in the scriptures is that "God is

love." (1 John 4:8.) The gospel of Christ has also been referred to as the gospel of love. Love, then, is and should be the relationship between man and God and between man and mankind. In his teachings, the Savior indicated that the law of love forms the basis of all the laws and commandments: "Thou shalt love the Lord thy God with all thy heart, and with all thy soul, and with all thy mind. This is the first and great commandment. And the second is like unto it, Thou shalt love thy neighbour as thyself. On these two commandments hang all the law and the prophets." (Matt. 22:37-40.)

Selected Quotations

"What is the distinguishing characteristic of our Heavenly Father? John gave us a clue when he said: 'Beloved, let us love one another: for love is of God; and every one that loveth is born of God and knoweth God. He that loveth not knoweth not God; for *God is love.*' (1 John 4:7-8. Italics added.)

"This was so very difficult for me to understand before the missionaries knocked on my door, for, from this scripture and others quite similar, it appeared that God and love were one and the same. Is God, then, just an emotion? You can't see love. You may see the effect of love or the lack of it, but love is not a corporate entity. When I learned the truth—that God is an exalted man of flesh and bone and spirit—then I understood what John was saying: that love is God's distinguishing characteristic.

"God loves us. We know it. The scriptures declare it, and from the experiences of each one of us, we know it to be true. Almost no one doubts this fact. God loves us, but why? Why does God love *us* when we often do not deserve his love?

"I don't know why God loves us, but I believe the scriptures give us a clue. God doesn't love us because *we* are good. God loves us because *he* is good. God is good and so he loves us, and those who are the best love the best. . . .

"I have seen this godlike quality of unselfish love in all the best men I have known or read about. Jesus wept over those who rejected him and prayed for those who crucified him.

"Joseph Smith's heart was filled with love and compassion for all men, even for his persecutors. All the prophets have had this great quality. . . .

"Only as we live in obedience to these commandments will we be able to know real love for others and real joy ourselves." (Hartman Rector, Jr., *IE,* December 1969, pp. 81-82.)

"It is a time-honored adage that love begets love. Let us pour forth love—show forth our kindness unto all mankind, and the Lord will reward us with everlasting increase; cast our bread upon the waters and we shall receive it after many days, increased to a hundredfold. . . . I do not dwell upon your faults, and you shall not upon mine. Charity which is love, covereth a multitude of sins [1 Pet. 4:8]." (Joseph Smith, *HC* 5:517.)

"True love is a process. True love requires personal action. Love must be continuing to be real. Love takes time. . . . We must at regular and appropriate intervals speak and reassure others of our love and the long time it takes to prove it by our actions. Real love does take time. The Great Shepherd had the same thoughts in mind when he taught, 'If ye love me, *keep* my commandments' (John 14:15; italics added) and 'If ye love me *feed* my sheep' (John 21:16; italics added). Love demands action if it is to be continuing. Love is a process. Love is not a declaration. Love is not an announcement. Love is not a passing fancy. Love is not an expediency. Love is not a convenience. 'If ye love me, keep my commandments' and 'If ye love me feed my sheep' are God-given proclamations that should remind us we can often best show our love through the processes of *feeding* and *keeping*." (Marvin J. Ashton, *Ensign,* November 1975, p. 108.)

"A lonely young Persian student was in Munich, Germany, struggling to find a meaning to life. He was deeply disturbed by the materialism and selfishness that seemed to fill the world, and especially postwar Europe. He heard a knock at the door, and two humble Mormon elders stood before him. He was not the least interested in religion. In fact, cynicism and doubt had filled his soul until he was very nearly persuaded that there was no God nor any real meaning to life. The only thing that interested him about these two young men was their English accent. He had mastered four languages, but English was not one of them.

"He invited them in, but as they started their discussion, he cautioned: 'I don't want to hear about your God, nor do I want to hear about how your religion got started. I only want

to know one thing: what do you people do for one another?'
He waited, and a look of doubt crossed his dark features, as
the elders exchanged glances.

"Finally, the spokesman for the two said softly, 'We love
one another.'

"Nothing he could have said would have been more elec-
trifying than this simple utterance had upon this young
Persian, for the Holy Ghost immediately bore testimony to
his soul that these missionaries were true servants of the
Lord. Shortly thereafter he was baptized, and he presently is
in this country receiving his doctorate degree at a local
university—all because a young Mormon missionary
declared a simple truth, 'We love one another.'

"Virtually all religions tell us to love one another, but the
restored Church tells us *how* to love one another. The home
teaching visits, the inspired Welfare Program, the unselfish
service performed in the temples, and the worldwide
missionary system demonstrate in a very practical way the
teaching of the Savior: 'Thou shalt love thy neighbour as
thyself.'(Matt. 22:39.)" (Henry D. Taylor, *IE,* June 1969,
p. 64.)

Scriptural References: D&C 4:5; 12:8; 20:19; 34:3; 38:24;
42:22, 29, 38, 45; 59:5-6; 76:116; 88:123; 95:12; 121:41, 45;
Moses 7:33; Lev. 19:18; Deut. 6:5; 30:6; John 3:16; 5:42;
13:34; 14:15; 15:10, 12-13; 2 Ne. 26:30; 31:20; 3 Ne. 12:44.

Marriage

The first marriage (Adam and Eve) and all subsequent
marriages performed on this earth by the power of God are
intended to be eternal. Marriage is designed not only for this
earth, but for all eternity. Earlier prophets taught the concept
of eternal marriage, but unfortunately many ministers of religion do not teach this concept today. In his revelations
contained in the Doctrine and Covenants the Lord reemphasized the importance and the eternal nature of the marriage
covenant.

Selected Quotations

"Now let us consider the first marriage that was
performed after the earth was organized. Adam, the first
man, had been created. . . . We then find this recorded: 'And
the Lord God said, It is not good that man should be alone; I
will make him an help meet for him.' After the Lord had

formed Eve, he 'brought her unto the man. And Adam said, This is now bone of my bones and flesh of my flesh; she shall be called woman because she was taken out of man. Therefore shall a man leave his father and his mother, and shall cleave unto his wife and they shall be one flesh.' (Gen. 2:18, 22-24.) These words were undoubtedly just what they sound like. They were very likely the words spoken by Adam reciting the vows of the first marriage upon this earth. . . .

"Here was a marriage performed by the Lord between two immortal beings, for until sin entered the world their bodies were not subject to death. He made them one, not merely for time, nor for any definite period; they were to be one throughout the eternal ages. If you were to say that because Adam and Eve transgressed and became subject to death that this eternal union was broken, then just remember that the purpose of the atonement by Jesus Christ was to restore that which was lost by the fall. Their restoration then to each other after the resurrection would not require a remarriage, for death to them was not a divorce; it was only a temporary separation. Resurrection to immortality meant for them a reunion and an eternal bond never again to be severed. . . .

"If marriage then was for the purpose of the organizing of spirits before the world was formed and for 'multiplying and replenishing the earth' on which we now live, surely there must likewise be a divine purpose in its being continued after the resurrection. This purpose is declared by the Lord to be for 'a continuation of the seeds forever and ever.' (D&C 132:19.)" (Harold B. Lee, *Youth and The Church,* pp. 128-29.)

"Marriage in the temple for time and eternity should be the goal of every member of the Church, for marriage is ordained of God. Marriage is a commandment. Marriage was instituted by divine edict. [49:15-17 quoted.]

"Marriage is a sacred relationship entered into primarily for the rearing of a family, in fulfillment of the commandments of the Lord. Marriage with children, and the beautiful family relationship which can come of it, is the fulfillment of life. . . . The Lord intended that marriage performed for eternity in the temple should endure forever. This was his plan. . . .

"What therefore God hath joined together, let not man

put asunder.' (Mark 10:9.) It is evident from the scriptures that marriage performed in the Lord's way should not be dissolved." (James A. Cullimore, *Ensign,* June 1971, p. 93.)

"To those who might decry marriage or postpone it or forbid it Paul spoke, condemning them. It is generally selfishness, cold and self-centered, which leads people to shun marriage responsibility. There are many who talk and write against marriage. Even some of our own delay marriage and argue against it. To all who are deceived by these 'doctrines of devils,' we urge the return to normalcy. We call upon all people to accept normal marriage as a basis for true happiness. The Lord did not give sex to man for a plaything. Basically marriage presupposes a family. [Ps. 127:3, 5 quoted.]

"Certainly anyone who purposely denies himself or herself honorable parenthood is to be pitied, for the great joy of parenthood is fundamental in the normal, full life." (Spencer W. Kimball, *Ensign,* May 1974, p. 6.)

"Not all sins of this permissive world are with the youth. I was shocked recently when I read a movie magazine. The man spoke of marriage as a legalistic, paper-signing institution, and said: 'It should be abolished. Without the social pressures in the state, it could be utopia.' He asked the woman. She said: 'Marriage should be done away with. I already know people who are living quietly together without marriage, but I haven't yet seen the effect of this on children as they grow up in such a society.'

"These are not the only ones who are advocating living together without marriage. We call this to the attention of our people with all the strength we possess.

"We say again: We members of the Church marry. All normal people should marry. (There could be a few exceptions.) All normal married couples should become parents. We remember the scripture which says: 'Whoso forbiddeth to marry is not ordained of God, for marriage is ordained of God unto man. Wherefore, it is lawful that he should have one wife, and they twain shall be one flesh, and all this that the earth might answer the end of its creation.' (D&C 49:15-16.)

"The earth cannot justify nor continue its life without marriage and the family. Sex without marriage, for all people, young or older, is an abomination to the Lord, and it is most unfortunate that many people have blinded their eyes to these great truths." (Spencer W. Kimball, *Ensign,* November 1974, p. 8.)

Scriptural References: D&C 49:15; 131:2; 132:16; Gen. 2:24; 6:2; Matt. 19:5-6; 22:30; 1 Cor. 6:16; 7:2; Jacob 3:7.

Meet; "meet in mine eyes"

Earlier definitions of the word *meet,* which are now listed as archaic in some modern dictionaries, include the idea of being proper, fit, acceptable, permissible, right, necessary, or desirable. Thus, the statement it is "not meet that I should command in all things" (D&C 58:26) essentially means that it is not necessary or desirable for the Lord to tell us everything we should know.

Scriptural References: D&C 19:8; 41:6-8; 58:26; 64:26; 84:58; 88:24; 89:5; 90:30; 121:16; Moses 3:18, 20; Abr. 5:14, 21; Jer. 26:14; 27:5; Matt. 3:8; 15:26; 1 Cor. 15:9; 16:4; Alma 5:54; 9:30; 12:15; 13:13.

Melchizedek Priesthood (*see also* Priesthood)

The Holy Priesthood after the Order of the Son of God is the title of the priesthood of God. However, in order to avoid the too-frequent repetition of the name of Deity, the Lord has permitted this priesthood to be referred to as the Melchizedek Priesthood, which comprehends or includes the Aaronic Priesthood.

Melchizedek was a righteous high priest who lived on the earth about 2,000 years before Christ. He is mentioned in both the Old Testament and the New Testament, but most of our information on Melchizedek comes either from the modern scriptures or from the prophets of this dispensation.

Selected Quotations

"The history of the Melchizedek Priesthood did not begin with this earth. The prophets understood the premortality existence of priesthood. The Apostle Paul expressed it when he said, 'Without father, without mother, without descent, having neither beginning of days nor end of life; but made like unto the Son of God; abideth a priest continually.' (Heb. 7:3.) That men who are called of God to the authority of the ministry on earth may have been selected for such an appointment even before they took mortal bodies is clearly evident from the scriptures. (*Articles of Faith,* p. 194.) In support of this doctrine, I bring you now three statements: two scriptural quotations and one from the Prophet. [Abr. 3:22-23; Alma 13:3-4 quoted.]

"Now these are made clear by this statement of the Prophet: 'Every man who has a calling to minister to the inhabitants of the world was ordained to that very purpose in the Grand Council of heaven before this world was. (Now note this.) I suppose I was ordained to this very office in that Grand Council. It is the testimony that I want that I am God's servant and this people His people.' (*TPJS*, p. 365.)" (Harold B. Lee, *ASIF*, pp. 4-5.)

"Was the Priesthood of Melchizedek taken away when Moses died? All Priesthood is Melchizedek, but there are different portions or degrees of it. That portion which brought Moses to speak with God face to face was taken away; but that which brought the ministry of angels remained. All the prophets had the Melchizedek Priesthood." (Joseph Smith, *TPJS*, pp. 180-81.)

"The mission and authority of the greater Priesthood are here set forth. It administers in the gospel, and reveals the 'mysteries of the kingdom'—even the knowledge concerning God, without which there would be no eternal life (D&C 84:19). It administers the ordinances of the gospel, in which the power of godliness is manifest (v. 20); and it holds the authority which enables man to see God, even the Father, and live (v. 22). To quote from the *History of the Church:*

" 'President Joseph Smith, Jun., addressed the assembly and said, the Melchizedek High Priesthood was no other than the Priesthood of the Son of God; that there are certain ordinances which belong to the Priesthood, from which flow certain results; and the Presidents or Presidency are over the Church; and revelations of the mind and will of God to the Church, are to come through the Presidency. This is the order of heaven, and the power and privilege of the Priesthood. It is also the privilege of any officer in the Church to obtain revelations, so far as relates to his particular calling and duty in the Church. All are bound by the principles of virtue and happiness, but one great privilege of the Priesthood is to obtain revelations of the mind and will of God. It is also the privilege of the Melchizedek Priesthood, to reprove, rebuke, and admonish, as well as to receive revelation' (*HC* 2:477)." (Smith and Sjodahl, *DCC*, p. 502.)

"There are in this greater priesthood five offices or callings—elder, seventy, high priest, patriarch, and apostle—yet the priesthood is the same; and the priesthood is greater than any of its offices. We are a kingdom of brethren, a congregation of equals, all of whom are entitled to receive all of the blessings of the priesthood. There are no blessings reserved for apostles that are not freely available to all the elders of the kingdom; blessings come because of obedience and personal righteousness, not because of administrative positions.

"I shall speak of these blessings—the ten priesthood blessings—which are available to all of us who hold the holy Melchizedek Priesthood.

"Blessing one: We are members of the one true and living Church upon the face of the whole earth, and we have received the fulness of the everlasting gospel. . . .

"Blessing two: We have received the gift of the Holy Ghost, and we are entitled to receive the gifts of the Spirit—those wondrous spiritual endowments which set us apart from the world and raise us above carnal things. . . .

"Blessing three: We can be sanctified by the Spirit, have dross and evil burned out of us as though by fire, become clean and spotless, and be fit to dwell with gods and angels. . . .

"Blessing four: We can stand in the place and stead of the Lord Jesus Christ in administering salvation to the children of men. . . .

"Blessing five: We have power to become the sons of God, to be adopted into the family of the Lord Jesus Christ, to have him as our Father, to be one with him as he is one with his Father. . . .

"Blessing six: We can enter into the patriarchal order, the order of eternal marriage, the order which enables the family unit to continue everlastingly in celestial glory. . . .

"Blessing seven: We have power to govern all things, both temporal and spiritual, both the kingdoms of the world, and the elements and storms and powers of the earth. . . .

"Blessing eight: We have power, through the priesthood, to gain eternal life, the greatest of all the gifts of God. . . .

"Blessing nine: We have power to make our calling and election sure, so that while we yet dwell in mortality, having overcome the world and been true and faithful in all things, we shall be sealed up unto eternal life and have the unconditional promise of eternal life in the presence of Him whose we are. . . .

"Blessing ten: We have the power—and it is our privilege—so to live, that becoming pure in heart, we shall see the face of God while we yet dwell as mortals in a world of sin and sorrow. . . .

"These, then, are the ten blessings of the priesthood, the Holy Priesthood, after the order of the Son of God, the priesthood which the saints in ancient days called after Melchizedek to avoid the too frequent repetition of the name of Deity." (Bruce R. McConkie, *Ensign,* November 1977, pp. 33, 35.)

Scriptural References: D&C 84:17, 19, 25, 40; 86:10; 107:2, 17, 22, 65, 69, 79; 113:6; 121:21; 124:28; 127:8; 131:2; Moses 6:7; JS-H 1:38; Num. 16:10; 1 Pet. 2:9; 2 Ne. 6:2; 3 Ne. 18:37; Moro. 2:2.

Meridian of time

The word *meridian* means middle; *meridian of time* refers to the middle of time or to the time when Jesus Christ lived upon the earth.

Selected Quotations

"Our Savior came in the meridian of time. That dispensation is called the dispensation of the meridian of time. This means that it was about half-way from the *beginning of 'time' to the end of 'time.'* Anyone who desires can figure it for himself, that our Lord came about 4,000 years from the time of the fall. The millennium is to come some time following the 2,000 years after his coming. Then there is to be the millennium for 1,000 years, and following that a *'little season,'* the length of which is not revealed, but which may *bring 'time' to its end* about 8,000 years from the beginning." (Joseph Fielding Smith, *DS* 1:81.)

Scriptural References: D&C 20:26; 39:3; Moses 5:57; 6:57, 62; 7:46.

Might, mind, and strength

The powerful descriptive action words *might, mind* and *strength* are used in both ancient and modern scriptures to indicate the breadth and depth of commitment we should make to the Lord and to his work.

Moses was commanded to teach the children of Israel,

"Thou shalt love the Lord thy God with all thine heart, and with all thy soul, and with all thy might" (Deut. 6:5), and in the New Testament the Savior identified this as "the first and great commandment" (Matt. 22:38; see also Mark 12:30, 33 and Luke 10:27).

The three words *might, mind,* and *strength* are combined in at least three verses of the Doctrine and Covenants (11:20, 20:31, and 33:7), and the word *heart* is added to them in at least three other references: 4:2, 59:5, and 98:47.

In a later revelation, the Lord gives the following commandment to the saints in Zion: "Thou shalt love the Lord thy God with all thy heart, with all thy might, mind, and strength; and in the name of Jesus Christ thou shalt serve him. Thou shalt love thy neighbor as thyself." (D&C 59:5-6.)

Scriptural References: D&C 4:2, 4; 11:20; 20:31; 59:5; Mark 12:30, 33; Luke 10:27; Mosiah 2:11; Moro. 10:32.

Millennium

The dictionary defines millennium as "a period of 1,000 years." The millennium referred to in Revelation 20 and other scriptures refers to the 1,000-year period when Christ shall reign personally upon the earth and conditions of righteousness and happiness will exist. The gospel and the Church have been restored in this dispensation to help prepare a people to be worthy to live with Jesus Christ when he comes to inaugurate the millennium and rule as King of kings and Lord of lords.

Selected Quotations

"When Christ comes the Saints who are on the earth will be quickened and caught up to meet him. This does not mean that those who are living in mortality at that time will be changed and pass through the resurrection, for mortals must remain on the earth until after the thousand years are ended. A change, nevertheless, will come over all who remain on the earth; they will be quickened so that they will not be subject unto death until they are old. Men shall die when they are an hundred years of age, and the change shall be made suddenly to the immortal state. Graves will not be made during this thousand years, and Satan shall have no power to tempt any man. Children shall grow up 'as calves of the stall' [Mal. 4:2] unto righteousness, that is without sin or the temptations which are so prevalent today. Even the animal kingdom shall experience a great change, for the enmity of beasts shall disappear, . . . and they shall not hurt nor destroy in all my holy mountain: for the earth shall be full of the knowledge of the Lord, as the waters cover the sea. [Isa. 11:6-9.]" (Joseph Fielding Smith, *WP,* pp. 288-89.)

"Some members of the Church have an erroneous idea that when the millennium comes all the people are going to be swept off the earth except righteous members of the Church. That is not so. There will be millions of people, Catholics, Protestants, agnostics, Mohammedans, people of all classes, and of all beliefs, still permitted to remain upon the face of the earth, but they will be those who have lived clean lives, those who have been free from wickedness and corruption. All who belong, by virtue of their good lives, to the terrestrial order, as well as those who have kept the celestial law, will remain upon the face of the earth during the millennium." (Joseph Fielding Smith, *DS* 1:86-87.)

"Christ and the resurrected Saints will reign over the earth during the thousand years. They will not probably dwell upon the earth, but will visit it when they please, or when it is necessary to govern it. There will be wicked men on the earth during the thousand years. The heathen nations who will not come up to worship will be visited with the judgments of God, and must eventually be destroyed from the earth." (Joseph Smith, *HC* 5:212.)

"But our testimony would not be complete if we did not reaffirm our faith in the second coming of Christ, in the millennium which is to come, when he will reign as King of kings, and Lord of lords. That this climactic event is not far distant is indicated by the signs of the times, by wars and rumors of wars, by the satanic schemes of evil men who would enslave not only the bodies but also the minds of all who dare refuse to subscribe to the idealogies invented by the anti-Christ. [D&C 133.]" (Hugh B. Brown, *CR,* October 1960, pp. 93-94.)

Scriptural References: D&C 43:30; 77:6-7; 88:101, 110; Moses 7:64; A of F 1:10; Isa. 65:18-23; Dan. 7:14; Micah 4:1-8; Mal. 3, 4; Rev. 20:1-3, 7.

Miracles (*see also* Gifts of the Spirit)

A miracle is not in violation of natural law; rather it is the application of natural law at a level that man in his present condition is not able to fully understand. Some dictionary definitions of miracle are "an extraordinary event manifesting divine intervention in human affairs" and "an extremely outstanding or unusual event, thing, or accomplishment."

True miracles from God are the result of faith. Therefore, as Moroni has indicated, if miracles are lacking in the world then faith must be lacking. (Moroni 7:37.)

Selected Quotations

"They who doubt the possibility of miracles are indeed without the power to perform them. But this does not prove that believers lack that power. Miracles are the fruits of faith— 'These signs shall follow them that believe.' (Mark 16:17.) The gist of the matter is this: These doubters have done away with God, or have tried to do away with him, and consequently are unable to conceive of a higher power than they themselves possess. . . .

"Miracles are extraordinary results flowing from superior means and methods of doing things. When a man wants light he strikes a match, or presses a button, or turns a switch, and lo! there is light. When God wants light, he says: 'Let there be light.' It is simply a matter of knowing how to do things in a superior way, and having the power to do them. Man is gradually acquiring this power. It is a far call from the tallow dip to the electric light. But the end is not yet. Improvements will continue to be made, and some day, perhaps men may be able to make light just as the Lord makes it. Paradoxically, it might be said that the time will come when miracles will be so common that there will be none.

"Miracles belong to no particular time or place. Wherever and whenever there is a legitimate demand for the exercise of divine power, that power will act, and marvels will result. We worship a God of miracles, and he changeth not, but is the same yesterday, today and forever. (Morm. 9:11, 17-20.) There is but one valid reason for the absence of miracles among any people, and that is the absence of faith. 'All things are possible to them that believe.' (Mark 9:23.)" (Orson F. Whitney, *CR*, April 1925, pp. 17, 20-22.)

"Miracles are not primarily intended, surely they are not needed, to prove the power of God; the simpler occurrences, the more ordinary works of creation do that. But unto the heart already softened and purified by the testimony of the truth, to the mind enlightened through the Spirit's power and conscious of obedient service in the requirements of the Gospel, the voice of miracles comes with cheering tidings, with fresh and more abundant evidences of the magnanimity of an all-merciful God." (James E. Talmage, *AF*, p. 219.)

"It may be asked, how are we to distinguish between the miracles wrought by the power of God, and those wrought by the power of Satan? We answer in the language of Paul, 'he that is spiritual judgeth all things.' (1 Cor. 2:15.) But as the greater part of the world are not spiritual, we will point out other rules by which to distinguish the two powers. Wherever miracles are wrought by the power of God, *there* will be found a true and righteous doctrine, unmixed with error: wherever miracles are wrought by the power of the devil, *there* will be found more or less false doctrine. Wherever miracles are wrought by the servants of God, they will do them in the name of Jesus Christ, after having obeyed the ordinances of the gospel; when the servants of the devil do miracles, if they pretend to do them in the name of Christ, it will be found by examination that they have not obeyed the ordinances of Christ, and therefore He suffers the devil to deceive them; but it is oftener the case that they do not perform them in the name of Christ, neither in the way that He has appointed, as in the case of mesmerism, clairvoyance, etc. Those who do miracles by the power of God, generally have a message to publish to the people by authority from God. The most of those who do miracles by the power of the devil, pretend to no message whatever; or if they pretend to have a message to deliver to the people, it will be found, on inspection, to be mixed with error." (Orson Pratt, *MDOP*, pp. 256-58.)

"It has been asserted that miracles are impossible, because they are contrary to the laws of nature, and that the supernatural element in the history of religion is, in our enlightened age, the main difficulty in the way of its acceptance. It is assumed that the so-called laws of nature are immutable, and that nothing can take place that appears to be contrary to such laws. To this objection the answer is, that we do not know *all* the laws of nature. We can, therefore, not maintain that the miracles performed by the servants of the Lord are not in perfect accord with some law of which we are ignorant. All we can say is that they do not belong to any of the classes of ordinary events with which men are familiar. But that is far from saying that they are impossible. As a matter of fact, violations of the best established laws of nature appear to be occurring constantly. We raise a weight from the ground. That seems to be contrary to the law of gravitation. Our bodies, for years, resist decay because of the action of the life-force within. That seems to be contrary to chemical laws governing matter. One force counteracts another; and besides, God's universe is not exclusively controlled by physical forces. Superior to these, directing and controlling them, is the divine will. As a captain, with a word of command, turns his immense ship in whatever direction he chooses, and controls his engines and everything, so God directs and controls His universe and all that pertains thereto, not contrary to, but in conformity with, laws and forces known to Him, even though unknown to us." (Smith and Sjodahl, *DCC*, p. 516.)

Scriptural References: D&C 24:13; 35:8; 45:8; 46:21; Num. 14:22; John 2:11, 23; 3:2; 12:37; Moro. 7:27, 37; 10:12.

Missionary service; missionary work; every man to warn his neighbor

Any person who is truly converted to the gospel of Jesus Christ will naturally and anxiously want to share these truths with others. Also, the Lord has given commandments to his saints that, inasmuch as they have been warned of the impending destruction preceding the second coming of Jesus Christ, they have the responsibility to warn the others. Missionary service, then, has been one of the distinguishing characteristics of the true Church in this dispensation.

Selected quotations

"I will say as Paul did, 'Woe be unto me if I preach not the Gospel.' (1 Cor. 9:16.) I will say the same for the Apostles, the High Priests, the Seventies, and the Elders, so far as they are called to declare the word of life and salvation to this generation; the judgment of God will rest upon us if we do not do it. You may ask why. I answer, because a dispensation of the Gospel of Jesus Christ has never been given to man in ancient days or in this age, for any other purpose than for the salvation of the human family." (Wilford Woodruff, *JD* 22:204.)

"When we come into the Church, we covenant in the

waters of baptism that we will do missionary work. We enter into a solemn contract with Deity that we will bear testimony of the restoration of the gospel on every appropriate occasion. We agree 'to stand as witnesses of God at all times and in all things, and in all places' that we 'may be in, even until death.' (Mosiah 18:9.) We are also bound by the command that the Lord has given by revelation in this day, that 'it becometh every man who hath been warned to warn his neighbor.' (D&C 88:81.) Thus we have an affirmative, positive, definite obligation resting upon us to do missionary work. This matter of carrying the gospel message to the world is not something that we can choose to do or not, if and when we may find it to be convenient. We are under covenant to do it 'at all times . . . and in all places . . . even until death.' (Mosiah 18:9.)

"We are indebted, each of us individually, to the missionaries who brought the gospel to us or to our ancestors; many of us owe these missionaries more than we owe anyone else. We received from them the pearl of great price. We have an obligation to discharge our debt, and one of the very best ways in which we can do this is to go forth ourselves as missionaries, or otherwise to use our talents and our means to see that others of our Father's children have the opportunity to receive that which has been restored in this day." (Bruce R. McConkie, *CR*, October 1960, pp. 54-55.)

"*It is generally understood that every member of the Church should be a missionary.* He is probably not authorized to go from house to house, but he is authorized, by virtue of his membership, to set a proper example as a good neighbor." (David O. McKay, *CR*, October 1958, p. 93.)

"Perhaps the greatest reason for missionary work is to give the world its chance to hear and accept the gospel. The scriptures are replete with commands and promises and calls and rewards for teaching the gospel. I use the word *command* deliberately for it seems to be an insistent directive from which we, singly and collectively, cannot escape. . . .

"I wonder if we are doing all we can. Are we complacent in our approach to teaching all the world? We have been proselyting now 144 years. Are we prepared to lengthen our stride? To enlarge our vision? . . ." (Spencer W. Kimball, *Ensign*, October 1974, pp. 4-5, 13.)

Scriptural References: D&C 42:11; 50:17; 62:5; 71:1; 75:4; 84:61; 88:81; 90:11; 107:25; 133:8, 38; Moses 8:19; Matt. 28:19; Mark 16:15.

Music; hymns; "song of the righteous is a prayer unto me"

Music is an art that evidently has always been associated with the gospel of Jesus Christ. Appreciation of and the ability to perform music has helped to enrich and strengthen spirituality. In this dispensation, the Lord has indicated that "the song of the righteous is a prayer unto me."(D&C 25:12.)

As is the case in so many other areas, however, Lucifer has attempted to use music to lead people away from the true spirit of worship. Care must therefore be taken concerning the type and spirit of our music, including the music performed in our Church meetings.

Selected Quotations

"Recently the First Presidency restated this counsel: 'Through music, man's ability to express himself extends beyond the limits of the spoken language in both subtlety and power. Music can be used to exalt and inspire or to carry messages of degradation and destruction. It is therefore important that as Latter-day Saints we at all times apply the principles of the gospel and seek the guidance of the Spirit when selecting the music with which we surround ourselves.' (*Priesthood Bulletin,* August, 1973.)" (Boyd K. Packer, *Ensign,* January 1974, p. 25.)

Scriptural References: D&C 25:12; 66:11; 84:98; 101:18; 109:39; 128:22; 133:33, 56; 136:28; Job 38:7; Ps. 40:3; 98:1; Isa. 12:5; 42:10; Matt. 26:30; Act 16:25; Mosiah 2:28; Ether 6:9.

Mysteries; mysteries of God; mysteries of the kingdom

One dictionary definition of *mystery* is "a religious truth that man can know by revelation alone and cannot fully understand." Actually there are no mysteries to God, because he understands and comprehends all things. Our Heavenly Father would like to reveal all of his truths to his children so they could receive the blessings associated with obedience to his laws. However, in his infinite wisdom, God also knows that some persons not only would not keep these laws, but might also use them for unrighteous purposes to their own damnation. He has indicated that he will reveal his truths "line upon line, precept upon precept, here a little and there a little . . . unto him that receiveth I will give more." (2 Ne. 28:30.)

In this dispensation, the Lord has promised that these un-revealed truths (mysteries) will be revealed as the people learn to faithfully keep the commandments and teachings he has already given.

Selected Quotations

"We are called to hold the keys of the mysteries of those things that have been kept hid from the foundation of the world until now. Some have tasted a little of these things, many of which are to be poured down from heaven upon the heads of babes; yea, upon the weak, obscure and despised ones of the earth. [D&C 128:18.] Therefore we beseech of you, brethren, that you bear with those who do not feel themselves more worthy than yourselves, while we exhort one another to a reformation with one and all, both old and young . . . let honesty, and sobriety, and candor, and solemnity, and virtue, and pureness, and meekness, and sim-plicity crown our heads in every place; and, in fine, become as little children, without malice, guile or hypocrisy." (Jo-seph Smith, *HC* 3:296.)

"The Lord has promised to reveal his mysteries to those who serve him in faithfulness. . . . There are no mysteries pertaining to the Gospel, only as we, in our weakness, fail to comprehend Gospel truth. The Gospel is very simple, so that even children at the age of accountability may understand it. Without question, there are principles which in this life we cannot understand, but when the fulness comes we will see that all is plain and reasonable and within our comprehen-sion. The 'simple' principles of the Gospel, such as baptism, the atonement, are mysteries to those who do not have the guidance of the spirit of the Lord." (Joseph Fielding Smith, *CHMR* 1:40.)

"Many men will say, 'I will never forsake you, but will stand by you at all times.' But the moment you teach them some of the mysteries of the kingdom of God that are retained in the heavens and are to be revealed to the children of men when they are prepared for them, they will be the first to stone you and put you to death." (Joseph Smith, *HC* 5:424.)

"A mystery is a truth that cannot be known except through divine revelation—a sacred secret. In the days of Paul the important truth that Gentiles were to be admitted to the Kingdom of God without observing the Law of Moses was a 'mystery' (Eph. 1:9-11; Col. 1:25-27). In our day such great truths as those pertaining to the restoration of the Priesthood, the work for the dead, and the re-establishment of the Church are 'mysteries,' because they could not have been discovered except by revelation.

"It should be noted that when God revealed a truth to anyone, through the Prophet Joseph, President Brigham Young, or any of their successors, that truth was just as true, and just as binding, as if Peter, James, John, Gabriel, or Michael had been sent with the message. He who does not believe the word of God through a mortal messenger, would not believe one from the other side of mortality (Luke 16:31)." (Smith and Sjodahl, *DCC*, p. 141.)

Scriptural References: 1 Cor. 2:7; 4:1; 13:2; Eph. 3:9; 5:32; 6:19; Alma 10:5; 12:9; 26:22; 37:4; 40:3.

Natural; natural to the earth

A thing is natural if it is in the same essential condition as the things around it. At the present time the earth is temporarily in a telestial mortal condition, and generally speaking the people who are living on the earth are carnal, sensual, and devilish. Thus, all of these terms could be used as synonyms for *natural*. In 29:35 we read that the commandments of God "are not natural nor temporal, neither carnal nor sensual," and 67:10 indicates that man cannot see God "with the carnal neither natural mind, but with the spiritual." In this life, natural could be considered almost as an opposite or antonym of spiritual.

Selected Quotations

"The human mind takes cognizance of things material and temporal, and, within its limitations, is capable of introspection as also of reasoning and speculating in the abstract. Paul knew all this and much more, as his words demonstrate: [1 Cor. 2:13-14 quoted.]

"The 'natural man,' by which the writer of the epistle means the man whose spiritual powers lie undeveloped and dormant, can not understand spiritual things, thoughts or sayings, for they are all foolishness to him. The physical body may be developed highly, even abnormally, while mind and spirit are weak and dull. So too the mind may function actively, while the other attributes of the spirit are torpid.

"On this basis Paul affirmed that 'the preaching of the cross' is but foolishness to the 'natural man': while, unto those who had so far opened their eyes, their ears, their hearts as to perceive and comprehend spiritually, the 'preaching of the cross' was veritably 'the power of God.' (1 Cor. 1:18.)

"Men qualified to teach according to this spiritual order are less frequently found among the worldly-wise than among the humble and such as may be called weak and unlearned." (James E. Talmage, *Sunday Night Talks by Radio,* pp. 473-76.)

"The Prophet Joseph Smith declared that all evil done by man was voluntary. (TPJS, p. 187.) Brigham Young taught the same doctrine. (DBY, p. 85.) President Joseph F. Smith (*GD,* p. 69) and all other leaders of the Restored Church have taught that by the actions of men possessed of free agency, good or evil comes into the world. Thus, the whole question of evil is referred to the will of man. He who desires good, and seeks to become the master of his will, will do good; while he who desires evil, and uses his will for that purpose, does evil. Men who love darkness do so because their deeds are evil. [10:20-21; 112:23.]" (John A. Widtsoe, *ER* 1:257.)

Scriptural References: D&C 29:35, 43; 58:3; 67:10, 12; 88:28; 128:14; Moses 1:10-11, 14; 6:36; Rom. 1:26-27, 31; 11:21, 24; 1 Cor. 2:13-14; 15:44, 46; 2 Tim. 3:3; James 1:23; 2 Pet. 2:12; Jacob 5; Mosiah 3:19; Alma 19:6; 26:21; 41:4, 12.

Nauvoo, Illinois

Nauvoo, Illinois, was the major gathering place of the Saints between 1839 and the great exodus westward in 1846. It was built from a village previously known as Commerce, Illinois. According to Joseph Smith, the word *Nauvoo* means "beautiful."

Scriptural References: D&C 124:60, 109, 111, 117, 119, 121; 125:3-4.

New heaven and a new earth

In relationship to its present condition, the earth will be "new" or different during the millennium, when it will be "renewed and receive its paradisiacal glory." (Article of Faith 10.) At that time the earth will be in a physical terrestrial condition, as it was in the days of "paradise" or the Garden of Eden. At the end of the millennium and after "a short season," the earth will die and be resurrected to a celestial glory; it will then be *another* "new" earth.

President Joseph Fielding Smith has indicated that the new heaven and earth at the beginning of the millennium is the one mentioned in the tenth Article of Faith and is discussed in sections 63 (verses 50-51), 101 (verses 23-31), and 133 (verses 22-24) and in Isaiah 65:17-25. The "new heaven and earth" after the end of the millennium when the earth dies and receives its resurrected glory is discussed in sections 29 (verses 22-25), 77 (verses 1-2), 88 (verses 14-26, 101), and 130 (verse 7) and in Isaiah chapters 24 and 51.

The term *new heaven* would suggest that the new earth will be in a different place of the universe as compared to our present telestial earth. The heavens of the new earth will be new or different in the sense that the stars, planets, and so forth will be in different positions in relationship to the earth.

Selected Quotations

"A new heaven and a new earth are promised by the sacred writers. Or, in other words, the planetary systems are to be changed, purified, refined, exalted, and glorified, in the similitude of the resurrection, by which all physical evil or imperfections will be done away." (Parley P. Pratt, *KT,* p. 60.)

"This earth is filling the measure of its creation. (D&C 88:18-26.) Today it is passing through its mortal state. The time will come when it shall die and pass away, as do all things upon it. [Isaiah 24 and 51.] . . . Here we have predictions that the earth shall pass away, die, and all its inhabitants shall also die in like manner. This truth was not generally and correctly understood until the Lord made known in revelations to Joseph Smith that this should be the case. When Isaiah said the earth should 'fall and not rise again,' the interpretation is that it should not be restored to the same mortal or temporal condition. When the earth passes away and is dissolved, it will pass through a similar condition which the human body does in death, but, like the human body, so shall the earth itself be restored in the resurrection and become a celestial body, through the mercy and mission of Jesus Christ. This reference to a new heaven and earth, spoken of in Sec. 29:22-23, and 77:1-2, is not the same as that spoken of by Isaiah in Chap. 65:17. The 'new heavens and new earth' referred to in this scripture, and also in Sec. 101:23-31, had reference to the change which shall come to the earth and all upon it, at the beginning of the Millennial reign, as we declare in the tenth article of the Articles of Faith. This is the renewed earth when it shall receive its paradisiacal glory, or be restored as it was before the fall of man. (See Compendium, art. *Millennial Reign,* p. 202.) 'The new heaven and new earth' . . . in section 29 is the final change, or resurrection, of the earth, after the 'little season' which shall follow the Millennium. When this time comes all things are to be restored by and through the resurrection." (Joseph Fielding Smith, *CHMR* 1:143-44.)

Scriptural References: D&C 29:23, 24; 63:49; 101:25; Ezra 11:19; 18:31; 36:26; Rev. 21:1; 3 Ne. 12:47; 15:2, 3; Ether 13:9.

New Jerusalem

Both the New Testament and the modern scriptures speak of a New Jerusalem to be built in the latter days. Some have assumed that this refers to only one new city, but a careful reading indicates that there are several "new" Jerusalems, including (1) the city in Enoch's day, which will come with Jesus Christ at the time of his second coming; (2) the old city of Jerusalem in Israel, which will be rebuilt and thus will become new; and (3) a city called New Jerusalem, which will be built in Zion—the Americas. All of these new Jerusalems are mentioned in the revelations of the Doctrine and Covenants.

Selected Quotations

" '. . . What is the interpretation of Revelation 21:1, 2 with reference to the New Jerusalem coming down from God out of heaven?' . . .

"The prevailing notion in the world is that this is the city of Jerusalem, the ancient city of the Jews which in the day of regeneration will be renewed, but this is not the case. We read in the Book of Ether that the Lord revealed to him many of the same things which were seen by John. . . . In his vision, in many respects similar to that given to John, Enoch saw the old city of Jerusalem and also the new city which has not yet been built, and he wrote of them as follows. . . . [See Ether 13:2-11.]

"In the day of regeneration, when all things are made new, there will be three great cities that will be holy. One will be the Jerusalem of old which shall be rebuilt according to the prophecy of Ezekiel. One will be the city of Zion, or of Enoch, which was taken from the earth when Enoch was translated and which will be restored; and the city Zion, or New Jerusalem, which is to be built by the seed of Joseph on this the American continent. [Moses 7:62-64 quoted.]

"After the close of the millennial reign we are informed that Satan, who was bound during the millennium, shall be loosed and go forth to deceive the nations. Then will come the end. The earth will die and be purified and receive its resurrection. During this cleansing period the City Zion, or New Jerusalem, will be taken from the earth; and when the earth is prepared for the celestial glory, the city will come down according to the prediction in the Book of Revelation." (Joseph Fielding Smith, *AGQ* 2:103, 105-6.)

Scriptural References: D&C 42:9, 62, 67; 45:66; 84:2, 4; 133:56; Moses 7:62; Rev. 3:12; 21:2; 3 Ne. 20:22; 21:20-25; Ether 13:3-11.

Oath and covenant of the priesthood (*see also* Priesthood)

All members of the Church make covenants with the Lord at the time of baptism, confirmation, and partaking of the sacrament. When worthy and qualified men receive the priesthood—the power and authority to act in the name of and in behalf of God—they take upon themselves the oath and covenant of the priesthood. This term is used in section 84 and has also been thoroughly explained by modern prophets, seers, and revelators.

Selected Quotations

"A covenant is an agreement between two or more parties. An oath is a sworn attestation to the inviolability of the promises in the agreement. In the covenant of the priesthood the parties are the Father and the receiver of the priesthood.

Each party to the covenant undertakes certain obligations. The receiver undertakes to magnify his calling in the priesthood. The Father, by oath and covenant, promises the receiver that if he does so magnify his priesthood he will be sanctified by the Spirit unto the renewing of his body (see D&C 84:33); that he will become a member of '. . . the church and kingdom, and the elect of God,' (84:34) and receive the '. . . Father's kingdom; therefore,' said the Savior, 'all that my Father hath shall be given unto him.' (84:38.) . . .

"But these blessings do not come by ordination alone. Ordination to the priesthood is a prerequisite to receiving them, but it does not guarantee them. For a man actually to obtain them, he must faithfully discharge the obligation which is placed upon him when he receives the priesthood; that is, he must magnify his calling.

"It is apparent from this revelation [84:33-34] that the only way a man can make the life, for which mortality is designed, is to obtain and magnify the Melchizedek Priesthood. With '. . . eternal life, . . . the greatest of all the gifts of God' (D&C 14:7) depending upon it, it is of utmost importance that we keep clearly in mind what the magnifying of our callings in the priesthood requires of us. I am persuaded that it requires at least the following three things:

"1. That we obtain a knowledge of the gospel.

"2. That we comply in our personal living with the standards of the gospel.

"3. That we give dedicated service." (Marion G. Romney, *IE,* June 1962, pp. 416-17.)

"Christ is the great prototype where priesthood is concerned, as he is with reference to baptism and all other things. And so, even as the Father swears with an oath that his Son shall inherit all things through the priesthood, so he swears with an oath that all of us who magnify our callings in that same priesthood shall receive all that the Father hath. This is the promise of exaltation offered to every man who holds the Melchizedek Priesthood, but it is a conditional promise, a promise conditioned upon our magnifying our callings in the priesthood and living by every word that proceedeth forth from the mouth of God. . . . The Aaronic Priesthood is a preparatory priesthood to qualify us to make the covenant and receive the oath that attends this higher priesthood." (Joseph Fielding Smith, *CR,* October 1970, pp. 90-92.)

Scriptural References: D&C 84:33-41; 124:47; Num. 25:13; Neh. 13:29; Mal. 2:4; Heb. 7:20-21.

Obedience; law of obedience

Obedience is a principle of the gospel and is a requirement to gain heaven; in a sense, obedience might be considered a virtue in and of itself. Inasmuch as every blessing—and thus all happiness and joy—is conditioned (predicated) upon obedience to law, it is obvious that a loving, kind, merciful Heavenly Father who wants his children to be happy would hope and expect that they would obey those laws upon which such happiness is based. God requires us to be obedient, but this does not mean that he forces obedience. We are still free to choose wrong, but we must suffer the consequences of such disobedience; also, those who continue to wilfully disobey will never be able to meet the requirements of heaven.

Selected Quotations

"Obedience is a requirement of heaven and is therefore a principle of the gospel. [D&C 82:10; 130:20-21.] Are all required to be obedient? Yes, all. What, against their will? O no, not by any means. There is no power given to man nor means lawful to be used to compel men to obey the will of God, against their wish, except persuasion and good advice, but there is a penalty attached to disobedience which all must suffer who will not obey the obvious truths or laws of heaven." (Joseph F. Smith, *JD* 19:193.)

"Obedience is the first law of God. It is most important that we should be obedient to the word and will of the Lord. It was that which entitled the Son of God to be anointed above His brethren; for He was in all things most perfect and obedient. . . . The Lord is not going to give us everything without our doing something. He requires of us a broken heart, a contrite spirit, and an obedience to the mind and will of the Lord. [D&C 59:8; 82:10.]" (Francis M. Lyman, *CR,* October 1899, p. 35.)

"Children must learn *obedience,* and parents must exact obedience from them. Love your children, let them know that you love them; but remember that it is no favor to a child to let him do things he should not do. . . . We do not suggest blind obedience, but obedience by faith in those things which may not be fully understood by man's limited comprehension, but which in the infinite wisdom of God are for man's benefit and blessing." (N. Eldon Tanner, *Ensign,* November 1977, pp. 43-44.)

"There are several ways the Lord has set for us to learn obedience, so we may prove ourselves and merit His approval and blessings here and eternal glory with Him in the worlds to come.

"First of all, we have not been left to walk alone. The Lord has clearly revealed His will concerning His children and shown us His plan of redemption. His laws are explicitly recorded in the standard works of the Church. . . .

"A second way we learn obedience is by following the counsel of living prophets and other appointed Church leaders. . . .

"Third, we learn obedience by disciplining our lives in all things. One process by which we discipline ourselves is by repentance. . . .

"Finally, we learn obedience, as the Savior did, by the things which we suffer. . . .

"Keeping the commandments of God is not a difficult burden when we do it out of love of Him who has so graciously blessed us. . . . Our willingness to comply with the commandments of God is a witness of our faith in Him and our love for Him." (Delbert L. Stapley, *Ensign,* November 1977, pp. 18-21.)

Scriptural References: D&C 89:18; 105:6; 130:19, 21; 132:50; A of F 1:2; Num. 27:20; 2 Cor. 2:9; Jacob 7:27.

Olive Leaf

The title *Olive Leaf* was applied by the Prophet Joseph Smith to the revelation published as section 88.

Scriptural References: See superscription to section 88.

Only Begotten; Jesus Christ as the Only Begotten Son of God (*see also* Jesus Christ)

Every person who will ever live on this earth is a spiritual son or daughter of our Father in heaven. With the exception of Jesus Christ, each of us have received our physical bodies on this earth from a physical mortal man and a physical mortal woman. Each person inherits mortality (being subject to physical death) from both his mortal father and his mortal mother.

The Father of the physical body of Jesus Christ was not a mortal man, but our immortal Father in heaven. Jesus Christ is the only person on this earth whose physical body was begotten by our Heavenly Father; thus he is rightfully referred to as the Only Begotten Son of God in the flesh.

Selected Quotations

"We should understand this, that Jesus the Christ came into the world, in the Meridian of Time, to be the Only Begotten Son of God in the flesh. . . . Jesus as we call him, the Nazarene, the son of Mary, . . . was the Son of God, who is the Father of his spirit. So, in the beginning he was with God and was the firstborn of this great family [D&C 93:21], and on the earth he was the Only Begotten of the Father in the flesh. [D&C 29:42.]" (Charles W. Penrose, *CR*, April 1921, pp. 10-11.)

"When the time came that His first-born, the Savior, should come into the world and take a tabernacle, the Father came Himself and favoured that spirit with a tabernacle instead of letting any other man do it. The Savior was begotten by the Father of His spirit, by the same Being who is the Father of our spirits." (Brigham Young, *JD* 4:218.)

"I believe firmly that Jesus Christ is the Only Begotten Son of God in the flesh. He taught this doctrine to his disciples. He did not teach them that he was the Son of the Holy Ghost, but the Son of the Father. Truly, all things are done by the *power* of the Holy Ghost. It was through this power that Jesus was brought into this world, but not as the Son of the Holy Ghost, but the Son of God. . . . Christ was begotten of God." (Joseph Fielding Smith, *DS* 1:18.)

Scriptural References: D&C 21:21; 29:42, 46; 49:5; 76:13, 23, 25, 35, 57; 93:11; 124:123; Moses 1; 2:1, 26-27; 3:18; 4:1-3, 28; 5:7-9, 57; 6:52-62; 7:50-62; John 1:18; 3:6, 18; 1 Jn. 4:9; 2 Ne. 25:12; Jacob 4:5, 11; Alma 5:48; 9:26; 12:33, 34; 13:5, 9.

Ordinance

An ordinance of the gospel is a principle that requires the authorized action of one who is ordained. Some principles do not require the action of the priesthood—i.e., faith, repentance, prayer. If the principle requires the direct action of one who has been ordained to the priesthood, then it might be referred to as an ordinance. Baptism is both a principle and an ordinance, as are such *rites* and *ceremonies* as confirmation, the sacrament of the Lord's Supper, and celestial marriage.

Selected Quotations

"Abraham is said to have kept the commandments and ordinances of God. (Gen. 26:5.) The same is said of Jehoshaphat. (2 Chron. 17:4.) In Hebrews 9:1, 'ordinances' means the requirements of the ceremonial law, as distinct from 'Commandments,' which refers to moral precepts. The ordinances of the gospel are, more especially, baptism, the laying on of hands for the reception of the Holy Spirit, the sacrament, and the rules and regulations of the Church given by divine inspiration. He who is sent of God obeys God's ordinances, as well as His commandments." (Smith and Sjodahl, *DCC,* p. 306.)

"Ordinances instituted in the heavens before the foundation of the world, in the priesthood, for the salvation of men, are not to be altered or changed. All must be saved on the same principles." (Joseph Smith, *HC* 5:423.)

Scriptural References: D&C 21:11; 77:14; 88:139-40; 124:30-39, 134; 128:5-12; Moses 5:59; A of F 1:4; Alma 13:8; 50:8.

Ordinations

Modern usage in The Church of Jesus Christ of Latter-day Saints is that an *ordination* refers to receiving a particular office in the priesthood. The priesthood itself is *conferred* upon a person; he is *ordained* to an office in the priesthood; and he may be *set apart* to a particular area of responsibility (i.e., as a president of the elders quorum).

Selected Quotations

"As to the question of authority, nearly everything depends upon it. No ordinance can be performed to the acceptance of God without divine authority. . . . Some suppose this authority may be derived from the Bible, but nothing could be more absurd. . . . If by reading and believing the Bible this authority could be obtained, all who read the Bible and believed it would have it—one equally with another. . . . God Almighty is the only source from whence this knowledge, power and authority can be obtained and that through the operations of the Holy Ghost." (Joseph F. Smith, *JD* 19:191.)

Scriptural References: D&C 20:41-43; 53:3; 55:1; 68:25-27; A of F 1:4, 5; Alma 6:1.

Parables (*see also titles of individual parables—i.e.,* Tares)

The dictionary indicates that a parable is "a short story that illustrates a moral attitude or a religious teaching." It has also been defined as an earthly story with a heavenly meaning. The Savior frequently used parables in his teachings, and he explained some of his reasons for this in Matthew 13.

In his revelations in this dispensation, the Savior frequently reinforced his earlier parables by repeating them, explaining them, and applying them to the conditions and circumstances of our day. Following are some of the parables included in the revelations contained in the Doctrine and Covenants; for additional information on each of the parables, check the materials listed for the indicated verses.

Fig-tree—35:16; 45:34-38.

Man and his sons, whom he treated differently—38:26-27.

Ten virgins—45:56-58; 63:54.

Wheat and the tares—86:1-7; 101:65-66.

Man and his servants whom he sent to labor at different hours—88:51-61. (See also material listed for 33:3.)

Nobleman and his servants whom he instructed to build a watchtower in his vineyard—101:43-62; 103:21.

Woman and the unjust judge—101:81-84.

Scriptural References: JS-M 1:27, 38; Ps. 78:2; Matt. 13:3-53.

Patriarch; patriarchal blessings

The word *patriarch* comes to English from the Latin and the French and essentially means *father. Webster's New Collegiate Dictionary* (1977 ed.) also includes the following definition: "a Mormon of the Melchizedek priesthood empowered to perform the ordinances of the church and pronounce blessings within a stake or other prescribed jurisdiction."

The word does not appear a single time in the King James Version of the Old Testament and appears in only two books of the New Testament (Acts 2:29; 7:8, 9; and Heb. 7:4). The New Testament word *evangelist,* which has been given the same meaning as patriarch by some, appears only three times (Acts 21:8; Eph. 4:11; 2 Tim. 4:5).

The Doctrine and Covenants lists *patriarch* only three

times (124:91, 124; 135:1) and *patriarchal* once (124:92).

Most of the information concerning the office of patriarch and the purposes of patriarchal blessings comes from subsequent quotations and explanations of the Prophet Joseph Smith and others of the General Authorities.

Patriarch

"An Evangelist is a Patriarch, even the oldest man of the blood of Joseph or of the seed of Abraham. Wherever the Church of Christ is established in the earth, there should be a Patriarch for the benefit of the posterity of the Saints, as it was with Jacob in giving his patriarchal blessing unto his sons, etc." (Joseph Smith, *HC* 3:381.)

"Evangelists are patriarchs and they hold the right to bless and pronounce by the spirit of revelation the lineage of members of the Church. . . . There is in the Church the office of patriarch to, or of, the Church, sometimes called the 'presiding' patriarch. This office was first conferred upon Joseph Smith, Sen., in this dispensation, and was given to him by revelation and right of lineage. This office by divine appointment comes down by lineage and rightfully belongs to the family of Hyrum, son of Joseph Smith, Sen., and descends by the law of primogeniture. Joseph, son of Israel, because of the transgression of his older brethren, received this birthright and it was conferred upon his son, Ephraim, and has continued down through that lineage." (Joseph Fielding Smith, *CHMR* 2:20-21.)

"A Patriarch to the church is appointed to bless those who are orphans, or have no father in the church to bless them. . . . Where the Church is so extensive . . . other patriarchs have been ordained . . . to assist the Patriarch to the church." (John Taylor, *Times and Seasons* 6:928.)

Patriarchal Blessings

"Patriarchal blessings contemplate an inspired declaration of the lineage of the recipient, and also where so moved upon by the Spirit, an inspired and prophetic statement of the life mission of the recipient, together with such blessings, cautions, and admonitions as the patriarch may be prompted to give for the accomplishment of such life's mission, it being always made clear that the realization of all promised blessings is conditioned upon faithfulness to the gospel of our

Lord, whose servant the patriarch is." (First Presidency, Letter to Stake Presidents, June 28, 1958.)

"A patriarchal blessing today, given by an ordained patriarch, should contain a declaration of lineage, that is, the tribe of Israel through which the promises of inheritance shall come, even as assignments of inheritances were given in ancient Israel. . . . It is required that patriarchal blessings be recorded in the Church records." (Eldred G. Smith, *CR*, April 1952, pp. 38-39.)

"A patriarchal blessing is a sacred document to the person who has received it and is never given for publication and, as all patriarchal blessings, should be kept as a private possession to the one who has received it." (Harold B. Lee, *Ensign*, January 1973, p. 105.)

"These are happy days, the days of the patriarchs, and it is our great hope that every person, including the older youth, will be given the opportunity of having a patriarchal blessing, which is recorded in the official records of the Church.

"I have great confidence in the patriarchs and in their blessings. When the patriarch is a faithful Latter-day Saint and remains close to the Lord and is a student of the scriptures, the promises which he makes under his special authority and calling will be fulfilled, if the recipient of the blessing is faithful and true.

"Of course, it is the right of every father and his duty as patriarch of his own family to give a father's blessing to his children, and it is our hope that every father will give a sacred blessing to each of his children, especially as they are leaving home to go to school or on missions or to be married, which blessing should then be noted in the individual's private journal." (Spencer W. Kimball, *Ensign*, November 1977, p. 4.)

Scriptural References: D&C 124:91-96, 124; 135:1; Abr. 1:25-26; A of F 1:6; Acts 2:29; 7:8-9; 21:8; Eph. 4:11; 2 Tim. 4:5; Heb. 7:4.

Perdition; sons of perdition; Lucifer (*see also* Satan)

The word *perdition* means "lost"; when the term is used to refer to a person, it means "the lost one." Lucier is perdition—the lost one—and the people who follow after him are the sons of perdition. Generally the term *son of perdition* is used to refer to anyone who is evil or wicked. It is used by

Latter-day Saints to refer to those who have committed the unpardonable sin (the sin against the Holy Ghost) and thus will not inherit any degree of glory.

Selected Quotations

"A man cannot commit the unpardonable sin after the dissolution of the body, and there is a way possible for escape. . . .

"No man can commit the unpardonable sin after the dissolution of the body, nor in this life, until he receives the Holy Ghost; but they must do it in this world. Hence the salvation of Jesus Christ was wrought out for all men, in order to triumph over the devil; for he stood up as a Savior. All will suffer until they obey Christ himself. [D&C 19:15-19.]

"All sins shall be forgiven, except the sin against the Holy Ghost; for Jesus will save all except the sons of perdition. [Matt. 12:31-32.] What must a man do to commit the unpardonable sin? He must receive the Holy Ghost, have the heavens opened unto him, and know God, and then sin against him. After a man has sinned against the Holy Ghost, there is no repentance for him. He has got to say that the sun does not shine while he sees it; he has got to deny Jesus Christ when the heavens have been opened unto him, and to deny the plan of salvation with his eyes open to the truth of it; and from that time he begins to be an enemy. [D&C 132:27.] This is the case with many apostates of The Church of Jesus Christ of Latter-day Saints." (Joseph Smith, *HC* 6:313-14.)

"Commission of the unpardonable sin consists in crucifying unto oneself the Son of God afresh and putting him to open shame. (Heb. 6:4-8; D&C 76:34-35.) To commit this unpardonable crime a man must receive the gospel, gain from the Holy Ghost by revelation the absolute knowledge of the divinity of Christ, and then deny 'the new and everlasting covenant by which he was sanctified, calling it an unholy thing, and doing despite to the Spirit of grace.' (*TPJS*, p. 128.) He thereby commits murder by assenting unto the Lord's death, that is, having a perfect knowledge of the truth he comes out in open rebellion and places himself in a position wherein he would have crucified Christ knowing perfectly the while that he was the Son of God. Christ is thus crucified afresh and put to open shame. (D&C 132:27.)" (Bruce R. McConkie, *MD*, pp. 816-17.)

"In many minds there has been a great misapprehension on the question of the resurrection. Some have had the idea . . . that the sons of perdition will not be resurrected at all. They base this idea, and draw this conclusion, from the 38th and 39th paragraphs of Section 76 of the book of Doctrine and Covenants. . . .

"A careful reading of these verses, however, and especially of the preceding paragraphs, will show that the Lord does not, in this language, exclude even the sons of perdition from the resurrection. It is plain that the intention is to refer to them explicitly as the only ones on whom the second death shall have any power: 'for *all the rest* shall be brought forth by the resurrection of the dead, through the triumph and glory of the Lamb.' This excluded class are the only ones on whom the second death shall have any power, and 'the only ones who shall not be redeemed in the due time of the Lord after the sufferings of his wrath.'

"This is by no means to say that they are to have no resurrection. Jesus our Lord and Savior died for all, and all will be resurrected." (George Q. Cannon, *JI* 35:123-24.)

"Evidently many among us have made a dreadful mistake, but not unpardonable, in thinking that the sons of perdition will be very few. We have heard it said at times that they will be so few that they probably could be 'counted on the fingers of one hand.' Where this thought originated we may not know. From the reading of the scriptures it appears that there will be a large number; far too many even if there were but one, for their punishment is most severe without any question." (Joseph Fielding Smith, *AGQ* 1:78.)

Scriptural References: D&C 76:26, 32, 43; Moses 5:24; Job 17:12; Philip. 1:28; 2 Thes. 2:3; 1 Tim. 6:9; Heb. 10:39; 2 Pet. 3:7; Rev. 17:8, 11; 3 Ne. 27:32; 29:7.

Poor; responsibility to care for the poor

The Lord prepared the earth so that it could take care of all the physical needs of man. In this dispensation, he has indicated that "there is enough and to spare." (104:17.) The Lord expects the needs of the worthy poor to be taken care of by their families and his church. He has stated that children and wives have claim upon their fathers and husbands for their maintenance, and where there are no fathers and husbands the children and wives have claim upon the Church. The Lord has indicated the way and means whereby the needs of the poor should be provided. The Lord has also instructed that the idler should not eat the food or wear the clothes of the worker, and "the idler shall not have place in the church, except he repent and mend his ways." (75:29.)

Selected Quotations

"The poor we have always with us. It was said by Abraham Lincoln that God must love the poor because he has made so many of them. The Savior seemed to think a great deal of the poor. He came to preach the Gospel to them, to administer to their wants, to heal the sick, to cast out devils, to open the eyes of the blind. His life and his ministry was devoted to the poor. You will find, if you study closely the revelations of God found in the Book of Covenants, that a great amount of space is devoted to the poor. [D&C 42:30-42, 71; 56:16-18; 58:8-11; 78:3, 82:12; 83:6; 109:55; 136:8.] We are reminded of them continually; that we shall divide our substance with them. The fast day has been instituted, in part, for that purpose." (Rudger Clawson, *CR*, April 1899, p. 4.)

"We are striving to the best of our ability to provide for the poor; that is, for God's poor. You know there are several kinds of poor, and we want to provide out of the funds of the tithing and of the offerings of the Saints as far as we possibly can, for the honest and the worthy poor, and not for the drunken poor or for those who bring poverty, and distress upon themselves by 'riotous living,' extravagance, folly and sin. They should be put to work by some means or power, and kept at work until they learn to abstain from that which is vicious, and they will observe and do that which is essential to life and to the well-being of mankind." (Joseph F. Smith, *CR*, October 1915, p. 4.)

"When an individual cannot care for himself, his family should provide every assistance possible; and when the family of the needy person has done *all it can do* to provide money or commodities, the bishop is empowered to assist. According to the *Welfare Services Handbook*, the bishop of each ward has 'the sole mandate to care for, and the sole discretion in caring for the poor [and needy] of the Church. . . . It is his duty and his only to determine to whom, when, how and how much shall be given to any member of his ward from Church funds [or commodities]. . . . This is his high and solemn obligation imposed by the Lord Himself. Whoever and whatever the help he calls in to assist him to perform this service, he is still responsible.' (*Welfare Services Handbook,* p. 6.)" (H. Burke Peterson, *Ensign,* November 1976, p. 114.)

"In this modern world plagued with counterfeits for the Lord's plan, we must not be misled into supposing that we can discharge our obligations to the poor and the needy by shifting the responsibility to some governmental or other public agency. Only by voluntarily giving out of an abundant love for our neighbors can we develop that charity characterized by Mormon as 'the pure love of Christ.' (Moro. 7:47.) This we must develop if we would obtain eternal life." (Marion G. Romney, *CR,* October 1972, p. 115.)

Scriptural References: D&C 38:35; 42:30-31, 34, 37, 39, 71; 44:6; 56:16-19; 82:12; 83:6; 84:112; 124:21, 75, 89; Luke 4:18; 6:20; 7:22, 18:22; 19:8; 21:2-3; Alma 4:13; 5:55; 32:2-9; 3 Ne. 13:1.

Post-earthly spirit world

The post-earthly spirit world (the place where the spirit goes when the body dies physically) is *not* the same place as the pre-earthly spirit world (where the spirit lived before it came to the earth in a physical body). Some Latter-day Saints have wrongly concluded that these two places are the same because of an incorrect interpretation of Alma's words to Corianton that "the spirits of all men, as soon as they are departed from this mortal body . . . whether they be good or evil, are taken home to that God who gave them life." (Alma 40:11.) Several modern prophets have indicated that this scripture does *not* mean that the spirits of the departed go into the actual physical presence of our Heavenly Father where they existed before their earthly experience; rather, the scripture means that upon death the spirits of the deceased go back into a spiritual existence where they can see, hear, and understand spiritual things, much as they could before the earthly experience while they lived in the presence of God.

There are at least two major divisions in the post-earthly spirit world:

1. *Paradise*—This part of the spirit world is inhabited by righteous spirits who are awaiting their resurrection. They are in a state of happiness, rest (from their sorrows and troubles), and peace. (See 2 Cor. 12:4; Alma 40:11-12; Moro. 10:34; D&C 77:2, 5.)

2. *Outer darkness or hell*—The wicked (wilfully disobedient) go into outer darkness where they are in a state of "awful, fearful looking for the fiery indignation of the wrath of God upon them." (Alma 40:14.)

In a general sense, the whole post-earthly spirit world is a spirit prison because no disembodied spirit can enjoy a fulness of joy until it is resurrected with its physical body. (D&C 93:33-34.) Even the spirits of the righteous in paradise are in a spirit prison, and it was to these spirits that the Savior went to preach while his body was in the tomb. (1 Pet. 3:18-21; 4:6; D&C 76:73-74; JFS-V 1:1-60.)

In a more specific sense the term *spirit prison* is used to refer to that part of the post-earthly spirit world where the wicked dwell. (Moses 7:37-39.)

Selected Quotations

"As for my going into the immediate presence of God when I die, I do not expect it, but I expect to go into the world of spirits and associate with my brethren, and preach the Gospel in the spiritual world, and prepare myself in every necessary way to receive my body again, and then enter through the wall into the celestial world. I never shall come into the presence of my Father and God until I have received my resurrected body, neither will any other person." (Heber C. Kimball, *JD* 3:112-13.)

"We will take the best men we can find—when they pass through the veil they are in happiness, they are in glory, they go among the disembodied spirits; but they do not go where there are resurrected bodies, for they cannot live there. . . . They also go into the spiritual world to live with spirits. Do they commune with the Father and Son? The Father communes with them as He pleases, through the means of angels, or otherwise the Son and Holy Ghost. . . .

"No spirit of Saint or sinner, of the Prophet or him that kills the Prophet, is prepared for their final state: All pass through the veil from this state and go into the world of spirits; and there they dwell, waiting for their final destiny." (Brigham Young, *JD* 6:293-94.)

"The great misery of departed spirits in the world of spirits, where they go after death, is to know that they come short of the glory that others enjoy and that they might have enjoyed themselves, and they are their own accusers." (Joseph Smith, *HC* 5:425.)

Scriptural Reference: Alma 40:11-14.

Prayer; ask, seek, knock; communication with God

Before the Lord sent his children upon the earth, he provided means by which he could communicate with them (through the Holy Ghost, prophets, scriptures, etc.) and by which they could communicate with him (prayer). He has counseled us to "ask, seek, knock" and has promised that if we ask in faith with "nothing wavering," he will answer our prayers for our good.

Selected Quotations

"Man's needs are many. He has little, if any, power of himself to supply them. Therefore, he turns to God for the necessary help. This he can properly do, for the Lord, who has placed man on earth with limited powers, has declared Himself ready to assist His children. He has given them the privilege to address Divinity, with the assurance of being heard. Indeed, He has requested them to approach Him in prayer for guidance in solving life's problems.

"Prayer is really the beginning of wisdom. By prayer, communion between man and God is established and maintained. It brings man and his Maker into close association. Earnest, sincere prayer places man in tune with heaven and with the Beings who dwell therein. The knowledge and power thus gained from the unseen world are very real. . . .

"Every prayer is heard, and every sincere prayer is answered. They who pray should be content to await the answer at the time and in the manner comporting with God's wisdom. He knows what is for our good and bestows His blessings accordingly. The testimony of untold millions that their prayers have been heard is a convincing testimony that God hears and answers prayers.

"A prayer is not complete unless gratitude for blessings received is expressed. It is by the power of the Lord that we 'live and move and have our being.' [Acts 17:28.] This should be frankly stated gratefully as we pray to our Father in heaven." (John A. Widtsoe, *ER* 1:311-13.)

"Henry Ward Beecher once said, 'It is not well for a man to pray cream and live skim milk.' That was a century ago. There is now before us a danger that many may pray skim milk and live *that* not at all.

"Our modern times seem to suggest that prayerful devotion and reverence for holiness is unreasonable or undesirable, or both. And yet, skeptical 'modern' men have need for prayer. Perilous moments, great responsibility, deep anxiety, overwhelming grief—these challenges that shake us out of old complacencies and established routines will bring to the surface our native impulses. If we let them, they will humble us, soften us, and turn us to respectful prayer.

"If prayer is only a spasmodic cry at the time of crisis, then it is utterly selfish, and we come to think of God as a repairman or a service agency to help us only in our emergencies. We should remember the Most High day and night—always—not only at times when all other assistance has failed and we desperately need help. If there is any element in human life on which we have a record of miraculous success and inestimable worth to the human soul, it is prayerful, reverential, devout communication with our Heavenly Father." (Howard W. Hunter, *Ensign,* November 1977, p. 52.)

"Learn how to pray and how to receive answers to your prayers. When you pray over some things, you must patiently wait a long, long time before you will receive an answer. Some prayers, for your own safety, must be answered immediately, and some promptings will even come when you haven't prayed at all. Once you really determine to follow that guide, your testimony will grow and you will find provisions set out along the way in unexpected places, as evidence that someone knew that you would be traveling that way." (Boyd K. Packer, *CR,* April 1976, p. 47.)

"May I be bold enough to suggest that your Heavenly Father knows you personally and can call you by name. . . . This thought itself is admittedly almost beyond the comprehension of mortal understanding, but please, let us not limit the Creator of heaven and earth in any way, for his powers are limitless, and the basic concept must hold that a father knows his children.

"As a child of God kneels to pray, that individual must believe implicitly that his prayer is being heard by him to whom the prayer is addressed. The thought that our Heavenly Father is too busy or that our message is being recorded by celestial computers for possible future consideration is unthinkable and inconsistent with all we have been taught by his holy prophets." (Robert L. Simpson, *IE,* June 1970, p. 82.)

"Prayer does not consist of words altogether. True, faithful, earnest prayer consists more in the feeling that rises from the heart and from the inward desire of our spirits to supplicate the Lord in humility and in faith, that we may receive his blessings. It matters not how simple the words may be, if our desires are genuine and we come before the Lord with a broken heart and a contrite spirit to ask him for that which we need. . . .

"Do not learn to pray with your lips only. Do not learn a prayer by heart, and say it every morning and evening. . . . A great many people fall into the rut of saying over a ceremonious prayer. They begin at a certain point, and they touch at all the points along the road until they get to the winding-up scene; and when they have done, I do not know whether the prayer has ascended beyond the ceiling of the room or not." (Joseph F. Smith, *CR*, October 1899, pp. 69, 71-72.)

"May I . . . suggest some ways to improve our communication with our Heavenly Father.

"1. *We should pray frequently.* . . .

"2. *We should find an appropriate place where we can meditate and pray.* . . .

"3. *We should prepare ourselves for prayer.* . . .

"4. *Our prayers should be meaningful and pertinent.* . . .

"In all of our prayers it is well to use the sacred pronouns of the scriptures—*Thee, Thou, Thy,* and *Thine*—when addressing Deity in prayer, instead of the more common pronouns of *you, your,* and *yours.* In this arrangement we show greater respect to Deity. . . .

"5. *After making a request through prayer, we have a responsibility to assist in its being granted.* We should listen. Perhaps while we are on our knees, the Lord wants to counsel us." (Ezra Taft Benson, *Ensign,* May 1977, pp. 32-33.)

Scriptural References: D&C 29:2; 42:14; 43:12; 52:9; 59:14; 63:64-65; 81:3; 84:61; 88:76, 119: 93:51-52; Matt. 5:44; 6:7; Alma 34:39; 58:10; Moro. 2:2.

Pre-earthly existence; council in heaven; from the foundation of the earth

According to the Inspired Version of the Bible, the Bible at one time clearly and definitely taught the pre-earthly existence of all mankind. Unfortunately, many of the plain and precious references concerning this subject in the book of Genesis have either been lost or deleted from the biblical text.

Modern scriptures, particularly the Pearl of Great Price, but also the Doctrine and Covenants, have helped to restore the truth that we are all spirit children of our Heavenly Father and we lived with him before we came to the earth. Life on this earth (our second estate) is simply the continuation of our pre-earthly existence (our first estate). Life will continue after our death from this earth, first in the post-earthly spirit world and then in the resurrected state.

Selected Quotations

"The mind or the intelligence which man possesses is co-equal with God Himself. . . . I am dwelling on the immortality of the spirit of man. Is it logical to say that the intelligence of spirits is immortal and yet that it had a beginning? The intelligence of spirits had no beginning, neither will it have an end. That is good logic. That which has a beginning may have an end. There never was a time when there were not spirits; for they are co-equal (co-eternal) with our Father in heaven. . . . Intelligence is eternal and exists upon a self-existent principle. It is a spirit from age to age, and there is no creation about it." (Joseph Smith, *TPJS*, pp. 353-54.)

" 'The spirit of man is not a created being; it existed from eternity, and will exist to eternity. Anything created cannot be eternal; and earth, water, etc., had their existence in an elementary state, from eternity.' (*HC* 3:387.) We learn by this that the intelligent part of man always existed. We are all born sons and daughters of God in the spirit. . . .

"It is a glorious thing to know that we are in very deed the begotten children of God, the Father, in the spirit and that Jesus Christ is the first born in the spirit and the only begotten of the Father in the flesh." (Joseph Fielding Smith, *CHMR* 2:221-23.)

"The doctrine of the pre-existence,—revealed so plainly, particularly in latter days, pours a wonderful flood of light upon the otherwise mysterious problem of man's origin. It shows that man, as a spirit, was begotten and born of heavenly parents, and reared to maturity in the eternal mansions of the Father, prior to coming upon the earth in a temporal body to undergo an experience in mortality. It teaches that all men existed in the spirit before any man existed in the flesh, and that all who have inhabited the earth since Adam have taken bodies and become souls in a like manner. . . . Man is the child of God, formed in the divine image and endowed with divine attributes, and even as the infant of an earthly father and mother is capable in due time of becoming a man, so the undeveloped offspring of celestial parentage is capable, by experience through ages and aeons, of evolving into a God." (First Presidency, *Messages of the First Presidency* 4:205-6.)

"Man is a dual being; and his life, a plan of God. Man has a *natural* body and a *spiritual* body. Man's body is but the tabernacle in which his spirit dwells. Too many, far too many, are prone to regard the body as the man, and consequently to direct their efforts to the gratifying of the body's pleasures, its appetites, its desires, its passions. Too few recognize that the real man is an immortal spirit, which 'intelligence or the light of truth,' animated as an individual entity before the body was begotten, and that this spiritual entity with all its distinguishing traits will continue after the body ceases to respond to its earthly environment." (David O. McKay, *Instructor* 100:122.)

"During the ages in which we dwelt in the pre-mortal state we not only developed our various characteristics and showed our worthiness and ability, or the lack of it, but we were also where such progress could be observed. . . . Under such conditions it was natural for our Father to discern and choose those who were most worthy and evaluate the talents of each individual. He knew not only what each of us could do, but what each of us would do when put to the test and when responsibility was given us. Then, when the time came for our habitation on mortal earth, all things were prepared and the servants of the Lord chosen and ordained to their respective missions." (Joseph Fielding Smith, *WP,* pp. 50-51.)

"We have no scriptural justification . . . for the belief that we had the privilege of choosing our parents and our life companions in the spirit world. This belief has been advocated by some, and it is possible that in some instances it is true, but it would require too great a stretch of the imagination to believe it to be so in all, or even in the majority of cases. Most likely we came where those in authority decided to send us. Our agency may not have been exercised to the extent of making choice of parents and posterity." (Joseph Fielding Smith, *WP,* pp. 44-45.)

Scriptural References: D&C 29:36-38; 38:1; 49:7; 76:25-27; 93:29; Moses 3:5; 4:1-4; 6:36; Abr. 3:22-28; JFS-V 1:53; Job 12:10; Eccl. 12:7; Jer. 1:4-5; Luke 10:17-20; John 1:2; 8:58; 9:1-2; 16:28; 17:5; Eph. 1:4; Heb. 12:9; Jude 1:6; Rev. 12:7-9; 3 Ne. 26:5; Ether 3:16.

Priesthood; priesthood of God (*see also* Aaronic Priesthood; Keys of priesthood; Melchizedek Priesthood; Oath and covenant of the priesthood; Priesthood offices)

The priesthood of God is the power and authority to act for and in the name of God. The revelations of the latter days provide detailed definitions and explanations of this priesthood, list many of the offices in the priesthood, and explain many of the duties of priesthood members.

Selected Quotations

"The priesthood of the Son of God is the law by which the worlds are, were, and will continue for ever and ever. It is that system which brings worlds into existence and peoples them, gives them their revolutions—their days, weeks, months, years, their seasons and times and by which they . . . go into a higher state of existence." (Brigham Young, *JD* 15:127.)

"It is nothing more nor less than the power of God delegated to man by which man can act in the earth for the salvation of the human family, in the name of the Father and the Son and the Holy Ghost, and act legitimately; not assuming that authority, not borrowing it from generations that are dead and gone, but authority that has been given in this day in which we live by ministering angels and spirits from above, direct from the presence of Almighty God." (Joseph F. Smith, *CR,* October 1904, p. 5.)

"The Holy Priesthood is the channel through which God communicates and deals with man upon the earth; and the heavenly messengers that have visited the earth to communicate with man are men who held and honored the priesthood while in the flesh; and everything that God has caused to be done for the salvation of man, from the coming of man upon the earth to the redemption of the world, has been and will be by virtue of the everlasting priesthood." (Wilford Woodruff, *MS* 51:657.)

"Women do not hold the priesthood. Some have thought that they might and do to some extent. I shall read two statements to indicate what the Church's position is with reference to the place of woman as she relates to the Priesthood. President Joseph Fielding Smith, quoting from his father [Joseph F. Smith], says:

Does a wife hold the priesthood of her husband, and may she lay hands on the sick with him, with authority? A wife does not hold the priesthood with her husband, but she enjoys the benefits thereof with him; and if she is requested to lay hands on the sick with him . . . she may do so with perfect propriety. . . . When this is done the wife is adding her faith to the administration of her husband. The wife would lay on hands just as would a member of the Aaronic Priesthood, or a faithful brother without the priesthood, she in this manner giving support by faith to the ordinance performed by her husband. (Joseph Fielding Smith, *DS* 3:177.)

"I want you to get the distinction that he makes there—the husband performs the ordinance by the authority of the priesthood, and she (if she joins with him in such an experience) would do it only to add her faith to his, but not by any authority of the priesthood. Brother Widtsoe has added another note to this matter when he says:

By divine fiat, the Priesthood is conferred on the men. This means that organization must prevail in the family, the ultimate unit of the Church. The husband, the Priesthood bearer, presides over the family; the Priesthood conferred upon him is intended for the blessing of the whole family. Every member shares in the gift bestowed, but under a proper organization. No man who understands the gospel believes that he is greater than his wife, or more beloved of the Lord, because he holds the Priesthood, but rather that he is under the responsibility of speaking and acting for the family in official matters. It is a protection to the woman who, because of her motherhood, is under a large physical and spiritual obligation. Motherhood is an eternal part of Priesthood. (John A. Widtsoe, *ER,* pp. 307-8.)" (Harold B. Lee, *ASIF,* BYU, July 17, 1958.)

Scriptural References: D&C (check index for subject); Moses 6:7; Abr. 1:4, 18, 26-27, 31; 2:9, 11; JS-H 2:38, 69-74; Ex. 40:15; Num. 25:13; Heb. 7:24; 1 Pet. 2:9; Alma 13:8.

Priesthood offices (*see also* Church offices and presiding quorums; Priesthood)

Several offices in the priesthood have been identified in the revelations of this dispensation. In the Aaronic Priesthood are the offices of deacon, teacher, priest, and bishop; the first two of these comprised the Levitical Priesthood in ancient times. In the Melchizedek Priesthood are the offices of elder, seventy, high priest, patriarch, apostle, and president of the Church.

Terminology used in regard to the bestowal of the priesthood and its keys indicates that a person has the priesthood *conferred* upon him (Aaronic Priesthood, etc.); he is *ordained* to an office in the priesthood (deacon, etc.); and he is *set apart* to a particular position (president of the deacons quorum, etc.).

Apostle

"The title 'Apostle' is one of special significance and sanctity; it has been given of God, and belongs only to those who have been called and ordained as 'special witnesses of the name of Christ in all the world, thus differing from other officers in the Church in the duties of their calling.' (D&C 107:23.) By derivation the word 'Apostle' is the English equivalent of the Greek 'apostolos,' indicating a messenger, an ambassador, or literally 'one who is sent.' It signifies that he who is rightly so called, speaks and acts not of himself, but as the representative of a higher power whence his commission issued; and in this sense the title is that of a servant, rather than of a superior. Even the Christ, however, is called an Apostle, with reference to His ministry in the flesh (Heb. 3:1); and this appellation is justified by His repeated declarations that He came to earth to do not His own will but that of the Father by whom He was sent. [John 4:34; 5:30; 6:38-39.]

"So great is the sanctity of this special calling, that the title 'Apostle' should not be used lightly as the common or ordinary form of address applied to living men called to this office. The quorum or council of the Twelve Apostles as existent in the Church today may better be spoken of as the 'Quorum of the Twelve,' the 'Council of the Twelve,' or simply as the 'Twelve,' and not as the 'Twelve Apostles,' except as particular occasion may warrant the use of the more sacred term. It is advised that the title 'Apostle' be not applied as a prefix to the name of any member of the Council of the Twelve; but that such a one be addressed or spoken of as Brother _____ or Elder _____, and when necessary or desirable, as in announcing his presence in a public assembly, an explanatory clause may be added, thus,

'Elder _____ one of the Council of the Twelve.' "
(James E. Talmage, *Liahona or Elders' Journal* 11:580-81.)

"What ordination should a man receive to possess all the keys and powers of the Holy Priesthood that were delivered to the sons of Adam? He should be ordained an Apostle of Jesus Christ. That office puts him in possession of every key, every power, every authority, communication, benefit, blessing, glory, and kingdom that was ever revealed to man. That pertains to the office of an Apostle of Jesus Christ." (Brigham Young, *JD* 9:87.)

Patriarch

"The calling of a patriarch or an evangelist is to bless the people or members of the Church. We read of evangelists in the New Testament but find nothing there to indicate what the particular duties of this calling in the priesthood are. [Acts 21:8; Eph. 4:11; 2 Tim. 4:5.] This information has come to us only through the revelations of the Lord to the Prophet Joseph Smith. The Lord instructed the Twelve Apostles of his Church in this dispensation 'to ordain evangelical ministers, as they shall be designated unto them by revelation' in all large branches of the Church. (See D&C 107:39.)" (LeGrand Richards, *MWW,* p. 125.)

High Priest

"A High Priest is a member of the same Melchizedek Priesthood with the Presidency, but not of the same power or authority in the church." (Joseph Smith, *HC* 2:477.)

"The duty of a High Priest is to administer in spiritual and holy things, and to hold communion with God." (Joseph Smith, *HC* 1:338.)

"We have in each stake of Zion an organization called the High Priests' quorum, to which all High Priests of the Church belong, including the presidency and high councilors of the stake, and also the Bishops and their counselors, all the Patriarchs and all others who have been ordained to the office of High Priest in the Church." (Joseph F. Smith, *CR,* October 1904, pp. 3-4.)

Seventy

"Seventies are primarily traveling elders, especially ordained to promulgate the Gospel among the nations of the earth, 'unto the Gentiles first, and also unto the Jews.' . . . A full quorum comprises seventy members, including seven presidents." (James E. Talmage, *AF,* p. 207.)

"Effective immediately, stake presidents may ordain seventies and set apart presidents of seventy in their stakes . . . This should eliminate many long delays and create a good working relationship between the stake leaders and their seventies, and we hope that new emphasis may come to missionary work." (Spencer W. Kimball, *Ensign,* May 1974, p. 86.)

Elder

"A person who is ordained to the office of an Elder in this kingdom has the same Priesthood that the High Priests, that the Twelve Apostles, that the Seventies, and that the First Presidency hold . . . but every man in his order and place, possessing a portion of the same Priesthood, according to the gifts and callings to each." (Brigham Young, *JD* 9:89.)

"The duty of the Elder is to be a standing minister in Zion, to administer in spiritual things, to administer the sacrament, to baptize, to lay on hands for the reception of the Holy Ghost, to take the lead of all meetings when no higher authority is present, and to conduct them under the influence and power of the Holy Ghost." (Rudger Clawson, *CR,* April 1902, p. 29.)

"The First Presidency and the Council of the Twelve have approved the organization of an elders quorum in every ward and independent branch. The elders, regardless of number, up to 96, residing in a particular ward or independent branch, may be constituted as an elders quorum, with a presidency. Where there are more than 96 elders, the quorum should be divided. It is felt by the Brethren that this great reservoir of power and strength can best be used to its greatest value to have strong, active quorums of elders in the more local jurisdictions." (Spencer W. Kimball, *Ensign,* May 1974, p. 86.)

"*Elder* is a title comprising all who hold the Melchizedek Priesthood. (1 Tim. 5:17.) Apostles are elders, as are also bishops. (Tit. 1:5-7.)" (Brigham Young, *JD* 9:89.)

Bishop

"The Bishop, as such, is a Priest who presides over the Aaronic Priesthood, and his duty is to administer in temporal affairs." (Smith and Sjodahl, *DCC,* p. 710.)

"I conceive it to be the duty of a Bishop to be the executive officer of the ward, to deal in temporal affairs, and to be a common judge in Israel, and to sit in the Bishop's court and adjudicate and regulate the affairs of his ward, with his counselors. It is the duty of the Bishop particularly to see that the presidencies of the quorums of the Lesser Priesthood are active and faithful. Let him see also that the presidencies of the auxiliary organizations are faithful in the performance of their duty." (Rudger Clawson, *CR,* April 1902, p. 30.)

"There is no retrograde movement in ordaining a High Priest to the office of a Bishop, for, properly speaking, he is set apart to act in that office. . . .

". . . The duties and powers of a Bishop cease the very moment he steps over the Aaronic Priesthood, which is to officiate in temporal things; when he passes this he immediately begins to officiate by the authority and power of the Melchizedek Priesthood, though he may not know it." (Brigham Young, *JD* 10:96-97.)

"Each ward should have one or more quorums of priests (forty-eight), teachers (twenty-four), and deacons (twelve), each with a presidency of three [except the priests quorum]. The ward bishopric presides in a general way over all the quorums of the Aaronic Priesthood in the ward, and over all church members, as individuals, residing therein. The bishop of the ward is ex-officio president of the priest's quorum." (Orson F. Whitney, *SNT,* p. 228.)

Priest

"The duties of a Priest are here enumerated. His office is the most advanced in the Aaronic Priesthood. In the Mosaic dispensation the Priests were ordained to instruct and pray for the people, and to offer sacrifices for them." (Smith and Sjodahl, *DCC,* p. 108.)

"The duty of the Priest is to preach, teach and expound the scriptures, to baptize, to administer the sacrament, to visit the homes of the people, to pray with them vocally, and to teach them all family duties." (Rudger Clawson, *CR,* April 1902, p. 29.)

"From a retrospect of the requirements of the servants of God to preach the Gospel, if a Priest understands his duty, his calling, and ministry, and preaches by the Holy Ghost, his enjoyment is as great as if he were one of the Presidency;

and his services are necessary in the body, as are also those of Teachers and Deacons." (Joseph Smith, *HC* 2:478.)

Teacher

"The duty of the Teacher is to watch over the Church, to be with the Church constantly, and strengthen it, to see that iniquity doth not abound, to see that there is no evil-speaking, or backbiting, and to preach, teach, exhort, and expound; and he is to be assisted in his duties by the Deacon; but the Teacher and the Deacon have no authority to baptize, or administer the sacrament. They do have the authority, however, to preach the gospel, to show forth a good example, to warn the people and invite all to come unto Christ." (Rudger Clawson, *CR,* April 1902, p. 29.)

Deacon

"The duty of Deacons is to assist the Teachers. A Deacon holds the power and authority first bestowed in the Aaronic Priesthood. One who performs those duties well, thereby qualifies himself for the more advanced positions.

"It was customary in Paul's days to ordain mature men to the office of Deacons, because the conditions of the Saints were such that only elderly people could be used to advantage. The Church was new, and adults were converted; perhaps only few, if any, were born and educated in the Church. . . . In our day . . . the Priesthood is conferred on boys of twelve and thirteen who are found faithful and worthy. . . . The appointment of boys to the Deaconship is done under the direction of the constituted authority of the Lord, though the exact date of its beginning is perhaps not on record." (Smith and Sjodahl, *DCC,* p. 108.)

Scriptural References: D&C (check index for subject); JS-H 2:72; Ex. 3:16; Philip. 1:1; 1 Tim. 3:8, 10, 12-13; 2 Ne. 5:26; Jacob 1:18, Jarom 1:11; Moro. 4:1.

Prophecy (*see also* Gifts of the Spirit)

The gift of prophecy from God is one of the unfailing signs of the true church. There are at least three prerequisites to prophecy:

1. *The foreknowledge of God.* If God does not know what is going to happen, then it would be impossible for him to reveal these things to his children upon the earth. The scriptures, particularly the modern scriptures, indicate that God

does indeed know everything and "there is not anything save he [God] knows it." (2 Ne. 9:20.) Section 130 (verse 7) of the Doctrine and Covenants indicates that all things past, present, and future are continually before the Lord.

2. *The principle of revelation.* Even though our Heavenly Father knows all things, prophecy would be impossible on the earth if there were not a power or means—revelation—by which he could reveal his knowledge. The true church will always believe in revelation, in "all that God has revealed, all that he does now reveal, and . . . that He will yet reveal many great and important things pertaining to the Kingdom of God." (A of F 1:9.)

3. *The existence of a prophet upon the earth.* Even though our Heavenly Father knows everything and even though the principle of revelation is true, yet prophecy would be impossible if there were not a worthy and qualified person upon the earth to receive the mind and will of God. Thus, the existence of a prophet upon the earth is a vital link in prophecy. "Surely the Lord God will do nothing, but he revealeth his secret unto his servants the prophets." (Amos 3:7.)

Selected Quotations

"There is no office growing out of this Priesthood that is or can be greater than the Priesthood itself. It is from the Priesthood that the office derives its authority and power. No office gives authority to the Priesthood. No office adds to the power of the Priesthood. But all offices in the Church derive their power, their virtue, their authority, from the Priesthood. . . .

"The office of an Elder, of a High Priest, of a Seventy—all the offices in the Church are simply appendages to the Melchizedek Priesthood, and grow out of it." (Joseph F. Smith, *CR,* October 1903, pp. 82, 87.)

"The first office held in this dispensation was that of Elder. Joseph Smith was ordained by Oliver Cowdery to be the first Elder of the Church, and Oliver Cowdery was ordained to be the second Elder of the Church on the 6th day of April, 1830. Following this ordination, as the Church increased in membership, deacons, teachers, and priests were ordained, also other elders. On the third day of June, 1831, the first high priests were ordained. Among this number was Joseph Smith the Prophet. He was ordained at his request to the office of high priest, under the hand of Lyman Wight, who had been previously ordained to the office by Joseph Smith the Prophet." (Joseph Fielding Smith, *CHMR* 1:61-62.)

"As Joseph F. Smith clearly stated regarding the President of the church: 'Every officer in the Church is under his direction, and he is directed of God.' (*Gospel Doctrine*, p. 174.) Let us always remember this. The President of the Church holds the keys of the Melchizedek Priesthood, and there is no business or office in the Church that the President of the Church may not fill. In fact, every office in the Church belongs to the President. The Lord, in speaking to the Prophet Joseph Smith, said: 'And again, the duty of the President of the office of the High Priesthood is to preside over the whole church, and to be like unto Moses—Behold, here is wisdom; yea, to be a seer, a revelator, a translator, and a prophet, having all the gifts of God which he bestows upon the head of the church.' (D&C 107:91-92.)" (N. Eldon Tanner, *Ensign,* January 1973, p. 103.)

"The President of the Church has a . . . special spiritual endowment . . . for he is the prophet, seer, and revelator for the whole Church.

"Here we must have in mind—must know—that only the President of the Church, the Presiding High Priest, is sustained as prophet, seer, and revelator for the Church, and he alone has the right to receive revelations for the Church, either new or amendatory, or to give authoritative interpretations of scriptures that shall be binding on the Church, or change in any way the existing doctrines of the Church. He is God's sole mouthpiece on earth for The Church of Jesus Christ of Latter-day Saints, the only true Church. He alone may declare the mind and will of God to his people. No officer of any other Church in the world has this high right and lofty prerogative.

"So when any other person, irrespective of who he is, undertakes to do any of these things, you may know he is not 'moved upon by the Holy Ghost,' in so speaking unless he has special authorization from the President of the Church. [D&C 20:9-11; 90:1-4, 9, 12-16; 107:8, 65-66, 91-92; 115:19; 124:125; *HC* 2:477; 6:363.]" (J. Reuben Clark Jr., *ASIF,* BYU, July 7, 1954.)

"Now what authority does President Kimball have? As

President of the Church, he holds all of the keys and powers ever given by the angels to the Prophet Joseph Smith in the restoration of the gospel in this last dispensation. He has received these powers by the laying on of hands of those in authority. . . . The powers given by the angels to the Prophet Joseph Smith remained with the Church, and they still remain with the Church. They are centered always in one man, the President of the Church, the prophet, seer, and revelator. It could not be any other way. This is the Lord's pattern. This is the way he directs and conducts his work." (Mark E. Petersen, *Ensign*, May 1974, p. 56.)

"Prophecy does not come to us simply that we may know that which is to transpire. The Lord sends inspired men to outline to us the future in order that, having that knowledge, we may be brought to repentance; that we may avoid, by repentance, the inevitable judgments which come to men because of their wickedness, that we may become partakers of the blessings which are vouchsafed to all those who repent and serve the Lord. This is the purpose of prophecy, this is the spirit of prophecy, and the prophets have always been with God's children from the beginning of time, and they are with them today to warn and admonish them and to point out to them the way in which they should walk. A prophet is not only one who foretells events that are to come, but one who, inspired of the Lord, instructs people in that which they ought to do in the day of their own probation, that they may be brought back into the presence of the Lord." (Anthony W. Ivins, *CR*, October 1914, p. 92.)

"The Gift of Prophecy distinguishes its possessor as a prophet—literally, one who speaks for another, specifically, one who speaks for God. . . . To prophesy is to receive and declare the word of God, and the statement of His will to the people. The function of prediction, often regarded as the sole essential of prophecy, is but one among many characteristics of this divinely given power. The prophet may have as much concern with the past as with the present or the future; he may use his gift in teaching through the experience of preceding events as in foretelling occurrences." (James E. Talmage, *AF*, p. 228.)

Scriptural References: D&C 1:38; 11:25; 20:26; 21:5; 46:22; 131:5; A of F 1: 5, 7; Amos 3:7; 7:15; 1 Cor. 12:10; 13:2; 14:3, 5, 22; 1 Tim. 4:14; 2 Pet. 1:10-21; Rev. 19:10; 1 Ne. 22:2; 2 Ne. 25:4; Jacob 4:6; Alma 45:9.

Prophet; President of the Church; President of the High Priesthood (*see also* Priesthood offices; Prophecy)

A prophet of God is one who speaks for God. There could
be many prophets in the true church if they are worthy and
qualified to speak for God in their respective areas of
responsibility. There is only one prophet at a time upon the
earth who is qualified to speak for the entire church. When
the definite article *the* is used before the word *prophet* to
designate a person now living on the earth, this title could
appropiately refer to only one person: the prophet of the
Church. Other titles that could also be used to refer to this
person are *the President of the Church* or *the President of the
High Priesthood.*

Selected Quotations

"The word Prophet defined in the Hebrew language
means one who has been called to denounce sin and foretell
the consequences and punishment of it. He is to be above all
else a preacher of righteousness, to call the people back from
idolatry to faith in the living God, and when moved upon by
the Spirit of the Lord, to foretell coming events. But more
particularly a prophet is to be an expounder of present duties
and an interpreter of the meaning and application of the
written word." (Anthony W. Ivins, *CR,* October 1933, p. 84.)

"To be a prophet of the Lord, one does not need to 'be
everything to all men.' He does not need to be youthful and
athletic, an industrialist, a financier, nor an agriculturist; he
does not need to be a musician, a poet, an entertainer, nor a
banker, a physician, nor a college president, a military
general, nor a scientist. He does not need to be a linguist to
speak French and Japanese, German and Spanish, but he
must understand the divine language and be able to receive
messages from heaven.

"He need not be an orator, for God can make his own.
The Lord can present his divine messages through weak men
made strong. He subsituted a strong voice for the quiet,
timid one of Moses, and gave to the young man Enoch
power which made men tremble in his presence, for Enoch
walked with God as Moses walked with God. . . .

"What the world needs is a prophet-leader who gives
example—clean, full of faith, godlike in his attitudes with an
untarnished name, a beloved husband, a true father. A
prophet needs to be more than a priest or a minister or an

elder. His voice becomes the voice of God to reveal new programs, new truths, new solutions. I make no claim of infallibility for him, but he does need to be recognized of God, an authoritative person. He is no pretender as numerous are who presumptuously assume position without appointment and authority that is not given. He must speak like his Lord: '. . . as one having authority, and not as the scribes.' (Matt. 7:29.)

"He must be bold enough to speak truth even against popular clamor for lessening restrictions. He must be certain of his divine appointment, of his celestial ordination, and his authority to call to service, to ordain, to pass keys which fit eternal locks. He must have commanding power like prophets of old: '. . . to seal both on earth and in heaven, the unbelieving and rebellious . . . unto the day when the wrath of God shall be poured out upon the wicked without measure' (D&C 1:8-9), and rare powers: '. . . that whatsoever you seal on earth shall be sealed in heaven; and whatsoever you bind on earth, in my name and by my word, saith the Lord, it shall be eternally bound in the heavens; and whosesoever sins you remit on earth shall be remitted eternally in the heavens; and whosesoever sins you retain on earth shall be retained in heaven' (D&C 132:46).

"What is needed is more a Moses than a Pharaoh; an Elijah than a Belshazzar; a Paul than a Pontius Pilate. He needs not be an architect to construct houses and schools and highrise buildings but he will be one who builds structures to span time and eternity and to bridge the gap between man and his Maker.

"When the world has followed prophets, it has moved forward; when it has ignored them, the results have been stagnation, servitude, death." (Spencer W. Kimball, *IE,* June 1970, pp. 93-94.)

"The Prophet Joseph Smith writes in his journal, 'This morning . . . I visited with a brother and sister from Michigan, who thought that "a prophet is always a prophet"; but I told them that a prophet is a prophet only when he was acting as such.' (Joseph Smith, *History of the Church,* 5:265.)

"That statement makes a clear distinction between official and unofficial actions and utterances of officers of the Church. In this recorded statement the Prophet Joseph Smith recognizes his special right and duty, as the President and Prophet of the Church, under the inspiration of the

Lord, to speak authoritatively and officially for the enlightenment and guidance of the Church. But he claims also the right, as other men, to labor and rest, to work and play, to visit and discuss, to present his opinions and hear the opinion of others, to counsel and bless as a member of the Church." (John A. Widtsoe, *ER*, p. 236.)

Scriptural References: D&C 20:67; 102:9; 107:65, 76, 82.

Purse or scrip

Modern dictionaries indicate that the word *scrip* is archaic, meaning "a small bag or wallet." Modern usage lists another definition as "paper currency." Thus, when a missionary is instructed to go forth without purse or scrip, he is not to be burdened by taking excessive money with him, but is to rely upon the Lord and those whom he teaches to supply him with the necessities of life. The custom of traveling without purse or scrip was followed in New Testament times and in the early part of this dispensation.

Selected Quotations

"To go without 'purse and scrip' is, in modern language, to travel without money and trunk. 'Scrip' is a 'satchel,' a 'knapsack.' When our Lord sent His Apostles on their first missionary journey, He charged them not to take with them money or money belts; nor 'scrip,' such as David carried when he went to meet Goliath; nor a change of clothes. Simplicity was to be one of their characteristics." (Smith and Sjodahl, *DCC*, p. 126.)

"When I went out first as a boy I took nothing with me but the clothes I had on, except a bundle of tracts and a pair of pants and a shirt to use in baptizing. I had faith I could bring people into the Church, and I wanted something I could put on to baptize them in. . . . Indeed, all my ministry among the people of the world was literally 'without purse or scrip.' Now I do not say that this should be done now. I believe that as circumstances change, the Lord changes his commandments, to correspond therewith. As Jesus taught, a great many of you who went out in the world took 'neither brass nor gold nor silver in your purses nor scrip for your journey, nor two coats ' [Matt. 10:9-10], 'for the labourer is worthy of his hire,' but afterwards he said: 'When I sent you out without purse or scrip, did you lack anything?' And they said, Nay, Lord—but now he said, 'He that has no purse let him get one and he that hath no sword let him buy one.' [Luke 22:36.] Circumstances had changed and so the word was changed. He didn't change, but the circumstances being changed the word of the Lord was different. So in these times conditions have changed very much from those times." (Charles W. Penrose, *CR*, October 1921, p. 17.)

Scriptural References: D&C 24:18; 84:78, 86; Luke 22:35.

Quickly; "I come quickly" (*see also* Second Coming)

The term *"I come quickly"* refers to the nearness of the second coming of Jesus Christ and is found in at least 13 sections of the Doctrine and Covenants. Although nearly 150 years have passed since some of these revelations were given, yet that is a relatively short period of time when compared to the nearly 6,000 years that the earth has existed in a telestial condition. The recent fulfillment of many of the prophecies pertaining to the second coming indicate that event is indeed near.

Selected Quotations

" 'I come quickly.' This is a scriptural expression that occurs frequently, especially in the book of Revelation. This is 'speaking after the manner of the Lord.' (D&C 63:53.) This does not mean that immediately the Lord will make his appearance, but when he does come he will come suddenly, when he is least expected. He told his disciples that the day would come when men were unawares, as the thief in the night. For this reason we should watch and pray, 'For as a snare shall it come on all them that dwell on the face of the whole earth.' (Luke 21:34-35.) There is no excuse for any of us, then, not to be prepared, for we have been fully and frequently warned." (Joseph Fielding Smith, *CHMR* 1:157.)

Scriptural References: D&C 33:18; 34:12; 35; 37; 39:34; 41:4; 49:28; 51:20; 54:10; 68:35; 87:8; 88:126; 99:5; 112:34; Rev. 2:5, 16; 3:11; 11:14; 22:7, 12, 20.

Records; importance of record keeping; personal records

From the early days of the Church, the Lord has taught the importance of keeping complete and accurate records so far as the Church is concerned. Also, in recent times the prophets have stressed the importance of keeping family and personal records. Good records serve several useful functions. Not only do they provide reference to past decisions and actions, but they also provide valuable information to later generations.

Selected Quotations

"The matter of record keeping is one of the most important duties devolving on the Church. In the early days of the Church, because of lack of experience, this duty was neglected, therefore many important historical events were not recorded. Even today it is difficult to impress upon clerks in stakes, wards and missions the importance of proper record keeping. There has, however, been a vast improvement in recent years. The Church today endeavors to keep a record of each individual member and file that record in the archives where it may be preserved. On the day of the organization of the Church the Lord impressed the small body of members with the importance of record keeping, and this duty the Church has endeavored to perform truthfully ever since." (Joseph Fielding Smith, *CHMR* 1:103.)

"I have never spent any of my time more profitably for the benefit of mankind than in my journal writing, for a great portion of the Church history has been compiled from my journals and some of the most glorious gospel sermons, truths, and revelations that were given from God to this people through the mouth of the Prophets Joseph and Brigham, Heber and the Twelve could not be found upon the earth on record only in my journals and they are compiled in the Church history and transmitted to the saints of God in all future generations. Does not this pay me for my troubles? It does." (Wilford Woodruff, Diary, Mar. 17, 1857.)

"We urge our young people to begin today to write and keep records of all the important things in their own lives and also the lives of their antecedents in the event that their parents should fail to record all the important incidents in their own lives. Your own private journal should record the way you face up to challenges that beset you. Do not suppose life changes so much that your experiences will not be interesting to your posterity. Experiences of work, relations with people and an awareness of the rightness and wrongness of actions will always be relevant. . . .

"No one is commonplace, and I doubt if you can ever read a biography from which you cannot learn something from the difficulties overcome and the struggles made to succeed. These are the measuring rods for the progress of humanity.

"As we read the stories of great men, we discover that they did not become famous overnight nor were they born professionals or skilled craftsmen. The story of how they became what they are may be helpful to us all.

"What could you do better for your children and your children's children than to record the story of your life, your triumphs over adversity, your recovery after a fall, your progress when all seemed black, your rejoicing when you had finally achieved?

"Get a notebook, . . . a journal that will last through all time, and maybe the angels may quote from it for eternity. Begin today and write in it your goings and comings, your deepest thoughts, your achievements and your failures, your associations and your triumphs, your impressions and your testimonies. Remember, the Savior chastised those who failed to record important events." (Spencer W. Kimball, *NE*, October 1975, pp. 4-5.)

"A word about personal journals and records: We urge every person in the Church to keep a diary or a journal from youth up, all through his life. Would every family, as they now hold their home evenings, train their children from young childhood to keep a journal of the important activities of their lives, and certainly when they begin to leave home for schooling and missions?" (Spencer W. Kimball, *Ensign*, November 1977, p. 4.)

Scriptural References: D&C 127:9; Enos 1:15-16; 3 Ne. 23:7-13.

Religion; ethics

In the First Vision, the Lord indicated that the creeds of the churches were an abomination in his sight because the professors of these creeds drew near unto the Lord "with their lips, but their hearts" were far removed from him. (JS-H 1:19.) Many of these creeds are built on ethical considerations, but too often they do not deal with the truly religious life.

Selected Quotations

"We have had in the world throughout the ages two opposing types of guides for human conduct. One we call ethics and the other we call religion. An ethical man is good because it pays him to be good; because it promotes the peace of the community. An ethical man is virtuous because otherwise he contracts disease, and disease, personal or community, is not desirable. Such is ethics—calculating, selfish. Religion tells another story: I must be good because in the great economy of God, in the great program laid out for the salvation of human kind, in which I am involved with all my brethren and sisters, it is required that I must be righteous and virtuous. Obedience to the law leads to infinite results, both on earth and in the life to come. I must be virtuous, not merely because I protect my self, but because I live then in harmony with the greater law that proceeds from the author of law." (John A. Widtsoe, *CR,* April 1934, pp. 115-16.)

"There is a great difference between ethics and religion. There is a distinction between one whose life is based on mere ethics and one who lives a truly religious life. We have a need for ethics, but true religion includes the truths of ethics and goes far beyond. True religion has its roots in the belief in a supreme being. Christian religion is based upon a belief in God the Eternal Father and in his Son Jesus Christ and in the word of the Lord as contained in scripture. Religion also goes beyond theology. It is more than just a belief in Deity; it is the practice of the belief. James E. Talmage said, 'One may be deeply versed in theological lore, and yet be lacking in religious and even moral character. If theology be theory then religion is practice; if theology be precept, religion is example.' (*Articles of Faith,* p. 5.) . . . This encompasses the choosing of right over wrong, following good, and abstaining from evil. Ethics alone will not accomplish all these things for us, but an active religion will add to ethics the principles and ordinances of the gospel, which, if obeyed, will open the doors of eternal salvation, provided such religion is ordained of God and not of man's creation." (Howard W. Hunter, *IE,* December 1969, pp. 96-97.)

Scriptural Reference: James 1:26-27.

Repent; repentance; "preach nothing but repentance to this generation"

The principle of repentance is basic to all of the other principles and ordinances of the gospel. The basic meaning of the word *repent* is "to change" or "to turn from." Often only one side of repentance is stressed—the turning away from doing those things that are wrong. Another important aspect of repentance is to start doing those things that are right; this also involves a change, or repentance. All a missionary need preach is repentance. The investigator should stop doing those things he has been doing that are wrong and start doing those things he has not been doing that are right.

Selected Quotations

"The Prophet Joseph Smith specified as the first principles and ordinances of the gospel, 'first, Faith in the Lord Jesus Christ; second, Repentance; third, Baptism by immersion for the remission of sins; fourth, Laying on of hands for the gift of the Holy Ghost.' (A of F 1:4.)

"These four principles and ordinances form the arch to the entrance of The Church of Jesus Christ of Latter-day Saints. Compliance with them is the process by which one receives that rebirth of the water and of the Spirit without which, as Jesus taught Nicodemus, a man can neither see nor enter into the kingdom of God. In one sense, repentance is the keystone in that arch. Unless followed by repentance, professed faith in the Lord Jesus Christ is impotent; unless preceded by repentance, baptism is a futile mockery, effecting no remission of sins; and without repenting, no one actually receives the companionship of the Holy Spirit of God, notwithstanding the laying on of hands for the gift of the Holy Ghost." (Marion G. Romney, *IE,* March 1956, p. 88.)

"Repentance is a glorious principle. It also is a gift of God. True repentance cannot come without the exercise of faith. It is possible for a man to get so deeply saturated in sin that he cannot repent. This is the condition of Lucifer and those who followed him. This is likewise the condition which overtakes sons of Perdition in this life. . . .

"What a terrible thing it would be if there was no principle of repentance and forgiveness for sin, and if we had to go through eternity with the weight of our transgressions upon us. Through the free gift of God and the atonement of Jesus Christ, all may repent and receive remission of their sins through obedience to the Gospel." (Joseph Fielding Smith, *CHMR* 2:210-11.)

"The call to repentance from sin is to all men and not to the members of the Church only, and not to those only whose sins are considered major ones. And the call promises forgiveness of sin to those who respond. What a farce it would be to call people to repentance if there were no forgiveness, and what a waste of the life of Christ if it failed to bring the opportunity for salvation and exaltation!

"Sometimes a guilt consciousness overpowers a person with such a heaviness that when a repentant one looks back and sees the ugliness, the loathsomeness of the transgression, he is almost overwhelmed and wonders, 'Can the Lord ever forgive me? Can I ever forgive myself?' But when one reaches the depths of despondency and feels the hopelessness of his position, and when he cries out to God for mercy in helplessness but in faith, there comes a still, small, but penetrating voice whispering to his soul, 'Thy sins are forgiven thee.' " (Spencer W. Kimball, *MF*, p. 344.)

"How wonderful that God should endow us with this sensitive yet strong guide we call a conscience! Someone has aptly remarked that 'conscience is a celestial spark which God has put into every man for the purpose of saving his soul.' Certainly it is the instrument which awakens the soul to consciousness of sin, spurs a person to make up his mind to adjust, to convict himself of the transgression without soft-pedaling or minimizing the error, to be willing to face facts, meet the issue and pay necessary penalties—and until the person is in this frame of mind he has not begun to repent. To be sorry is an approach, to abandon the act of error is a beginning, but until one's conscience has been sufficiently stirred to cause him to move in the matter, so long as there are excuses and rationalizations, one has hardly begun his approach to forgiveness. . . .

"Often people indicate that they have repented when all they have done is to express regret for a wrong act. But true repentance is marked by that godly sorrow that changes, transforms, and saves. To be sorry is not enough." (Spencer W. Kimball, *MF*, pp. 152-53.)

Scriptural References: D&C (check index); Book of Mormon (check index).

Respecter of persons; "God is no respecter of persons"
The scriptural statement "God is no respecter of persons"

does not mean that God does not have respect for persons; rather it emphasizes that he is absolutely impartial in his judgments, just as he counseled Moses: "Ye shall not respect persons in judgment." (Deut. 1:17.) Every person who keeps a law is entitled to the blessing attending such obedience; in a similar manner, every person who breaks a law must either repent of his disobedience or suffer the penalty attached to that law. God does not and cannot allow mercy to rob justice. God can have respect for one person over another only to the degree that the first person is more righteous (obedient to law) than the other.

Selected Quotations

"The Lord is no respecter of persons. However, let us not misinterpret this saying. It does not mean that the Lord does not respect those who obey him in all things more than he does the ungodly. Without question the Lord does respect those who love him and keep his commandments more than he does those who rebel against him. The proper interpretation of this passage (1:35) is that the Lord is not partial and grants to each man, if he will repent, the same privileges and opportunities of salvation and exaltation. He is just to every man, both the righteous and the wicked. He will receive any soul who will turn from iniquity to righteousness, and will love him with a just love and bless him with all that the Father has to give; but let it not be thought that he will grant the same blessings to those who will not obey him and keep his law. If the Lord did bless the rebellious as he does the righteous, without their repentance, then he would be a respecter of persons. His justice and his mercy are perfect. Justice, says Alma, 'exerciseth all her demands, and also mercy claimeth all which is her own; and thus, none but the truly repentant are saved. What, do ye suppose that mercy can rob justice? I say unto you, Nay; not one whit. If so, God would cease to be God.' (Alma 42:24-25.)" (Joseph Fielding Smith, *CHMR* 1:255.)

Scriptural References: D&C 1:35; 38:16, 26; Acts 10:34; Moro. 8:12.

Restoration; restitution of all things; restoration of all things

In order for a thing to be restored to a certain place or condition, it must have been in the place or condition previously. When the scriptures indicate that there will be a "restoration of all things" concerning the gospel, this means that all truths, principles, ordinances, priesthood powers and keys, etc., that were part of any earlier gospel dispensations will be restored in this the dispensation of the fulness of times. The New Testament translators sometimes used the word *restitution* instead of *restoration* (Acts 3:21), but the basic meaning is the same.

Selected Quotations

"It is the pronouncement of The Church of Jesus Christ of Latter-day Saints that this is the Dispensation of the Fulness of Times, and that through the 'restitution of all things' the Lord has made provision to 'gather together in one all things in Christ, both which are in heaven, and which are on earth.' This 'restitution of all things' will, however, not be complete until the end of the thousand years of the personal reign of Christ upon the earth when death will be destroyed. (See 1 Cor. 15:24-26.)" (LeGrand Richards, *MWW*, p. 36.)

Scriptural References: D&C 27:6; 86:10; Isa. 29:13-14; Matt. 17:11; Acts 3:19-21; Rev. 14:6-7; 2 Ne. 3:6-15; 30:1-8.

Resurrection; first resurrection; resurrection of the just

The resurrection (rising from the dead) of Jesus Christ is one of the most important events that has ever happened or that will ever happen on this earth. It not only provided proof that Jesus Christ was and is the divine Son of God, but it burst the chains of physical death for all mankind. "As in Adam all die, even so in Christ shall all be made alive." (1 Cor. 15:22.) Jesus Christ was the first person on this earth to be resurrected from the dead; hence, the scriptures refer to him as the firstfruits of them that sleep. (1 Cor. 15:23.) All those who were resurrected immediately after the resurrection of Jesus Christ came forth in the first resurrection, because it was the first opportunity they had of being resurrected. The righteous and the just will come forth the *first opportunity* they will have to be resurrected. Thus, the terms "first resurrection" and "resurrection of the just" mean essentially the same.

Selected Quotations

"Though all men are assured of a resurrection, all will not be resurrected at the same time, and there will be varying degrees of glory for immortal persons. All will come forth from the grave. 'But every man in his own order' (1 Cor.

15:23), as Paul expresses it. Joseph Smith said: 'In the resurrection, some are raised to be angels, others are raised to become gods.' (*TPJS*, p. 312.)

"Two great resurrections await the inhabitants of the earth: one is the first resurrection, the resurrection of life, the resurrection of the just; the other is the second resurrection, the resurrection of damnation, the resurrection of the unjust. (John 5:28-29; Rev. 20; D&C 76.) But even within these two separate resurrections, there is an order in which the dead will come forth. Those being resurrected with celestial bodies whose destiny is to inherit a celestial kingdom, will come forth in the morning of the first resurrection. Their graves shall be opened and they shall be caught up to meet the Lord at his Second Coming. They are Christ's, the first-fruits, and they shall descend with him to reign as kings and priests during the millennial era. (D&C 29:13; 43:18; 76:50-70; 88:97-98; 1 Thess. 4:16-17; Rev. 20:3-7.)

" 'And after this another angel shall sound, which is the second trump; and then cometh the redemption of those who are Christ's at his coming; who have received their part in that prison which is prepared for them, that they might receive the gospel, and be judged according to men in the flesh.' (D&C 88:99.) This is the afternoon of the first resurrection; it takes place after our Lord has ushered in the millennium. Those coming forth at that time do so with terrestrial bodies and are thus destined to inherit a terrestrial glory in eternity. (D&C 76:71-80.)

"At the end of the millennium, the second resurrection begins. In the forepart of this resurrection of the unjust those destined to come forth will be 'the spirits of men who are to be judged, and are found under condemnation; And these are the rest of the dead; and they live not again until the thousand years are ended, neither again, until the end of the earth.' (D&C 88:100-101.) These are the ones who have earned telestial bodies who were wicked and carnal in mortality, and who have suffered the wrath of God in hell 'until the last resurrection, until the Lord, even Christ the Lamb, shall have finished his work.' (D&C 76:85.) Their final destiny is to inherit a telestial glory. (D&C 76:81-112.)

"Finally, in the latter end of the resurrection of damnation, the sons of perdition, those who 'remain filthy still' (D&C 88:102), shall come forth from their graves. (2 Ne. 9:14-16.)" (Bruce R. McConkie, *MD*, pp. 639-40.)

"As concerning the resurrection, I will merely say that all men will come from the grave as they lie down, whether old or young; there will not be 'added unto their stature one cubit,' neither taken from it; all will be raised by the power of God, having spirit in their bodies, and not blood. Children will be enthroned in the presence of God and the lamb with bodies of the same stature that they had on earth, having been redeemed by the blood of the Lamb; they will there enjoy the fulness of that light, glory and intelligence, which is prepared in the celestial kingdom. 'Blessed are the dead who die in the Lord, for they rest from their labors and their works do follow them.' [Rev. 14:23.]" (Joseph Smith, *HC* 4:555-56.)

"Those from whom we have to part here, we will meet again and see as they are. We will meet the same identical being that we associated with here in the flesh—not some other soul, some other being, or the same being in some other form, but the same identity and the same form and likeness, the same person we knew and were associated with in our mortal existence. . . . Deformity will be removed; defects will be eliminated, and men and women shall attain to the perfection of their spirits, to the perfection that God designed in the beginning." (Joseph F. Smith, *GD,* p. 23.)

"I want to impress . . . the fact that the resurrection will prove to be just as natural as birth; that the coming together of those particles that belong to us and belong to one another, each in a distinct organization, although similar in many respects to others, and the formation or reformation of our own personality, is just as sure as that we lay down our lives. As we rise in the morning from our night's rest, so it will be with us in the resurrection." (Charles W. Penrose, *IE,* July 1919, pp. 752, 754.)

"Joseph Smith taught the doctrine that the infant child that was laid away in death would come up in the resurrection as a child; pointing to the mother of a lifeless child, he said to her: 'You will have the joy, the pleasure, and satisfaction of nurturing this child, after its resurrection, until it reaches the full stature of its spirit.' There is growth, there is development, after the resurrection from death. . . . The body remains undeveloped in the grave, but the spirit returns to God who gave it. Afterwards, in the resurrection, the spirit and body will be reunited; the body will develop and grow to the full stature of the spirit; and the resurrected soul will go on to perfection." (Joseph F. Smith, *GD*, pp. 455-56.)

Scriptural References: D&C 76:22-23 (also check index); Job. 14:14; 19:25-27; Matt. 27:52-53; Acts 1:1-3; 26:22-23; 1 Cor. 15:3-8, 19-23; 2 Ne. 9:4-9; Hel. 14:15-18; Morm. 9:11-14.

Revelation; spirit of revelation (*see also* Gifts of the Spirit)

The principle of revelation is one of the major means employed by God to communicate with man. God may reveal things directly to a person, or he may reveal truths to a prophet who then may teach the people. Continuous revelation is one of the signs of a living God communicating with his living church.

Selected Quotations

"The Spirit of Revelation is in connection with these blessings. A person may profit by noticing the first intimation of the spirit of revelation; for instance, when you feel pure intelligence flowing into you, it may give you sudden strokes of ideas, so that by noticing it, you may find it fulfilled the same day or soon; (i.e.) those things that were presented unto your minds by the Spirit of God, will come to pass; and thus by learning the Spirit of God and understanding it, you may grow into the principle of revelation, until you become perfect in Christ Jesus. (Joseph Smith, *TPJS*, p. 151.)

"The things of God can only be understood by the Spirit of God and the Spirit of God is a revealing spirit. The Master promised before he left the earth to send another Comforter which would lead men into all truth. [John 15:16; 16:7.] Divine revelation has always been a characteristic of the living Church—it is absolutely essential to its continued existence in an organized state on the earth." (Hugh B. Brown, *CR*, September 1961, pp. 93-94.)

"Would you like a formula to tell you how to get personal revelation? It might be written in many ways. My formula is simply this: (1) Search the scriptures. (2) Keep the commandments. (3) Ask in faith. Any person who will do this will get his heart so in tune with the Infinite that there will come into his being, from the 'still small voice,' the eternal realities of religion. And as he progresses and advances and comes nearer to God, there will be a day when he will entertain angels, when he will see visions, and the final end is to view the face of God. *Religion is a thing of the spirit.* Use all your intellectuality to help you, but in the final analysis, you have to get in tune with the Lord." (Bruce R. McConkie, *BYUSY*, 1966, p. 8.)

"Of all things, that for which we should be most grateful today is that the heavens are indeed open and that the restored church of Jesus Christ is founded upon the rock of revelation. Continuous revelation is indeed the very lifeblood of the gospel of the living Lord and Savior, Jesus Christ. . . .

"How this confused world of today needs revelation from God. With war and pestilence and famine, with poverty, desolation, with more and more graft, dishonesty, and immorality, certainly the people of this world need revelation from God as never before. How absurd it would be to think that the Lord would give to a small handful of people in Palestine and the Old World his precious direction through revelation and now, in our extremity, close the heavens.

"However, it is the sad truth that if prophets and people are unreachable, the Lord generally does nothing for them. Having given them free agency, their Heavenly Father calls, persuades, and directs aright his children, but waits for their upreaching hands, their solemn prayers, their sincere, dedicated approach to him. If they are heedless, they are left floundering in midnight's darkness when they could have the noonday sun. . . .

"I bear witness to the world today that more than a century and a half ago the iron ceiling was shattered; the heavens were once again opened, and since that time revelations have been continuous. . . .

"The foreverness of this kingdom and the revelations which it brought into existence are absolute realities. Never again will the sun go down; never again will all men prove totally unworthy of communication with their Maker. Never again will God be hidden from his children on the earth. Revelation is here to remain. . . .

"I say, in the deepest of humility, but also by the power and force of a burning testimony in my soul, that from the prophet of the Restoration to the prophet of our own year, the communication line is unbroken, the authority is continuous, and light, brilliant and penetrating, continues to shine. The sound of the voice of the Lord is a continuous melody and a thunderous appeal. For nearly a century and a half there has been no interruption. Man never needs to stand alone. Every faithful person may have the inspiration for his own limited kingdom. But the Lord definitely calls prophets today and reveals his secrets unto them as he did yesterday, he does today, and will do tomorrow: that is the way it is." (Spencer W. Kimball, *Ensign*, May 1977, pp. 76-78.)

Scriptural References: D&C 8:2-3; 9:7-9; 43:2-7; 76:5-10; 82:2-4; 121:26-32; A of F 1:7, 9; Prov. 29:18; Amos 3:7; Matt. 16:13-19; 1 Cor. 2:9-11; 12:3; Jacob 4:8-10; Mosiah 8:13-18; Alma 5:43-47; Moro. 10:4-5.

Riches; riches of this earth

The Lord created the heavens and the earth and all things that are in the heavens and the earth. All material things essentially belong to God, as he is the Creator of the basic elements from which all things are made. "The earth is the Lord's, and the fulness thereof." (Ps. 24:1.) God could create additional things for the blessing of his church and his saints if this were necessary. He has given man the opportunity of creating things out of the elements He has provided. Man should not place his major attention or interest upon such material things, however, for the major purpose of man's existence is to develop spiritually so he can regain the presence of our Heavenly Father. Thus, if man is blessed with an abundance of material riches, he should use these for the blessing of others.

Selected Quotations

"Remember . . . the greatest gift that God can bestow upon us [is] eternal life, and it is worth more than all the houses and lands or the gold and the silver upon the earth. For by and by we will go to the grave, and that puts an end to worldly possessions, as far as our using them is concerned. The grave finds a home for all flesh, and no man can take his houses and lands, his gold and silver, or anything else of a worldly character with him. We brought none of these things with us when we came from our previous state. . . . All the knowledge that we can accumulate from experience and observation, and from the revelations of God to man, goes to show that the riches of this world are fleeting and transitory; while he that has eternal life abiding in him is rich indeed. [D&C 6:7.]" (Wilford Woodruff, *JD* 22:234.)

"As for gold and silver, they are of very little account compared with eternal life. When we die we must leave the riches of this world behind. We were born naked and we will go out of the world in the same condition. We cannot take with us houses, gold, silver, or any of this world's goods. [Alma 39:14.] We will even leave our tabernacles for somebody to bury." (Wilford Woodruff, *JD* 21:127.)

"We do not look upon wealth in itself as a curse. We believe that those who can handle means rightly can do much to bless their fellows. But he who is ruled by the love of money is tempted to commit sin. The love of money is the root of all evil. [1 Tim. 6:10.] There is hardly a commandment but is violated through this seeking for riches." (Anthon H. Lund, CR, April 1903, p. 24.)

Scriptural References: D&C 6:7; 11:7; 38:39; 56:16; Luke 8:14; Jacob 2:18; Mosiah 11:14; 12:29; Alma 39:14; Hel. 13:21-23.

Riches of eternity

The term "riches of eternity" refers to the attainment of eternal life and everything associated with this type of life in the presence of our Heavenly Father: "Behold, he that hath eternal life is rich." (D&C 6:7; 11:7; 43:25.)

Selected Quotations

"All those who wish to possess true riches, desire the riches that will endure. Then look at the subject of salvation, where you will find true riches. They are to be found in the principles of the Gospel of salvation, and are not to be found anywhere else. . . . The only true riches in existence are for you and me to secure for ourselves a holy resurrection; then we have command of the gold and the silver, and can place it where we please, and in whose hands we please. . . .

"The power which belongs to the true riches is gained by pursuing a righteous course, by maintaining an upright deportment towards all men, and especially towards the household of faith, yielding to each other, giving freely of that which the Lord has given to you.

"Remember, that true riches—life, happiness, and salvation, is to secure for ourselves a part in the first resurrection, where we are out of the reach of death, and him that hath the power of it; then we are exalted to thrones, and have power to organize element. Yes, they that are faithful, and that overcome, shall be crowned with crowns of eternal glory. They shall see the time when their cities shall be paved with gold; for there is no end to the precious metals, they are in the native element, and there is an eternity of it. If you want a world of the most precious substance, you will have nothing to do but say the word, and it is done. You can then say to the elements, 'produce ye the best oranges, lemons, apples, figs, grapes, and every other good fruit.' " (Brigham Young, *JD* 1:269, 272-73, 276.)

"To those who live for tomorrow, the rewards are beyond their conception. And even though some of the blessings are for future enjoyment, is it not far better to enjoy the spiritual luxuries of tomorrow, which is an eternity, rather than to revel in the physical comforts of today?

"Peace, joy, satisfaction, happiness, growth, contentment, all come with the righteous living of the commandments of God. The one who delights in all of the worldly luxuries of today, at the expense of spirituality, is living but for the moment. His day is coming. Retribution is sure. . . .

"When one realizes the vastness, the richness, the glory of that 'all' [Luke 15:31] which the Lord promises to bestow upon his faithful, it is worth all it costs in patience, faith, sacrifice, sweat and tears. The blessings of eternity contemplated in this 'all' bring to men immortality and everlasting life, eternal growth, divine leadership, eternal increase, perfection, and with it all—Godhood." (Spencer W. Kimball, *CR*, April 1952, pp. 23-24.)

Scriptural References: D&C 38:39; 67:2; 68:31; 78:18.

Right hand; righteous on the right hand of God

For some reason that is not explained completely in our present scriptures, the term *right hand* has always indicated a favorable or preferred position. When the Savior was resurrected, he sat down "on the right hand of the Father" (20:24); the twelve apostles will stand at the right hand of Jesus Christ when he comes in power and glory at the time of his second coming (29:12); and the righteous will be gathered on the right hand of the Savior "unto eternal life" (29:27). On the other hand (intended partially as a pun), the wicked are designated as being on the left hand of the Lord (D&C 19:5; 29:27).

Selected Quotations

"*Use of right hand in ordinances.* The custom, evidently by divine direction, from the very earliest time, has been to associate the right hand with the taking of oaths, and in witnessing or acknowledging obligations. The right hand has been used, in preference to the left hand, in officiating in sacred ordinances where only one hand is used.

"The earliest reference we have to the superiority of the right hand over the left, in blessing, is found in the blessing of Jacob to his two grandsons, Ephraim and Manasseh, when he placed his hand 'wittingly' upon the heads of the boys. (Gen. 48:13-14.)

"Earlier, when Abraham sent his servant to Abraham's own kindred to find a wife for Isaac, he had the servant place his hand under his (Abraham's) thigh, and swear to him that he would accomplish his mission. Evidently, this was the servant's right hand.

"The Lord said through Isaiah: 'Fear thou not; for I am with thee: be not dismayed; for I am thy God: I will strengthen thee; yea, I will help thee; yea, I will uphold thee with the *right hand* of my righteousness.' (Isa. 41:10.)

"In the Psalms we read: 'The Lord said unto my Lord, Sit thou at my *right hand*, until I make thine enemies thy footstool.' (Ps. 110:1.)

"It is the custom to extend the right hand in token of fellowship. The right hand is called the *dexter*, and the left, the *sinister*; dexter means *right* and sinister means *left*. Dexter, or right, means *favorable* or *propitious*. Sinister is associated with evil, rather than good. Sinister means *perverse*.

"We take the sacrament with the right hand. We sustain the authorities with the right hand. We make acknowledgment with the right hand raised." (Joseph Fielding Smith, *DS* 3:107-8.)

Scriptural References: D&C 20:24; 29:12, 27; 49:6; 66:12; 76:20, 23; 84:88; 104:7; 109:71; 124:19; 133:56; Moses 7:56-57; JS-M 1:1; Gen. 48:13-14; Isa. 41:10; Ps. 110:1; Matt. 20:23; 22:44; 25:33-34; 26:64; 27:38; Mosiah 5:9; 26:23-24; 3 Ne. 22:3; 29:4, 9.

Rock; Rock of heaven; Stone of Israel (*see also* Jesus Christ)

The word *rock* is used by the Savior on several occasions to refer to himself, to the gospel, or to a principle of the gospel. In all of these uses, the word evokes the image of stability, dependability, strength, and permanence, which should be associated with Jesus Christ and his teachings. The title "stone of Israel" (D&C 50:44) is used in much the same sense in referring to the Savior.

Perhaps the most frequently quoted scripture containing the word *rock* is Matthew 16:17-18: "Blessed art thou, Simon Bar-jona; for flesh and blood hath not revealed it unto thee, but my Father which is in heaven. And I also say unto thee, That thou art Peter, and upon this rock I will build my church; and the gates of hell shall not prevail against it."

Unfortunately, the meaning of the word *rock* in this scripture has been interpreted in different ways by various religious groups. Some have mentioned that the antecedent is Peter, while others have felt it referred to the principle of revelation. The Lord uses the same term in several of his latter-day revelations (11:16, 24; 18:4-5, 17; 33:12-13), and it is abundantly clear that he is speaking of the gospel or of a principle of the gospel (revelation) rather than of the man Peter. When the term is used to refer to a person, it usually refers to Jesus Christ. (See D&C 50:44.)

The Prophet Joseph Smith explained the meaning of the word: "Jesus says, 'Upon this rock I will build my Church, and the gates of hell shall not prevail against it.' What rock? Revelation." (*HC* 5:258.)

Scriptural References: D&C 6:34; 10:69; 11:16, 24; 18:4, 5, 17; 33:13; 50:44; 128:10; Moses 7:53; Gen. 49:29; Deut. 32:3-4, 18, 30-31; 2 Sam. 22:47; 23:3; Ps. 18:2, 31, 46; 28:1; 31:3; 42:9; 62:2, 6-7; 71:3; 78:35; 89:26; 92:15; 94:22; Matt. 16:18; 1 Pet. 2:1-9; 1 Ne. 13:36; 2 Ne. 4:30, 35; 9:45; Jacob 7:25; Hel. 5:12; 3 Ne. 11:39-40.

Root; branch; "neither root nor branch"

In common usage, *root* refers to the "underground part of a seed plant" and also means "base or foundation or origin." When it is used to refer to people, the dictionary suggests it is "one or more progenitors of a group of descendants." The scriptural term that a particular group of people would "be wasted away, both root and branch" (109:52) would indicate that both progenitors and descendants would be lost.

Selected Quotations

"Malachi went on to say they 'shall burn as stubble.' This means that they shall be destroyed. By whom? Malachi explains, 'They that come shall burn them, saith the Lord of Hosts.' . . .

"But what is meant by the expression 'that it shall leave them neither root nor branch'? This expression simply means that wicked and indifferent persons who reject the gospel of Jesus Christ will have no family inheritance or patriarchal lineage—neither root (ancestors or progenitors) nor branch (children or posterity). Such persons cannot be received into the celestial kingdom of glory of resurrected beings, but must be content with a lesser blessing." (Theodore M. Burton, *CR*, April 1965, p. 112.)

Scriptural References: D&C 97:7; 109:52; 113:5; 133:64; JS-M 1:37; Isa. 5:24; 11:10; 27:6; 37:31; 40:24; 53: 2; Rom. 11:16-18; 15:12; Jacob 5; Mosiah 14:2; Alma 32; 3 Ne. 25:1.

Sabaoth; Lord of Sabaoth

The word *sabaoth* is a Greek form of a Hebrew word (*tsebaoth*), which means "armies." Jesus Christ is the Lord of Sabaoth, or Lord of Armies, also translated as Lord of Hosts. (Isa. 1:9; Rom. 9:29; James 5:4.) The Lord of Sabaoth (Jesus Christ) is also "the creator of the first day, the beginning and the end." (D&C 95:7.)

Scriptural References: D&C 87:7; 88:2; 95:7; 98:2; Rom. 9:29; James 5:4.

Sabbath; Sabbath day; the Lord's day (*see also* Ten Commandments)

The basic Hebrew root of the word *sabbath* is "seventh," and until the time of Jesus Christ the Sabbath day was also the seventh day of the week—Saturday. In time sabbath came to mean "day of rest." Since the time of the Savior, most Christians have observed their day of rest on the first day of the week, Sunday, which has also become known as the Lord's day. It was on the first day of the week, Sunday, that the Lord was resurrected, and on the following Sunday he also appeared to his apostles.

From at least the time of creation, one day of the week has been designated as a holy day, a day of worship when appropriate attention should be given to the Lord of creation and to the principles of righteousness taught by him. Sabbath observance is an eternal principle, and the commandments of the Lord pertaining to its observance apply as much today as they did anciently.

Selected Quotations

"Sunday is worship day. It is holy. This is a Christian nation, and the Lord has promised that as long as we keep him in mind and worship him this country will stand—this Government will stand. No other nation can take it or destroy it. But if we forget him, God's promises are not binding.

"Why should Sunday be observed as a day of rest? First, Sunday is essential to the true development and strength of body. . . .

"A second purpose for keeping holy the Sabbath day is: 'That thou mayest more fully keep thyself unspotted from the world.' . . .

"There is a third reason. Keeping holy the Sabbath Day is a law of God, resounding through the ages from Mount Sinai. You cannot transgress the law of God without circumscribing your spirit." (David O. McKay, *CR*, October 1956, pp. 90-91.)

"The Sabbath is not a day for indolent lounging about the house or puttering around in the garden, but is a day for consistent attendance at meetings for the worship of the Lord, drinking at the fountain of knowledge and instruction, enjoying the family, and finding uplift in music and song. 'It is a day for reading the scriptures, visiting the sick, visiting relatives and friends, doing home teaching, working on genealogy records, taking a nap, writing letters to missionaries and servicemen or relatives, preparation for the following week's church lessons, games with the small children, fasting for a purpose, writing devotional poetry, and other worthwhile activities of great variety." (Spencer W. Kimball, *FPM*, pp. 270-71.)

"We note that in our Christian world in many places we still have business establishments open for business on the sacred Sabbath. We are sure the cure for this lies in ourselves, the buying public. Certainly the stores and business houses would not remain open if we, the people, failed to purchase from them. Will you all please reconsider this matter. Take it to your home evenings and discuss it with your children. It would be wonderful if every family determined that henceforth no Sabbath purchase would be made.

"When we love the Lord, why do we still break his laws? We implore you, then, earnestly, to discontinue the purchase of things on the Sabbath day." (Spencer W. Kimball, *Ensign*, November 1975, p. 6.)

" I wonder if money earned upon the Sabbath, when it is unnecessary Sabbath earning, might not also be unclean money. I realize that some people must work on the Sabbath; and when they do, if they are compelled, that is, of course, a different situation. But men and women who will deliberately use the Sabbath day to develop business propositions, to increase their holdings, to increase their income, I fear for them. . . . There are people who work on the Sabbath, not through complusion, but because the income is attractive, and others who work voluntarily to get the 'time and a half' that Sabbath work gives them. . . . The Savior knew that the ox gets in the mire on the Sabbath, but he knew also that no ox deliberately goes into the mire every week." (Spencer W. Kimball, *CR*, October 1953, pp. 54-56.)

Scriptural References: D&C 59:9; 68:29; 127:10; Ex. 20:8-11; Isa. 56:2; 58:13; Jer. 17:21; Matt. 12:8; Mark 2:27; 3:4; Luke 6:5; 14:5; Jarom 1:5; Mosiah 13:16; 18:23.

Sacrament; sacrament of the Lord's Supper; fruit of the vine

A sacrament is a *sacred event*. The sacrament of the Lord's Supper is that sacred event or ordinance which was instituted in remembrance of the atoning sacrifice of Jesus Christ.

Jesus Christ accomplished two major things in his atonement. He atoned (or paid for) the spiritual death that was first introduced into this world when Adam and Eve transgressed the law of God and that comes upon each of us whenever we commit sin. This part of the atonement was performed in the Garden of Gethsemane when Jesus Christ bled at every pore in his agony and suffering. In order to help us remember this part of the atonement, we have been commanded to partake of a liquid to remind us of the blood

Jesus Christ shed for us. In New Testament times, the former-day saints used the "fruit of the vine" ("fruit of the cup")—evidently grape juice—as this liquid. In our day the Lord has indicated that "it mattereth not what ye shall eat or what ye shall drink when ye partake of the sacrament, if it so be that ye do it with an eye single to my glory—remembering unto the Father my body which was laid down for you, and my blood which was shed for the remission of your sins." (D&C 27:2.)

Jesus Christ also atoned for the physical death that was the consequence of Adam and Eve partaking of the tree of life. This part of the atonement was accomplished at Calvary and at the tomb at the time of the resurrection. To remind us of this aspect of the atonement, the Lord has instructed us to partake of bread to remind us of his resurrected body.

Selected Quotations

"The covenant made by members of the Church each time they partake of the Sacrament, should constantly be uppermost in their minds. Never should they eat the bread or drink the water without a full realization of just what they are doing and what it means to them. The covenant made embraces the following:

"First, that through the sanctified bread and water, we too, sanctify ourselves in partaking of it before our Heavenly Father, and in the name of Jesus Christ.

"Second, that we eat in remembrance of his broken body and of his blood which was shed for us.

"Third, that we are willing to take upon us the name of the Son, and not be ashamed of him. We belong to the Church of Jesus Christ, and if faithful have taken upon us his name.

"Fourth, we covenant that we will always remember him. This embodies the willingness to love and honor him.

"Fifth, that we will keep his commandments which he has given us.

"These things we covenant to do when we partake of these emblems; moreover, we renew the covenant each week, if we perform our duty. The promise made to us, if we will do these things, is that we shall always have his Spirit to be with us.

"No member of the Church can fail to make this covenant and renew it week by week, and retain the Spirit of the Lord.

The Sacrament meeting of the Church is the most important meeting which we have, and is sadly neglected by many members. We go to this service, if we understand the purpose of it, not primarily to hear someone speak, important though that may be, but first, and most important, to renew this covenant with our Father in heaven in the name of Jesus Christ. Those who persist in their absence from this service will eventually lose the Spirit, and if they do not repent will eventually find themselves denying the faith." (Joseph Fielding Smith, *CHMR* 1:131-32.)

"Now partaking of the sacrament is not to be a mere passive experience. We are not to remember the Lord's suffering and death only as we may remember some purely secular historical event. Participating in the sacrament service is meant to be a vital and a spiritualizing experience. Speaking of it, the Savior said: 'And it shall be a testimony unto the Father that ye do always remember me.' (3 Nephi 18:7.)

"In order to testify, one's mind has to function, and it must be concentrated upon the thing to be testified. And we are not only to partake of the emblems of the sacrament in remembrance of the Redeemer, testifying that we do always remember him, but we are also thereby to witness unto the Father that we are willing to take upon us the name of his Son and that we will keep his commandments. This amounts to a virtual renewal of the covenant of baptism." (Marion G. Romney, *CR,* April 1946, pp. 39-40.)

"All little children virtually belong to the Church until they are eight years of age. Should they die before that age, they would enter the celestial kingdom. [D&C 29:46-47; 74:6.] The Savior said: 'Of such is the kingdom of heaven.' (Matt. 19:14.) Then why should they be deprived of the sacrament?

"Non-members cannot comply with the covenants embodied in the blessings of the sacrament and, therefore, should not partake of it. They are old enough to reason and should understand that the sacrament, so far as adults are concerned, is for those who have repented of their sins in the waters of baptism.

"It would be proper in a meeting to say, 'The sacrament will now be administered to the members of the Church,' in cases where there are non-members present; otherwise nothing need be said of this nature. If non-members are present and partake of the sacrament, we would not do anything to prevent it, for evidently they would take it in good faith, notwithstanding the nature of the covenant.

"The Lord has said that we should not permit anyone to partake of the sacrament unworthily. This means, as I understand it, anyone in the Church who has been in transgression of some kind and who has not repented. It would also apply to the apostate." (Joseph Fielding Smith, *DS* 2:350.)

Scriptural References: D&C 20:46, 58, 68, 75, 78; 27:2, 5; 46:4; 59:9; 62:4; 89:6, 16; Matt. 26:26-29; John 6:54; Acts 2:42; 20:7; 1 Cor. 11:26-30; 3 Ne. 18:7, 29; 20:3; 26:13; Moro. 4:3; 5:2; 6:6.

Sacrifice; *law of sacrifice*

The law of sacrifice is based on the premise that everything belongs to the Lord—the earth and the bounties thereof and even our lives. If we truly loved the Lord, we should be willing to return all of these to him if he required them of us. Sacrifice is a test for man in this mortal probation only. When viewed from an eternal perspective, it will be evident there is no sacrifice in giving up these earthly things if a greater gift—eternal life—is received in return.

Selected Quotations

"A religion that does not require the sacrifice of all things never has power sufficient to produce the faith necessary unto life and salvation. . . . It was through this sacrifice, and this only, that God has ordained that men should enjoy eternal life; and it is through the medium of the sacrifice of all earthly things that men do actually know that they are doing the things that are well pleasing in the sight of God. . . . Those, then, who make the sacrifice, will have the testimony that their course is pleasing in the sight of God; and those who have this testimony will have faith to lay hold on eternal life, and will be enabled, through faith, to endure unto the end, and receive the crown that is laid up for them that love the appearing of our Lord Jesus Christ. But those who do not make the sacrifice cannot enjoy this faith, because men are dependent upon this sacrifice in order to obtain this faith: therefore, they cannot lay hold upon eternal life, because the revelations of God do not guarantee unto them the authority

so to do, and without this guarantee faith could not exist."
(Joseph Smith, *Lectures on Faith,* p. 6.)

"It is written: 'He who is not able to abide the law of a celestial kingdom cannot abide a celestial glory.' (D&C 88:22.) The law of sacrifice is a celestial law; so also is the law of consecration. Thus to gain that celestial reward which we so devoutly desire, we must be *able* to live these two laws.

"Sacrifice and consecration are inseparably intertwined. The law of consecration is that we consecrate our time, our talents, and our money and property to the cause of the Church; such are to be available to the extent they are needed to further the Lord's interests on earth.

"The law of sacrifice is that we are willing to sacrifice all that we have for the truth's sake—our character and reputation; our honor and applause; our good name among men; our houses, lands, and families: all things, even our very lives if need be. . . . Few of us are called upon to sacrifice much of what we possess, and at the moment there is only an occasional martyr in the cause of revealed religion. But what the scriptural account means is that to gain celestial salvation we must be *able* to live these laws to the full if we are called upon to do so. Implicit in this is the reality that we must in fact live them to the extent we are called upon so to do." (Bruce R. McConkie, *CR,* April 1975, pp. 74-75.)

Scriptural References: D&C 59:8; 64:23; 97:8; 1 Sam. 15:22; Rom. 12:1; 2 Ne. 2:7; Alma 34:10-11.

Salt and savor; "salt of the earth and the savor of men"

Salt played an important role in the diet, customs, and practices of ancient Israel. It was not only used as an appetizing condiment in the food of man and beast (Job 6:6), but was also frequently used in the various religious offerings of the Israelites. An inferior type of salt was used in the decomposition of waste (Matt. 5:13; Luke 14:35), and an excess of salt was sowed on the soil of a destroyed city to cause sterility (Judg. 9:45). The "covenant of salt" (Lev. 2:13; Num. 18:19; 2 Chr. 13:5) indicates that anciently salt was a symbol of faithfulness, steadfastness, and purity.

The word *savor* refers to the physical senses of tasting and smelling; it also means "to have experience of" and "to delight in." In some of his parables, the Savior referred to the righteous saints as "the salt of the earth" and as "the savor of men."

Selected Quotations

"How do we lose the savor that followers of the Lord should have? We lose it as we cease to serve Him, or even by becoming casual in our obedience. For example, if we become careless about attending our meetings, do we not lose some of the savor that good salt should have? If we neglect our prayers, our tithes and offerings, what becomes of our savor? . . .

"If we do not share the gospel with our neighbors, what becomes of our savor? If we violate God's holy Sabbath day, does that cause a sweet savor to arise from us, or do we cast a stench into His face? If we are dishonest, unkind, or vengeful, do we not offend the Deity? And if we lose our virtue— that priceless gift of chastity—what becomes of our savor? Is not cleanliness next to godliness? Does not filth banish purity? Does not unchastity insult the Lord? Is it not a 'savor that stinketh'?

"If we are guilty of infidelity in our family, or are otherwise cruel in our home, do we exude a sweet savor or a stench? If we oppose Church policies and defy our chosen leaders, what becomes of our 'sweet savor'? Can there be any sweetness in disloyalty? If we withdraw from the Church and accept the destructive teachings of false prophets, do we not abdicate our place in the Lord's kingdom? And does that give the Lord a sweet savor?" (Mark E. Petersen, *Ensign,* November 1976, pp. 50-51.)

Scriptural References: D&C 101:39, 40; 103:10; Matt. 5:13; Mark 9:49-50; Luke 14:34; 3 Ne. 12:13; 16:15.

Salvation; saved in the kingdom of God

The basic meaning of *salvation* is "saved." The resurrection provides salvation from physical death, for example, in the sense that it saves all mankind from the permanent effects of physical death. Inasmuch as this kind of salvation eventually comes upon all mankind, it is sometimes referred to as unconditional or general salvation. However, a person could be saved from physical death and yet be subject to the spiritual death in one degree or another. Therefore, full salvation is conditional upon the person's obedience to the principles and ordinances of the gospel. As Amulek stated, "How can ye be saved, except ye inherit the kingdom of heaven?" (Alma 11:37.)

Selected Quotations

"Salvation is nothing more nor less than to triumph over all our enemies and put them under our feet. And when we have power to put all enemies under our feet in this world, and a knowledge to triumph over all evil spirits in the world to come, then we are saved, as in the case of Jesus, who was to reign until He had put all enemies under His feet, and the last enemy was death." (Joseph Smith, *TPJS,* p. 297.)

"Salvation is the greatest gift; it includes all other gifts. All other gifts are subservient to it. Salvation means deliverance from outward dangers, victory over enemies, remission of sins through acceptance of Christ and obedience to His laws, and eternal exaltation. (Compare Exodus 14:13; 1 Sam. 14:45; Luke 1:77; 19:9.) 'Wherefore let him that thinketh he standeth take heed lest he fall.' (1 Cor. 10:12.)" (Joseph Smith, *HC* 5:403.)

Scriptural References: D&C 6:13; 18:17; 45:58; 68:4; 93:8; 123:17; 131:6; 133:4; Moses 6:5; A of F 1:3; Jonah 2:9; Luke 3:6; Acts 13:47; Rom. 10:10; 2 Cor. 7:10; Philip. 2:12, 1 Thes. 5:9, 2 Tim. 3:15; Heb. 5:9; 1 Pet. 1:10; 2 Ne. 26:27; Mosiah 3:18; Alma 34:15.

Sanctify; sanctification; sanctification through the grace of Jesus Christ

Sanctify means "to free from sin," "to purify." Sanctification is a state of purity, holiness, and saintliness that comes through the cleansing power of the Holy Ghost. It can only be obtained by keeping the principles and ordinances of the gospel as indicated in the following statement by the Savior: "Repent, all ye ends of the earth, and come unto me and be baptized in my name, that ye may be sanctified by the reception of the Holy Ghost, that ye may stand spotless before me at the last day. Verily, verily, I say unto you, this is my gospel." (3 Ne. 27:20-21.)

Selected Quotations

"I will put my own definition to the term sanctification, and say it consists in overcoming every sin and bringing all into subjection to the law of Christ. God has placed in us a pure spirit; when this reigns predominant, without let or hindrance, and triumphs over the flesh and rules and governs and controls as the Lord controls the heavens and the earth, this I call the blessing of sanctification. Will sin be perfectly destroyed? No, it will not, for it is not so designed in the economy of heaven.

"Do not suppose that we shall ever in the flesh be free from temptations to sin. Some suppose that they can in the flesh be sanctified body and spirit and become so pure that they will never again feel the effects of the power of the adversary of truth. Were it possible for a person to attain to this degree of perfection in the flesh, he could not die, neither remain in a world where sin predominates. Sin has entered into the world, and death by sin. [Rom. 5:12.] I think we shall more or less feel the effects of sin so long as we live, and finally have to pass the ordeals of death. . . . We should so live as to make the world and all its natural blessings subservient to our reasonable wants and holy desires." (Brigham Young, *JD* 10:173.)

"To be *sanctified* is to become clean, pure, and spotless; to be free from the blood and sins of the world; to become a new creature of the Holy Ghost, one whose body has been renewed by the rebirth of the Spirit. *Sanctification* is a state of saintliness, a state attained only by conformity to the laws and ordinances of the gospel. The plan of salvation is the system and means provided whereby men may sanctify their souls and thereby become worthy of a celestial inheritance." (Bruce R. McConkie, *MD,* p. 675.)

Scriptural References: D&C 20:31, 34, 77, 79 (also check index for *sanctified*); 100:15; John 17:17, 19; 3 Ne. 27:20; 28:39.

Satan; devil; Lucifer; buffetings of Satan; Satan to be bound; Satan to tremble (*see also* Perdition)

Satan is the adversary to the great eternal plan of progression of our Heavenly Father and of Jesus Christ. In the pre-earthly existence, Satan was known as Lucifer; he is also called the devil. He is described as being a liar from the beginning and is called the father of lies. He is an evil personage of spirit who is trying to destroy the plans and works of God.

Selected Quotations

"Lucifer was from the 'the beginning.' In the great Council in heaven he proposed to redeem mankind by compulsion, if God would give him His honor. That proposition was rejected by the Council, and another, made by the

Beloved Son, was adopted. Satan, instead of yielding to the majority, in accordance with the rule of the kingdom of heaven, rebelled and, at the head of other rebellious spirits, endeavored to carry out his plan, in opposition to that which had been accepted. Then he was 'cast down' and became Satan (Pearl of Great Price, Book of Moses, 4:1-4)." (Smith and Sjodahl, *DCC*, p. 51.)

"When the devil and his host were sent from heaven because of disobedience, they came to this world. And wherever the children of men are, there also those evil spirits exist to tempt the children of men to do evil, and everything that leads to destruction and misery, and woe originates from that source, but everything that leads to exaltation, virtue, holiness, goodness, glory, immortality, and eternal life is from the hand of God. The Lord is the strongest power, and He will prevail at last." (Wilford Woodruff, *JD* 11:66.)

"We came to this earth that we might have a body and present it pure before God in the celestial kingdom. The great principle of happiness consists in having a body. The devil has no body, and herein is his punishment. He is pleased when he can obtain the tabernacle of man, and when cast out by the Savior he asked to go into the herd of swine, showing that he would prefer a swine's body to having none.

"All beings who have bodies have power over those who have not. . . . The devil has no power over us only as we permit him. The moment we revolt at anything which comes from God, the devil takes power." (Joseph Smith, *TPJS*, p. 181.)

"Satan is trying to keep us from the full enjoyment which comes from keeping the commandments of God. We must never forget, and we must teach our children to know, that Satan is real and determined to destroy us. He knows the importance and significance of the family unit. He knows that entire civilizations have survived or disappeared depending on whether the family life was strong or weak. We can keep him out of our homes by living and teaching our children to live the principles of the gospel of Jesus Christ, thereby resisting temptation when it comes, as it surely will." (N. Eldon Tanner, *Ensign*, January 1974, p. 10.)

"Satan and his forces were never more strongly arrayed than today. He is cunning. He is successful. One of the most subtle and effective tools he is using among us today is the convincing of some that they have arrived, they have reached their destination, they have earned a rest, they aren't needed anymore, they are out of danger, they are beyond temptation, and they can take pride in their accomplishments." (Marvin J. Ashton, *CR*, April 1972, p. 61.)

Scriptural References: D&C (check index for *devil* and *satan*); Job 1:6-12; 2:1-7; Ps. 109:6; Zech. 3:1-2; Mark 1:13; 3:23, 26; 4:15; 8:33; Rev. 2:9, 13, 24; 3:9; 12:9; 20:2, 7.

Saviors; saviors of men; saviors on mount Zion

The basic meaning of the word *saviors* is "to save someone from something." The Savior of all mankind did something for all men that we could not do for ourselves: he broke the bands of physical death and thus provided for the resurrection of all.

Every blessing is predicated upon obedience to a law. However, many people have lived on the earth when some of the laws of the gospel were not available to them. For example, baptism by immersion for the remission of sin by one holding the proper authority is required of every person who has arrived at the age of accountability in order to enter into the kingdom of heaven. (John 3:5.) Some people have lived and died without ever having the opportunity of being baptized.

Because of the principle of ordinance work for the dead, including baptism (see 1 Cor. 15:29), it is possible today for worthy members of the Church to go into the temple and be baptized for and in behalf of a deceased person. The member of the Church is doing something for the deceased person that the departed cannot do for himself; thus, in a real and vital sense the member of the Church is a savior of the deceased person *in that particular thing.* In this and other ways, worthy members of the Church can become "saviors of men."

Selected Quotations

" 'And saviors shall come up on mount Zion to judge the mount of Esau; and the kingdom shall be the Lord's.' (Obadiah 21.) [Note: Obadiah was a contemporary of Elijah.] . . . The keys are to be delivered, the spirit of Elijah is to come, the Gospel to be established, the Saints of God gathered, Zion built up, and the Saints to come up as saviors on Mount Zion.

"But how are they to become saviors on Mount Zion? By building their temples, erecting their baptismal fonts, and going forth and receiving all the ordinances, baptisms, confirmations, washings, anointings, ordinations and sealing powers upon their heads, in behalf of all their progenitors who are dead, and redeem them that they may come forth in the first resurrection and be exalted to thrones of glory with them; and herein is the chain that binds the hearts of the fathers to the children, and the children to the fathers, which fulfills the mission of Elijah. . . .

"The Saints have not too much time to save and redeem their dead, and gather together their living relatives, that they may be saved also, before the earth will be smitten, and the consumption decreed falls upon the world.

"I would advise all the Saints to go with their might and gather together all their living relatives to this place, that they may be sealed and saved, that they may be prepared against the day that the destroying angel goes forth."(Joseph Smith, *TPJS,* p. 330.)

Scriptural References: D&C 103:9-10; Obad. 1:21.

Scepter; scepter of power

A scepter is "a staff or baton" used as an emblem of authority.

Scriptural References: D&C 85:7; 106:6; 121:46; Gen. 49:10; Num. 24:17; Ps. 45:6; Heb. 1:8.

Scripture; scriptures; importance of reading the scriptures; standard works

Scripture might be defined as the will of God as revealed to man. In this sense, scripture could be spoken or written. However, some scripture has been written down and accepted as official canon by members of the Church. It then becomes part of the *scriptures* or the *standard works* of the Church.

Selected Quotations

"Search the scriptures. Treasure up gospel truths. Enjoy the words of eternal life in this life, and hope for immortal glory in the life to come. Read, ponder, and pray about all that the prophets have written. Such is the course which the

Lord invites men to pursue where his holy word is concerned." (Bruce R. McConkie, *Ensign,* November 1975, p. 17.)

"A great teacher once said, 'He who does not read has no advantage over him who cannot read.' Illiteracy in the gospel seems almost inexcusable in this day of enlightenment and modern teaching techniques, especially among those of us who are committed in the waters of baptism and who reconfirm that commitment each week as we partake of the sacrament." (Robert L. Simpson, *Ensign,* November 1975, p. 13.)

"If you want to know what the Lord would have the Saints know and to have his guidance and direction for the next six months, get a copy of the proceedings of this conference, and you will have the latest word of the Lord as far as the Saints are concerned. And [also] all others who are not of us, but who believe what has been said has been 'the mind of the Lord, the will of the Lord, and the voice of the Lord, and the power of God unto salvation.' (See D&C 68:4.)" (Harold B. Lee, *Ensign,* January 1974, p. 128.)

"Let me tell you of one of the goals that I made when I was still but a lad. When I heard a Church leader from Salt Lake City tell us at conference that we should read the scriptures, and I recognized that I had never read the Bible, that very night at the conclusion of that very sermon I walked to my home a block away and climbed up in my little attic room in the top of the house and lighted a little coal-oil lamp that was on the little table, and I read the first chapters of Genesis. A year later I closed the Bible, having read every chapter in that big and glorious book.

"I found that this Bible that I was reading had in it 66 books, and then I was nearly dissuaded when I found that it had in it 1,189 chapters, and then I also found that it had 1,519 pages. It was formidable, but I knew if others did it that I could do it.

"I found that there were certain parts that were hard for a 14-year-old boy to understand. There were some pages that were not especially interesting to me, but when I had read the 66 books and 1,189 chapters and 1,519 pages, I had a glowing satisfaction that I had made a goal and that I had achieved it.

"Now I am not telling you this story to boast; I am merely

using this as an example to say that if I could do it by coal-oil light, you can do it by electric light. I have always been glad I read the Bible from cover to cover." (Spencer W. Kimball, *Ensign,* May 1974, p. 88.)

Scriptural References: D&C 1:37; 11:22; 18:4; 21:4; 26:1; JS-M 1:37; Luke 16:31; 24:27; 2 Pet. 1:20; 3 Ne. 10:14; 23:1.

Sealing power (*see also* Elijah)

The sealing power of the priesthood enables acts to be performed on earth that will be sealed in heaven. This power includes all of the ordinances for both the living and the dead and is the means by which children can be sealed to parents to form a patriarchal priesthood chain from each worthy person back to Adam.

Selected Quotations

"This family unit is so important that the Lord has made it known to us that all the families of the earth must be sealed together. By the time of the end of the millennium, all of Adam's posterity who accept the gospel must be sealed together as one family by the power of the priesthood, which is the power to seal on earth, and it shall be sealed in heaven, and to bind on earth, and it shall be bound in heaven.

"Every person who comes to the earth must have an opportunity to receive all the blessings of these sealings if he will accept them, sometime before the end of the millennium. There could not be a just God if it were otherwise. These sealing blessings are obtained, first, through the ordinance of baptism into the church of Jesus Christ. Then the wife is to be sealed to the husband for time and all eternity, and those children who are born outside of this wedlock must be sealed to their parents, that they may receive the blessings as though they were born under the new and everlasting covenant.

"Those who have died without this law may have the privilege of receiving this blessing by proxy. That is where our responsibility comes in. We must first teach the gospel to the living. Then we must gather the records of those of our families who died without the law, that this great and important work can be done for them." (Eldred G. Smith, *Ensign,* November 1975, pp. 106-7.)

Scriptural References: D&C 1:8; 132:46; 2 Ne. 33:15; Hel. 10:7.

Season; "for a little season"

The word *season* is generally used to refer to one of the seasons of the year: spring, summer, fall, and winter. The word can also be used to refer to a more general period of time or to a particular condition. The Lord indicated that the Prophet Joseph Smith should stop his translation "for a season" (5:30), that his elders "should wait for a little season" (105:9, 13), and that after the millennium the devil "shall be loosed for a little season" (88:111).

Scriptural References: D&C 29:22; 42:5; 43:31; 51:16; 63:42; 71:2; 88:71, 111; 100:13; 103:4; 105:9, 13, 21; 112:18; 127:1; Rev. 6:11; 20:3; Jacob 5:71, 76-77; 3 Ne. 27:11.

Second Coming (*see also* Calamities before Second Coming)

According to the Angel Moroni, one of the major reasons for the "great and marvelous works" of the last days is to prepare a people to be worthy to live with Jesus Christ when he comes again. The second coming of Jesus Christ has been prophesied from the beginning of this earth and will inaugurate the millennial conditions of peace and righteousness upon the earth.

Lucifer does not want the second coming to take place, for at that time all of the wicked on the earth will be destroyed and Lucifer will lose his power. Thus, he is doing and will continue to do everything he can to prevent the second coming. This opposition, together with the general wickedness of people upon the earth, will result in great calamities and destructions before the second coming.

Concerning these impending calamities, the Lord has said: "I the Lord, knowing the calamity which should come upon the inhabitants of the earth, called upon my servant Joseph Smith, Jun., and spake unto him from heaven . . . and also . . . others, that they should proclaim these things unto the world." (D&C 1:17-18.) One specific calamity mentioned is that "the hour . . . is nigh at hand, when peace shall be taken from the earth, and the devil shall have power over his dominion." (1:35.)

Other warnings of calamities are included in other revelations, including a desolating scourge that will cover the land (5:19; 45:31), wars in the United States and in other lands (45:26, 63; 63:33; 87:1-8), the sea will heave itself beyond its bounds, engulfing mighty cities (88:90), great destructions will be caused by lightnings, thunders, and earthquakes

(43:25; 45:33; 87:6; 88:89-90), the sun will be darkened and the moon turned into blood (29:14; 34:9; 45:42; 88:87; 133:49), a great hailstorm will be sent forth to destroy the crops of the earth (29:16; 43:25; 109:30), and flies and maggots shall eat the flesh of the inhabitants of the earth (29:18).

"I was once praying earnestly upon this subject [time of the coming of the Son of Man], and a voice said unto me, 'My son, if thou livest until thou art eighty-five years of age, thou shalt see the face of the Son of Man.' I was left to draw on my own conclusions concerning this; and I took the liberty to conclude that if I had lived to that time, He would make His appearance. But I do not say whether He will make his appearance or I shall go where He is. I prophesy in the name of the Lord God, and let it be written—the Son of Man will not come in the clouds of heaven till I am eighty-five years old. . . . It is not the design of the Almighty to come upon the earth and crush it and grind it to powder but he will reveal it to His servants the prophets. . . .

"Judah must return, Jerusalem must be rebuilt, and the waters of the Dead Sea be healed. [Ezek. 47:8-12.] It will take some time to rebuild the walls of the city and the temple, &c.; and all this must be done before the Son of Man will make His appearance. There will be wars and rumors of wars, signs in the heavens above and on the earth beneath, the sun turned into darkness and the moon to blood, earth-quakes in divers places, the seas heaving beyond their bounds. [D&C 29:14-20; 34:9; 45:31-42; 88:87-91]; then will appear one grand sign of the Son of Man in heaven. [D&C 88:93.] But what will the world do? They will say it is a planet, a comet, &c. But the Son of Man will come as the sign of the coming of the Son of Man, which will be as the light of the morning cometh out of the east. [D&C 43:20-27.]" (Joseph Smith, *HC* 5:336-37.)

"Men profess to prophesy. I will prophesy that the signs of the coming of the Son of Man are already commenced. One pestilence will desolate after another. We shall soon have war and bloodshed. The moon will be turned into blood. I testify of these things, and that the coming of the Son of Man is nigh, even at your doors." (Joseph Smith, *HC* 3:390.)

"By the 'second advent' we understand not the personal appearing of the Son of God to a few, such as His visitation to Saul of Tarsus [Acts 9:3-6; 26:13-16], to Joseph Smith in

1820 [Joseph Smith-History 1:11-20], and again in the Kirtland Temple in 1836 [D&C 110-111]; nor later manifestations to his worthy servants as specifically promised [D&C
35:20-21; 67:11-14; 88:67-68; 76:22-24]; but His yet future
coming in power and great glory, accompanied by hosts of
resurrected and glorified beings, to execute judgment upon
the earth and to inaugurate a reign of righteousness." (James
E. Talmage, *JS*, p. 780.)

"Before the end shall come, the sun shall be darkened,
and the moon be turned to blood, and the stars shall refuse
their shining, and some shall fall, and great destruction
awaits the wicked. There are some, even in the Church, unfortunately, who think that such expressions are cruel, and
they are not willing to accept them as coming from a 'merciful God.' However, man brings the punishment upon
himself and the judgments of the Almighty are bound to
follow. 'Yea, wo be unto the Gentiles except they repent; for
it shall come to pass in that day, saith the Father, that I will
cut off the horses out of the midst of thee, and I will destroy
thy chariots. And I will cut off the cities of the land, and
throw down all thy strongholds. . . . For it shall come to pass,
saith the Father, that at that day whosoever will not repent
and come unto my Beloved Son, them will I cut off from
among my people, O House of Israel; and I will execute
vengeance and fury upon them, even as upon the heathen,
such as they have not heard.' (3 Nephi 21:14-21. Compare
Micah 5:9-15.) Again the Lord has said that the elders
should go forth in power, 'Yea, verily, to seal them up (i.e.,
the wicked) unto the day when the wrath of God shall be
poured out upon the wicked without measure.' (D&C 1:9.)

"We are promised that one of the great signs preceding
the coming of the Lord will be that the sun shall be darkened
and the moon turned to blood. Of course, the turning of the
moon to blood is a figure, and it will appear as a body of
blood. The earth, likewise, will reel to and fro as a drunken
man and then shall appear the sign of the Son of Man in the
heavens. (Matt. 24:29-30.) It will then be the time of the
gathering of the righteous 'from one end of heaven to the
other.' It will be at this time, most likely, when the great city
of Enoch will return. . . .

"The prophets all through the ages, when predicting the
time of the second coming of our Lord, have spoken of the

destruction of the wicked. Isaiah, in his twenty-fourth chapter, said: 'Therefore hath the curse devoured the earth, and they that dwell therein are desolate; therefore the inhabitants of the earth are burned, and few men left.' Malachi speaks of the day coming that shall burn as an oven; 'and all the proud, yea, and all that do wickedly, shall be stubble; and the day that cometh shall burn them up, saith the Lord of hosts, that it shall leave them neither root nor branch.' (Joseph Fielding Smith, *CHMR* 1:156-57.)

Scriptural References: Check the index of Doctrine and Covenants for *Coming of the Son of Man* and *Coming, the Lord's Second.*

Seer; prophet, seer, and revelator (*see also* Prophet)

A seer is one who sees, a *see-er.* The Book of Mormon indicates that a seer is a person who has the right to use the "holy interpreters" or the Urim and Thummim. (Mosiah 8:13-17; Mosiah 28:10-16.) Ammon also testified that "a seer is a revelator and a prophet also; and a gift which is greater can no man have." (Mosiah 8:16.) The members of the First Presidency and Council of the Twelve Apostles, together with the Patriarch to the Church, are sustained by members of the Church as "prophet, seers, and revelators."

Selected Quotations

"The President of the Church is sustained by the people as 'Prophet, Seer, and Revelator, and President of the Church of Jesus Christ of Latter-day Saints.' This is in compliance with the revealed word of God. The first revelation received by Joseph Smith after the organization of the Church on April 6, 1830, specifically declares that 'there shall be a record kept among you; and in it thou shalt be called a seer, a translator, a prophet, an apostle of Jesus Christ, an elder of the church through the will of God the Father, and the grace of your Lord Jesus Christ.' (D&C 21:1.) . . .

"The counselors to the President and the Council of the Twelve Apostles and, usually, the Patriarch to the Church, are also sustained as 'prophets, seers, and revelators.' This conforms to the Priesthood conferred upon them, and to their official calling in the Church. . . .

"When others besides the President of the Church hold the title 'prophet, seer, and revelator,' it follows that the 'power and authority' thus represented are called into action only by appointment from the President of the Church, otherwise there might be a conflict of authority. This is well illustrated in the practice of the Church. For example, a man may be ordained a High Priest, an office in which the right of presidency is inherent, but he presides only when called to do so. It is even so with the exercise of authority under these sacred titles. . . .

"A seer is one who sees with spiritual eyes. He perceives the meaning of that which seems obscure to others; therefore he is an interpreter and clarifier of eternal truth. He foresees the future from the past and present. This he does by the power of the Lord operating through him directly, or indirectly with the aid of divine instruments such as the Urim and Thummim. In short, he is one who sees, who walks in the Lord's light with open eyes. (Mosiah 8:15-17.) . . .

"A revelator makes known, with the Lord's help, something before unknown. It may be new or forgotten truth, or a new or forgotten application of known truth to man's need. Always, the revelator deals with truth, certain truth (D&C 100:11) and always it comes with the divine stamp of approval. Revelation may be received in various ways, but it always presupposes that the revelator has so lived and conducted himself as to be in tune or harmony with the divine spirit of revelation, the spirit of truth, and therefore capable of receiving divine messages. . . .

"In summary: A prophet is a teacher of known truth; a seer is a perceiver of hidden truth, a revelator is a bearer of new truth. In the widest sense, the one most commonly used, the title, prophet, includes the other titles and names of the prophet, a teacher, perceiver, and bearer of truth.

"One who bears the title of prophet, and they who sustain him as such, are first of all believers in God, and in a divine plan of salvation for the human family; and secondly, they commit themselves to the task of bringing to pass the purposes of the Almighty. They believe that the children of men are capable of receiving and obeying truth. Were it not so, the title 'prophet, seer, and revelator' would be empty, hollow words. As it is, they are clarion calls of the Church of Christ to a world walking in the dim shadows of misunderstanding." (John A. Widtsoe, *ER*, pp. 256-59.)

"A seer is greater than a prophet. [Mosiah 8:15.] One may be a prophet without being a seer; but a seer is essentially a prophet—if by 'prophet' is meant not only a spokesman, but likewise a foreteller. Joseph Smith was both prophet and seer.

"A seer is one who sees. But it is not the ordinary sight that is meant. The seeric gift is a supernatural endowment. Joseph was 'like unto Moses'; and Moses, who saw God face to face, explains how he saw him in these words: 'Now mine own eyes have beheld God; but not my natural, but my spiritual eyes, for my natural eyes could not have beheld; for I should have withered and died in his presence; but his glory was upon me; and I beheld his face, for I was transfigured before him.' (Moses 1:11.) Such is the testimony of the ancient seer, as brought to light by the seer of the latter days." (Orson F. Whitney, *SNT*, p. 39.)

Scriptural References: D&C 21:1; 107:92; 124:94, 125; 127:12: 135:3; Moses 6:36, 38; JS-H 1:35; 2 Chr. 9:29; 12:15; 16:7, 10; 19:2; 29:25, 30; 35:15; 2 Ne. 3:6-7, 11, 14; Mosiah 8:13, 15-17; 28:16.

Setting apart

The basic meaning of the term *setting apart* is "to distinguish" or "to make unique"; thus, "to set apart." In the Church today, the term is used to denote a blessing pronounced by authorized members of the priesthood upon the heads of persons, both male and female, who are "set apart" to positions of responsibility. Such actions must comply with the law of common consent. (D&C 20:65; 26:2; 28:13.)

Selected Quotations

"The setting apart is an established practice in the Church and men and women are 'set apart' to special reponsibility, in ecclesiastical, quorum, and auxiliary positions. All missionaries are set apart and it is remarkable how many of them speak often of the authority who officiate and of the blessings promised and their fulfilment. To some folk the setting apart seems a perfunctory act while others anticipate it eagerly, absorb every word of it, and let their lives be lifted thereby. The setting apart may be taken literally; it is a setting apart from sin, apart from the carnal; apart from every thing which is crude, low, vicious, cheap, or vulgar; set apart from the world to a higher plane of thought and activity. The blessing is conditional upon faithful performance." (Spencer W. Kimball, *CR*, October 1958, p. 57.)

Scriptural References: D&C 20:67; 107:22.

Sex sins; unchastity; adultery; abortion (*see also* Ten Commandments)

The power to procreate—to have children—is a God-given gift that is to be used in righteousness for divine purposes in this life. Our Heavenly Father does not bestow this gift until the person has matured to the age when he should have powers of discernment and know the difference between good and evil. Furthermore, he has specified clearly through the teachings of His prophets how, when, and for what purposes these powers are to be used. Violations of these principles are serious offenses in the sight of God.

Selected Quotations

"God is the same yesterday, today, and forever. He has never intended that we should change or update with our vision the moral issues which he established long ago. Sin is still sin and always will be. We stand for a life of cleanliness. From childhood through youth and to the grave, we proclaim the wickedness of sexual life of any kind before marriage, and we proclaim that every one in marriage should hold himself or herself to the covenants that were made.

"In other words, as we have frequently said, there should be total chastity of men and women before marriage and total fidelity in marriage. The fact that so-called sex revolutionists would change the order and change the status is repugnant to us. We abhor, with all our power, pornography, permissiveness, and the so-called freedom of the sexes, and we fear that those who have supported, taught, and encouraged the permissiveness that brings about this immoral behavior will someday come to a sad reckoning with Him who has established the standards.

"Again we repeat the stirring words of the Savior: 'Why call ye me, Lord, Lord, and do not the things which I say?' (Luke 6:46.)" (Spencer W. Kimball, *Ensign,* November 1975, pp. 6-7.)

"Again we see history repeating itself. When we see the pornography, the adulterous practices, homosexuality gone rampant, the looseness and permissiveness of an apparently increasing proportion of the people, we say the days of Satan have returned and history seems to repeat itself.

"When we see the depravity of numerous people of our

own society in their determination to force upon people vulgar presentations, filthy communications, unnatural practices, we wonder, has Satan reached forth with his wicked, evil hand to pull into his forces the people of this earth? Do we not have enough good people left to stamp out the evil which threatens our world? Why do we continue to compromise with evil and why do we continue to tolerate sin?" (Spencer W. Kimball, *Ensign*, May 1975, p. 109.)

"Since the sanctity of the body is so related to the sanctity of sex, why make the body so common? Why expose to the public eye this sacred thing which is the temple of God? I tell you, girls, when you expose your bodies, whether on the dance floor, or otherwise, you do yourselves a great injustice, and you likewise do your boy friend an injury. I wish you girls could sit behind the curtain sometimes when we have private interviews with boys, and these boys really express themselves, man to man, about how they feel concerning modesty of dress. I have talked to many of these boys. Some of them have told me that their moral downfall began with a girl's immodest dress. They were tempted, right on the dance floor, just by what they could see, just by what was not properly covered up." (Mark E. Petersen, *Toward a Better Life*, p. 125.)

Abortion

The sin of abortion has been linked with the taking of life in seriousness and has been clearly denounced by leaders of the Church.

"We decry abortions and ask our people to refrain from this serious transgression. We have stated the following regarding this sin: 'The Church [vigorously] opposes abortion and counsels its members not to submit to or perform an abortion. . . . Abortion must be considered one of the most revolting and sinful practices in this day, when we are witnessing the frightening evidence of permissiveness leading to sexual immorality. Members of the Church guilty of being parties to the sin of abortion must be subjected to the disciplinary action of the councils of the Church as circumstances warrant. The Lord stated in the 59th section, "Thou shalt not steal; neither commit adultery, nor kill, nor do anything like unto it." ' " (Spencer W. Kimball, *Ensign*, November 1975, p. 6.)

"I thank the Father that His Only Begotten Son did not say in defiant protest at Calvary, 'My body is my own!' I stand in admiration of women today who resist the fashion of abortion, by refusing to make the sacred womb a tomb!" (Neal A. Maxwell, *Ensign*, May 1978, p. 10.)

"Abortion, the taking of life, is one of the most grievous of sins. We have repeatedly affirmed the position of the Church in unalterably opposing all abortions, except in two rare instances: When conception is the result of forcible rape and when competent medical counsel indicates that a mother's health would otherwise be seriously jeopardized.

"Certainly the tragedy of abortion often begins with a visit to an X-rated motion picture theater or fingering through an obscene magazine. The path to the grievous sins of fornication, adultery, and homosexuality can begin, too, with the viewing of some of the sex- and violence-oriented programs now being shown on television, including network television.

"We must put on the armor of righteousness and resist with all our might these satanic influences. The time is now when members of The Church of Jesus Christ of Latter-day Saints must take a stand fearlessly and relentlessly for the Lord's ways as opposed to those of Satan." (Spencer W. Kimball, *Ensign*, November 1976, p. 6.)

Adultery

"To us of this Church, the Lord has declared that adulterers should not be admitted to membership (D&C 42:76); that adulterers in the Church, if unrepentant, should be cast out (D&C 42:75), but if repentant should be permitted to remain (D&C 42:74, 42:25) and, He said, 'By this ye may know if a man repenteth of his sins—behold, he will confess them and forsake them.' (D&C 58:43.)

"In the great revelation on the three heavenly glories, the Lord said, speaking of those who will inherit the lowest of these, or the telestial glory: 'These are they who are liars, and sorcerers, and adulterers, and whoremongers, and whosoever loves and makes a lie.' (D&C 76:103.)

"The doctrine of the Church is that sexual sin—the illicit sexual relations of men and women—stands, in its enormity, next to murder. The Lord has drawn no essential distinctions between fornication, adultery, and harlotry or prostitution. Each has fallen under His solemn and awful condemnation.

"You youths of Zion, you cannot associate in nonmarital, illicit sex relationships, which is fornication, and escape the punishments and the judgments which the Lord has declared against this sin. The day of reckoning will come just as certainly as night follows day. They who would palliate this crime and say that such indulgence is but a sinless gratification of a normal desire, like appeasing hunger and thirst, speak filthiness with their lips. Their counsel leads to destruction: their wisdom comes from the Father of Lies.

"You husbands and wives who have taken on solemn obligations of chastity in the holy temples of the Lord and who violate those sacred vows by illicit sexual relations with others, you not only commit the vile and loathsome sin of adultery, but you break the oath you yourselves made with the Lord Himself before you went to the altar for your sealing. You become subject to the penalties which the Lord has prescribed for those who breach their covenants with Him.

"Of the harlots and those who visit them, God speaks in terms of divine contempt. They are they who have bargained away an eternity of bliss for the momentary pleasures of the flesh. The Lord will have only a clean people. He has said, 'I, the Lord, will contend with Zion, and plead with her strong ones, and chasten her until she overcomes and is clean before me.' (D&C 90:36.) But they who sin may repent, and, they repenting, God will forgive them, for the Lord has said, 'Behold, he who has repented of his sins, the same is forgiven, and I, the Lord, remember them no more.' (D&C 58:42.)

"By virtue of the authority in us vested as the First Presidency of the Church, we warn our people who are offending, of the degradation, the wickedness, the punishment that attend upon unchastity; we urge you to remember the blessings which flow from the living of the clean life; we call upon you to keep, day in and day out, the way of strictest chastity, through which only can God's choice gifts come to you and His Spirit abide with you.

"How glorious is he who lives the chaste life. He walks unfearful in the full glare of the noonday sun, for he is without moral infirmity. He can be reached by no shafts of base calumny, for his armor is without flaw. His virtue cannot be challenged by any just accuser, for he lives above reproach. His cheek is never blotched with shame, for he is without hidden sin. He is honored and respected by all mankind, for he is beyond their censure. He is loved by the Lord, for he stands without blemish. The exaltations of eternities await his coming." (First Presidency, *CR*, October 1942, pp. 11-12.)

Birth Control

"The world teaches birth control. Tragically, many of our sisters subscribe to its pills and practices when they could easily provide earthly tabernacles for more of our Father's children. We know that every spirit assigned to this earth will come, whether through us or someone else. There are couples in the Church who think they are getting along just fine with their limited families but who will someday suffer the pains of remorse when they meet the spirits that might have been part of their posterity. The first commandment given to man was to multiply and replenish the earth with children. That commandment has never been altered, modified, or cancelled. The Lord did not say to multiply and replenish the earth if it is convenient, or if you are wealthy, or after you have gotten your schooling, or when there is peace on earth, or until you have four children. The Bible says, 'Lo, children are an heritage of the Lord: . . . Happy is the man that hath his quiver full of them. . . .' (Ps. 127:3, 5.) We believe God is glorified by having numerous children and a program of perfection for them. So also will God glorify that husband and wife who have a large posterity and who have tried to raise them up in righteousness.

"The precepts of men would have you believe that by limiting the population of the world, we can have peace and plenty. That is the doctrine of the devil. Small numbers do not insure peace; only righteousness does. After all, there were only a handful of men on the earth when Cain interrupted the peace of Adam's household by slaying Abel. On the other hand, the whole city of Enoch was peaceful; and it was taken into heaven because it was made up of righteous people.

"And so far as limiting the population in order to provide plenty is concerned, the Lord answered that falsehood in the Doctrine and Covenants when he said: 'For the earth is full, and there is enough and to spare; yea, I prepared all things, and have given unto the children of men to be agents unto themselves.' (D&C 104:17.)

"A major reason why there is famine in some parts of the world is because evil men have used the vehicle of govern-

ment to abridge the freedom that men need to produce
abundantly. True to form, many of the people who desire to
frustrate God's purposes of giving mortal tabernacles to his
spirit children through worldwide birth control are the very
same people who support the kinds of government that per-
petuate famine. They advocate an evil to cure the results of
the wickedness they support." (Ezra Taft Benson, *IE,* June
1969, pp. 43-44.)

"Those who have taken upon themselves the responsibility of wedded life should see to it that they do not abuse
the course of nature; that they do not destroy the principle of
life within them, nor violate any of the commandments of
God. The command which he gave in the beginning to multiply and replenish the earth is still in force upon the
children of men. Possibly no greater sin could be committed
by the people who have embraced this Gospel than to
prevent or to destroy life in the manner indicated. We are
born into the world that we may have life, and we live that
we may have a fulness of joy; we must obey the law of our
creation and the law by which we may obtain the consum-
mation of our righteous hopes and desires—eternal life."
(Joseph F. Smith, *GD,* p. 347.)

Homosexuality

"Homosexuality is an ugly sin, . . . defined as 'sexual
desire for those of the same sex or sexual relations between
individuals of the same sex,' whether men or women. It is a
sin of the ages. . . .

". . . If all the people in the world were to accept homosexuality, as it seems to have been accepted in Sodom
and Gomorrah, the practice would still be deep, dark sin.

"Those who would claim that the homosexual is a third
sex and that there is nothing wrong in such associations can
hardly believe in God or in his scriptures.

". . . Clearly it is hostile to God's purpose in that it negates
his first and great commandment to 'multiply and replenish
the earth.' If the abominable practice became universal it
would depopulate the earth in a single generation." (Spencer
W. Kimball, *MF,* pp. 78-79, 81.)

"A homosexual relationship is viewed by The Church of
Jesus Christ of Latter-day Saints as sin in the same degree as
adultery and fornication.

"In summarizing the intended destiny of man, the Lord has declared: 'For behold, this is my work and my glory—to bring to pass the immortality and eternal life of man.' (Moses 1:39.) Eternal life means returning to the Lord's exalted presence and enjoying the privilege of eternal increase. According to his revealed word, the only acceptable sexual relationship occurs within the family between a husband and a wife.

"Homosexuality in men and women runs counter to these divine objectives and, therefore, is to be avoided and forsaken. Church members involved to any degree must repent. 'By this ye may know if a man repenteth of his sins—behold, he will confess them and forsake them.' (D&C 58:43.) Failure to work closely with one's bishop or stake president in cases involving homosexual behavior will require prompt Church court action." (First Presidency, *Priesthood Bulletin,* February 1973.)

Masturbation

"Most youth come into contact early with masturbation. Many would-be authorities declare that it is natural and acceptable, and frequently young men I interview cite these advocates to justify their practice of it. To this we must respond that the world's norms in many areas—drinking, smoking, and sex experience generally, to mention only a few—depart increasingly from God's law. The Church has a different, higher norm. Thus prophets anciently and today condemn masturbation. It includes feelings of guilt and shame. It is detrimental to spirituality. It indicates slavery to the flesh, not that mastery of it and the growth toward godhood which is the object of our mortal life. Our modern prophet has indicated that no young man should be called on a mission who is not free from this practice." (Spencer W. Kimball, *MF*, p. 77.)

Necking and Petting

"Among the most common sexual sins our young people commit are necking and petting. Not only do these improper relations often lead to fornication, pregnancy, and abortions—all ugly sins—but in and of themselves they are pernicious evils, and it is often difficult for youth to distinguish where one ends and another begins. They awaken lust and stir evil thoughts and sex desires. They are but parts of the whole family of related sins and indiscretions. Paul wrote as if to modern young people who deceive themselves that their necking and petting are but expressions of love: 'Wherefore God also gave them up to uncleanness through the lusts of their own hearts, to dishonour their own bodies between themselves.' (Rom. 1:24.) How could the evils of petting be more completely described?

"Too often, young people dismiss their petting with a shrug of their shoulders as a *little* indiscretion, while admitting that fornication is a base transgression. Too many of them are shocked, or feign to be, when told that what they have done in the name of petting was in reality fornication. The dividing line is a thin, blurry one, and Paul probably referred to these sins ranging from petting to fornication when he said 'For it is a shame even to speak of those things which are done of them in secret.' (Eph. 5:12.) And the Lord perhaps was referring to this evil when in our own time he was reiterating the Ten Commandments: '. . . Neither commit adultery, nor kill, nor do anything like unto it.' (D&C 59:6.). . .

"Those who have received the Holy Ghost after baptism certainly know that all bodily contacts of this kind are pernicious and abominable. They recognize too that the God of yesterday, today, and tomorrow continues to demand continence and to require that people come to the marriage altar as virgins, clean and free from sex experience.

"Almost like twins, 'petting'—and especially 'heavy petting'—and fornication are alike. Also like twins, the one precedes the other, but most of the same characteristics are there. The same passions are aroused and, with but slight difference, similar bodily contacts are made. And from it are likely to come the same frustrations, sorrows, anguish, and remorse." (Spencer W. Kimball, *MF,* pp. 65-67.)

Pornography

"We hope that our parents and leaders will not tolerate pornography. It is really garbage, but today is peddled as normal and satisfactory food. Many writers seem to take delight in polluting the atmosphere with it. Seemingly, it cannot be stopped by legislation. There is a link between pornography and the low, sexual drives and perversions. We live in a culture which venerates the orgasm, streaking, trading wives, and similar crazes. How low can humans plunge!

We pray with our Lord that we may be kept from being in the world. It is sad that decent people are thrown into a filthy area of mental and spiritual pollution. We call upon all of our people to do all in their power to offset this ugly revolution.

"It is ridiculous to imply that pornography has no effect. There is a definite relationship to crime. Murder, robbery, rape, prostitution, and commercialized vice are fed on this immorality. Sex statistics seem to reflect a relationship between crime and pornography.

"It is utterly without redeeming social value. We urge our families to protect their children in every way possible. We live in a permissive world, but we must make certain we do not become a part of that permissive world, that degenerate world. We are shocked at the depths to which many people of this world go to assert their freedom. We fear that the trends of permissiveness toward immorality are destroying the moral fabric of our generation." (Spencer W. Kimball, *Ensign*, November 1974, p. 7.)

Sex Changes

"Some people are ignorant or vicious and apparently attempting to destroy the concept of masculinity and femininity. More and more girls dress, groom, and act like men. More and more men dress, groom, and act like women. The high purposes of life are damaged and destroyed by the growing unisex theory. God made man in his own image, male and female made he them. With relatively few accidents of nature, we are born male or female. The Lord knew best. Certainly, men and women who would change their sex status will answer to their Maker." (Spencer W. Kimball, *Ensign*, November 1974, p. 8.)

Scriptural References: D&C 42:24, 74; 63:17; 76:103; Ex. 20:14; Lev. 20:10; Matt. 5:28; 15:19; 19:9; Acts 15:20; 1 Cor. 6:9; Col. 3:5; 1 Thes. 4:3; 2 Tim. 3:3; Alma 39:5; 3 Ne. 12:28, 32.

Signs (*see also* Miracles, for related material)

Signs are not given to replace faith; they are given to help in the development of faith that is already present. "Signs shall follow them that believe." (Mark 16:17.) One of the major purposes for our mortal existence is to give us the opportunity to learn to walk by faith. A veil of forgetfulness is placed over our minds when we are born into this world so that we will not remember our previous existence with our Father in heaven. Therefore, we must exercise faith in him and in his prophets and his scriptures before we can come to know him as we did before we came to the earth.

If man should arrive at a knowledge of God only through signs rather than through faith, one of the major purposes of our mortal existence would not be realized. Also, when we ask for signs we are trying to change, modify, or adulterate the eternal plan of our Heavenly Father. It is indeed a wicked and adulterous generation which seeks for a sign. (Matt. 12:39.)

Selected Quotations

"I will give you one of the *Keys* of the mysteries of the Kingdom. It is an eternal principle, that has existed with God from all eternity: That man who rises up to condemn others, finding fault with the Church, saying that they are out of the way, while he himself is righteous, then know assuredly, that that man is in the high road to apostasy; and if he does not repent, will apostatize, as God lives. The principle is as correct as the one that Jesus put forth in saying that he who seeketh a sign is an adulterous person; and that principle is eternal, undeviating, and firm as the pillars of heaven; for whenever you see a man seeking after a sign, you may set it down that he is an adulterous man." (Joseph Smith, *HC* 3:385.)

"When the voice of the Good Shepherd is heard, the honest in heart believe and receive it. It is good to taste with the inward taste, to see with the inward eyes, and to enjoy with the sensations of the ever-living spirit. No person, unless he is an adulterer, a fornicator, covetous, or an idolator, will ever require a miracle; in other words, no good, honest person ever will." (Brigham Young, *DBY*, p. 340.)

"It is a wicked and adulterous generation that seeketh after a sign. Show me Latter-day Saints who have to feed upon miracles, signs and visions in order to keep them steadfast in the Church, and I will show you members of the Church who are not in good standing before God, and who are walking in slippery paths. It is not by marvelous manifestations unto us that we shall be established in the truth, but it is by humility and faithful obedience to the commandments and laws of God." (Joseph F. Smith, *CR,* April 1900, pp. 40-41.)

Scriptural References: D&C 63:7-12; 68:10-11; 84:65; 124:98; Mark 16:17-20; John 4:48; Acts 2:19-22; Jacob 7:13-14; Alma 30:43-51.

Sin; bondage of sin

Sin is the violation of divine law. Every law has an equal and opposite consequence. Whenever a law is kept (righteousness), the consequence is a blessing that results in joy and happiness. Whenever a law is broken (sin or wickedness), the consequence is a punishment that results in misery and unhappiness. When a person breaks a law (sins), he becomes subject to that law, for the law has power over him (the sinner). Thus, he is in the bondage of sin.

Scriptural References: D&C (check index); Rom. 6:18, 23; Mosiah 27:29.

Solemn assembly

A solemn assembly is a special meeting called by the Lord through His prophets to give special instructions or blessings to the Saints. Such assemblies are not held for the world, but only for those who are earnestly striving to become sanctified through obedience to gospel principles and ordinances. All temple dedications are solemn assemblies, but the Lord may also indicate to his prophet when additional such sacred meetings should be held. The Bible mentions several solemn assemblies that were held in ancient times: Lev. 23:36; Num. 29:35; Deut. 16:8; 2 Chr. 7:9; Neh. 8:18; Isaiah 1:10-14; Ezekiel 45:17; 46:11.

Selected Quotations

"Today we have participated in a solemn assembly. Solemn assemblies have been known among the Saints since the days of Israel. They have been of various kinds but generally have been associated with the dedication of a temple or a special meeting appointed for the sustaining of a new First Presidency or a meeting for the priesthood to sustain a revelation, such as the tithing revelation to President Lorenzo Snow....

"Joseph Smith and Brigham Young were first sustained by a congregation, including a fully organized priesthood.

Brigham Young was sustained on March 27, 1846, and was 'unanimously elected president over the whole Camp of Israel . . .' by the council. (B. H. Roberts, *CHC* 3:52.) Later he was sustained, and the Hosanna Shout was given.

"Each of the presidents of the Church has been sustained by the priesthood of the Church in solemn assembly down to and including President Harold B. Lee, who was sustained October 6, 1972.

"Joseph Smith led the first solemn assembly, and after closing his discourse, he called upon the several quorums, commencing with the presidency, to manifest by rising, their willingness to acknowledge him as the prophet and seer and uphold him as such by their prayers and faith. All the quorums in turn cheerfully complied with this request. He then called upon all the congregation of Saints also to give their assent by rising to their feet. He then proceeded to have the quorums of the priesthood and then the Saints in general stand to signify their sustaining; the leaders of the Church and the councils of the Church were similarly approved.

"Joseph Smith said: 'The vote was unanimous in every instance, and I prophesied to all, that inasmuch as they would uphold these men in their several stations, (alluding to the different quorums of the Church), the Lord would bless them . . . in the name of Jesus Christ, the blessings of heaven should be theirs; and when the Lord's anointed go forth to proclaim the word, bearing testimony to this generation, if they receive it they shall be blessed, but if not, the judgments of God will follow close upon them until that city or that house which rejects them shall be desolate.' Then the Hosanna Shout was given." (Spencer W. Kimball, *Ensign*, May 1974, pp. 45-46.)

Scriptural References: D&C 88:70, 117; 95:7; 108:4; 109:6, 10; 124:39; 133:6; Lev. 23:36; Num. 29:35; Deut. 16:8; 2 Kgs. 10:20; 2 Chr. 7:9; Neh. 8:18; Isa. 1:13; Ezek. 14:17; 46:11; Joel 1:14; 2:15; Amos 5:21.

Son Ahman (*see also* Jesus Christ; Son of Man; Adam-ondi-Ahman)

In the language taught by God to Adam (the Adamic language), *Ahman* is the name of God the Father. *Son Ahman* means the Son of God the Father, or Only Begotten Son of God. Jesus Christ uses this title to designate himself in two revelations—D&C 78:20 and 95:17.

Selected Quotations

"There is one revelation that this people are not generally acquainted with. I think it has never been published, but probably it will be in the Church History. It is given in questions and answers. The first question is, 'What is the name of God in the pure language?' The answer says, 'Ahman.' 'What is the name of the Son of God?" Answer, 'Son Ahman—the greatest of all the parts of God excepting Ahman.' " (Orson Pratt, *JD* 2:342.)

"We also learn from the closing verses of this revelation that Jesus Christ is also called Son Ahman. (See D&C 95:17.) Therefore his name is connected with the name of the place where Adam dwelt. For that reason Elder Orson Pratt gives it the interpretation of 'The Valley of God.' " (Joseph Fielding Smith, *CHMR* 1:310.)

Scriptural References: D&C 78:20; 95:17.

Son of Man (*see also* Jesus Christ; Son Ahman)

"Man of Holiness" is the name of God the Father in the Adamic language; the "name of his Only Begotten is the Son of Man, even Jesus Christ, a righteous Judge, who shall come in the meridian of time." (Moses 6:57.) Son of Man (with a capital M) is Jesus Christ and is a shortened version of Son of Man of Holiness.

Selected Quotations

"As the Prophet Joseph said to the Church in early days, so now says the Church unto the world—if the heavens could be rent, and you could see the Eternal Father sitting on His throne, you would see Him like a man in form. That the Eternal Father has called himself a Man is plainly apparent in the testimony of Enoch the Seer; and in the same scripture Jesus Christ is designated 'The Son of Man' even before the time of the flood; 'for in the language of Adam, Man of Holiness is His name, and the name of His Only Begotten is the Son of Man, even Jesus Christ.' (Moses 6:57; compare 7:24, 47, and 54.) In a certain revelation to Enoch, the Eternal Father thus spake: 'Behold, I am God; Man of Holiness is my name, Man of Counsel is my name, also.' (Moses 7:35.) Thus does the light of modern revelation illuminate the dark passages of old." (James E. Talmage, CR, April 1915, p. 123.)

Scriptural References: D&C 45:39; 49:6, 22; 58:65; 61:38;

63:53; 64:23; 65:5; 68:11; 76:16; 109:5; 122:8; 130:14, 15, 17;
Moses 6:57; 7:24, 47, 56, 59, 65; Abr. 3:27; JS-M 1:26, 36-37,
41, 43, 48; Matt. 16:23; 17:9, 12, 22; 18:11; 19:28; 20:18, 28;
24:27, 30, 37, 39, 44; 25:13, 31; 26:2, 24, 45, 64.

Spirit of revelation *(see also* Gifts of the Spirit; Revelation)

The spirit of revelation is a gift of the Holy Spirit, which
can be given to man to help him discern when he is receiving
revelation from God. It can be a valuable guide to man to
help direct him throughout his life.

Selected Quotations

"A person may profit by noticing the first intimation of the
spirit of revelation; for instance, when you feel pure intelligence flowing unto you, it may give you sudden strokes
of ideas, so that by noticing it, you may find it fulfilled the
same day or soon; (i. e.) those things that were presented into
your minds by the Spirit of God [D&C 85:6; Enos 10], will
come to pass; and thus by learning the Spirit of God and
understanding it, you may grow into the principle of revelation, until you become perfect in Christ Jesus." (Joseph
Smith, *HC* 3:381.)

"Revelation may be given to every member of the
Church. The Prophet said that every man should be a
prophet; that the testimony of Jesus is the spirit of prophecy.
It is not only the privilege but the duty of each member of
the Church to know the truth which will make him free. This
he cannot know unless it is revealed to him. Moroni has
promised every person who humbly and sincerely reads the
Book of Mormon that he may know by revelation that it is
true. The gift of the Holy Ghost is given to the members of
the Church so that they may have the spirit of prophecy and
revelation. Let it be understood however, that they will not
receive revelation for the guidance of the Church. That gift is
reserved for and vested in the man who holds the keys of the
Priesthood. But the members of the Church are entitled to
receive revelation which is needful for their progress, and if
they will hearken to the Spirit of truth and walk humbly
before the Lord, they will not fall short of this spiritual
guidance. Members of the Church, who neglect their duty
and who are indifferent to the commandments, place
themselves in danger of being deceived. Failing to obtain the
guiding influence of the Holy Ghost, they become liable to

the enticing influence of deceivers because they lack the ability to discern between truth and error. Alma called attention to this in his instruction to Zeezrom. These words it is well for us all to heed. [Alma 12:9-11.]" (Joseph Fielding Smith, *CHMR* 2:217-18.)

"The Lord would not permit me to occupy this position one day of my life, unless I was susceptible to the Holy Spirit and to the revelations of God. It is too late in the day for this church to stand without revelation. Not only the President of the Church should possess this gift and give it unto the people, but his counselors and the Apostles and all men that bear the Holy Priesthood, if they magnify their calling, should possess that gift for themselves and to assist them in their duties, although they may not be called to give revelations to lead and direct the Church. The spirit of revelation belongs to the Priesthood." (Wilford Woodruff, *MS* 56:324.)

Scriptural References: D&C 8:3; 11:25; Eph. 1:17; Alma 4:20; 5:46; 8:24; 9:21; 17:3; 23:6; 43:2; 45:10; Hel. 4:12, 23; 3 Ne. 3:19.

Spirit prison (*see also* Post-earthly spirit world)

When physical death occurs, the spirit of man goes into the post-earthly spirit world, where it is assigned either to paradise or to "outer darkness," depending upon the faithfulness of the man during his mortal probation. (See Alma 40:11-14.) In a sense, both of these places are prisons in that they are places of confinement, for the spirit is limited without its physical body as to what it can do, and the spirit does not regain its physical body until the resurrection. When the spirit is thus separated from its body, it cannot "receive a fulness of joy." (D&C 93:34.) It was to righteous spirits in the limited prison of paradise that the Savior went to preach his gospel as stated by Peter (1 Pet. 3:18-21; 4:6), by Joseph Smith and Sidney Rigdon (D&C 76:73-75), and by Joseph F. Smith (JFS-V 1:28-31).

However, those spirits assigned to "outer darkness" are much more limited as to what they can do. Their portion of the spirit prison has been referred to as hell. Before the atonement of Jesus Christ, there was a gulf between the righteous and the wicked in the post-earthly spirit world, but that gulf was bridged by Jesus Christ as revealed in one of the latest revelations to be canonized by the Church: Joseph

F. Smith—Vision of the Redemption of the Dead, in the Pearl of Great Price.

Scriptural References: D&C 38:5; 76:73; 88:99-100; 128:122; Moses 7:38, 57; JFS-V 1:20, 28, 29, 42, 57; Isa. 24:22; 49:9; 61:1; Luke 4:18; 1 Pet. 3:19; 4:6; 1 Ne. 21:9; Alma 40:13-14.

Spiritual; spiritual death; spiritual life (*see also* Death)

When used by itself and not preceding a noun, the word *spiritual* is frequently used in the Doctrine and Covenants as the opposite of such terms as *natural, temporal, carnal,* and *sensual.* In section 29 the Lord indicates that his commandments "are spiritual; they are not natural nor temporal, neither carnal nor sensual." (29:35.) When used preceding a noun the word *spiritual* emphasizes the importance and/or seriousness of the term. *Spiritual death* refers to the most serious type of death—death as to the things pertaining to righteousness. *Spiritual life* is the opposite—to be alive as to things pertaining to righteousness, to be in the presence of God.

Selected Quotations

"Now what is a spiritual body? It is one that is quickened by spirit and not by blood. Our Father in heaven and our Savior and all those who have passed through the resurrection have physical bodies of flesh and bones, but their bodies are quickened by spirit and not by blood, hence they are spiritual bodies and not blood bodies. The immortal body is quickened by spirit, but the mortal body is quickened by blood." (Joseph Fielding Smith, *DS* 1:76-77.)

Scriptural References: D&C 29:31-35, 41; 67:10; 70:12; 72:14; 77:2; 88:27; 107:8, 18, 32, 80; 128:14; 2 Ne. 9:12; Alma 12:16; 42:9; Hel. 14:16, 18.

Stake

The word *stake* is commonly used in the Church to refer to the administrative unit composed of wards and/or branches. Also, priesthood quorums and auxiliaries function within stakes.

Selected Quotations

"The expression 'stake of Zion,' first used in the revelation given in November 1831 (D&C 68) is taken from the expression in Isaiah: 'Look upon Zion, the city of our solemnities; thine eyes shall see Jerusalem a quiet habitation, a tabernacle that shall not be taken down; not one of the stakes thereof shall ever be removed, neither shall any of the cords thereof be broken.' (Isa. 33:20.) Again: 'Enlarge the place of thy tent and let them stretch forth the curtains of thine habitation: spare not, lengthen thy cords, and strengthen thy stakes.' (Isa. 54:2.) Isaiah speaks of Zion as a tent, or tabernacle, having in mind the Tabernacle which was built and carried in the wilderness in the days of Moses, and the cords are the binding cables that extend from the tent, or tabernacle, to the stakes which are fastened in the ground. Now [D&C 82:13] the Lord revealed that Zion was to be built and surrounding her would be the stakes helping to bind and keep her in place. This figure of speech has almost been lost through the intervening years, but it retains its significance, or beauty. To speak of Zion, the new Jerusalem, or even that section where the city will be built, as a stake of Zion, is a sad mistake. Zion is the tent, the stakes of Zion are the binding pegs that support her. Zion, therefore, cannot be a stake, it would be as improper to call a tent a stake as to apply this term to Zion." (Joseph Fielding Smith, *CHMR* 1:321-22.)

"A stake organization consists of the following: A presidency of three high priests; a high council of twelve high priests; a stake clerk; one or more patriarchs; a high priests' quorum with the stake presidency serving as its presidency, with a secretary; one or more quorums of seventy, each with seven presidents and a secretary; elders' quorums with a presidency and a secretary." (LeGrand Richards, *MWW*, p. 166.)

Scriptural References: D&C 68:25-26; 82:13-14; 101:21; 109:39, 59; 119:7; 124:2, 36, 134, 142; 125:4; 133:9; Isa. 33:20; 54; 3 Ne. 22:2; Moro. 10:31.

Stand ye in holy places

The term *stand in holy places* also has the meaning of "do what is right." In other words, it can refer to a condition as well as to a place.

Selected Quotations

"In these days of our generation, many of you are asking: Where is safety? The word of the Lord is not silent. He has admonished us: 'But my disciples shall stand in holy places, and shall not be moved; but among the wicked, men shall lift up their voices and curse God and die.' (D&C 45:32.)

"The Lord has told us where these 'holy places' are: 'And it shall come to pass among the wicked, that every man that will not take his sword against his neighbor must needs flee unto Zion for safety.' (D&C 45:68.) . . .

"As one studies the Lord's commandments and attending promises upon compliance therewith, one gets some definite ideas as to how we might 'stand in holy places,' as the Lord commands—if we will be preserved with such protection as accords with his holy purposes, in order that we might be numbered among the 'pure in heart' who constitute Zion. . . . As one studies the commandments of God, it seems to be made crystal clear that the all-important thing is not where we live but whether or not our hearts are pure." (Harold B. Lee, *CR*, October 1968, pp. 61-62.)

"I was down in Kelsey, Texas, last November, and I heard a group of anxious people asking, 'Is now the day for us to come up to Zion, where we can come to the mountain of the Lord, where we can be protected from our enemies?' I pondered that question, I prayed about it. What should we say to those people who were in their anxiety? I have studied it a bit, I have learned something of what the Spirit has taught, and I know now that the place of safety in this world is not in any given place; it doesn't make so much difference where we live; but the all-important thing is how we live, and I have found that security can come to Israel only when we keep the commandments, when they live so that they can enjoy the companionship, the direction, the comfort, and the guidance of the Holy Spirit of the Lord, when they are willing to listen to these men whom God has set here to preside as His mouthpieces, and when we obey the counsels of the Church." (Harold B. Lee, *CR*, April 1943, pp. 128-29.)

Scriptural References: D&C 45:32; 87:8; 101:24, 64; 124:39; Heb. 9:24.

Stars shall fall from heaven (*see also* Calamities before second coming; Second coming)

One of the predicted events associated with the second coming of Jesus Christ is that "the stars shall fall from heaven." (29:14; see also 45:42; Joel 2:30-31; Matt. 24:29.)

This event is usually mentioned in the scriptures as occurring at about the same time as "the sun shall be darkened, and the moon shall be turned into blood." (29:14.)

Some of the prophets of this dispensation have suggested that when the earth fell in the days of Adam it was actually placed in a new part of the universe. Thus, when the earth regains its paradisiacal glory, it will move to its former location, changing its relationship to the sun (which shall then be "darkened" in proportion to the new means by which the earth will receive its light) and to the moon (which will then evidently be much farther away and will appear to be red in somewhat the same way Mars is sometimes described as the red planet). As the earth moves through the stars of its present heaven to its new position, these stars will appear to be falling in relationship to the movement of the earth.

Scriptural References: D&C 45:39-42; Joel 2:30-31.

Stealing (*see also* Ten Commandments)

The commandment against stealing has been deemed so important by the Lord that it was not only included in the Decalogue (the Ten Commandments), but also unrepentant thieves are not to remain as members of the Church: "Thou shall not steal; and he that stealeth and will not repent shall be cast out." (D&C 42:20; 59:6; Ex. 20:15; Matt. 19:18; 2 Ne. 26:32.) The ownership of all good things can eventually be traced to the Lord, for he is the Creator of "the heavens and the earth, and all things which in them are." (3 Ne. 9:15.) Thus, the thief steals not only from his fellowman, but from God.

Selected Quotations

"It is astonishing how many men and women who have always lived good lives will yield to temptation to take that which does not belong to them. For the past few years we have been passing through a change. There seems to have been a letting down in the matter of honesty. Our Heavenly Father knew that we would need this commandment when he gave it. . . .

" 'Thou shalt not steal.' This commandment was given to ancient Israel and punishment was meted out to those in that day who were dishonest. It is binding upon us today and I want to say to you that the punishment that is meted out to those who are dishonest in our day, when they are apprehended and hailed before the courts of the land and punished for their crimes, is insignificant when compared with the spiritual punishment that befalls us when we transgress the law of honesty and violate that commandment of God." (George Albert Smith, *CR*, October 1932, pp. 24-26.)

"Our faith has been greatly strained, as we have learned of the profligate stealing in some communities, where millions of dollars are taken by shoplifters from our merchants. In the end, the public must eventually pay. Why would any man, woman, or child steal from the friendly merchants and his folks and neighbors? This is unbelievable. And great losses are sustained with the incredible amount of vandalism. It was the Lord who gave us the injunction: 'Thou shalt not steal.' (Ex. 20:15.)" (Spencer W. Kimball, *Ensign*, November 1977, pp. 4-5.)

Scriptural References: D&C 42:20, 85; 59:6; Ex. 20:15; Matt. 19:18; Mosiah 2:13; 13:22; 29:14.

Steward; stewardship; "wise steward"

A steward is a manager, a supervisor, a director, an agent. The word is frequently used in regard to the management of physical possession or of land (stewardship). However, in his revelations, the Lord also uses these terms in regard to the scriptures and revelations (70:3), to literary efforts (72:20), to responsibilities in the priesthood (42:70), and to receiving the commandments of the Lord in general. A "wise steward" is one who magnifies his position and wisely administers his stewardship.

Selected Quotations

"Every leader in his place is accountable for his stewardship. . . . We shall have to give an account before the God of heaven when we go into the spirit world and meet Him there for the use of this Priesthood and the keys of the kingdom which . . . have been committed unto the hands of this people, and God will hold us responsible for the use we make of these blessings, privileges, and powers which we enjoy in connection therewith. The eyes of God and his angels, and of every man who dwells in the Celestial World are watching us and the courses we pursue." (Harold B. Lee, *CR*, April 1963, pp. 80-81.)

Scriptural References: D&C 42:32, 70; 51:19; 64:40; 69:5; 70:4, 9; 72:3; 78:22; 82:11; 101:90; 104:11; 124:14; 136:27; Luke 16:2; 1 Cor. 4:2; Titus 1:7; 1 Pet. 4:10.

Storehouse; bishop's storehouse

Scriptural references to the bishop's storehouse include the idea of a system of taking care of the physical needs of the poor as well as to a building where necessary commodities might be stored. At the present time, the system of bishop's storehouses is part of the welfare services plan of the Church.

Selected Quotations

"The Church storehouse system is an organization of physical warehouses and transportation facilities, with operating and managing personnel. This system is set up to receive, store, transport, exchange, and distribute food and nonfood commodities to those in need.

"A fundamental unit of the Church storehouse system is the local bishops storehouse. Bishops storehouses are Church-owned facilities from which local bishops obtain food, clothing, and other commodities to care for the poor and needy who are unable to care for themselves. Deseret Industries are used as storehouses to provide nonfood commodities. Each bishop in the Church should have access to a local storehouse stocked with essential commodities produced in the program to meet the needs of his people.

"The Lord, by revelation, has commanded that storehouses be established. The surpluses, or 'residue,' from the consecrated properties under the united order were to be kept in the storehouses 'to administer to the poor and the needy.' (D&C 42:34.) Later, the Lord instructed that the Presiding Bishop 'appoint a storehouse unto this church; and let all things both in money and in [food], which are more than is needful for the wants of this people, be kept in the hands of the bishop.' (D&C 51:13.)

". . . Our bishops storehouses are not intended to stock enough commodities to care for all the members of the Church. Storehouses are only established to care for the poor and the needy. For this reason, members of the Church have been instructed to personally store a year's supply of food, clothing, and, where possible, fuel. By following this counsel, most members will be prepared and able to care for themselves and their family members, and be able to share with others as may be needed." (Ezra Taft Benson, *Ensign*, May 1977, p. 82.)

"Storehouses bless the members of the Church by helping them live their covenants of sacrifice and consecration. Indeed, the Lord states in the eighty-third section of the Doctrine and Covenants that 'the storehouse shall be kept by the consecrations of the church.' (D&C 83:6.) President Clark reminds us: 'Our storehouses today under the welfare plan are kept, in fact, by the consecrations of the Church, that is, of the membership of the Church. The storehouses we have now are . . . stocked by the produce raised and materials fabricated for the purpose by the Church members. These contributions are truly consecrations, for they are freely and gratuitously given, with no claim back by the donor either as to the contributions themselves or to compensations therefor.' (President J. Reuben Clark, Jr., address at bishops' meeting, Oct. 6, 1944.)" (Victor L. Brown, *Ensign*, November 1976, p. 114.)

Scriptural References: D&C 42:34, 55; 51:3; 58:24, 37; 70:7, 11; 72:10; 78:3; 82:18; 83:5, 6; 90:23; 101:96; Mal. 3:10; Luke 12:24; 3 Ne. 24:10.

Strait; strait gate

The word *strait* should not be confused with *straight,* which is pronounced the same although spelled differently. *Strait* means "narrow, close fitting, limited in space or time." The strait gate leading to the kingdom of God on the earth (the Church) is narrow and restricted, meaning certain conditions must be met before the person can enter. Thus, "few there be that find it." Similarly, a strait gate protects all the ordinances of the gospel, including the path "that leadeth unto the exaltation and continuation of the lives." (D&C 132:22.)

Selected Quotations

"There are those who complain that to follow the straight and narrow path requires limitations, restrictions, overcoming, and doing without things that are very tempting. We must remember, however, that it guarantees victory and achievement of our goal, which is gained by setting a goal and being able to concentrate and follow an undeviating course.

"*Narrow* is a very meaningful word. Often people accuse us of being narrow-minded if we are following the straight and narrow path, which certainly does require self-restraint and self-denial. We must realize and be prepared to accept the fact that it confines us, restricts us, and limits us in certain areas. But let us fully realize that it does not fetter or shackle mankind. On the contrary, it is the way to emancipation, independence, and liberty." (N. Eldon Tanner, *Ensign,* May 1975, p. 76.)

Scriptural References: D&C 22:2; 132:22; Matt. 7:13-14; Luke 13:24; Jacob 6:11; 3 Ne. 14:13-14; 27:33.

Succession to the office of President

The procedure is well established that upon the death of the President of the Church, the President of the Council of the Twelve Apostles becomes the presiding officer of the Church on the earth. He continues in this position until the Quorum of the First Presidency is reorganized and until the new President of the Church is ordained and set apart to his new position.

It is also a well-established procedure in the Church that the President of the Council of the Twelve will become the new President of the Church. In fact, he is already the presiding officer of the Church in his position as President of the Twelve as long as there is no Quorum of the First Presidency organized above him; as President of the Quorum of the First Presidency, he continues in the role of the presiding officer.

The prophets, seers, and revelators of this century have clearly and definitely taught that this order of succession to the presidency of the Church is the will of the Lord and will continue. Thus the Council of the Twelve Apostles provides important training opportunities for future presidents of the Church.

Selected Quotations

"To those who ask the question: How is the President of the Church chosen or elected? the correct and simple answer should be a quotation of the fifth Article of Faith: 'We believe that a man must be called of God, by prophecy, and by the laying on of hands, by those who are in authority, to preach the Gospel and administer in the ordinances thereof.'

"The beginning of the call of one to be President of the Church actually begins when he is called, ordained, and set apart to become a member of the Quorum of the Twelve Apostles. Such a call by prophecy, or in other words, by the inspiration of the Lord to the one holding the keys of presidency, and the subsequent ordination and setting apart by the laying on of hands by that same authority, places each apostle in a priesthood quorum of twelve men holding the apostleship.

"Each apostle so ordained under the hands of the President of the Church, who holds the keys of the kingdom of God in concert with all other ordained apostles, has given to him the priesthood authority necessary to hold every position in the Church, even to a position of presidency over the Church if he were called by the presiding authority and sustained by a vote of a constituent assembly of the membership of the Church.

"The Prophet Joseph Smith declared that 'where the president is not, there is no First Presidency.' Immediately following the death of a President, the next ranking body, the Quorum of the Twelve Apostles, becomes the presiding authority, with the President of the Twelve automatically becoming the acting President of the Church until a President of the Church is officially ordained and sustained in his office.

"Early in this dispensation, because of certain conditions, the Council of Twelve continued to preside as a body for as long as three years before the reorganization was effected. As conditions in the Church became more stabilized, the reorganization was effected promptly following the passing of the President of the Church.

"All members of the First Presidency and the Twelve are regularly sustained as 'prophets, seers, and revelators,' as you have done today. This means that any one of the apostles, so chosen and ordained, could preside over the Church if he were 'chosen by the body [which has been interpreted to mean, the entire Quorum of the Twelve], appointed and ordained to that office, and upheld by the confidence, faith, and prayer of the church,' to quote from a revelation on this subject, on one condition, and that being that he was the senior member, or the president, of that body. (See D&C 107:22.)

"Occasionally the question is asked as to whether or not one other than the senior member of the Twelve could become President. Some thought on this matter would suggest that any other than the senior member could become President of the Church only if the Lord reveals to that President of the Twelve that someone other than himself could be selected. The Lord revealed to the first prophet of this dispensation the orderly plan from the Church leadership by a predetermined organization of the earthly kingdom of God. [D&C 107:22-24 quoted.]

"With reference to this subject, the fourth President of the Church, Wilford Woodruff, made a few observations in a letter to President Heber J. Grant, then a member of the Twelve, under date of March 28, 1887. I quote from that letter: '. . . when the President of the Church dies, who then is the Presiding Authority of the Church? It is the Quorum of the Twelve Apostles (ordained and organized by the revelations of God and none else). Then while these Twelve Apostles preside over the Church, who is the President of the Church[?] It is the President of the Twelve Apostles. And he is virtually as much the President of the Church while presiding over Twelve men as he is when organized as the Presidency of the Church, and presiding over two men.' And this principle has been carried out now for 140 years—ever since the organization of the Church." (Harold B. Lee, *IE*, June 1970, pp. 28-29.)

"Do you know of any reason in case of the death of the President of the Church why the Twelve Apostles should not choose some other than the President of the Twelve to be the President of the Church?

"I know of several reasons why they should not. First, at the death of the President of the Church the Twelve Apostles become the presiding authority of the Church, and the president of the Twelve is really the President of the Church, by virtue of his office as much while presiding over the Twelve Apostles as while presiding over his two counselors. . . . Second, in case of the death of the President of the Church it takes a majority of the Twelve Apostles to appoint the President of the Church, and it is very unreasonable to suppose that the majority of that quorum could be converted to depart from the course marked out by inspiration and followed by the Apostles at the death of Christ and by the Twelve Apostles at the death of Joseph Smith." (Wilford Woodruff, in Matthias F. Cowley, *Wilford Woodruff*, p. 561.)

"We frequently hear discussions in our classes and between brethren to the effect that any man could be called, if the authorities should choose him, to preside over the Church, and that it is not the fixed order to take the senior apostle to preside, and any member of that quorum could be appointed. The fact is that the senior apostle automatically becomes the presiding officer of the Church on the death of the President. If some other man were to be chosen, then the senior would have to receive the revelation setting himself aside. President John Taylor has made this very plain. Says President Taylor, speaking of the time following President Young's death: 'I occupied the senior position in the quorum, and occupying that position which was thoroughly understood by the quorum of the twelve, on the death of President Young, as the twelve assumed the presidency, and I was their president, it placed me in a position of president of the Church, or, as expressed in our conference meeting: "As president of the quorum of the twelve apostles, as one of the twelve apostles, and of the presidency of the Church of Jesus Christ of Latter-day Saints." In this manner, also, was President Brigham Young sustained, at the general conference held in Nauvoo, in October following the martyrdom of the Prophet Joseph Smith.' (*Gospel Kingdom,* p. 192.) The counselors in the presidency cease to be counselors when the President dies and take their regular place among their brethren." (Joseph Fielding Smith, *CHMR* 1:189-90.)

Scriptural References: D&C 107:22-30; 112:14-32.

Suffer; "suffer it to be so"

Some of the accepted meanings of the word *suffer* are "to permit" and "to allow." It is used in these senses numerous times both in ancient and modern scriptures.

Scriptural References: D&C 10:14, 43; 61:8; 109:49; Luke 8:32; 9:22, 41, 59; 17:25; 18:16; 22:15, 51; 24:46.

Summer is nigh (*see also* Second coming)

Summer has been given as a symbol in the parable of the fig tree for the time of the second coming of Jesus Christ: When the fig tree puts forth its leaves, then you know that summer is nigh. In this sense, the term *summer is nigh* refers to the closeness of the second coming of Jesus Christ. The word *summer* is also used as a symbol of the time of harvest, a time when work can be done, or as a symbol of this mortal earthly probation. The Lord warns us to work while we can;

otherwise "the summer shall be past, and the harvest ended, and your souls not saved." (45:2.)

Selected Quotations

"In a revelation to the people of the Church, March 7, 1831, the Lord speaks of the signs of His coming, and counsels diligence: 'Ye look and behold the fig-trees, and ye see them with your eyes, and ye say when they begin to shoot forth, and their leaves are yet tender, that summer is now nigh at hand; Even so it shall be in that day when they shall see all these things, then shall they know that the hour is nigh.' . . . [D&C 45:37-44 quoted.]

"A distinctive characteristic of the revelations given in the present dispensation, regarding the second coming of our Lord, is the emphatic and oft-repeated declaration that the event is near at hand. The call is, 'Prepare ye, prepare ye, for that which is to come; for the Lord is nigh.' Instead of the cry of one man in the wilderness of Judea, the voice of thousands is heard authoritatively warning the nations and inviting them to repent and flee to Zion for safety. The fig-tree is rapidly putting forth its leaves; the signs in heaven and earth are increasing; the great and dreadful day of the Lord is near." (James E. Talmage, *AF,* pp. 361-62.)

Scriptural References: D&C 35:16; 45:2, 37; 56:16.

Sustain (*see also* Common consent)

The basic meaning of *sustain* is "to support, to buoy up, to allow, or to admit as valid." In the Church, we sustain a person by our actions as well as by the formal procedure of the uplifted hand.

Selected Quotations

"What is meant by sustaining a person? Do we understand it? It is a very simple thing to me; I do not know how it is with you. For instance, if a man be a teacher, and I vote that I will sustain him in his position, when he visits me in an official capacity I will welcome him and treat him with consideration, kindness and respect, and if I need counsel I will ask it at his hand, and I will do everything I can to sustain him. That would be proper and a principle of righteousness, and I would not say anything derogatory to his character. If that is not correct I have it yet to learn. And then, if anybody in my presence were to whisper something about him disparaging to his reputation, I would say, 'Look here! Are you a saint?' Yes. Did you hold up your hand to sustain him? Yes. Then why do you not do it? Now, I would call an action of that kind sustaining him. If any man make an attack upon his reputation—for all men's reputations are of importance to them—I would defend him in some such way. When we vote for men in the solemn way in which we do, shall we abide by our covenants? or shall we violate them? If we violate them we become covenant-breakers. We break our faith before God and our brethren, in regard to the acts of men whom we have covenanted to sustain. But supposing he should do something wrong, supposing he should be found lying or cheating, or defrauding somebody; or stealing or anything else, or even become impure in his habits, would you still sustain him? It would be my duty then to talk with him as I would with anybody else, and tell him that I had understood that things were thus and so, and that under these circumstances I could not sustain him; and if I found that I had been misinformed I would withdraw my charge; but if not, it would then be my duty to see that justice was administered to him, that he was brought before the proper tribunal to answer for the things he had done; and in the absence of that I would have no business to talk about him." (John Taylor, *JD* 21:207-8.)

"Do you ever think of the inconsistency of raising your right hand in solemn witness before God that you will sustain certain men who have been called and ordained, in the manner appointed of God, as your leaders, as prophets unto the people, verily as revelators, and then, though perchance you come together and hear their words, going away and pay no attention to them? When one speaks with the power of his Priesthood, and in the authority of his office, then what he speaks is binding upon himself and all who hear. Ofttimes I tremble, literally, as I consider what I am doing when addressing the Latter-day Saints, for I know that what I say unto them is binding upon me, and that I shall be judged by the precepts that I impress upon them; and what I say under such conditions is likewise binding upon those who hear.

"You cannot, we cannot, pass by lightly the words that come by way of counsel and instruction from the ordained servants of God, and escape the inevitable penalty of that neglect. Nevertheless, we have our agency; we may choose to disobey, but we must take the consequences of that choice." (James E. Talmage, *CR*, October 1921, pp. 187-88.)

Scriptural References: D&C 20:63; 38:34; 102:9; 107:22; 124:144; 134:5; Num. 27:19.

Swearing; taking the name of God in vain (*see also* Ten Commandments)

Swearing or taking an oath can either be used for righteous or for unrighteous purposes. In a good sense, the making of a covenant is a form of taking an oath or making a promise with God. However, as is so often the case, wicked people, often with the encouragement and help of the devil, have prostituted or changed the original good intent of the taking of a sacred oath by swearing or taking an oath *in vain* or in a *profane way.* As in ancient times, the Lord has warned against blaspheming the name of Deity: "Thou shalt not take the name of the Lord thy God in vain; for the Lord will not hold him guiltless that taketh his name in vain." (Ex. 20:7; D&C 63:61-62.) Profanity makes common, degrades, and shows contempt for the things of God.

Selected Quotations

"To take the name of God in vain, . . . is to use that name lightly, to use it emptily, to use it without effect, so far as the intent is concerned—but nevertheless, with awful effect upon the profane user. We are apt to think that this has reference to the speaking of the name of God only, and in that particular respect the commandment [Exod. 20:7] is sufficiently weighty and important to us. . . .

"I listen with horror to profane swearing. One cannot escape it wholly, go where one will; that is to say, as one has to meet diverse associations one is sure to encounter it. Of profanity I have not yet heard one word of defense. It is wholly demoralizing, wholly base, to say nothing of the sacrilege and blasphemy ofttimes associated in the linking of the name of Deity with our perverse expressions. . . .

"But another phase of taking the name of God in vain is that referred to in the scripture . . . 'And ye shall not swear by my name falsely.' [Lev. 19:12.] How that is disregarded in the world we know. In the courts of the land, yes, . . . in the courts of justice, the oath is administered, 'So help you God,' and we witness every day practically, instances of such solemn adjuration being disregarded as soon as spoken; we see men perjuring themselves, defiling, polluting the name of God even on the witness stand. We have come to think that perjury in our courts is something to be condoned, palliated, and in some minds extolled, if by it some personal advantage can be gained.

"I ask your attention to another way which the name of God is taken in vain, and that by the presumption of men who profess to speak in his name without authority. The Lord has been particularly careful as to those whom he commissions to use his name, . . . and having thus commissioned a man . . . to speak in his name, he, the Lord, holds himself bound by what is done by that agent if it is done righteously in his holy name. [D&C 1:38.] . . .

"And now there is yet another instance, method, way by which we are too prone to take the name of God in vain and in this connection, I call your attention to the thirtieth chapter of Proverbs, verses seven to nine inclusive . . .

" 'Two things have I required of thee; deny me them not before I die:

" 'Remove far from me vanity and lies: give me neither poverty nor riches; feed me with food convenient for me:

" 'Lest I be full and deny thee, and say, Who is the Lord? or lest I be poor, and steal, and take the name of my God in vain.'

"What association is there between the crime of theft and that of taking the name of God in vain, so closely brought together here? . . . Do we take the name of God in vain by stealing? Latter-day Saints, this applies to us. Is not the name of the Lord written in our foreheads? Where can a Latter-day Saint go without bearing the name of the Lord with him? And if he steal, he is stealing before the Lord and with his name displayed, thus polluting the name of the Lord, for he has taken that name upon himself.

"By way of summary:

"1. We may take the name of God in vain by profane speech.

"2. We take it in vain when we swear falsely, not being true to our oaths and promises.

"3. We take it in vain in a blasphemous sense when we presume to speak in that name without authority.

"4. And we take his name in vain whenever we willfully do aught that is in defiance of his commandments, since we have taken his name upon ourselves." (James E. Talmage, *CR*, October 1931, pp. 50-53.)

"Sometimes good-hearted people are in the habit of joking a good deal about sacred things, and there is scarcely anything that is held by them too sacred to speak lightly of in some form. They do this in the presence of their children, and their children take advantage of it; and while they go but an inch, so to speak, their children go the full length. They see that their parents do not hold sacred things which are sacred; they joke about them and speak lightly of them in the presence of their children, . . . The children grow up to feel that even their parents . . . do not hold sacred those things that they call sacred. The parents joke about these things and speak lightly of them and the children take advantage of it." (Joseph F. Smith, *CR,* October 1909, p. 5.)

Scriptural References: Ex. 20:7; Lev. 18:21; 19:12; Matt. 5:34; Mark 6:23; James 5:12; 1 Ne. 20:1; Alma 49:27; 3 Ne. 12:33; 24:5; Morm. 3:10; Ether 8:14.

Sword; sword of God; "sword is bathed in heaven"; "sharper than a two-edged sword" (*see also* Armor of God)

The sword was an effective weapon of offense during many of the wars fought in Old Testament times. It became a symbol of power and might. Some swords even had sharp edges on both sides of the blade, making them more fearsome weapons of war. The word of the Lord is powerful and great, and all of his words shall be fulfilled. The Lord cautions us to pay attention to and be careful with his words, for they are "quick and powerful, sharper than a two-edged sword." (D&C 11:2.)

The term that the sword of the Lord "is bathed in heaven" is used in both ancient and modern scriptures. Isaiah recorded the words of the Lord as follows: "For my sword shall be bathed in heaven: behold, it shall come down upon Idumea, and upon the people of my curse, to judgment." (Isa. 34:5.)

John recorded in the book of Revelation that the Savior will bring a sharp sword to "smite the nations" when he comes to judge the world. (Rev. 19:11-21.)

Selected Quotations

" 'For the word of the Lord is quick and powerful, and sharper than any two-edged sword, piercing even to the dividing asunder of soul and spirit and of the joints and marrow, and is a discerner of the thoughts and intents of the heart.' [Heb. 4:12.]

"The truth of this may seem difficult to realize, but when the 'still small voice' of the Lord speaks to men it is overwhelming. We have the story of Elijah, who withstood the great wind when the Lord passed by; that rent the mountains, likewise the earthquake which shook the earth, and then fire, but the Lord was not in the fire, and then the Lord spoke by the 'still small voice.' Then Elijah wrapped his face in his mantle, for the fear of the Lord came upon him. When the Lord comes he will speak, and the rocks will be rent, the mountains will be laid low, and the valleys exalted, and men will try to hide themselves from his presence. They will not be able to stand the piercing of the 'still small voice,' unless the Spirit of the Lord is upon them." (Joseph Fielding Smith, *CHMR* 1:56.)

Scriptural References: D&C 1:13; 6:2; 11:2; 12:2; 14:2; 27:18; 33:1; 35:14; 110:10; 121:5; Heb. 4:12.

Tares; the tares and the wheat (*see also* Parables)

The Lord taught that wheat was the staff of life, and often in his parables he would use the example of wheat, a grain that was well known and commonly used by the people being taught. However, the tare is a noxious plant that looks similar to wheat and is difficult to distinguish from wheat until late in the growing season. The Lord used this similarity as a teaching device in helping the people to see the difference between good and evil in the end and also to learn how to deal with some aspects of evil in everyday life. In a more general sense, the word *tare* has come to mean weeds or anything undesirable.

Selected Quotations

"I am convinced that the Latter-day Saints are the 'wheat,' and they have been, and are being gathered out of the midst of the 'tares' of the earth. They are the salt of the earth, and the gathering of the wheat from the midst of the tares is almost completed. There remains but the gleaning of the wheat; and when the wheat is gathered the tares shall be bound in bundles, and the burning time remaineth for them. The Lord gathered this people out from the midst of the nations of the earth to preserve them from the desolations that would come.

"I bear witness to you that the angels of God, who hold the power delegated to them to pour out his judgments upon the wicked, marvel at God's leniency and patience to this generation. That is why they cried: 'Why are we not permitted to go forth?' They are stayed and held back." (Melvin J. Ballard, *CR*, October 1920, p. 78.)

Scriptural References: D&C 38:12; 86:1, 3, 6-7; 88:94; 101:65-66; Matt. 13:25-40.

Teaching; teachers; "teach one another" (*see also* Gifts of the Spirit)

The teacher has a great and awesome responsibility, for he is helping to determine the thoughts and frequently the actions of present and of future generations. He has influence over many people, and this influence may have eternal consequences.

Selected Quotations

"What is a teacher? The teacher is a prophet. He lays the foundation of tomorrow. The teacher is an artist. He works with the precious clay of unfolding personality. The teacher is a friend. His heart responds to the faith and devotion of his students. The teacher is a citizen. He is selected and licensed for the improvement of society. The teacher is an interpreter. Out of his mature and wider life, he seeks to guide the young.

"The teacher is a builder. He works with the higher and finer values of civilization. The teacher is a culture-bearer. He leads the way toward worthier tastes, saner attitudes, more gracious manners, higher intelligence. The teacher is a planner. He sees the young lives before him as a part of a great system that shall grow stronger in the light of truth. The teacher is a pioneer. He is always interpreting and attempting the impossible, and usually winning out.

"The teacher is a reformer. He seeks to improve the handicaps that weaken and destroy life. The teacher is a believer. He has an abiding faith in God and in the improvability of the race. It was James Truslow Adams who said, 'There are obviously two educations. One should teach us how to make a living, and the other how to live.'

"We are engaged in teaching people how to live. Elbert Hubbard said, 'You can't teach anybody anything. You can only help him find himself.' That was the genius of the Savior. He taught us divine principles we could apply to ourselves and thus solve our personal problems. The Savior had no peer as a teacher." (Paul H. Dunn, *Ensign*, December 1971, p. 119.)

"A wise man, when asked to list three cardinal points that exemplified the lives of the great teachers of all time and that would be a guide to new teachers, said: 'First, teach by example. Second, teach by example. Third, teach by example.' Our Savior, Jesus Christ, is the greatest example the world has ever known, and his teachings endure throughout the ages because the precepts he taught were emphasized by the example of his own life." (Delbert L. Stapley, *IE*, June 1969, p. 69.)

"May I challenge you in the words from the epistle of James to be 'doers of the word, and not hearers only' (Jas. 1:22), remembering:

> *I hear and I forget;*
> *I see and I remember;*
> *I do and I learn.*

"Others then will follow your example. Commandments will be lived. Lives will be blessed.

"In Galilee there taught a master teacher, even Jesus Christ the Lord. He left his footprints in the sands of the seashore, but he left his teaching principles in the hearts and in the lives of all whom he taught. He instructed his disciples of that day, and to us he speaks the same words, 'Follow thou me.' Then, as now, foolish, unwise persons will stop their ears, close their eyes, and turn away their hearts. Let us remember, there is no deafness so permanent as the deafness which will not hear. These is no blindness so incurable as the blindness which will not see. There is no ignorance so deep as the ignorance that will not know." (Thomas S. Monson, *IE*, December 1970, pp. 102-3.)

"What miracles an impact teacher can achieve by giving honest appreciation and a sense of self-worth! The parent or teacher who honestly satisfies this heart hunger will hold a child or a class in the palm of his hand.

"Some years ago when Aldin Porter was president of the Boise North Stake, he dropped by the home of Glen Clayton, who was the Scoutmaster in his ward. Glen and his son were working together repairing a bicycle. President Porter stood and talked to them for a few minutes and then left. Several hours later he returned and the father and son were still working on the bike together. President Porter said,

'Glen, with the wages you make per hour you could have bought a new bike, considering the time you have spent repairing this old one.'

"Glen stood up and said, 'I'm not repairing a bike, I'm training a boy!'

"That year twenty-one boys achieved the rank of Eagle Scout in Glen's troop. Impact teachers do not teach lessons, they teach souls. . . .

"Ezekiel said that the fathers have eaten sour grapes and it hath set the children's teeth on edge. (See Ezek. 18:2.) Paraphrasing Presiding Lee's statement, 'The greatest teaching we will ever do is within the walls of our own home.' We have a sacred trust to teach our children the principles of truth; but equally important is to love and care in following the way of the Master.

"Impact teachers are not cast in a certain mold in the spirit world and introduced on earth's scene at just the proper time. Every leader in the kingdom can become an impact teacher. Your notoriety may not reach much past the quorum or class, but your influence may be felt in the eternities. . . . The impact teacher cares with an attitude of pure charity. The impact teacher asks, 'What would the Savior do when faced with this problem?' " (Vaughn J. Featherstone, *Ensign,* November 1976, pp. 103-5.)

Scriptural References: D&C 20:53; 42:14, 70; 43:15-16; 68:28; 88:77, 118; Ps. 32:8; Prov. 9:9; 22:6, Mosiah 4:15; 23:14.

Telestial (*see also* Degrees of glory)

The telestial is the lowest of the three major degrees of glory.

Selected Quotations

"The adjective 'telestial' has not become current in the language; its use is at present confined to the theology of The Church of Jesus Christ of Latter-day Saints. It is applied as a distinguishing term to the lowest of the three kingdoms of glory provided for the redeemed. The only English word approaching it in form is the adjective 'telestic,' which is defined thus: 'tending toward the end or final accomplishment; tending to accomplish a purpose.'

"In this connection the following note, from Elder J. M. Sjodahl to the author may be profitably studied: 'Paul speaking of the several times of resurrection (1 Cor. 15:22-25) says of the last: "then cometh the end, when he shall have delivered up the kingdom of God," etc. The word translated *end* is *telos,* and the glory of those who are resurrected last may therefore properly be called *telestial,* as related to *telos.* Their resurrection is the end, the finish, the completion, of the resurrection series.' " (James E. Talmage, *AF,* p. 521.)

"Those who partake of the telestial kingdom are the unclean inhabitants of the earth; those who have defiled themselves with immoral practices, the liars, sorcerers, thieves, blasphemers, and all who have loved wickedness. Because of their evil practices they bring down upon themselves the wrath of God. These are turned over to Satan and become subject to his rule and suffer his buffetings until the day of the earth, or their redemption which is the resurrection which will not come until the end of the earth, or the 'fulness of times,' or when our Savior has finished his work; then they shall be brought forth after they have paid the 'uttermost farthing,' and have learned by the things they have suffered that 'crime does not pay.' " (Smith and Sjodahl, *DCC,* p. 465.)

"Can they [people of the telestial glory] come where God and Christ dwell? No, worlds without end they cannot come there. Can they go into the presence of the heathen where the glory is that of the moon? No, they cannot even come there. When they are delivered from the power of Satan and endless death and brought forth, where do they go? If they do not go into the presence of God the Father, if they are not counted worthy to enter into the terrestrial world among the heathens, where will they go? God has provided mansions for them according to their works here in this world. Having suffered the vengeance of eternal fire for the space of a thousand years and upwards, and suffered the extreme penalty of the law of God, they can now be brought forth to inherit a place where they can be administered unto by terrestrial beings and by Angels holding the Priesthood, and where they can receive the Holy Ghost." (Orson Pratt, *JD* 15:322-23.)

Scriptural References: D&C 76:81-98, 109; 88:21-24, 31; 1 Cor. 15:40.

Temple; temples; "the Lord will come suddenly to his temple"

The Lord's house (temple) is a holy sanctuary where sacred ordinances and ceremonies are performed and where eternal truths are taught pertaining to the exaltation and eternal life of man. It is literally a *House of the Lord* upon the earth where the Lord's Spirit may be in attendance, where he can personally appear, or where he can send heavenly messengers. Ancient prophets testified that one of the signs before the second coming of Jesus Christ is that the Lord would come suddenly to His temple.

Selected Quotations

"Temple work . . . gives a wonderful opportunity for keeping alive our spiritual knowledge and strength. The mighty perspective of eternity is unraveled before us in the holy temples; we see time from its infinite beginning to its endless end; and the dream of eternal life is unfolded before us. Then I see more clearly my place amidst the things of the universe, my place among the purposes of God; I am better able to place myself where I belong, and I am better able to value and to weigh, to separate and to organize the common, ordinary duties of my life, so that the little things shall not oppress me or take away my vision of the greater things that God has given us." (John A. Widtsoe, *CR*, April 1922, pp. 97-98.)

"President Young said: 'To accomplish this work there will have to be not only one temple, but thousands of them, and thousands and tens of thousands of men and women will go into those temples and officiate for people who have lived as far back as the Lord shall reveal.' (JD 3:372.). . .

"Then the Prophet Wilford Woodruff said: 'When the Savior comes, a thousand years will be devoted to this work of redemption and temples will appear all over this land of Joseph—North and South America—and also in Europe and elsewhere.' (*JD* 19:230.)" (LeGrand Richards, *Ensign*, November 1974, p. 54.)

Scriptural References: D&C 36:8; 42:36; 133:2; Mal. 3:1-3; 3 Ne. 24:1.

Temporal (*see also* Natural)

The basic root of the word *temporal* is *tempor,* having to do with time. A dictionary definition of *temporal* is "of or relating to time as opposed to eternity." The Lord is not bound by time. All of his laws and commandments pertain to eternity as well as to this earth life; hence, they are not temporal. In a revelation given in September 1830, the Lord stated: "Not at any time have I given unto you a law which was temporal . . . for my commandments are spiritual; they are not natural nor temporal, neither carnal nor sensual." (29:34-35.) In one eternal sense, temporal ("temporary; bound by time") is the opposite of spiritual ("eternal; valid forever").

Selected Quotations

"The Lord has to do with those things that are temporal as well as those that are spiritual; for He has declared that 'for brass he will bring gold, and for stones iron, and for iron he will bring silver" [Isa. 60:17], and He will beautify Zion and cause her to shine and be made glorious. . . . The Lord is in the temporal as well as in the spiritual things of His kingdom, and will be if we keep His commandments and seek to sanctify them in his service. That is the point. As with Him, all things will be spiritual to us, if we use them to the glory of God and the benefit of our fellow creatures." (Charles W. Penrose, *CR,* April 1906, pp. 90-91.)

Scriptural References: D&C 14:11; 24:9; 29:31-35, 42; 63:38; 70:11, 12, 14; 77:2, 6; 89:2; 107:68, 71; Moses 6:63; 7:42; 2 Cor. 4:18; 1 Ne. 15:31-32; 22:3, 6; 2 Ne. 2:5; 9:11; Mosiah 2:41; Alma 7:23; 11:42; 12:16, 24, 31; 36:4; 37:43; 42:8-9; Hel. 14:16; Morm. 9:13.

Ten Commandments

The Ten Commandments were given in ancient times [Ex. 20:3-17] but have been repeated and reemphasized by the Lord in this dispensation [D&C 42:18-29].

Selected Quotations

"Some people hold that the Ten Commandments belong to a by-gone age. That cannot be so, for I remember that the Lord in this generation reiterated to the Prophet Joseph Smith the principles that are found in the Ten Commandments as reported by Moses; and he made them more emphatic, for he said not only, 'Thou shalt not steal; thou shalt not lie'; but added, that 'he who steals or lies shall be cast out unless he repents.' [Sec. 42:20-21.]" (John A. Widtsoe, *CR,* April 1937, p. 67.)

"There is a cure for the earth's illness, an infallible one. . . . The diagnosis is sure, and the remedy certain. Today's prophet stands in the same position between God and the people as did Isaiah, Samuel, and even Moses who gave to the world the Ten Commandments. But a controlling majority of the people of this world have relegated them to the past.

" '*Thou shalt have no other gods before me.*' (Ex. 20:3.) Yet today we worship the gods of wood and stone and metal. Not always are they in the form of a golden calf, but equally real as objects of protection and worship. They are houses, lands, bank accounts, leisure. They are boats, cars, and luxuries. They are bombs and ships and armaments. We bow down to the god of mammon, the god of luxuries, the god of dissipation.

" '*Thou shalt not take the name of the Lord thy God in vain. . . .*' (Ex. 20:7.) Yet on the corner, in public places, on work projects, at banquet tables, there come ringing into our ears the sacred names of Deity without solemnity.

" '*Remember the sabbath day, to keep it holy.*' (Ex. 20:8.) Yet work goes on, merchandise is sold, athletic entertainments, fishing, hunting go forward without regard to commandments. Conventions, unnecessary travel, family picnics, the Sabbath is violated generally. . . . The taverns are full, the beaches crowded, the grandstands packed, man servants and maid servants hired to duty, the ski lifts busy, canyon picnic tables loaded. Scriptures are read little, and the holy day becomes a holiday.

" '*Six days shalt thou labour. . . .*' (Ex. 20:9.) Yet ever-increasing hours of leisure provide ever-increasing opportunities for Sabbath breaking and commandment ignoring, and strikes and lobbying go on to increase damaging leisure and decrease work hours further.

" '*Thou shalt not commit adultery.*' (Ex. 20:14.) Yet common sin and idolatry run hand in hand. Free love and indiscretions and deviations of every nature are common in our day. Illegitimate births are said to reach as high as one in ten, yet promiscuity far exceeds illegitimacy. This ugly deviation is found among youth and married people. Divorce, ever on the increase, jumping from one divorce for thirty-six weddings in Civil War days now has reached somewhere near one to four. Flirtations, rationalized to be innocent ones, are the root of numerous of the divorces and other ills.

" '*Thou shalt not steal.*' (Ex. 20:15.) Yet in high places and in low, in government office and in business, in everyday life, men have rationalized until consciences seem to have been seared in the matter of honesty. Yet here are bribery, fraud, deceit, theft, padding of expense accounts, tax evasions, installment buying beyond ability to pay, and gambling running into the billions.

"The outlook is bleak, but the impending tragedy can be averted. But it can be only through a great repentance and transformation." (Spencer W. Kimball, *CR,* September 1961, pp. 30-34.)

"These directions and warnings have not been the arbitrary edicts of a vindictive tyrant. They are the teachings, counsels, and pleadings of a solicitous, loving Heavenly Father. They prescribe the one and only means to peace and happiness in this earth. They declare irrevocable law, compliance with which is indispensable to peace and progress: the earth itself responds to man's obedience or disobedience to the teachings of God, who made the earth." (Marion G. Romney, *Ensign,* May 1977, p. 52.)

Scriptural References: D&C 42:18-29; Ex. 20; Deut. 5.

Terrestrial (*see also* Degrees of glory)

The terrestrial is the middle of the three degrees of glory.

Selected Quotations

"But how about these terrestrials, can they come up into the celestial? No, their intelligence and knowledge have not prepared and adapted them to dwell with those who reign in celestial glory, consequently they cannot even be angels in that glory. They have not obeyed the law that pertains to that glory, and hence they couldn't abide it. But will there be blessings administered to them by those who dwell in celestial glory? Yes, angels will be sent forth from the celestial world to minister to those who inherit the glory of the moon, bearing messages of joy and peace and of all that which is calculated to exalt, to redeem and ennoble those who have been resurrected into a terrestrial glory. They can receive the Spirit of the Lord there and the ministration of angels there. [Sec. 76:87.] . . . Those in the terrestrial world have the privilege of beholding Jesus sometimes—they can receive the presence of the Son, but not the fulness of the Father." (Orson Pratt, *JD* 15:322-23.)

"Many noble and great bodies will possess this kingdom, receiving to an extent the glory of God as administered by the Son, but not of a fulness. These, for the most part, will be men who, during earth-life existence, sought the excellence of men; and some who gave of their time, talents and endeavor to the ways of man-made ideals of culture, science, and education, but thought not to include God and his ways in their search for a complete life. They received more of the Spirit of the world and of the wisdom which men teacheth, and, yet, are just men, however, neglecting that spirit which is of God." (Alvin R. Dyer, *Who Am I?*, pp. 552-53.)

"Members of the Church who have testimonies and who live clean and upright lives, but who are not courageous and valiant, do not gain the celestial kingdom. Theirs is a terrestrial inheritance. Of them the revelation says, 'These are they who are not valiant in the testimony of Jesus; wherefore, they obtain not the crown over the kingdom of our God.' (D&C 76:79.) . . . Now what does it mean to be valiant in the testimony of Jesus? It is to be courageous and bold; to use all our strength, energy, and ability in the warfare with the world: to fight the good fight of faith. . . . The great cornerstone of valiance in the cause of righteousness is obedience to the whole law of the whole gospel.

"To be valiant in the testimony of Jesus is to 'come unto Christ, and be perfected in him'; it is to deny ourselves 'of all ungodliness,' and 'love God' with all our 'might, mind and strength.' (Moro. 10:32.) To be valiant in the testimony of Jesus is to believe in Christ and his gospel with unshakable conviction. It is to know of the verity and divinity of the Lord's work on earth.

"But this is not all. It is more than believing and knowing. We must be doers of the word and not hearers only. . . . To be valiant in the testimony of Jesus is to 'press forward with a steadfastness in Christ, having a perfect brightness of hope, and a love of God and of all men.' It is to 'endure to the end.' (2 Nephi 31:20.) It is to live our religion, to practice what we preach, to keep the commandments. It is the manifestation of 'pure religion' in the lives of men; it is visiting 'the fatherless and widows in their affliction' and keeping ourselves 'unspotted from the world.' (James 1:27.)

"To be valiant in the testimony of Jesus is to bridle our passions, control our appetites, and rise above carnal and evil things. It is to overcome the world as did he who is our prototype and who himself was the most valiant of all our Father's children. It is to be morally clean, to pay our tithes and offerings, to honor the Sabbath day, to pray with full purpose of heart, to lay our all upon the altar if called upon to do so.

"To be valiant in the testimony of Jesus is to take the Lord's side on every issue. It is to vote as he would vote. It is to think what he thinks, to believe what he believes, to say what he would say and do what he would do in the same situation. It is to have the mind of Christ and be one with him as he is one with his Father." (Bruce R. McConkie, *Ensign,* November 1974, pp. 33-35.)

Scriptural References: D&C 76:71-97; 88:21-23, 30; 1 Cor. 15:40.

Testimony

One of the major reasons why we came upon this physical world with a veil of forgetfulness over our minds is so we can learn for ourselves that God is our Heavenly Father and that Jesus Christ is his Divine Son. The things of God are known only by the Spirit of God. The gaining of a testimony is a great blessing, and every blessing is predicated upon obedience to law. Every person on this earth should be interested in learning the steps and laws that must be followed in order to gain a testimony; the wise person will then live those laws so that the testimony can come. "This is life eternal, that they might know thee the only true God, and Jesus Christ, whom thou hast sent." (John 17:3.)

Selected Quotations

"Every member of the Church is entitled to know that God our Heavenly Father lives; that he is not dead. He is also entitled to know that our elder brother, Jesus Christ, is the Savior and Redeemer of the world, and that he has opened the door for us, that we, through our individual acts, may receive salvation and exaltation and dwell once again in the presence of our Heavenly Father. This assurance and witness must be earnestly sought. Heber C. Kimball, a counselor to President Brigham Young, warned the Saints in 1856 that many trials would come to test their faith; that the time would come that no man or woman would be able to endure on borrowed light. Each must gain a personal knowledge of the truth and be guided by the light within himself." (Henry D. Taylor, *Ensign,* June 1971, p. 108.)

"It seems to me . . . that there runs in some blood strains a higher susceptibility to the refining and saving influences of

testimony than in other strains. I don't know that I understand it, but I have thought that the significance of the
' blood of Israel ' is that there is in that great blood strain,
following the blessings and promises of God, a susceptibility
to the influence of the Holy Spirit that does not run in other
strains. . . . I believe that it [testimony] is inheritable, and
that the tendency to faith may descend from father to son. It
seems to me that Paul had that in mind when writing to
Timothy, he said in substance: 'I do perceive in thee the
faith that was in thy grandmother Lois' [2 Timothy 1:5], thus
recognizing that this tendency to faith, this susceptibility to
testimony courses along in the very blood strains of the
race." (Stephen L Richards, *CR,* October 1925, pp. 118-19.)

Scriptural References: D&C 62:3; 76:22, 50, 74, 79; 84:62,
81, 88; 100:10; 124:20; 136:39; Moses 7:27, 62; JS-H 1:26;
JFS-V 1:12; Ps. 19:7; Acts 14:3; 1 Cor. 1:6; 2:1; 12:3; 2 Cor.
1:12; Gal. 1:12; 2 Tim. 1:8; Rev. 12:11; 19:10; Alma 4:20;
6:8; 7:13.

Thoughts; "none else save God knowest thy thoughts"

Thoughts have a profound influence on the character, personality, and eventual actions of man. The Lord is concerned
with our thoughts and warns us that we will be held accountable for them.

Evil thoughts are a sin (Prov. 15:26; 24:9), and they
frequently lead to further sinful action: "Out of the heart of
men, proceed evil thoughts, adulteries, fornications, mur-
ders, Thefts, covetousness, wickedness, deceit, lasciviousness,
an evil eye, blasphemy, pride, foolishness: All these evil
things come from within." (Mark 7:21-23.)

Good thoughts can lead one to God by building faith and
confidence in the individual as he learns to master his
thoughts and increases his confidence in God, who can know
the thoughts of man. Thus "let virtue garnish thy thoughts
unceasingly; then shall thy confidence wax strong in the
presence of God." (121:45.)

Selected Quotations

"A man is literally what he thinks, his character being the
complete sum of all his thoughts. . . .

"Not only does a person become what he thinks, but often
he comes to look like it. If he worships the God of War, hard
lines tend to develop on his countenance. If he worships the

God of Lust, dissipation will mark his features. If he worships the God of Peace and Truth, serenity will crown his visage. . . .

"Inescapably we reap what we sow. If a farmer wants to raise wheat he must sow wheat, if he wishes fruit he must plant fruit trees, and so with any other crop. The principle is equally binding in the mental and spiritual spheres. . . .

"This relationship of character to thought cannot be too strongly emphasized. How could a person possibly become what he is *not* thinking? Nor is any thought, when persistently entertained, too small to have its effect. The 'divinity that shapes our ends' is indeed in ourselves. It is one's very self." (Spencer W. Kimball, *MF*, p. 103.)

"We may succeed in hiding our affairs from men; but it is written that for every word and every secret thought we shall have to give an account in the day when accounts have to be rendered before God, when hypocrisy and fraud of any kind will not avail us; for by our words and by our works we shall be justified, or by them we shall be condemned." (John Taylor, *JD* 24:232.)

"William James, the great Harvard psychologist, once asked this question, how would you like to create your own mind? But isn't that about what usually happens? Professor James explains that the mind is made up by what it feeds upon. He said that the mind, like the dyer's hand, is colored by what it holds. If I hold in my hand a sponge full of purple dye, my hand becomes purple. And if I hold in my mind and heart great ideas of faith and enthusiasm, my whole personality is changed accordingly.

"If we think negative thoughts, we develop negative minds. If we think depraved thoughts, we develop depraved minds. On the other hand, if we think celestial thoughts, which are the kind of thoughts that God thinks, then we develop celestial minds." (Sterling W. Sill, *Ensign*, May 1978, p. 66.)

"As I have flown over the beautiful land of South America, time and time again I have been impressed with the aerial view of the mighty Amazon River. Not only is this Amazon the greatest river in the world, but even many of its tributaries are great rivers in their own right and are navigable for many miles.

"One interesting feature about these rivers is their

different colors. The Madeira, for example, is called a white river because its waters carry fine clay particles along its course. The black color of the Rio Negro comes from decaying organic materials picked up in the forests through which it passes. Still other rivers flow over white sands and often appear emerald green or turquoise blue.

"Just as these rivers are colored by the substances picked up as they flow along, so the streams of our thoughts are colored by the material through which they are channeled. The scriptures indicate that as a man 'thinketh in his heart, so is he.' (Prov. 23:7.) The material we read has a great effect on the nature of our thoughts. We therefore need to be concerned not only with avoiding unwholesome literature, but we must fill our minds with pure knowledge, and we must see that our children do the same." (J. Thomas Fyans, *Ensign*, May 1975, p. 88.)

"Choose from among the sacred music of the Church a favorite hymn, one with words that are uplifting and music that is reverent, one that makes you feel something akin to inspiration. . . . Perhaps 'I am a Child of God' would do. Go over it in your mind carefully. Memorize it. Even though you have had no musical training, you can think through a hymn.

"Now, use this hymn as the place for your thoughts to go. Make it your emergency channel. Whenever you find these shady actors have slipped from the sidelines of your thinking onto the stage of your mind, put on this record, as it were. As the music begins and as the words form in your thoughts, the unworthy ones will slip shamefully away. It will change the whole mood on the stage of your mind. Because it is uplifting and clean, the baser thoughts will disappear. For while virtue, by choice, *will not* associate with filth, evil *cannot* tolerate the presence of light.

"In due time you will find yourself, on occasion, humming the music inwardly. As you retrace your thoughts, you discover some influence from the world about you encouraged an unworthy thought to move on stage in your mind, and the music almost automatically began." (Boyd K. Packer, *CR*, October 1973, pp. 24-25.)

Scriptural References: D&C 6:16; 33:1; 88:109; Ps. 94:11; Matt. 9:4; 12:25; Luke 5:22; 6:8; 11:17; 1 Cor. 3:20; Jacob 2:5; Alma 12:3-14.

Time; importance of time (*for information on "times and seasons" see material for* 121:12.)

Our time upon the earth is very brief and limited when compared with the eternities before and the eternities after this life. God through His prophets has accordingly counseled us to use our earthly time wisely.

Selected Quotations

" 'David hasted, and ran toward the army to meet the Philistine.' (1 Sam. 17:48.) I think it is significant that the scriptures indicate this young boy who was on the Lord's errand did not merely saunter, nor walk, but he actually *ran* and conquered. David had faith.

"The scriptures are replete with examples of other great men of God who maintained this same rapid pace and felt this same sense of urgency as they served the Lord. When Abraham saw three messengers of God approaching, 'he *ran* to meet them.' (Gen. 18:2. Italics added.) When the angel announced the birth of the Savior to the shepherds, these men '*came with haste,* and found Mary, and Joseph, and the babe lying in a manger.' (Luke 2:16. Italics added.) When Mary Magdalene entered the empty tomb and *ran* to tell Peter and John what had happened, the two apostles '*ran* both together' to see. (John 20:2-4. Italics added.)" (J. Thomas Fyans, *Ensign,* May 1975, pp. 88-89.)

"We are here that we may increase also in righteousness, and in all things that are essential to salvation. We are here to lay the foundation for these purposes, and we have not time to waste; we cannot spare one moment; every hour needs to be utilized, and most precious they will appear to us when we come near to the end. When a man who has neglected his duties feels that there are only a few years, or a few weeks, more time allotted to him, how he does want to live; how he wishes he had gone to the temple; how he wishes he had performed a mission abroad, or more missions; how he wishes he had been devoted all his life to the work of the Lord. Perhaps he has a taste of the joy of having done a little, has worked a few years—forty or fifty— but wishes he had done more. He has spent, possibly, too much of his time endeavoring to gather means." (Francis M. Lyman, *CR,* April 1904, p. 12.)

Scriptural References: D&C 26:1; 41:9; 60:13; Abr. 3:4;

Ps. 89:47; 90:4; Eccl. 3:1; 8:5; 2 Pet. 3:8; Alma 12:24; 34:22; 40:8; 42:4.

Tithe; tithing; law of tithing (*see also* material for section 119)

The basic meaning of *tithe* is "one-tenth." A *tithing* has been defined as "one-tenth of one's increase." The law of tithing was practiced in both Old Testament and New Testament times and has been reinstituted in this dispensation.

Selected Quotations

"The tithe is God's law for his children, yet the payment is entirely voluntary. In this respect it does not differ from the law of the Sabbath or from any other of his laws. We may refuse to obey any or all of them. Our obedience is voluntary, but our refusal to pay does not abrogate or repeal the law.

"If tithing is a voluntary matter, is it a gift or a payment of an obligation? There is a substantial difference between the two. A gift is a voluntary transfer of money or property without consideration. It is gratuitous. No one owes the obligation to make a gift. If tithing is a gift, we could give whatever we please, or make no gift at all. It would place our Heavenly Father in the very same category as the street beggar to whom we might toss a coin in passing.

"The Lord has established the law of tithing, and because it is his law, it becomes our obligation to observe it if we love him and have a desire to keep his commandments and receive his blessings. In this way it becomes a debt. The man who doesn't pay his tithing because he is in debt should ask himself if he is not also in debt to the Lord. . . .

"The payment of tithing strengthens faith, increases spirituality and spiritual capacity, and solidifies testimony. It gives the satisfaction of knowing one is complying with the will of the Lord. It brings the blessings that come from sharing with others through the purposes for which tithing is used. We cannot afford to deny ourselves these blessings. We cannot afford not to pay our tithing. We have a definite relationship to the future as well as to the present. What we give, and how we give, and the way we meet our obligations to the Lord has eternal significance.

"A testimony of the law of tithing comes from living it. Like all others of God's laws, when we live them we receive the blessings." (Howard W. Hunter, *CR,* April 1964, pp. 33-36.)

"Inquiries are received at the office of the First Presidency from time to time from officers and members of the Church asking for information as to what is considered a proper tithe. For your guidance in this matter, please be advised that we have uniformly replied that the simplest statement we know of is the statement of the Lord himself, namely, that the members of the Church should pay 'one-tenth of all their interest annually,' which is understood to mean income. No one is justified in making any other statement than this.

"We feel that every member of the Church is entitled to make his own decision as to what he thinks he owes the Lord and to make payment accordingly." (First Presidency, letter to stake presidents and bishops, Mar. 19, 1970.)

"Strictly speaking there is no such thing as a *part tithing.* Tithing is a tenth, and unless a person contributes the tenth, he has only made a contribution to the tithing funds of the Church. Somewhat inappropriately the term *part-tithepayer* is used with reference to those making such contributions." (Bruce R. McConkie, *MD,* pp. 798-99.)

Scriptural References: D&C 64:23; 85:3; 97:12; 119:4; Gen. 14:20; 28:22; Lev. 27:30; Num. 18:26; Deut. 12:6; 14:22; 26:12; 2 Chr. 31:5; Neh. 10:38; 12:44; Prov. 3:9; Mal. 3:8; Matt. 23:23; Luke 18:12; Heb. 7:2; Alma 13:15; 3 Ne. 24:8.

Today; "now it is called today"

The word *today,* when used in connection to the second coming of Jesus Christ, refers to the period between the present time and the second coming.

Selected Quotations

"Only through watchfulness and prayer may the signs of the times be correctly interpreted and the imminence of the Lord's appearing be apprehended. To the unwatchful and the wicked the event will be as sudden and unexpected as the coming of a thief in the night. But we are not left without definite information as to precedent signs. . . .

"War shall become so general that every man who will not take arms against his neighbor must of necessity flee to the land of Zion for safety. [D&C 45:66-71.] Ephraim shall assemble in Zion on the western continent, and Judah shall be again established in the east; and the cities of Zion and

Jerusalem shall be the capitals of the world empire, over which Messiah shall reign in undisputed authority. The Lost Tribes shall be brought forth from the place where God has hidden them through the centuries and receive their long deferred blessings at the hands of Ephraim. The people of Israel shall be restored from their scattered condition. [D&C 133:7-14, 21-35.]" (James E. Talmage, *JC*, pp. 785-86.)

"This is a day for action. This is the time for decision, not tomorrow, not next week. This is the time to make our covenant with the Lord. Now is the time for those who have been noncommittal or who have had a half-hearted interest to come out boldly and declare belief in Christ and be willing to demonstrate faith by works." (Howard W. Hunter, *CR*, October 1960, p. 109.)

Scriptural References: D&C 45:6; 64:23-25.

Tongues; speaking in tongues; interpretation of tongues (*see also* Gifts of the Spirit)

The gifts of speaking in tongues and the interpretation of tongues are gifts of the Holy Ghost that are given for the edification of man. These gifts have many applications, but they can also be easily counterfeited by Satan. The Lord, through His prophets, has given careful instructions in regard to the use of these gifts.

Selected Quotations

"Do not indulge too much in the exercise of the gift of tongues, or the devil will take advantage of the innocent and unwary. You may speak in tongues for your comfort, but I lay this down for a rule, that if anything is taught by the gift of tongues, it is not to be received for doctrine." (Joseph Smith, *HC* 4:607.)

"Be not so curious about tongues, do not speak in tongues except there be an interpreter present; the ultimate design of tongues is to speak to foreigners, and if persons are very anxious to display their intelligence, let them speak to such in their own tongues. The gifts of God are all useful in their place, but when they are applied to that which God does not intend, they prove an injury, a snare and a curse instead of a blessing." (Joseph Smith, *HC* 5:31-32.)

"Can I interpret tongues? Yes, because that gift is in me, and I have not forfeited it. Is it in brother Brigham [Young]? Yes, and so is every gift that God ever gave to His ancient

Apostles. . . . He has the spirit in him, and so have his Counsellors, that can discern your spirits and gifts, whether they are of God or of the devil. When any of you get up to speak in tongues, whether you do so by the power of God or of the devil, I can tell you which source that tongue came from, and if it is from the Lord I can interpret it." (Heber C. Kimball, *JD* 4:170-71.)

Scriptural References: D&C 46:24-25; 109:36; A of F 1:7; Mark 16:7; Acts 2:4, 11; 10:46; 19:6; 1 Cor. 12:10, 28, 30; 13:1, 8; 14:5-6, 18, 21-23, 39; Omni 1:25; Alma 9:21; 3 Ne. 29:6; Morm. 9:7, 24; Moro. 10:15-16.

Trump; "voice (sound) of a trump"

The trumpet is a musical instrument that can be made to produce a loud, blaring sound that can be heard for a considerable distance. Sometimes the expression "sound of a trumpet" is used in the scriptures in a literal sense—an actual trumpet will be blown and the actual sound of the trumpet will be heard. On other occasions, however, the expression is used only in the figurative sense that the message will be loud and clear, just as the sound of the trumpet can be loud and clear.

Selected Quotations

"After these great judgments [D&C 88:88-91] are poured upon the nations of the earth, then will be fulfilled the words which I have read. [D&C 88:92, quoted.] After these angels have flown through the midst of heaven calling upon the inhabitants of the earth to prepare for the coming of the Bridegroom, seven more angels are to sound their trumps. The first one sounds, and his proclamation is concerning great Babylon. [D&C 88:94, quoted.]

"There must be something connected with the sounding of this trump that is miraculous in order that all nations may hear it. Any sound that can be produced by mortal man does not reach, generally speaking, over about thirty miles from where it originates, which is a very small space indeed. But there will be something connected with the sounding of the trump of the first of the seven angels which will manifest a power which we know nothing of. The sound of that trump will be heard by all people, nations, kindreds and tongues in the four quarters of our globe. I do not know that the sound will be so much louder than some we have heard, but it will be carried by some miraculous power so that all people will hear it.

" 'Immediately after the sounding of this trump, there will be silence in heaven for the space of half an hour.' Whether the half hour here spoken is according to our reckoning— thirty minutes, or whether it be according to the reckoning of the Lord we do not know. We know that the word hour is used in some portions of the Scriptures to represent quite a lengthy period of time. For instance, we, the Latter-day Saints, are living in the eleventh hour, that is the eleventh period of time [Sec. 33:3] and for aught we know the half hour during which silence is to prevail in heaven may be quite an extensive period of time. During the period of silence all things are perfectly still; no angels flying during that half hour; no trumpets sounding; no noise in the heavens above; but immediately after this great silence the curtain of heaven shall be unfolded as a scroll is unfolded." (Orson Pratt, *JD* 16:327-28.)

Scriptural References: D&C 24:12; 29:4; 30:9; 33:2; 34:6; 36:1; 42:6; 75:4; JS-M 1:37; Ps. 47:5; 1 Col. 15:52; 1 Thes. 4:16; Alma 29:1.

Truth; Light of Truth; Spirit of Truth

The meaning and extent of truth has been a favorite topic of discussion for philosophers over the years. The question "What is truth?" was asked of Jesus Christ when he lived upon the earth, but the present New Testament does not include his answer. (See John 18:38.) In the Doctrine and Covenants, the Lord has defined truth as "knowledge of things as they are, and as they were, and as they are to come." (93:24.)

The Savior frequently used the word *truth* in regard to himself, for he is a God of truth: "I am the way, the truth, and the life." (John 14:6; Ether 4:12.) The prophets indicate that the Savior "is full of grace and truth" (2 Ne. 2:6; John 1:14, 17; D&C 93:11), and he came to the earth to "bear witness unto the truth" (John 18:37). Jesus Christ is also identified by the title *Spirit of truth*— "I am the Spirit of truth." (D&C 93:26.) The apostle John quoted the Savior: "When he, the spirit of truth, is come, he will guide you into all truth." (John 16:13.) The Holy Ghost, who has the responsibility to be a witness for Jesus Christ and to testify of truth, might also be designated by the title *Spirit of truth.*

Selected Quotations

"What is truth? Here I must give you an inspired definition, a definition that came from an unsophisticated boy-prophet, but one which rivals the definitions of the greatest scholars and of all time. [D&C 93:24, quoted.] How is such knowledge to be obtained? Through science and education? Yes, in part, but not wholly. And why not completely? Because most of the knowledge of things 'as they were' and 'as they are to come' is without the realm and province of science, as well as much knowledge of 'things as they are.' Science, then, can give us but fragments of truth, not the whole truth. And the whole truth is necessary if we are to be provided with proper criteria by which to do our choosing.

"How then, is the whole truth to be secured? The key is to be found in another revelation, 'the Spirit of truth is of God.' [D&C 93:26.] That being so, we must, of necessity have God's aid in the acquisition of truth. His aid comes through faith and prayer. Faith contemplates the acceptance of spiritual reality of a world outside the domain of science. It involves methods and processes different from those of scientific research. It postulates humility and dependence on divine power, the antipathies of egotism and self-sufficiency. A contrite heart is a fertile field for planting the seeds of truth. In such a field they come to fruition in a knowledge, understanding, and conviction of the great concepts of life which defy the reason and philosophy of the arrogant and self-sufficient who will not stoop to the methods of the humble." (Stephen L Richards, *CR,* April 1939, pp. 40-41.)

"In the Church we have no fear that any discovery of new truths will ever be in conflict with these standards—with any fundamental basic principle which we advocate in the Gospel. Truth is always consistent. This fact gives to us as members of the Church a feeling of great security, a feeling of peace, a feeling of assurance. We know beyond any question that the truths which we advocate, the truths of the gospel restored to the earth through the Prophet Joseph, are in very deed the truths of heaven. These truths will always be consistent with the discovery of any new truths, whether discovered in the laboratory, through research of the scientist, or whether revealed from heaven through prophets of God. Time is always on the side of truth." (Ezra Taft Benson, *CR,* April 1958, p. 60.)

"Freedom is based on truth, and no man is completely free as long as any part of his belief is based on error, for the chains of error bind his mind. This is why it is so important for us to learn all the truth we can from all the sources we can." (N. Eldon Tanner, *Ensign,* May 1978, p. 14.)

"A truth of the gospel is not a truth until you live it. You do not really believe in tithing, and it is not a truth of the gospel to you until you pay it. The Word of Wisdom to you is not a truth of the gospel until you keep it. The Sabbath day is not a holy day unless you observe it. Fasting and paying fast offerings, consecrating your fast, is not a truth of the gospel unless you live it." (Harold B. Lee, *BYUSY,* 1961, p. 10.)

Scriptural References: D&C 6:15; 50:17, 19, 21; 88:6; 93:9, 11, 23, 26, 29; 107:71; 124:9; Moses 1:6; Ps. 117:2; John 14:17; 15:26; 16:13; Alma 30:46.

Twinkling of an eye

Twinkling of an eye is an expression used in the scriptures to indicate that when a certain thing happens it will occur quickly, immediately—virtually in the time it would take for a person to blink his eyes.

Scriptural References: D&C 43:32; 63:51; 101:31; 1 Cor. 15:52; 3 Ne. 28:8.

United Order; order of Enoch (*see also* Consecration; Enoch)

A distinction should be made between the law of consecration and the united order (or order of Enoch), which is concerned with the financial and monetary portions of the law of consecration.

The law of consecration is a celestial law wherein the righteous willingly and wholeheartedly consecrate their all—time, strength, talents, possessions—to the establishment, upbuilding, and maintenance of the Lord's work and kingdom. It is the law by which the city of Zion will be established in the last days.

Many of the saints in ancient times and some of the saints in the early part of this dispensation were given the opportunity to live the financial portions of this law by having "all things in common." Full practice of the financial law would help one to develop those attributes of godliness which enable one to live the law of consecration and prepare for eternal life in the celestial kingdom.

Selected Quotations

"In this last dispensation, before the church had been organized nine months the Lord directed the Saints to take care of the poor. At the same time he told them that if they did not do so, they were not his disciples. (See D&C 38.) Five weeks later, on February 9, 1831, he revealed the united order. (See D&C 42.) Within a month thereafter, he spoke again on the subject, saying to the brethren that, pending the establishment of the order, they must 'visit the poor and the needy and administer to their relief.' (D&C 44:6.)

"During the next three years and four months, the Saints had settled Independence, Missouri, made an attempt to live the united order, failed to do so, and been expelled from their properties in Jackson County, and Zion's Camp had gone to Missouri from Kirtland with the purpose of restoring them to their homes. This the expedition was unable to do. On Fishing River, Missouri, June 22, 1834, the Lord explained the reason for the failure of their putting the Saints back in their homes, as follows: [D&C 105:16 quoted.]

"The requirement to live the united order at that time was then withdrawn. The lesser law of tithing was revealed, which, with the law of the fast, has prevailed and persisted in the Church until now." (Spencer W. Kimball, *Ensign,* November 1975, p. 125.)

"Out of the answers to [Joseph Smith's] prayers on the subject [of help for the poor] was revealed an ideal economic system, commonly known as the 'United Order.' It rejected the weaknesses of the many similar attempts and introduced new, almost revolutionary methods of operation.

"Its objective was to provide every man who is willing to work with the necessities and the comforts of life, thus abolishing poverty from the earth. It was to be a cooperative plan but directly opposed to modern communism, since it recognized man as a free agent, respected the rights of private property, and preserved and encouraged individual initiative. The United Order thus established rests upon four basic principles.

"First, the earth is the Lord's. Men are only stewards of their possessions. All that man has should be used therefore in accordance with the Lord's expressed will.

"Second, all men are children of God—of a divine family. Therefore, the Lord requires that they must help one another as needs arise, provided that he who will not work shall have no claim upon his brother.

"Third, every man must be respected as a free agent. He may enter the order at his pleasure. Once in the order, he must be allowed to use, fully, and as he pleases, any properties placed in his hands. He may leave the order at his pleasure.

"Fourth, the government of the order is vested in a central agency, sustained by the members of the order, presided over by the bishop, his counselors, and such helpers as may be needed. This central agency would have power to adjust the disputes normally arising among strongly individualized human beings.

"The operation of the order under these four heads is extremely simple. Those who join the order would place all their possessions, irrevocably, in a common treasury—the rich man, his wealth; the poor man, his penny. Then each member would receive a sufficient portion, called 'an inheritance,' from the common treasury, to enable him to continue in his trade, business, or profession as he may desire. The farmer would receive land and implements; the tradesman, tools and materials; the merchant, the necessary capital; the professional man, instruments, books, etc. Members who work for others would receive proportionate interests in the enterprises they serve. No one would be without property—all would have an inheritance.

"A person's inheritance would be his personal property, to operate permanently and freely for his benefit and that of his family. Should he withdraw from the order, his inheritance would go with him, but he would have no claim upon that which he had placed in the common treasury. [D&C 51:3-6.] At the end of the year, or a set period, the member who had earned more than his business and family needs required would place the surplus in the common treasury. Thus, for example, large fortunes would be administered by the order as a whole rather than by one individual. The member who, despite intelligent diligence, had lost from his operations would have his loss made up by the general treasury for another start, or he might with his consent be placed in some activity better fitting his gifts.

"In short, the general treasury would set up every man in his preferred field and would care for and help those unable to profit from their inheritance. The general treasury, holding the surpluses of the members, would also finance the erection of public buildings and make possible all community enterprises decided upon by the order. [D&C 104:60-77.]

"This remarkable economic order was tried out in Ohio and Missouri, chiefly in 1832-1834. The Church was then organizing settlements in Missouri. Though practiced only a short time, about two years, it showed possibilities of great success. However, in those pioneer days, under severe persecution from neighbors, and with undisciplined selfishness of certain members, the people could not give the order a fair trial." (John A. Widtsoe, *JS,* pp. 191-94.)

Scriptural References: D&C 76:57; 92:1; 104:48, 53.

Urim and Thummim

The words *Urim* and *Thummim* are transliterations of the plural Hebrew words which have the general meaning of "lights" and "perfections." The Urim and Thummim used by the Prophet Joseph Smith in the translation of the Book of Mormon consisted of "two transparent stones set in the rim of a bow fastened to a breastplate." (Joseph Smith in the Wentworth letter; *HC* 4:537.)

These two stones were possessed by the brother of Jared in Book of Mormon times. (Ether 3:22-28.) Old Testament prophets also had a Urim and Thummim (Ex. 28:30; Lev. 8:8; Num. 27:21; Deut. 33:8; 1 Sam. 28:6; Ezra 2:63; Neh. 7:65), as did some of the prophets and historians of the Book of Mormon (Omni 1:20-21; Mosiah 8:13-19; 28:11-20; Alma 37:23-24; Ether 4:1-7).

The inspired writings of Joseph Smith indicate that when the earth is sanctified, it "will be a Urim and Thummim to the inhabitants who dwell thereon." (D&C 130:9.)

Selected Quotations

"When Moroni told Joseph Smith of the record deposited in the Hill Cumorah, he said:

Also, that there were two stones in silver bows—and these stones, fastened to a breastplate, constituted what is called the Urim and Thummim—deposited with the plates; and the possession and use of these stones were what constituted "seers" in ancient or former times; and that God had prepared them for the purpose of translating the book. (JS-H 1:35)

"...The use of the Urim and Thummim was known to the prophets of old:

Urim and Thummim, (i.e. "Light and Perfection") mentioned as the means by which the High Priest inquired of the Lord, Ex. 28:30; Lev. 8:8; Num. 27:21; Deut. 33:8; 1 Sam. 28:6. The Urim and Thummim were clearly material objects of some kind; it has been suggested that they were (I) stones in the High Priest's breast-plate, (II) sacred dice, (III) little images of "truth" and "justice" such as are found hung around the neck of an Egyptian priest's mummy. The Urim and Thummim did not exist after the Captivity—Ezra 2:63. (*A Concise Biblical Encyclopedia*, p. 154.)" (Le-Grand Richards, *MWW*, pp. 71-72.)

Scriptural References: D&C 10:1; 17:1; 130:9-10; Abr. 3:1, 4; JS-H 1:35, 42, 52, 59, 62; Ex. 28:30; Lev. 8:8; Num. 27:21; Deut. 33:8; 1 Sam. 28:6; Ezra 2:63; Neh. 7:65; Ether 3:22-28.

Vessels of the Lord; "be ye clean that bear the vessels of the Lord"

In ancient Israel, certain vessels (bowls, urns, vases, and other containers) and utensils were used in religious feasts and ceremonies. The vessels that were to be used in the temple had special significance and were handled only by those who were worthy and authorized and who had properly prepared themselves. In a somewhat similar manner, the Lord has indicated that his saints should come "out from among the wicked" (38:42) and leave the worldliness of Babylon so they will be worthy to "bear the vessels of the Lord" (see 133:5).

Selected Quotations

"My theme for these remarks is 'Be ye clean that bear the vessels of the Lord.' (D&C 133:5.)

" '... remember, O man, for all thy doings thou shalt be brought into judgment. Wherefore, if ye have sought to do wickedly in the days of your probation, then ye are found unclean before the judgment-seat of God; and no unclean thing can dwell with God; wherefore, ye must be cast off forever.' (1 Ne. 10:20-21.) Those are the words of Nephi.

" '... behold, I say unto you, the kingdom of God is not filthy, and there cannot any unclean thing enter into the kingdom of God. ...' (1 Ne. 15:34.)

"Six hundred years later the resurrected Jesus told his Nephite disciples that 'no unclean thing can enter into his kingdom; therefore nothing entereth into his rest save it be those who have washed their garments in my blood, because of their faith, and the repentance of all their sins, and their faithfulness unto the end.' (3 Ne. 27:19.)

"At the very beginning of this last dispensation, Jesus said to the brethren in conference assembled, '. . . go ye out from among the wicked. Save yourselves. Be ye clean that bear the vessels of the Lord. . . .' (D&C 38:42.)

"Within the same year he repeated, 'Go ye out from Babylon. Be ye clean that bear the vessels of the Lord.' (D&C 133:5.) These words call to mind Paul's declaration to the Corinthians: 'Know ye not that ye are the temple of God, and that the Spirit of God dwelleth in you? If any man defile the temple of God, him shall God destroy; for the temple of God is holy, which temple ye are.' (1 Cor. 3:16-17.)" (Marion G. Romney, *Ensign,* May 1974, pp. 79, 81.)

Scriptural References: D&C 38:42; 133:5; Isa. 52:11; 3 Ne. 20:41; Moro. 7:31.

Vineyard; "prune my vineyard" (*see also* Harvest symbols)

The vineyard is the harvest symbol usually used to represent the world—the earth and all of the people who live on the earth. At times the vineyard (the people of the world) has become corrupt, and it is necessary to prune it so the vine will be able to produce good fruit in abundance. The process of pruning involves the separation of one part of the plant from other parts. This could be achieved by calling out or separating the righteous from among the wicked or by the actual destruction of the wicked. It is usually in the former sense that the Lord instructs his servants (missionaries) to prune his vineyard. However, the Lord has also warned that when the pruning process is completed, the vines that continue to bring forth bad fruit will be burned. This evidently refers to the burning of the wicked, which will take place at the second coming when Jesus Christ will come in power and great glory.

Scriptural References: D&C 21:9; 24:19; 33:3-4; 39:13, 17; 72:2-19; 101:44-56; 103:21; 107:93; 2 Ne. 15:1-7; Jacob 5.

Virgins; parable of the ten virgins

The Savior gave the parable of the ten virgins in New Testament times (Matt. 25:1-13) and repeated it in this dispensation (D&C 45:56-59; 63:54). In all these instances, it is clear that this parable has to do with events associated with the second coming of Jesus Christ.

Selected Quotations

"The story itself is based on oriental marriage customs, with which the Lord's attentive listeners were familiar. It was and yet is common in those lands, particularly in connection with marriage festivities among the wealthy classes, for the bridegroom to go to the home of the bride, accompanied by his friends in processional array, and later to conduct the bride to her new home with a larger body of attendants composed of groomsmen, bridesmaids, relatives and friends. As the bridal party progressed, to the accompaniment of gladsome music, it was increased by little groups who had gathered in waiting at convenient places along the route, and particularly near the end of the course where organized companies came forth to meet the advancing procession. Wedding ceremonies were appointed for the evening and night hours; and the necessary use of torches and lamps gave brilliancy and added beauty to the scene." (James E. Talmage, *JC*, p. 577.)

"This was a parable [Matt. 25:1-13] as with many of the Master's teachings based upon customs with which the people, his hearers, were already familiar.

"The purpose of this lesson was to impress upon those called to the ministry and upon his followers and upon the world that there should be an increasing watchfulness and preparation for the day which he had predicted when the Lord would come again in judgment upon the earth.

"The bridegroom of the parable was the Master, the Savior of mankind. The marriage feast symbolized the second coming of the Savior to receive his Church unto himself. The virgins were those who were professed believers in Christ, because they were expectantly waiting for the coming of the bridegroom to the marriage feast, or they were connected with the Church and the events which were to transpire with reference to it.

"That this parable did refer particularly to the believers in Christ with a warning to them is further indicated by what the Lord has told us in modern revelation in which he said: [D&C 63:53-54, quoted], undoubtedly meaning a separation of the wicked from the righteous among the professing believers in the Lord Jesus Christ.

"The Lord defines the wise virgins of his parable in still another revelation in which he said: [D&C 45:57, quoted].

"Here is clearly indicated a truth we must all recognize, that among the people of God, the believers in the Savior of the world, there are those who are wise and keep the commandments, and yet there are those who are foolish, who are disobedient, and who neglect their duties. . . .

"The Lord gives us, each one, a lamp to carry, but whether or not we shall have oil in our lamps depends solely upon each one of us. Whether or not we keep the commandments and supply the needed oil to light our way and to guide us on our way depends upon each of us individually. We cannot borrow from our Church membership. We cannot borrow from an illustrious ancestry. Whether or not we have oil in our lamps, I repeat, depends solely upon each one of us; it is determined by our faithfulness in keeping the commandments of the Living God.

"We must buy from the only source from which we can obtain this kind of oil referred to by the Master—from the fountain of eternal supply." (Harold B. Lee, CR, October 1951, pp. 26-27, 30.)

"Now the question is, how can we keep oil in our lamps? By keeping the commandments of God, remembering our prayers, doing as we are told by the revelations of Jesus Christ, and otherwise assisting in building up Zion. When we are laboring for the kingdom of God, we will have oil in our lamps, our light will shine and we will feel the testimony of the spirit of God. On the other hand, if we set our hearts upon the things of the world and seek for the honors of men, we shall walk in the dark and not in the light. If we do not value our priesthood, and the work of this priesthood, the building up of the kingdom of God, . . . if we do not feel that these things are more valuable to us than the things of the world, we will have no oil in our lamps, no light, and we shall fail to be present at the marriage supper of the Lamb." (Wilford Woodruff, JD 22:208.)

"Live within your means. Get out of debt. Keep out of debt. Lay by for a rainy day which has always come and will come again. Practise and increase your habits of thrift, industry, economy, frugality. Remember that the parable of the ten virgins, the five that were wise and the five that were foolish, can be just as applicable to matters of the temporal world as those of the spiritual." (J. Reuben Clark, Jr., *CR*, October 1937, p. 107.)

Scriptural References: D&C 45:56; 63:54; Matt. 25:1-11.

Visions (*see also* Gifts of the Spirit)

Through visions, the Lord can reveal through the power of the Holy Ghost things past, present, and future to his prophets or others who qualify for this important gift of the Spirit. Receiving visions and revelations from God is one of the marks of the true Church.

Selected Quotations

"Holy men and holy women have had heavenly visions, by the hundreds and by the thousands, yea by the tens of thousands since this gospel was restored to the earth in our day." (Heber J. Grant, *CR*, October 1913, p. 92.)

"But what I want to say in regard to these matters is, that the Lord does communicate some things of importance to the children of men by means of visions and dreams as well as by the records of divine truth. And what is it all for? It is to teach us a principle. We may never see anything take place exactly as we see it in a dream or a vision, yet it is intended to teach us a principle." (Wilford Woodruff, *JD* 22:333.)

"God never bestows upon His people, or upon an individual, superior blessings without a severe trial to prove them, to prove that individual, or that people, to see whether they will keep their covenants with Him and keep in remembrance what He has shown them. Then the greater the vision, the greater the display of the power of the enemy . . .

"So when individuals are blessed with visions, revelations, and great manifestations, look out, then the devil is nigh you, and you will be tempted in proportion to the vision, revelation, or manifestation you have received." (Brigham Young, *JD* 3:205-6.)

Scriptural References: D&C 76:14, 28, 49, 113; 107: 93; 110:11-13; A of F 1:7; Prov. 29:18; Acts 10:3-19; 1 Ne. 1:16; 2 Ne. 4:23.

Voice of the Lord; voice of the Lord's Spirit

The voice of the Lord can be perceived by man either through his physical senses (the ear) or directly to his spirit (or mind). Sometimes the voice of the Lord is heard audibly but at other times it is perceived as a still small voice or as a whisper, and at still other times it is perceived only by its impressions upon the mind.

Scriptural References: D&C 1:2, 11, 14; 25:1; 52:1; 75:1; 84:46-47; 88:66; 97:1; 104:36; 105:36, 40; 112:22; Jer. 26:13; 38:20; 42:6, 13, 21; 43:4, 7; 44:23; Alma 5:16; 9:21; 13:22; 20:2; 43:49.

Ward

The only time the word *ward* is used in the Doctrine and Covenants is in reference to a recorder being appointed "in each ward of the city." (128:3.) The more extensive development of the ward as an integral ecclesiastical unit of the Church occurred after these early revelations were given.

Selected Quotations

"A ward organization is the unit that deals directly with the membership of the Church residing within ward boundaries, and is presided over by a bishop and two counselors, with a clerk or clerks to assist them. The bishopric directs the work of the Aaronic Priesthood quorums, keeps all quorums and auxiliaries fully organized, and sees that all the members are given an opportunity to labor in whatever capacity they are best qualified for, according to their special gifts and talents." (LeGrand Richards, *MWW*, p. 167.)

Scriptural References: D&C 128:3; Jer. 37:13; Acts 12:10.

Washing of feet; ordinances of washing feet (*see also* Feet)

At the time of the Last Supper, the Lord performed the gospel ordinance of washing of feet. Concerning this act, the Inspired Version records: "Now this was the custom of the Jews under their law; wherefore, Jesus did this that the law might be fulfilled." (John 13:10.)

Later the Lord told His apostles, "Ye also ought to wash one another's feet." (John 13:14.)

This ordinance of the gospel has been restored in this dispensation. When the School of the Prophets was organized, the Lord indicated that the members should "be received by the ordinance of the washing of feet, for unto this end [that ye might be clean from the blood of this generation] was the ordinance of the washing of feet instituted." (D&C 88:139.)

The ordinance of washing of the feet has now been incorporated in the ordinances that are revealed to be administered in the Lord's house.

The ordinance of washing of feet should not be confused with the instructions that elders serving as missionaries might cleanse their feet as a testimony against those who reject their testimony. Sometimes this involved the cleansing of feet with water (D&C 84:92-94; 99:4), but it is not the same as the ordinance of washing of feet.

Additional information on this subject may be found in *History of the Church* 1:312, 323; 2:308, 430-31, 475-76; *Jesus the Christ*, pp. 595 and 619; and *Mormon Doctrine*, pp. 829-32.

Scriptural References: D&C 60:15; 84:92; 88:74, 139; 99:4; Gen. 18:4; 19:2; 24:32; 43:24; John 13:5; 1 Tim. 5:10.

Watchmen; watchmen on the tower

The Lord's people have lived in many relatively flat lands. In some of these lands the people were instructed to build watchtowers on which a watchman could be placed to warn the people of an approaching enemy. The symbol of the watchman on the tower had great significance to the people, and they could very readily identify with the symbol and the principle being taught.

However, the practice of building and manning watchtowers would be ineffective (1) if the watchtower were never built, (2) if the watchman did not see the enemy coming, (3) if the watchman called out a warning when there was no enemy, (4) if the watchman saw the enemy but did not issue a warning, or (5) if the watchman issued the warning but the people did not hearken to it. All of these conditions were included at one time or another in the teachings of the Lord.

In regard to missionary work, when the Lord commands his servants to preach the gospel, it is the responsibility of the servants to obey the Lord. If the servants obey the Lord and teach the gospel, then the responsibility for accepting or rejecting the gospel shifts to those to whom the gospel is taught. If the servants do not teach the gospel when commanded, then the servants not only become responsible for their own disobedience, but they are also, in some way, responsible for the continued wickedness of those who would have received the gospel and repented if the gospel had been taught to them.

This is essentially the same teaching the Lord gave anciently to Ezekiel in his analogy of the watchman of Israel. (Ezek. 3:16-21 and 33:1-9.) It is also the admonition of Jacob the son of Lehi, in his explanation as to why he and his brother Joseph magnified their office "unto the Lord, taking upon us the responsibility, answering the sins of the people upon our own heads if we did not teach them the word of God with all diligence; wherefore, by laboring with our might their blood might not come upon our garments; otherwise their blood would come upon our garments, and we would not be found spotless at the last day." (Jacob 1:19.)

Selected Quotations

"I would like to speak of a dream or a parable taken from one of the prophets of the Old Testament, in which was depicted a watchman on a high tower overlooking the countryside, watching for enemies that might be coming to destroy, enemies that were in evidence by clouds of dust of approaching camels or horses, or whatever they had. The watchman was reporting hour by hour down to his lord in the courtyard. 'All is well, All is well,' or he reported if he saw any dangers.

"But in the dream or the parable the lord asked: 'But watchman, what of the night? Watchman, what of the night?' suggesting that more to be feared than the enemies that come in the daytime that you can see are the enemies that come in the night.

"Now it is about the enemies that come in the night I want just to make one reference.

"The term 'elder,' which is applied to all holders of the Melchizedek Priesthood, means a defender of the faith. That is our prime responsibility and calling. Every holder of the Melchizedek Priesthood is to be a defender of the faith.

"There are insidious forces among us that are constantly trying to knock at our doors and trying to lay traps for our young men and women, particularly those who are unwary and unsophisticated in the ways of the world. I speak of the battle against liquor by the drink, gambling, prostitution, pornography, and our efforts to aid Christian people who desire to have one day dedicated to keeping the Sabbath day holy. All we have to do is to remember what the Lord said in order to impress the importance of keeping the Sabbath day holy: 'And that thou mayest more fully keep thyself unspotted from the world, thou shalt go to the house of prayer and offer up thy sacraments upon my holy day.' (D&C 59:9.) Defenders of the faith should be alert, then, to see to it with all their influence that there is an opportunity given to the working man, the boy and the girl, the husband and the wife to have one day in the week when they can be with their families and have one day consecrated as a day of rest. Watchmen, be alert to the 'dangers of the night'!" (Harold B. Lee, *IE,* June 1970, p. 63.)

"We are the nation's watchmen—no other people collectively love the Constitution and honor it and hold it as a divinely inspired document as do the Latter-day Saints. The duty of the watchman is to watch over and safeguard his people. . . . As a generation of those who love this glorious country, we must ask ourselves, 'But watchman, what of the night?' Have our youth enough of the fires of freedom kindled in them to withstand the darkness? We must teach them in our homes, churches, and schools. The sound must go across this land from one end to the other." (Vaughn J. Featherstone, *Ensign,* November 1975, pp. 9-10.)

Scriptural References: D&C 101:45-46, 53-54, 57; 105:16, 30; 124:61; 2 Kgs. 17:9; 18:8; Isa. 62:6; Ezek. 33:3-6; Mosiah 12:22; 15:29; 3 Ne. 16:18; 20:32.

Weak things of the world

The Lord usually does not call as his prophets men who are already of great renown and who are highly learned in the ways of the world. Rather, he usually selects the young and/or relatively unlearned who are humble and worthy, and then tutors them. Joseph who was sold into Egypt, Daniel, Samuel the prophet, and Joseph Smith are all examples of prophets who were called in their youth and yet became powerful and great men under the tutelage and influence of the Lord.

In the true church today, the missionaries sent forth to teach are often quite young and relatively inexperienced in the ways of the world. Yet if they go forth humbly and worthily, the Spirit of the Lord can make them mighty in preaching and power.

Selected Quotations

"The Lord called Joseph Smith and others from among the weak things of the world, because he and his associates were contrite and humble. The great and mighty ones in the nations the Lord could not use because of their pride and self-righteousness. The Prophet discoursing on this question once said: 'There are a great many wise men and women, too, in our midst who are too wise to be taught; therefore they must die in their ignorance, and in the resurrection they will find their mistake. Many seal up the door of heaven by saying, So far God may reveal and I will believe.' (*TPJS,* p. 309.)

"The Lord's ways are not man's ways, and he cannot choose those who in their own judgment are too wise to be taught. Therefore he chooses those who are willing to be taught and he makes them mighty even to the breaking down of the great and mighty. In his mercy and justice he gives all men the means of escape from the dominion of Satan and the bondage of sin. Therefore he sent the Gospel and his Priesthood before the great and dreadful day should come. 'Surely,' said Amos, 'the Lord God will do nothing but he revealeth his secret unto his servants the prophets.' This restoration came that faith might increase, that the everlasting covenant, which had been broken might be established. When we think of our missionary system, we can see how the weak have gone forth among the strong ones and have prevailed. The mighty and strong ones have been broken down by the humble elders of the Church." (Joseph Fielding Smith, *CHMR* 1:255.)

Scriptural References: D&C 1:19, 23; 35:13; 89:3; 124:1; 133:58-59; 1 Cor. 1:27; Ether 12:27.

Welfare; welfare services

The scriptures would indicate that the Lord has always been concerned that the physical needs of the worthy be provided. Such principles and plans as the order of Enoch, the united order, tithing, and fast offering have been taught and utilized to help take care of the worthy poor, the sick, the handicapped, the fatherless, and the widow. During the past few decades, the plans and procedures through which these needs are to be met have been called welfare or welfare services. Of necessity, much of the attention of present Church leaders has been directed toward providing these physical and often spiritual needs.

Selected Quotations

"The welfare program in operation since 1936 is a continuing plan for the people of the Church until a more perfect and higher plan is revealed. When we demonstrate our faith, worthiness, willingness, and unity to live fully the principles of the welfare plan, it will lead and prepare us for the higher law of the celestial kingdom." (Delbert L. Stapley, *CR*, September 1955, pp. 14-15.)

"The principle of self-reliance or personal independence is fundamental to the happy life. In too many places, in too many ways, we are getting away from it. The substance of what I want to say is this: The same principle—self-reliance—has application to the spiritual and to the emotional.

"We have been taught to store a year's supply of food, clothing, and, if possible, fuel—*at home.* There has been no attempt to set up storerooms in every chapel. We know that in the crunch our members may not be able to get to the chapel for supplies.

"Can we not see that the same principle applies to inspiration and revelation, the solving of problems, to counsel, and to guidance? We need to have a source of it *stored in every home,* not just in the bishop's office. If we do not do that, we are quite as threatened spiritually as we should be were we to assume that the Church should supply all material needs.

"Unless we use care, we are on the verge of doing to ourselves emotionally (and, therefore, spiritually) what we have been working so hard for generations to avoid materially." (Boyd K. Packer, *Ensign,* May 1978, p. 91.)

" 'The Latter-day Saints believe not only in the gospel of spiritual salvation, but also in the gospel of temporal salvation. . . . We do not feel that it is possible for men to be really good and faithful Christian people unless they can also be good, faithful, honest and industrious people. Therefore, we preach the gospel of industry, the gospel of economy, the gospel of sobriety.' (Joseph F. Smith, *GD,* pp. 208-9.)

". . . When in 1936 the First Presidency re-enunciated these precepts in the form of the present-day welfare plan, they were merely extending to that generation a more complete opportunity for establishing the ideal of Zion. In this generation their words may have even deeper meaning.

" 'Our primary purpose,' said the First Presidency, 'was to set up, in so far as it might be possible, a system under which the curse of idleness would be done away with, the evils of a dole abolished, and independence, industry, thrift and self respect be once more established amongst our people. The aim of the Church is to help the people to help themselves. Work is to be reenthroned as the ruling principle of the lives of our Church membership.' (*CR,* October 1936, p. 3.)

"Welfare Services is not a program, but the essence of the gospel. *It is the gospel in action.* It is the crowning principle of a Christian life.

"So as to better visualize this process and firmly fix the specific principles that undergird this work, may I rehearse to you what I believe are its foundational truths.

"First is *love.* The measure of our love for our fellowman and, in a large sense, the measure of our love for the Lord, is what we do for one another and for the poor and the distressed. . . .

"Second is *service.* To serve is to abase oneself, to succor those in need of succor, and to impart of one's 'substance to the poor and the needy, feeding the hungry, and suffering all manner of afflictions, for Christ's sake.' (Alma 4:13.) . . .

"Third is *work.* Work brings happiness, self-esteem, and prosperity. It is the means of all accomplishment; it is the opposite of idleness. We are commanded to work. (See Gen. 3:19.) . . .

"Fourth is *self-reliance.* The Church and its members are commanded by the Lord to be self-reliant and independent. (See D&C 78:13-14.) . . .

"Fifth is *consecration,* which encompasses sacrifice. Consecration is the giving of one's time, talents, and means to care for those in need—whether spiritually or temporally—and in building the Lord's kingdom. . . .

"Sixth is *stewardship.* In the Church a stewardship is a sacred spiritual or temporal trust for which there is accountability. Because all things belong to the Lord, we are stewards over our bodies, minds, families, and properties. (See D&C 104:11-15.) A faithful steward is one who exercises righteous dominion, cares for his own, and looks to the poor and needy. (See D&C 104:15-18.)

"Now, turning from personal and family responsibilities to the Church's formal welfare activities . . . let me emphasize briefly several points.

"1. Make adequate provision for those who receive Church assistance to work or serve, according to their ability, for what they receive.

"2. Use good judgment in acquiring and managing your welfare production project. Be businesslike and frugal, recognizing that we are growing people—both givers and receivers—more than food and merchandise.

"3. Follow the Spirit in knowing to what extent individuals and families can and should care for themselves on their own.

"4. Use local resource persons to the fullest extent possible.

"5. Finally, regularly hold effective Welfare Committee meetings at all administrative levels." (Spencer W. Kimball, *Ensign,* November 1977, pp. 76-79.)

Scriptural References: D&C 38:35; 42:30-39; 51:5; 56:16; 104:16, 18.

Wine-press; Jesus Christ has trodden the wine-press alone

Before the invention of modern machinery, wine was made by the pressing of juice from grapes by the treading of human feet. Often this work was combined with religious celebrations and festivals and was a time of rejoicing. Usually several men would work together in this activity, singing and encouraging one another. (Isa. 16:10; Jer. 25:30; 48:33.) Sometimes the work would fall upon only one man, the others having become discouraged or turning to easier tasks.

In the scriptural analogy of the Lord having trodden the wine press alone (Rev. 14:15, 19-20; D&C 76:107; 88:106; 133:50), the implication seems to be that the appointed work will be done even if the Lord has to do it alone. Also, the analogy might also suggest that some things (the atonement performed in Gethsemane and at the time of the crucifixion and resurrection) could have been accomplished only by Jesus Christ.

Selected Quotations

"When Christ comes in his glory as conqueror and deliverer and to take vengeance upon the ungodly, he shall come as one who has trodden the winepress alone. It shall be the time of vengeance which is in his heart and all nations shall tremble at his presence. [D&C 45:74-75.] In that day he who has sanctified himself shall be saved, but he who has not shall be cut off from among the people. Then the words of Malachi (chap. 3-4) shall be fulfilled. The wicked shall be as stubble and shall be consumed, but the righteous shall be spared, and their children grow up as 'calves of the stall' without sin unto salvation. The thousand years of peace shall be ushered in and Christ shall reign as King of Kings and Lord of Lords. In that day when the unrighteous question his coming and the authority of his punishment the Lord shall answer them: [D&C 133:65-74, quoted.]" (Joseph Fielding Smith, *CHMR* 2:266.)

Scriptural References: D&C 76:107; 88:106; 133:50; Isa. 16:10; Jer. 25:30; 48:33; Rev. 14:15, 19-20.

Witnesses; law of witnesses; the three special witnesses of the Book of Mormon

The divine law of witnesses indicates that "in the mouth of two or three witnesses shall every word be established." (2 Cor. 13:1; see also Deut. 17:6; Matt. 18:15-16; John 8:12-29.) This law might be one of the reasons there are three members in the Godhead. As the Savior indicated: "the Father, and the Son, and the Holy Ghost are one. . . . I bear record of the Father, and the Father beareth record of me, and the Holy Ghost beareth record of the Father and me." (3 Ne. 11:27, 32.) One of the ways in which the members of the Godhead are one is that they witness or testify of each other.

The scriptures also testify of each other, and all the scriptures testify of Jesus Christ. The Book of Mormon has several modern witnesses to its authenticity: Joseph Smith, the three special witnesses, and the eight special witnesses. Such witnesses were provided by the Lord so that every word of his gospel might be established according to the divine law of witnesses.

Selected Quotations

"It was necessary . . . that there should be other witnesses and that Joseph Smith should not stand alone. . . . This is according to the law of witnesses which the Lord established in the very beginning. (See Deut. 19:15; John 5:30-32 and 8:12-14; 2 Cor. 13:1.) The consequences following the rejection of such strong, divine, and attested witness, is exceedingly great. After hearing such testimony as has been given by these witnesses and which is contained in the Book of Mormon itself, it should cause any person who has heard it to quake with fear in the very thought of rejecting any part of it. The Lord said to Nephi: 'Wherefore the Lord God will proceed to bring forth the words of the book; and in the mouth of as many witnesses as seemeth him good will he establish his word; and wo be unto him that rejecteth the word of God!' (2 Nephi 27:14.) Compare this with the testimony of Nephi in 2 Nephi 33:9 to end, and the testimony of Moroni in Moroni 10:27." (Joseph Fielding Smith, *CHMR* 1:73.)

"The witnesses of the Book of Mormon were true and faithful to their testimony throughout their lives. The time came, however, when all three of the special witnesses became estranged from Joseph Smith and departed from the Church because of their spirit of rebellion against the Prophet and the work. They were dealt with for their fellowship and excommunicated from the Church. While the Prophet lived, they retained their bitterness of spirit and remained aloof, but during all those years, and to the end of life, all three were steadfast in their testimony as found in the Book of Mormon. In the year 1848, after the Church had been driven from Nauvoo, Oliver Cowdery returned to the Church at Kanesville and humbly begged to be re-admitted as a member. Martin Harris also sought again a place and standing in the Church, and in the year 1870 he came to Utah to make his home. He died in 1875, at Clarkston, Utah at the age of 92 years. David Whitmer never came back to the Church, but shortly before his death, in refutation of the statements that had gone forth that he had denied his testimony, he published it again to the world, in which he said: 'It is recorded in the American Cyclopedia and the Encyclopedia Britannica, that I, David Whitmer, have denied my testimony as one of the Three Witnesses to the divinity of the Book of Mormon; and that the other two witnesses, Oliver Cowdery and Martin Harris, denied their testimony of that book. I will say once more to all mankind, that I have never at any time denied that testimony or any part thereof. I also testify to the world, that neither Oliver Cowdery nor Martin Harris ever at any time denied their testimony. They both died reaffirming the truth of the divine authenticity of the Book of Mormon.' " (Joseph Fielding Smith, *CHMR* 1:67-68.)

"One overwhelming thought . . . comes to our attention when we consider the action of these men and the boldness of the Prophet and the Church to take such drastic action against them. Had they entered into collusion with Joseph Smith with intent to deceive and practice a fraud, the first thing they would have done when the bitter spirit was upon them would be to denounce Joseph Smith and reveal the fraud. This is human nature and it never fails. Let it be said to their credit that the day never came when they denied the testimonies they had borne. Oliver Cowdery declared consistently even when out of the Church the truth of his witness to the Book of Mormon and to every other gift and blessing coming by heavenly manifestation. He never wavered in this testimony. Years later, when his spirit had been given time to cool, and in the very darkest hour of the history of the Church, when almost all men thought that the Church had gone to its destruction, Oliver Cowdery came back repentant, sorrowful, and asked to be reinstated as a member of the Church. This was not the act of one guilty of fraud. David Whitmer, although he never asked to come back to the Church, organized one of his own and continued to his dying day before great and small, to bear record to his testimony as a witness of this work. Again, I repeat, men do not take this course if they are guilty of evil practices and it stands forth and makes their testimony as given in the Book of Mormon even stronger than it would have done had they remained true to their covenants and obligations as members of the Church." (Joseph Fielding Smith, *CHMR* 2:81-82.)

Scriptural References: D&C 5:15; 6:28; 20:13; 42:80-81; 128:3, 20; Deut. 17:6; 19:15; Matt. 18:16; 2 Cor. 13:1; 2 Ne. 11:3; 27:12, 14, 22.

Women; motherhood; important role of mother

Women and men hold equal positions in The Church of Jesus Christ of Latter-day Saints so far as the greatest gift of God is concerned—eternal life. As Paul testified; "Neither is the man without the woman, neither the woman without the man, in the Lord." (1 Cor. 11:11.)

In this life, men and women play different roles in the family relationship. The man, as husband and father, has the major responsibility of providing the necessities of life for the family if he is able to do so. Both the wife and the children have claim upon the father and husband "for their maintenance." (D&C 83:1-6.)

The woman's role as mother makes her in a sense a co-creator with our Heavenly Father in providing physical bodies as earthly tabernacles for the spirit children of God. Also, the role of motherhood has always been held in the very highest regard by Church leaders and members.

Selected Quotations

"The Church of Jesus Christ of Latter-day Saints has sponsored the advancement of women from its very outset. It was the Prophet Joseph Smith who set forth the ideals for womanhood. He advocated liberally for women in the purest sense of the word, and he gave them liberty to fully express themselves as mothers, as nurses to the sick, as proponents of high community ideals, and as protectors of good morals.

"What more can any woman want for herself? What more could any man want for his wife? What more could any man want than to match that standard in his own conduct?

"The Prophet Joseph Smith gave us the Relief Society organization to advance these high purposes for Latter-day Saint women. That society today is a worldwide movement holding membership in national and world organizations for the advancement of women.

"Finally, when we sing that doctrinal hymn and anthem of affection, 'O My Father,' we get a sense of the ultimate in maternal modesty, of the restrained, queenly elegance of our Heavenly Mother, and knowing how profoundly our mortal mothers have shaped us here, do we suppose her influence on us as individuals to be less if we live so as to return there?" (Spencer W. Kimball, *Ensign,* May 1978, p. 6.)

"We know so little, brothers and sisters, about the reasons for the division of duties between womanhood and manhood as well as between motherhood and priesthood. These were divinely determined in another time and another place. We are accustomed to focusing on the men of God because theirs is the priesthood and leadership line. But paralleling that authority line is a stream of righteous influence reflecting the remarkable women of God who have existed in all ages and dispensations, including our own. Greatness is not measured by coverage in column inches, either in newspapers or in the scriptures. The story of the women of God, therefore, is, for now, an untold drama within a drama.

"We men know the women of God as wives, mothers, sisters, daughters, associates, and friends. You seem to tame us and to gentle us, and, yes, to teach us and to inspire us. For you, we have admiration as well as affection, because righteousness is not a matter of role, nor goodness a matter of gender. In the work of the Kingdom, men and women are not without each other, but do not envy each other, lest by reversals and renunciations of role we make a wasteland of both womanhood and manhood.

"Just as certain men were foreordained from before the foundations of the world, so were certain women appointed to certain tasks. Divine design—not chance—brought Mary forward to be the mother of Jesus. The boy prophet, Joseph Smith, was blessed not only with a great father but also with a superb mother, Lucy Mack, who influenced a whole dispensation.

"The charity of good women is such that their 'love makes no parade'; they are not glad 'when others go wrong'; they are too busy serving to sit statusfully about, waiting to be offended. Like Mary, they ponder trustingly those puzzlements that disable others. God trusts women so much that He lets them bear and care for His spirit children." (Neal A. Maxwell, *Ensign,* May 1978, p. 10.)

"We have special admiration for the unsung but unsullied single women among whom are some of the noblest daughters of God. These sisters know that God loves them, individually and distinctly. They make wise career choices even though they cannot now have the most choice career. Though in their second estate they do not have their first desire, they still overcome the world. These sisters who cannot now enrich the institution of their own marriage so often enrich other institutions in society. They do not withhold their blessings simply because some blessings are now withheld from them. Their trust in God is like that of the wives who are childless, but not by choice, but who in the justice of God will receive special blessings one day." (Neal A. Maxwell, *Ensign,* May 1978, p. 11.)

"Many of the sisters grieve because they are not blessed with offspring. You will see the time when you will have millions of children around you. If you are faithful to your covenants, you will be mothers of nations. . . . and when you have assisted in peopling one earth, there are millions of earths still in the course of creation. And when they have endured a thousand million times longer than this earth, it is only as it were the beginning of your creations. Be faithful, and if you are not blest with children this time, you will be hereafter." (Brigham Young, *JD* 8:208.)

Scriptural References: D&C 25:3; Prov. 31:10; Luke 1:28, 42; 1 Tim. 2:9; 1 Pet. 3:5, 7; 1 Ne. 17:20; Jacob 2:28; Alma 19:10.

Work; industry

The Church has always so emphasized the importance of work and industry that some people refer to it as a "second gospel"—the gospel of work. Work is a great eternal principle of progress that makes possible everything that has been accomplished or that will be accomplished in time (this life) and in eternity (the existence before this life and the existence after this life).

The Gods exert their physical, mental, and spiritual powers, all of which is work. Deity worked six days in creating the earth. (Ex. 20:8-11.) The Savior expended great energy (worked) in his ministry and in performing the atonement. He has taught: "My Father worketh hitherto, and I work" (John 5:17) and "I must work the works of him that sent me" (John 9:4). The Father has declared: "This is my work and my glory—to bring to pass the immortality and eternal life of man." (Moses 1:39.)

Man has been instructed by the Lord to work physically ("In the sweat of thy face shalt thou eat bread"—Gen. 3:19) and spiritually ("work out your own salvation with fear and trembling"—Philip. 2:12).

Selected Quotations

"We believe in work. We remember the fourth of the Ten Commandments says, 'Six days shalt thou labour, and do all thy work' (Exodus 20:9), and we are not sure that the rapidly decreasing work week is beneficial to mankind. We think the Lord knew what he was talking about. It would seem that we are play-conscious, travel-conscious, and our economy seems to be providing for the traveling public and the gaming public and the drinking public." (Spencer W. Kimball, *Ensign,* November 1974, p. 6.)

"Through the ages there have been many laws repealed, but we know of no divine repeal of the law of work. From the obscure life organs within the body to the building of the moon landing craft, work is one of the conditions of being alive. We have been told that everyday work is a purposeful activity requiring an expenditure of energy with some sacrifice of leisure. Sir William Osler, a great physician of Canada, said that *work* is the master word in ongoing life. It's the touchstone of progress, the measure of success, and the fount of hope. It is directly responsible, he said, for all advantages in medicine and technology. (See Harvey Cushing, *Life of Sir William Osler,* vol. 1, ch. 14.)" (Spencer W. Kimball, *Ensign,* May 1976, p. 126.)

"Work is a great thing. It is the law of this earth. When Adam was cast out, upon him was passed the glorious sentence, 'In the sweat of thy face shalt thou eat bread.' Man as he is would not and could not have existed except for the promulgation of this law. Work is a wonderful thing, no matter what that work may be. . . . If we can just get into our minds the dignity and the honor of work, no matter what that work may be, most of the ills from which we suffer will be solved. During the whole range of man's existence there has never yet been any plan by which men may live righteously in idleness, and no such plan, it is my faith, will ever be devised." (J. Reuben Clark, Jr., *CR,* October 1936, p. 112.)

"Now, as to a willingness to work: Nothing ever does itself. Nothing ever memorizes itself. Nothing ever accomplishes itself—without requisite effort. Carlyle said, 'Men do less than they ought, unless they do all that they can.' It is not enough just to try; we have to succeed. The Lord expects us to see things through." (Richard L. Evans, *CR,* April 1961, pp. 75-76.)

Scriptural References: D&C 42:42; 58:27; 68:30; 72:17; 82:18; Gen. 3:19; 1 Thes. 2:9; 4:11; Mosiah 2:14; 10:5; 23:5; 27:5.

World; in the world; of the world

Sometimes the words *earth* and *world* are used as though they are synonyms, but frequently the scriptures distinguish between the two. When this distinction is made, *earth* refers to the physical orb, whereas *world* refers to the civilization of mankind upon the earth. When *world* is used to represent the social conditions on the earth, it stands for worldliness, carnality, sensuality, wickedness, etc., for as Alma taught, since the fall of Adam all mankind has "become carnal, sensual, and devilish, by nature." (Alma 42:10.)

We are counseled that even though we are *in* the world we should not be *of* the world. The apostle John admonished, "Love not the world . . . the world passeth away, and the lust thereof." (1 Jn. 2:15, 17.) James taught, "Know ye not that the friendship of the world is enmity with God? whosoever therefore will be a friend of the world is the enemy of God." (James 4:4.)

Selected Quotations

"Now, what do we mean by the world? It is sometimes used as an indefinite term. I take it that the world refers to the inhabitants who are alienated from the saints of God. They are aliens to the Church, and it is the spirit of this alienation that we should keep ourselves free from." (David O. McKay, *CR*, October 1911, p. 58.)

"Why is it so difficult to accept things on faith? I think I can suggest an answer. It is because we are so conceited. Men of the world are in the world only because they adopt the philosophy of the world, which is the philosophy of self-sufficiency. It is not a humble philosophy—it is highly egotistical. It makes men themselves the arbiters of all things. They look to no higher source than themselves for the solution of all questions.

"Such a philosophy is diametrically opposed to the philosophy of Christ, which is that of faith. When men adopt his philosophy they are humble—they acknowledge an intelligence far superior to their own and they seek guidance and wisdom from that source. When they adopt the philosophy of faith, they come out of the world, for the world, as a term in theology, is not a place but a condition or state of mind and feeling. It requires courage to come out of the world and adopt the philosophy of faith." (Stephen L Richards, *CR*, April 1935, pp. 30-31.)

"This expression does not mean, as sometimes supposed, the destruction of the Earth, but the termination of a dispensation by some act of final judgment upon the inhabitants of the Earth. The flood was the 'end' of the antediluvian world. The destruction of Jerusalem by Titus was the end of 'the world' to which the first Christians were looking forward. The next 'end of the world' will be the overthrow of the kingdoms of the world and the establishment of the Millennium.

" 'The end of the world is the destruction of the wicked; the harvest and the end of the world have an allusion directly to the human family in the last days, instead of the Earth, as many have imagined' (Joseph Smith, *HC* 2:271.)" (Smith and Sjodahl, *DCC*, p. 92.)

Scriptural References: D&C 25:10; 121:35; Eccl. 3:11; John 15:18-19; 16:33; 17:16; Rom. 12:2; 1 Cor. 3:19; James 1:27; 4:4; 1 Jn. 2:15; Mosiah 3:19; 1 Ne. 6:5.

Worship

In section 93, the Lord reveals and explains some of the writings of John in the New Testament, and he declares: "I give unto you these sayings that you may understand and know how to worship, and know what you worship, that you may come unto the Father in my name, and in due time receive of his fulness." (V. 19.)

The commandment "Thou shalt worship the Lord thy God" is found in ancient and modern scriptures (Ex. 34:14; Matt. 4:10; Luke 4:8; Mosiah 18:25; D&C 20:17-19), and the commandment has also been extended to worship the Son: "Christ is the Holy One of Israel; wherefore ye must bow down before him, and worship him with all your might, mind, and strength, and your whole soul" (2 Ne. 25:29).

Selected Quotations

"What is Worship?—The derivation of the term suggests an answer. It comes to us as the lineal descendant of a pair of Anglo-Saxon words, *weorth,* meaning worthy, and *scipe,* the old form of *ship,* signifying condition or state, and connotes the thought of *worthy-ship.* The worship of which one is capable depends upon his comprehension of the worthiness characterizing the object of his reverence. Man's capacity for worship is a measure of his comprehension of God." (James E. Talmage, *AF,* pp. 395-96.)

"True and perfect worship consists in following in the steps of the Son of God; it consists in keeping the commandments and obeying the will of the Father to that degree that we advance from grace to grace until we are glorified in Christ as he is in his Father. It is far more than prayer and sermon and song. It is living and doing and obeying. It is emulating the life of the great Exemplar. With this principle before us, may I now illustrate some of the specifics of that divine worship which is pleasing to him whose we are?

"To worship the Lord is to follow after him, to seek his face, to believe his doctrine, and to think his thoughts. It is to walk in his paths, to be baptized as Christ was, to preach that gospel of the kingdom which fell from his lips, and to heal the sick and raise the dead as he did.

"To worship the Lord is to put first in our lives the things of his kingdom, to live by every word that proceedeth forth from the mouth of God, to center our whole hearts upon Christ and that salvation which comes because of him. It is to walk in the light as he is in the light, to do the things that he wants done, to do what he would do under similar circumstances, to be as he is.

"To worship the Lord is to walk in the Spirit, to rise above carnal things, to bridle our passions, and to overcome the world.

"It is to pay our tithes and offerings, to act as wise stewards in caring for those things which have been entrusted to our care, and to use our talents and means for the spreading of truth and the building up of his kingdom.

"To worship the Lord is to be married in the temple, to have children, to teach them the gospel, and to bring them up in light and truth. It is to perfect the family unit, to honor our father and our mother; it is for a man to love his wife with all his heart and to cleave unto her and none else.

"To worship the Lord is to visit the fatherless and the widows in their affliction and to keep ourselves unspotted from the world. It is to work on a welfare project, to administer to the sick, to go on a mission, to go home teaching, and to hold family home evening.

"To worship the Lord is to study the gospel, to treasure up light and truth, to ponder in our hearts the things of his kingdom, and to make them part of our lives. It is to pray with all the energy of our souls, to preach by the power of the Spirit, to sing songs of praise and thanksgiving.

"To worship is to work, to be actively engaged in a good cause, to be about our Father's business, to love and serve our fellowmen. It is to feed the hungry, to clothe the naked, to comfort those that mourn, and to hold up the hands that hang down and to strengthen the feeble knees.

"To worship the Lord is to stand valiantly in the cause of

truth and righteousness, to let our influence for good be felt in civic, cultural, educational, and governmental fields, and to support those laws and principles which further the Lord's interests on earth.

"To worship the Lord is to be of good cheer, to be courageous, to be valiant, to have the courage of our God-given convictions, and to keep the faith. It is ten thousand times ten thousand things. It is keeping the commandments of God. It is living the whole law of the whole gospel.

"To worship the Lord is to be like Christ until we receive from him the blessed assurance: 'Ye shall be even as I am.'

"These are sound principles. As we ponder them in our hearts, I am sure we shall know increasingly of their verity. True and perfect worship is in fact the supreme labor and purpose of man. God grant that we may write in our souls with a pen of fire the command of the Lord Jesus: 'Thou shalt worship the Lord thy God, and him only shalt thou serve' (Luke 4:8); and may we in fact and with living reality worship the Father in spirit and in truth, thereby gaining peace in this life and eternal life in the world to come." (Bruce R. McConkie, *Ensign*, December 1971, p. 130.)

Scriptural References: D&C 18:40; 20:19, 29; 59:5, 10; 76:21; 93:19; 101:22; 115:8; 133:39; 134:4, 6; Moses 1:15-20; 5:5; 6:49; Abr. 1:17; A of F 1:11; JFS-V 1:39; Ex. 20:3; 34:14; Matt. 2:2; 4:10; Alma 15:17; 31:12; 32:5; 33:3; 34:38; 43:10; 50:39; 3 Ne. 11:17; 17:10.

Zion; cause of Zion; "Zion shall rejoice upon the hills and flourish"

Throughout history, the word *Zion* has referred to several different places, peoples, and conditions. In Enoch's day, *Zion* referred both to the people (Moses 7:18) and to the city in which they lived (Moses 7:19). As is shown in the selected quotations from this dispensation, Zion has also been used to refer to a specific place, or general area, and to a condition.

Selected Quotations

"There are several meanings of the word Zion. It may have reference to the hill named Mt. Zion or by extension in the land of Jerusalem. It has sometimes been used, as by the prophet Micah to refer to the location of 'the mountain of the house of the Lord'—as some place apart from Jerusalem. [See Micah 4:2.] Zion was so called by Enoch in reference to the 'City of Holiness,' or the 'City of Enoch.' [See Moses 7:18-19.] The Land of Zion has been used to refer, in some connotations, to the Western Hemisphere. But there is another most significant use of the term by which the Church of God is called Zion, comprising, according to the Lord's own definition, 'the pure in heart.' (D&C 97:21.)" (Harold B. Lee, *CR,* October 1968, pp. 61-62.)

"You know there has been great discussion in relation to Zion—where it is, and where the gathering of the dispensation is, and which I am now going to tell you. The prophets have spoken and written upon it; but I will make a proclamation that will cover a broader ground. The whole of America is Zion itself from north to south, and is described by the Prophets, who declare that it is the Zion where the mountain of the Lord should be, and that it should be in the center of the land. When Elders shall take up and examine the old prophecies in the Bible, they will see it." (Joseph Smith, *HC* 6:318-19.)

"This American continent will be Zion; for it is so spoken of by the prophets. Jerusalem will be rebuilt and will be the place of gathering, and the tribe of Judah will gather there; but this continent of America is the land of Zion." (Brigham Young, *JD* 5:4.)

"Zion means, literally, a 'sunny place' or 'sunny mountain.' It first designated an eminence in Palestine on which Jerusalem is built. In the Doctrine and Covenants, Zion has three designations: First, the land of America; second, a specific place of gathering; and third, the pure in heart. . . .

"The Zion we build will pattern after the ideals of its inhabitants. To change men and the world, we must change their thinking, for the thing which a man *really believes* is the thing which he has *really thought;* that which he *actually thinks,* is the *thing which he lives.* Men do not go beyond their ideals; they often fall short of them, but they never go beyond them.

"Victor Hugo said: 'The future of any nation can be determined by the thoughts of its young men between the ages of 18 and 25.' Thus it is easy to understand why the Lord designates Zion as the 'pure in heart' [D&C 97:21], and only when we are such shall Zion 'flourish and the glory of the Lord be upon her.'

"The foundation of Zion, then, will be laid in the hearts of men: broad acres, mines, forests, factories, beautiful buildings, modern conveniences will be but means and accessories to the building of the human soul and the securing of happiness. We should choose, in building Zion, what we call the 'four cornerstones of Zion's inhabitants.'

"First: There must be a firm belief and acceptance of the truth that this universe is governed by intelligence and wisdom. . . .

"The second cornerstone is that the ultimate purpose in God's great plan is the perfecting of the individual. . . .

"The third cornerstone is a realization that the first and most essential thing in man's progress is freedom—free agency. . . .

"Fourth cornerstone: A sense of responsibility toward other individuals and the social group." (David O. McKay, *IE*, February 1959, 94:33.)

"The Zion the Lord seeks to establish through his covenant people . . . can be built up only among those who are the pure in heart, not a people torn by covetousness or greed, but a pure and selfless people. Not a people who are pure in appearance, rather a people who are pure in heart. Zion is to be in the world and not of the world, not dulled by a sense of carnal security, nor paralyzed by materialism. No, Zion is not things of the lower, but of the higher order, things that exalt the mind and sanctify the heart.

"Zion is 'every man seeking the interest of his neighbor, and doing all things with an eye single to the glory of God.' (D&C 82:19.) . . . Zion can be established only by those who are pure in heart, and who labor for Zion, for 'the laborer in Zion shall labor for Zion; for if they labor for money they shall perish.' (2 Ne. 26:31.)

"As important as it is to have this vision in mind, defining and describing Zion will not bring it about. That can only be done through consistent and concerted daily effort by every single member of the Church. No matter what the cost in toil or sacrifice, we must 'do it.' That is one of my favorite phrases: 'Do It.' May I suggest three fundamental things we must do if we are to 'bring again Zion,' three things for which we who labor for Zion must commit ourselves.

"First, we must eliminate the individual tendency to selfishness that snares the soul, shrinks the heart, and darkens the mind. . . .

"Second, we must cooperate completely and work in harmony one with the other. There must be unanimity in our decisions and unity in our actions. . . .

"Third, we must lay on the altar and sacrifice whatever is required by the Lord. We begin by offering a 'broken heart and a contrite spirit.' We follow this by giving our best effort in our assigned fields of labor and callings. We learn our duty and execute it fully. Finally we consecrate our time, talents, and means as called upon by our file leaders and as prompted by the whisperings of the Spirit. In the Church, as in the welfare system also, we can give expression to every ability, every righteous desire, every thoughtful impulse. Whether a volunteer, father, home teacher, bishop, or neighbor, whether a visiting teacher, mother, homemaker, or friend—there is ample opportunity to give our all. And as we give, we find that 'sacrifice brings forth the blessings of heaven!' (*Hymns,* no. 147.) And in the end, we learn it was no sacrifice at all." (Spencer W. Kimball, *Ensign,* May 1978, p. 81.)

Scriptural References: D&C 6:6; 21:7-8; 35:24; 38:4; 45:67-71; 105:5-9; 124:2-11; 133:18-32; Moses 7:18-69; A of F 1:10; 2 Chr. 5:2; Isa. 2:3; 52:1-2; Zech. 1:14, 17; 1 Ne. 22:14, 19; 2 Ne. 8:3-25; 14:3-5; 26:29-31; Mosiah 12:21-22; 15:14, 29; 3 Ne. 20:36-40.

APPENDIX B
PERSONS MENTIONED
IN THE DOCTRINE
AND COVENANTS

PERSONS MENTIONED IN THE DOCTRINE AND COVENANTS

This appendix contains an alphabetical list of all the persons living in the 1800s who are mentioned by name in the Doctrine and Covenants. Brief biographical sketches are also provided for several of these persons.

If the person is mentioned in only one or two sections, biographical information will usually be included in the materials for those sections. If the person is mentioned in several sections, however, or if he subsequently made a significant contribution to the Church, his biographical sketch will be included in this appendix.

Names of persons are listed alphabetically by surname (family name). When indicated, further information on particular persons can be found in *BE* (*Biographical Encyclopedia,* by Andrew Jenson), *ECH* (*Essentials in Church History,* by Joseph Fielding Smith), *HC* (*History of the Church*), or *CHC* (*Comprehensive History of the Church*).

Major N. Ashley is mentioned in 75:17.
Almon Babbitt is mentioned in 124:84.
Jesse Baker is mentioned in 124:137.
Wheeler Baldwin is mentioned in 52:31.
Heman Bassett is mentioned in 52:37.
John Cook Bennett is mentioned in 124:16-17.

First mayor of Nauvoo. Born Aug. 3, 1804, in Massachusetts, a son of J. and N. Bennett. Presented as Assistant President with the First Presidency April 8, 1841. (See *ECH,* p. 567.) Disfellowshipped May 25, 1842. Excommunicated from Church for immorality latter part of 1842. Published anti-LDS book, *The History of the Saints.* Died in Polk City, Iowa. (Additional information in *ECH,* pp. 226, 264-66, 278, 283, 569; *CHC* 2:47-50, 140-47, 154.)

"Though a great egotist, he was a man of education, address and ability. That he had little or no principle was not immediately apparent. Considerable of a diplomat and possessing some influence in political circles, he rendered valuable aid in securing the passage by the Illinois Legislature of the act incorporating the city of Nauvoo. Hence the honors bestowed upon him by the Mormon people. Prior to that, and subsequently, he was Quartermaster-General of Illinois. Bennett professed great sympathy for the Saints. He joined the Church and apparently was a sincere convert to the faith.

"Governor Thomas Ford, in his history of Illinois, styles Bennett 'probably the greatest scamp in the western country.' But this was not until long after the Mormons, thrice victimized, had become aware of his villainy." (Orson F. Whitney, *HU* 1:193-94.)

"Then he became one of the most bitter enemies of the Church. His slanders, his falsehoods and unscrupulous attacks, which included perjury and attempted assassination were the means of inflaming public opinion to such an extent that the tragedy at Carthage became possible." (Smith and Sjodahl, *DCC*, p. 110.)

Ezra T. Benson is mentioned in 136:12.

Samuel Bent is mentioned in 124:132.

Titus Billings is mentioned in 63:39.

Ezra Booth is mentioned in 52:23; 64:15-16.

Methodist minister impressed so much by a miracle that he asked for baptism. Ordained a high priest, and went to Missouri. Apostatized and started preaching and writing falsehoods against the Church, which prompted Joseph Smith and Oliver Cowdery to go on a mission to counteract these teachings (D&C 11). First apostate to publish statements against the Church. (Additional information in *ECH,* pp. 116, 120; *HC* 1:216.)

"Ezra Booth became particularly bitter. His apostasy culminated in the gathering of the mob that tried to assassinate the Prophet Joseph and Sidney Rigdon at Hiram." (Smith and Sjodahl, *DCC*, p. 390.)

Seymour Brunson is mentioned in 75:33; 124:132.

One of first elders of Church. Born Sept. 18, 1799, in Virginia, a son of Reuben Brunson and Salley Clark. Baptized January 1831; ordained elder Jan. 21, 1831, by John Whitmer. Served missions in Ohio, Virginia, and elsewhere. Chosen a member of the high council at Nauvoo when that stake was organized in October 1839, and continued to serve in that capacity until his death Aug. 10, 1840. Joseph Smith first taught the doctrine of baptism for the dead at his funeral. (Additional information in *BE* 3:331; *ECH,* pp. 174, 246, 252.)

"Andrew Jenson, *Historical Record,* notes that he was 'a lieutenant-colonel in the Nauvoo Legion, and a prominent Elder in the Church. . . . In 1838 he preferred the charges against Oliver Cowdery on which this prominent witness to the great Latter-day work was tried by the High Council at Far West.' " (Smith and Sjodahl, *DCC,* p. 439.)

Stephen Burnett is mentioned in 75:35; 80:1-5.

Philip Burroughs is mentioned in 30:10.

Josiah Butterfield is mentioned in 124:138.

Reynolds Cahoon is mentioned in 52:30; 61:35; 75:32; 94:14.

One of the first high priests ordained in this dispensation. First one to start digging the foundation for the Kirtland Temple. In 1838 appointed first counselor to John Smith, who first served as stake president at Adam-ondi-Ahman and later was president of all the Saints in the Iowa Territory. Selected in 1848 as counselor to Isaac Morley to preside over a company of Saints. When Joseph Smith blessed a baby boy of Brother and Sister Cahoon, he was inspired to name him Mahonri Moriancumer Cahoon, indicating that this given name was that of the brother of Jared in the Book of Mormon. (Additional information in *ECH,* pp. 106, 129, 250, 308.)

"Reynolds Cahoon held many important positions in the Church. In 1833 he was associated with Hyrum Smith and Jared Carter in a committee appointed to raise money for a house of the Lord in Kirtland, in which to accommodate the Elders who might come there to receive instructions before engaging in missionary work." (Smith and Sjodahl, *DCC,* p. 368.)

Gideon Carter is mentioned in 75:34.

Jared Carter is mentioned in 52:38; 79:1-4; 94:14; 102:3-4, 34.

John S. Carter is mentioned in 102:3-4, 34.

Simeon Carter is mentioned in 52:27; 75:30.

William Carter is mentioned in 52:31.

Joseph Coe is mentioned in 55:6; 102:3-4, 34.

Member of first high council in this dispensation, organized Feb. 17, 1834. Accompanied Joseph Smith, Sidney Rigdon, and others on missionary trip to Missouri in June 1831. Served on a committee (with Ezra Thayre) to purchase lands in Missouri. Joined other apostates in the fall of 1837 in an attempt to overthrow the Church. (Additional information in *ECH,* pp. 107, 128, 142, 167.)

"He was one of eight men present when the Temple site,

west of Independence, was dedicated, August 3rd, 1831. Unfortunately for himself, he did not remain in the Church. In the year 1837 he cast his lot with John F. Boynton, Luke S. Johnson, Warren Parrish, and others who had been disfellowshipped, and together they set up a church of their own, which they called the 'Church of Christ.' They alleged that Joseph Smith was a 'fallen prophet,' teaching false doctrines. For some time these dissenters took a leading part in the persecution of the Saints at Kirtland, but their efforts to build up a church came to naught. They were swept away, as chaff before the wind (Ps. 1:4)." (Smith and Sjodahl, *DCC*, p. 320.)

Zebedee Coltrin is mentioned in 52:29.

John Corrill is mentioned in 50:38; 52:7.

Served as second counselor to Presiding Bishop Edward Partridge from 1831 to 1837. Born Sept. 17, 1794, in Massachusetts. Baptized Jan. 10, 1831, and shortly thereafter was ordained an elder and called on a mission with Solomon Hancock. Was ordained a high priest June 3, 1831, by Lyman Wight. Called to go to Missouri (D&C 52:7) to preach the gospel. Imprisoned in Jackson County jail; offered himself as a ransom for the Church, together with others. Helped complete Kirtland Temple; present at its dedication. Appointed Church Historian April 6, 1838, along with Elias Higbee. Excommunicated March 17, 1839, at a conference in Quincy, Illinois. Published a 50-page pamphlet, "A Brief History of the Church of Latter-day Saints (commonly called Mormons), Including an Account of Their Doctrine and Discipline, with the Reasons of the Author for Leaving the Church." (Additional information in *BE* 1:241-42; *ECH,* pp. 106, 135-37, 146, 198, 596.)

"When the fires of persecution raged with terrifying fury, he faltered, and signified his intention of publishing a booklet called, *Mormonism Fairly Delineated,* the appearance of which the mob looked forward to with hopeful anticipation (*Historical Record,* p. 458)." (Smith and Sjodahl, *DCC,* p. 294.)

James Covill is mentioned in 40:1-3.

Oliver Cowdery is mentioned in 8:1-12; 18:1-21; 20:3; 21:10-12; 23:1-2; 25:6; 27:8; 32:2; 37:3; 47:3; 52:41; 55:4; 57:13; 58:58; 60:6, 17; 61:23, 30; 63:46; 68:32; 69:1-2, 4; 70:1; 82:11; 102:3, 34; 104:28-29, 34; 124:95.

One of the Three Witnesses to the Book of Mormon and
Second Elder of the Church. Born Oct. 3, 1806, in Vermont.
A schoolteacher in Manchester, N. Y., during the winter of
1828-29, where he heard the story of Joseph Smith. Met the
Prophet for the first time April 5, 1829, and served as his
scribe during much of the translation of the Book of
Mormon. Received three revelations (sections 6, 8, 9)
through the Prophet. Several other portions of the Doctrine
and Covenants are also directed to him. Present with Joseph
Smith when John the Baptist restored the Aaronic Priesthood May 15, 1829. One of the six charter members of the
Church April 6, 1830. Preached the first public discourse in
the history of the Church April 11, 1830. Ordained a high
priest Aug. 28, 1831; member of first high council in Church
organized Feb. 17, 1834. Served several missions for the
Church. Assisted other two special witnesses in selecting, ordaining, and setting apart members of the Council of the
Twelve. Present at dedication of Kirtland Temple, participating with the Prophet in visions of April 3, 1836, in which
he saw and heard the Savior, Moses, Elias, and Elijah (D&C
110). Made "Assistant President of the Church" Dec. 5, 1834,
and appointed assistant counselor to the First Presidency
Sept. 3, 1837. Tried before high council at Far West April 11,
1838, and subsequently excommunicated from Church.
Remained faithful to his testimony of the Book of Mormon;
rebaptized in October 1848. Died March 3, 1850, at home of
his brother-in-law, David Whitmer, in Richmond, Mo. (Additional information in *BE* 1:246-47.)

"It is said, and I presume correctly, that Oliver Cowdery
remarked at one time to Joseph Smith, 'If I should apostatize
and leave the Church, the Church would be broken up.' The
answer of the Prophet was, 'What and who are you? This is
the work of God, and if you turn against it and withdraw
from it, it will still roll on and you will not be missed.' It was
not long until Oliver turned away, but the work continued.
God raised up men from obscurity to step forth and shoulder
the burdens, and it was hardly known when and where he
went. In about ten years he came back again, came before a
local conference at Mosquito Creek, Pottawattomie Co.,
Iowa, Oct., 1848, and acknowledged his faults. He bore testimony of the mission of the Prophet, Joseph Smith, and of
the truth of the Book of Mormon; he exhorted the Saints to

follow the authority of the Holy Priesthood, which he assured them was with the Twelve Apostles. He said, 'when the Saints follow the main channel of the stream, they find themselves in deep water and always right, pursuing their journey with safety; but when they turned aside into sloughs and bayous, they are left to flounder in the mud and are lost, for the Angel of God said unto Joseph in my hearing that this Priesthood shall remain on the earth until the end.'

"Oliver declared he took pleasure in bearing this testimony to the largest congregation of Saints he had ever seen together. He was re-baptized and made arrangements to come to the mountains, but died soon after, while on a visit to the Whitmers, in Missouri." (George A. Smith, *JD* 13:347-48.)

Warren A. Cowdery is mentioned in 106:1.
Alpheus Cutler is mentioned in 124:132.
Amos Davies is mentioned in 124:111.
Asa Dodds is mentioned in 75:15.
David Dort is mentioned in 124:132.
Ruggles Eames is mentioned in 75:35.
James Foster is mentioned in 124:138.
Robert D. Foster is mentioned in 124:115.
Edson Fuller is mentioned in 52:28.
David Fullmer is mentioned in 124:132.
Isaac Galland is mentioned in 124:78, 79.
Sidney Gilbert is mentioned in 53:1; 57:6, 8, 9; 61:7, 9, 12; 64:18, 26; 90:35; 101:96.

Accompanied Joseph Smith, Sidney Rigdon, and others on mission to Missouri in 1831. Appointed agent for Church in receiving moneys and buying lands on which the Saints might locate in Missouri. With others, offered himself as ransom for Church during the Missouri persecution. (Additional information in *ECH,* pp. 107, 109, 135, 146.)

"Elder B. H. Roberts, in a footnote on Page [360], Volume 1, *A Comprehensive History of The Church of Jesus Christ of Latter-day Saints,* makes the remark that the Lord has had few more devoted servants in this dispensation than Algernon Sidney Gilbert. Where he was born is not known, but his father's family resided in Connecticut. For some years he was a successful merchant in Painesville, Ohio, and there the gospel found him in 1830. In the persecution that came upon the Saints in Jackson County he sacrificed all his goods. He was one of the six who offered their lives for their friends. He was a man of great practical sense, as is evidenced by the correspondence he and others engaged in with Governor Dunklin, on behalf of the brethren, but, nevertheless, he shrank from speaking publicly, and it appears that, when called to go on a mission to preach the gospel, he said he would rather die. Not long afterwards he was attacked by cholera, and the disease proved fatal." (Smith and Sjodahl, *DCC,* pp. 312-13.)

John Gould is mentioned in 100:14.

Oliver Granger is mentioned in 117:12, 15.

Selah J. Griffin is mentioned in 52:32; 56:5, 6.

Thomas Grover is mentioned in 124:132.

Levi W. Hancock is mentioned in 52:29; 124:138.

One of first seven presidents of seventies, from 1835 until his death in 1882. Ordained one of first seventies of Church Feb. 28, 1835. Born April 7, 1803, in Massachusetts, the youngest son and seventh child of Thomas Hancock. Baptized Nov. 16, 1830, by Parley P. Pratt. Called in June 1831 to travel to Missouri as missionary companion to Zebedee Coltrin. Participated in Mormon Battalion, where he served as chaplain. One of pioneer settlers in Utah. Ordained a patriarch about ten years before his death June 10, 1882, in Washington County, Utah. (Additional information in *BE* 1:188; *ECH,* pp. 152, 587.)

Solomon Hancock is mentioned in 52:27.

Emer Harris is mentioned in 75:30.

George W. Harris is mentioned in 124:132.

Martin Harris is mentioned in 5:1, 26, 32; 52:24; 58:35, 38; 70:1; 82:11; 102:3, 34; 104:24, 26.

One of Three Witnesses to the Book of Mormon. Born May 18, 1783, in New York. Met Joseph Smith in fall of 1827. Assisted financially and otherwise in translation and publication of the Book of Mormon. Took copies of characters of the plates of Mormon to Professor Charles Anthon. Received revelation (D&C 19) through Joseph Smith in March 1830. Baptized shortly after organization of Church; ordained a high priest June 3, 1831, at Kirtland, Ohio. Called that same month by revelation (D&C 52) to accompany Joseph Smith and other elders to Missouri. Asked by the Lord to set an example before the Church in giving his money to bishop (D&C 58:35). Member of first high council of Church organized in Kirtland, Ohio, Feb. 17, 1834; in 1835 assisted in selecting and ordaining Twelve Apostles. Was dropped from high council Sept. 3, 1837. Remained in Ohio when Saints moved to Missouri; became estranged from Church. In later years he indicated that the Church left him instead of his having left the Church. He finally moved to Utah in 1870. At the request of Brigham Young, he was rebaptized by Elder Edward Stevenson and confirmed by Elder Orson Pratt. Died in Cache County, Utah, July 10, 1875. (Additional information in *BE* 1:271-76; *ECH,* pp. 52, 73, 80, 83, 107, 173, 452.)

"Martin Harris (1783-1875), was the first of the witnesses to appear in the story of Joseph Smith. He was acquainted with the Smith family and, it is said, employed the boy Joseph on his farm. Martin Harris was a religiously-minded, prosperous farmer. He appears to have been a rather willful, but honest man, who wanted to be sure of everything he undertook. It was he who took the transcript of characters from the Book of Mormon plates to Professor Anthon for verification. He was one of the three witnesses who had most difficulty on the occasion when the plates were shown to them. He was not easily led. But so certain was he at last of the claims of Joseph Smith that he advanced $3,000 for the publication of the Book of Mormon. In a mistaken allegiance to Joseph Smith after the martyrdom he did not go westward with the Church. In his old age, however, he sought out the Church, bore to the members, in the valleys of the mountains, his oft-repeated testimony of the truth of Joseph Smith's claims, and died a faithful member of the Church." (John A. Widtsoe, *JS,* p. 53.)

"Martin Harris was a prosperous farmer and had means enough for the furtherance of the great latter-day work, but when he became disassociated from the Church, he did not continue to prosper. In 1870, at the age of 87 years, the Spirit prompted him to go to Utah. Elder Edward Stevenson, consequently, raised the money necessary among the Saints in Utah, and some of the Saints at Des Moines, Iowa, gave him a new suit of clothes. But Martin Harris, in his days of poverty, was never troubled with doubts. While prosperous, he frequently merited chastisement. He died in full fellowship with the Church, a faithful witness to the last." (Smith and Sjodahl, *DCC,* p. 97.)

Peter Haws is mentioned in 124:62, 70.
Henry Herriman is mentioned in 124:138.
John A. Hicks is mentioned in 124:137.
Elias Higbee is mentioned in 113:7.
Solomon Humphrey is mentioned in 52:35.
William Huntington is mentioned in 124:132.
Orson Hyde is mentioned in 68:1, 7; 75:13; 100:14; 102:3, 34; 103:40; 124:129.

Member of Council of Twelve Apostles 1835-78 and president of that quorum 1847-75. Born Jan. 8, 1805, in Connecticut, a son of Nathan Hyde and Sally Thorp. Became a religious leader in the Campbellite movement, studying under Sidney Rigdon. Baptized in the fall of 1831 and confirmed by Joseph Smith. Ordained a high priest by Oliver Cowdery Oct. 25, 1831. Served several missions in eastern parts of the country. Chosen as a member of the first high council Feb. 17, 1834. Chosen and ordained an apostle Feb. 15, 1835, under hands of the Three Witnesses. Served a mission in England 1837-38. Because he believed and supported the lies of Thomas B. Marsh when Marsh was excommunicated, Orson Hyde was dropped from the Council of the Twelve Apostles May 4, 1839; he was restored to the Twelve on June 27, 1839. In 1875 President Brigham Young placed him in the order of seniority in the Twelve that he would have held if he had first entered the Council of the Twelve in June 1839. At general conference in April 1840, sent on a mission to Jerusalem, where he dedicated that land Oct. 24, 1841, for the return of Judah's scattered remnants. Part of the expulsion from Nauvoo in 1846, but sent to England to help direct affairs of Church there. Helped settle Carson Valley (now in Nevada) and later resided in Sanpete County, Utah. Died Nov. 28, 1878. (Additional information in *BE* 1:80-82; *ECH*, pp. 136, 142, 152, 258-59.)

"Orson Hyde returned to the Church in June 1839, at Commerce, now Nauvoo, Illinois, and was reinstated in the council of the twelve. He was sorely repentant, and in tears of humility begged forgiveness from his brethren for the unfortunate part he had taken in this lying report with Thomas B. Marsh. He had been overcome by the spirit of darkness to the extent that he bore false witness against his brethren while under that influence. After his return to the Church, he faithfully performed his part to the end. . . . The consciousness of his guilt in this unfortunate act in Missouri, preyed upon his mind all his life, and many were the days he shed bitter tears because that chapter in his history could not be blotted out." (Joseph Fielding Smith, *CHMR* 2:124.)

George James is mentioned in 52:38.

Vienna Jaques is mentioned in 124:132.

Aaron Johnson is mentioned in 90:28.

John Johnson is mentioned in 96:6; 102:3, 34; 104:24, 34.

Conference of elders of Church held at his home November 1832, when members voted that they prized "the revelations to be worth to the Church the riches of the whole earth." Member of first high council organized in this dispensation, Feb. 17, 1834. (Additional information in *ECH,* pp. 119, 142.)

"John Johnson was one of the highly favored men in the early days of this dispensation, who did not remain faithful to the end, though at one time he was valiant in the cause.

"He had seen his wife miraculously healed by the Prophet Joseph. He opened his home at Hiram to Joseph and his family, while the Prophet was engaged in his great Biblical work. He defended Joseph against a murderous mob, risking his own life. In fact, his collar bone was broken, in the conflict, but he was instantly healed under the hands of David Whitmer. He became a member of the first High Council, and he saw two of his sons, Luke S. and Lyman E., rise to the exalted position of members of the Council of the Twelve Apostles. And yet, when the spirit of apostasy possessed so many Church members in Kirtland, in 1837 and 1838, he, as well as his sons, were affected by it. He died in Kirtland, July 30th, 1843, at the age of 64 years." (Smith and Sjodahl, *DCC,* p. 607.)

Luke Johnson is mentioned in 68:7; 75:9; 102:3, 34.

Member of Council of Twelve Apostles 1835-38. Born Nov. 3, 1807, in Vermont, a son of John Johnson and Elsa Jacobs. Baptized May 10, 1831, by Joseph Smith. Ordained a high priest Oct. 25, 1831, by Joseph Smith. In 1832-33 served as missionary in Ohio, Virginia, and Kentucky with Seymour Brunson and Hazen Aldrich. Member of first high council formed Feb. 17, 1834. Participated in Zion's Camp. Chosen and ordained one of Twelve Apostles at age 27 on Feb. 15, 1835, under hands of the Three Witnesses. Helped defend Prophet Joseph Smith on several occasions until 1836, when his "mind became darkened" and he was disfellowshipped at Kirtland Sept. 3, 1837. Later received back into fellowship, but then excommunicated at Far West April 13, 1838. Rebaptized at Nauvoo in 1846. Came to Utah as one of the first group of 143 pioneers. Settled in Tooele, where he served as bishop. Died Dec. 9, 1861, in house of his brother-in-law, Orson Hyde. (Additional information in *BE* 1:85-86; *ECH,* pp. 142, 167, 360, 571.)

"The Johnson family was one of the typical American families of old colonial times—the men were large, strong, brave, sensible, honest, well-to-do. 'My grandfather, Israel Johnson,' writes Luke Johnson in his autobiographical sketch, 'lived in Chesterfield, New Hampshire, and was much respected by his neighbors for his honesty, integrity and industry. My father, John Johnson, was born in Chesterfield, New Hampshire, April 11th, 1779. He followed the occupation of farming on a large scale, and was noted for paying his debts and living independently. He moved from Pomfret, Vermont, to Hiram, Portage county, Ohio. He was connected with the Methodist church for about five years previous to receiving the Gospel.' Luke Johnson then relates the circumstance of the Prophet, through the power of God, healing his mother of chronic rheumatism in the arm, which converted Ezra Booth . . . and then resumes: 'My father was satisfied in regard to the truth of "Mormonism," and was baptized by Joseph Smith, Jun., in the winter of 1830-31, and furnished him and his family a home, while he translated a portion of the Bible.' " (*HC* 1:260, footnote.)

Lyman Johnson is mentioned in 68:7; 75:14.

Member of Council of Twelve Apostles 1835-38. Born Oct. 24, 1811, in Vermont, a son of John Johnson and Elsa Jacobs. Baptized February 1831 by Sidney Rigdon. Ordained an elder Oct. 25, 1831, and a high priest Nov. 1, 1831. Called to do missionary work in 1831. Participated in Zion's Camp. Ordained apostle at age 23 on Feb. 14, 1835, by the Three Witnesses. Disfellowshipped Sept. 3, 1837, at Kirtland; restored to former standing a few days later. Excommunicated April 13, 1838, at Far West. Remained friendly to Saints, but was never rebaptized. Drowned Dec. 20, 1856, in Mississippi River. (Additional information in *BE* 1:91-92; *ECH,* pp. 152, 175, 571.)

"Lyman E. Johnson, the first to be called to the Apostle-

ship when the first Council of Twelve was organized, left the
Church, but he never had a really happy day after that. According to President Brigham Young he, on one occasion,
said, at a meeting of the Council:

" 'Brethren,—I will call you brethren—I will tell you the
truth. If I could believe Mormonism—it is no matter whether it is true or not—but If I could believe Mormonism as I
did when I traveled with you and preached, if I possessed the
world I would give it. I would give anything. I would suffer
my right hand to be cut off, if I could believe it again. Then I
was full of joy and gladness. My dreams were pleasant.
When I awoke in the morning, my spirit was cheerful. I was
happy by day and by night, full of peace and joy and thanksgiving. But now it is darkness, pain, sorrow, misery in the
extreme. I have never since seen a happy moment.' (*JD*
19:41)." (Smith and Sjodahl, *DCC,* p. 470.)

Heber C. Kimball is mentioned in 124:129.

First counselor to President Brigham Young from
December 1847 until June 1868. Born June 14, 1801, a son of
Solomon F. Kimball. Night of Sept. 22, 1827, had a vision
with John P. Greene, his neighbor, in which he saw armies
marching across heavens. Later learned that was the same
evening Joseph Smith received plates of Book of Mormon
from Moroni. Baptized Apr. 15, 1832; always faithful
member of the Church. Participated in Zion's Camp. Ordained apostle Feb. 14, 1835. Called to open British Mission.
Preached at first meeting in Salt Lake Valley. Sustained as
first counselor to President Brigham Young Dec. 27, 1847.
Died June 22, 1868. (Additional information in *ECH*—check
index, p. 644.)

Joseph Knight, Sr., is mentioned in 23:6. Section 12 is directed
to him.

An early supporter of Joseph Smith. Hired young Joseph,
and later provided provisions for the Prophet and Oliver
Cowdery, which enabled them to continue the translation of
the Book of Mormon. His horse and wagon were used by Joseph Smith to obtain the plates of Mormon from Cumorah.
Received a revelation (D&C 12) from the Lord through Joseph. Baptized the same day as Emma Smith in June 1830.
Hired lawyers to help defend Joseph Smith in court. Tried to
defend Joseph from the mobs.

Joseph Knight, Jr., wrote: "My father hired Joseph Smith

[in 1827]. Joseph and I worked and slept together. My father said Joseph was the best hand he ever hired. We found him a boy of truth . . . he made known to my father and I that he had seen a vision. . . . My father and I believed what he told us. I think we were the first (to believe) after his father's family." (*CHC* 1:85.)

Aug. 22, 1842, Joseph Smith wrote: "I contemplate the virtues and the good qualities of the faithful few, which I am now recording in the Book of the Law of the Lord—of such as have stood by me in every hour of peril, for these fifteen long years past—say, for instance, my aged and beloved brother, Joseph Knight, Sen., who was among the number of the first laboring in the commencement of the bringing forth of the work of the Lord, and of laying the foundation of the Church of Jesus Christ of Latter-day Saints. For fifteen years he has been faithful and true, and even-handed and exemplary, and virtuous and kind, never deviating to the right hand or to the left. Behold he is a righteous man, may God Almighty lengthen out the old man's days; and may his trembling, tortured, and broken body be renewed, and in the vigor of health turn upon him, if it be Thy will, consistently, O God; and it shall be said of him, by the sons of Zion, while there is one of them remaining, that this man was a faithful man in Israel; therefore his name shall never be forgotten." (*HC* 5:124-25.)

(Additional information in *HC* 1:47-48, 80, 88-89; 2:124; *ECH,* pp. 59, 85, 87; *CHC* 1:34, 85-97, 122, 205-13, 379.)

Newel Knight is mentioned in 52:32; 54:2; 56:6-7; 124:132.

Born Sept. 13, 1800, in Vermont, a son of Joseph Knight, Sr. One of earliest members of Church. Part of first miracle in Church when evil spirits were cast out of him by Joseph Smith. A few days later he had a vision of Redeemer and saw the organization and work of the Church. Labored on Kirtland Temple; suffered persecution in Missouri; driven from Nauvoo in 1846 and spent the winter among the Ponca Indians of northern Neb. Died Jan. 11, 1847. (Additional information in *ECH,* pp. 81-82, 84.)

"Newel Knight, a son of Joseph Knight, of Colesville, N.Y., attended the meetings of the Saints at Colesville and became interested in the gospel. The Prophet tried to prevail upon him to pray in public, but being timid, he refused, and the result was that an evil spirit seized him and distorted his face, twisted his limbs, and tossed him about fearfully. The afflicted youth earnestly besought the Prophet to cast out the evil spirit. Joseph did so in the name of the Lord. Newel Knight then came under the influence of the Holy Spirit, and visions of eternity were open to his view.

"The Knight family were Universalists, and this miracle, the first performed in the Church, must have made a deep impression upon them. Newel Knight says that under the influence of the Spirit of God he was lifted up bodily from the floor, so that his head pressed against the ceiling.

"Newel Knight was the leader of the Saints of the Colesville Branch in their migration from Ohio to Missouri. (See Sec. 54:2)." (Smith and Sjodahl, *DCC*, p. 309.)

Vinson Knight is mentioned in 124:74, 141.

William Law is mentioned in 124:82, 97, 107, 118, 126.

Second counselor to Joseph Smith, 1841-44. Born Sept. 8, 1809. Baptized in Canada and moved to Nauvoo in latter part of 1839. Called by revelation January 1841 to serve as second counselor to Joseph Smith, succeeding Hyrum Smith, who was called to the position of presiding Patriarch. Served mission in the East. Received endowments May 26, 1843. Took offense at statement of the Prophet "We have a Judas in our midst." Came out openly against the Church and was one of the promoters of the libel sheet *Nauvoo Expositor*. Excommunicated Apr. 18, 1844. Believed to be behind the mob that killed Joseph and Hyrum Smith. Interviewed in 1887 in Wisconsin, still exhibiting great animosity toward the Saints. Died Jan. 19, 1892, in Wisconsin. (Additional information in *BE* 1:53; *ECH,* pp. 297-98, 300, 567.)

"Wonderful opportunities were offered to Wm. Law, which he neglected to embrace. If he had done faithfully what God . . . gave him to do, he would have received the blessings promised, but when he failed to obey the Lord, even his appointment in the First Presidency could not save him from falling. When he lost the Spirit of God he became one of the most bitter enemies of the Church. Apostates and persecutors rallied around him, and he tried to form a church of his own of such material." (Smith and Sjodahl, *DCC,* p. 785.)

"When the doctrine of celestial marriage was revealed he turned away from the Church, and was one of the chief plotters against the Prophet and Patriarch and helped to bring them to martyrdom." (Joseph Fielding Smith, *CHMR* 4:83.)

Amasa Lyman is mentioned in 124:136; 136:14.

Member of Council of Twelve Apostles 1842-67 and appointed counselor to First Presidency about Feb. 4, 1843. Retired from First Presidency upon death of Joseph Smith June 27, 1844. Returned to the Council of the Twelve Aug. 12, 1844. Born Mar. 30, 1813, in New Hampshire, third son of Roswell Lyman and Martha Mason. Baptized Apr. 27, 1832. Ordained an elder Aug. 23, 1832, and subsequently served several missions, the first being to Ohio and Virginia. Ordained high priest December 1833. Participated in Zion's Camp. Ordained an apostle Aug. 20, 1842, by Brigham Young, at age 29. Attended special meeting Aug. 8, 1844, where Twelve Apostles were acknowledged as presiding quorum of Church. One of the pioneers to Utah, later serving missions to California and Great Britain. On Mar. 16, 1862, preached a sermon in Scotland in which he denied the atonement of Jesus Christ. Later called before First Presidency for preaching false doctrine, where he acknowledged his error. Subsequently taught similar false doctrines and was deprived of apostleship Oct. 6, 1867; was replaced by Joseph F. Smith. Excommunicated May 12, 1870. Died Feb. 4, 1877, at Fillmore, Utah. (Additional information in *BE* 1:96-99; *ECH*, pp. 200, 321, 440, 567, 572.)

William Marks is mentioned in 117:1, 10; 124:79-80.

First president of Nauvoo Stake, 1839-44. Born Nov. 15, 1792, in Vermont. First mentioned in Church history May 1837. Chosen member of high council in Kirtland Sept. 3, 1837. In a revelation to Joseph Smith (D&C 117:1, 10), called to reside with Saints in Missouri, but Saints were expelled before he arrived. Appointed to preside over stake of Zion at Commerce (Nauvoo) Oct. 5, 1839. Elected alderman of Nauvoo. After death of Joseph Smith, favored Sidney Rigdon and refused to recognize authority of Twelve Apostles. Rejected as president of the Nauvoo Stake Oct. 7, 1844. Stayed in the East when the Saints left for Great Salt Lake Valley. Affiliated with the Strangites, serving as a counselor to James J. Strang for several years. Associated in 1855 with John E. Page. In 1859 joined with promoters of Reorganized Church and became one of its leading members until his death May 22, 1872, at which time he was first counselor to the president of the Reorganized Church.

(Additional information in *BE* 1:283-84; *ECH,* pp. 222, 225, 320, 322.)

Thomas B. Marsh is mentioned in 52:22; 56:5; 75:31.

Member of Council of Twelve Apostles 1835-38 and first president of that quorum. Born Nov. 1, 1799, in Massachusetts. Visited in Palmyra, New York, just as the first 16 pages of Book of Mormon had been printed. After hearing that Church had been organized Apr. 6, 1830, moved to Palmyra and was baptized in September 1830 by David Whitmer. Ordained a high priest June 6, 1831, and subsequently served several missions in eastern part of the United States. Moved to Clay County, Mo., where he lived when Zion's Camp arrived. Chosen as member of high council in Missouri. In July and August 1837, accompanied Joseph Smith and Sidney Rigdon on mission to Canada, after which he again returned to Missouri, where he was appointed president "pro tem" of the Church along with David W. Patten. In August 1838, became disaffected with the Church over a trivial matter; excommunicated Mar. 17, 1839. Rebaptized in July 1857 and went to Utah that same year. Settled in Ogden, where he died as "a pauper and invalid." (Additional information in *BE* 1:74-76; *ECH,* pp. 152, 188-90, 570.)

"In 1857, he came to Salt Lake City, and asked forgiveness and reinstatement in the Church. President Young introduced him to the audience in the Bowery, on the 6th of September. He told the congregation that he had suffered greatly during his absence from the Church, but that he acknowledged the hand of the Lord in the chastisement he had received. He made the following significant remark concerning the beginning of his apostasy:

" 'I became jealous of the Prophet, and then I saw double and overlooked everything that was right, and spent all my time in looking for the evil. * * * I saw a beam in Brother Joseph's eye, but it was nothing but a mote, and my own eye was filled with the beam. * * * I talked with Brother Brigham and Brother Heber, and I wanted them to be mad like myself; and I saw they were not mad, and I got madder still because they were not. Brother Brigham, with a cautious look, said, "are you the leader of the Church, Brother Thomas?" I answered, "No!" "Well then," said he, "Why do you not let that alone?" Well, this was about the amount of my hypocrisy. I meddled with that which was not my business.' (*JD* 5:207).

"At the conclusion of his address he was by unanimous vote received into full fellowship as a member of the Church." (Smith and Sjodahl, *DCC*, pp. 164-67.)

"Thomas B. Marsh was commanded [D&C 31] to govern his house in meekness, and to be steadfast. In this he utterly failed. And for that reason he apostatized and became active in drawing the mob against the Saints in Missouri, in persecution. George A. Smith, in an address delivered in Salt Lake City, April 6th, 1856, tells the story. When the Saints were living in Far West, the wife of Marsh and Sister Harris agreed to exchange milk, in order to enable each of them to make a larger cheese than they could do separately. Each was to take to the other the 'strippings' as well as the rest of the milk. Mrs. Harris performed her part of the agreement, but Mrs. Marsh kept a pint of 'strippings' from each cow. When this became known the matter was brought before the Teachers, and these decided against Mrs. Marsh. An appeal was taken to the Bishop. He sustained the Teachers. If Marsh had obeyed the Revelation and governed his house in humility and with steadfastness, he would have righted the wrong done, but, instead of doing so, he appealed to the High Council. Marsh, who at the time was President of the Twelve, possibly thought that the Council would favor him, but that body confirmed the Bishop's decision. He was not yet satisfied, but appealed to the First Presidency, and Joseph, the Prophet, and his two Counsellors consented to review the case. They approved the finding of the High Council. Was Marsh satisfied then? No. With the persistency of Lucifer himself, he declared that he would uphold the character of his wife, 'even if he had to go to hell for it.' Elder George A. Smith observes:

" 'The then President of the Twelve Apostles, the man who should have been the first to do justice and cause reparation to be made for wrong, committed by any member of his family, took that position, and what next? He went before a magistrate and swore that the "Mormons" were hostile to the State of Missouri.'

"That affidavit brought from the government of Missouri an exterminating order, which drove some 15,000 Saints from their homes and habitations, and some thousands perished through suffering the exposure consequent on this state of affairs. (*JD* 3:284.)" (Smith and Sjodahl, *DCC*, p. 167.)

William E. M'Lellin is mentioned in 66:1; 68:7; 75:6; 90:35.

Member of Council of Twelve Apostles 1835-38. Born 1806 in Tennessee. Baptized and ordained an elder in 1831. Requested of Joseph Smith a revelation for himself (D&C 66). Criticized language of some of the revelations, and, at the challenge of the Prophet, tried to write a better revelation and failed. (See materials for 67:5-7; see also *ECH*, pp. 118-19.) In 1832-33 served a mission with Parley P. Pratt, but in a revelation Mar. 8, 1833, the Lord said He was not "well pleased with my servant William E. M'Lellin." Chosen as member of high council in Clay County, Mo., July 3, 1834. Chosen and ordained one of Twelve Apostles at time of organization of that quorum Feb. 15, 1835, by the Three Witnesses, at age 29. Said before a bishop's court at Far West on May 11, 1838, that he had no confidence in the presidency of the Church; was excommunicated. Later tried to establish a church of his own; then joined with mobbers against the Prophet. When Joseph Smith was in prison, M'Lellin and others robbed Joseph Smith's house and stable of considerable property. Died Apr. 24, 1883, at Independence, Jackson County, Mo. (Additional information in *BE* 1:82-83; *ECH*, pp. 118-19, 152, 175, 570.)

"While Joseph was in prison at Richmond, Mo., Mr. McLellin, who was a large and active man, went to the sheriff and asked for the privilege of flogging the Prophet; permission was granted, on `condition that Joseph would fight. The sheriff made McLellin's earnest request known to Joseph, who consented to fight, if his irons were taken off. McLellin then refused to fight, unless he could have a club, to which Joseph was perfectly willing; but the sheriff would not allow them to fight on such unequal terms. Bro. McLellin was a man of superficial education, though he had a good flow of language. He adopted the profession of medicine. He finally died in obscurity." (Andrew Jenson, *BE* 1:83.)

Daniel Miles is mentioned in 124:138.

George Miller is mentioned in 124:20, 62, 70.

Isaac Morley is mentioned in 52:23; 64:15-16, 20.

First counselor to Bishop Edward Partridge 1831-40. Born

March 11, 1786, in Massachusetts, a son of Thomas Morley and Editha Marsh. One of first converts to the Church; ordained a high priest June 3, 1831. Set apart later that month as counselor to Bishop Partridge, holding this position until the death of Bishop Partridge May 27, 1840, when he was released. Attended dedication of Kirtland Temple in March 1836, and in November 1837 was chosen patriarch of Far West, Mo. Later moved to Nauvoo and then emigrated to the Great Salt Lake Valley in 1848. Died June 24, 1865, at Fairview, Utah. (Additional information in *BE* 1:235-36; *ECH*, pp. 98, 135, 595.)

"Among the prominent men who in the early days of the Church joined its ranks at Kirtland, was Isaac Morley. Previous to that time, he was one of the leaders of a society that practiced communistic principles and was sometimes called the 'Morley Family,' because a number were living on his farm. He was ordained to the ministry at the same time as Sidney Rigdon, Lyman Wight, and Edward Partridge, by the brethren who passed through Kirtland on their Indian mission, and the newly baptized Saints in Kirtland and vicinity were left to their care. He passed through the many storms that swept over the Church and cast his lot with the Saints in Utah." (Smith and Sjodahl, *DCC*, p. 307.)

John Murdock is mentioned in 52:8; 99:1. Section 99 is directed to him.

Born in 1792. An early convert to the Church (fall of 1830), being baptized at about the same time as Sidney Rigdon and Frederick G. Williams. In June 1831, called on a mission to accompany Hyrum Smith (D&C 52:8). Helped obtain permission from citizens of Daviess County, Mo., to create a Mormon settlement at DeWitt. Served as the first bishop of the Salt Lake Fourteenth Ward. One of the first missionaries to Australia in 1851. Died in 1871. (Additional information in *ECH*, pp. 98, 397.)

Noah Packard is mentioned in 124:136.

Hiram Page is mentioned in 28:11.

John E. Page is mentioned in 118:6; 124:129.

Member of Council of Twelve Apostles 1838-49. Born Feb. 25, 1799, in New York, a son of Ebenezer and Rachel Page. Baptized Aug. 18, 1833, in Ohio. Ordained an elder in September 1833. Served a mission to Canada in 1836 and again in 1837. Went to Missouri in 1838, where he lost his wife and two children through extreme suffering at hands of mobs. Called by revelation to apostleship and ordained Dec. 19, 1838, at Far West, under the hands of Brigham Young and Heber C. Kimball, filling vacancy of Luke S. Johnson. Neglected to go to England when called in 1839. Called in April 1840 to accompany Orson Hyde to Jerusalem, but never did leave America. Later lived in Pittsburgh, Pa., where he organized several branches, but not according to approved pattern of the Church. Disfellowshipped at Nauvoo Feb. 9, 1846, and excommunicated June 27, 1846. Died in the fall of 1867 in Illinois. (Additional information in *BE* 1:92-93; *ECH,* pp. 179, 216, 230, 381, 572.)

Edward Partridge is mentioned in 41:9; 42:10; 50:39; 51:1, 3-4, 18; 52:24, 41; 58:14, 24, 62; 60:10; 64:17; 115:2; 124:19, 21.

First Presiding Bishop of the Church. Born Aug. 27, 1793 in Massachusetts. Became a Campbellite and was part of Sidney Rigdon's congregation. Baptized Dec. 11, 1830, by Joseph Smith, and shortly thereafter ordained an elder. Commanded by the Lord to preach the gospel (D&C 36). In February 1831 was called by revelation (D&C 41) to be a bishop to the Church; in this revelation the Lord said he was "like unto Nathanael of old, in whom there is no guile." Ordained a high priest June 3, 1831. Served as the only bishop in the Church until December 1831. Offered himself, with others, as ransom for the Church during the Missouri persecutions. Laid the southeast cornerstone for the temple at Far West. Appointed during the Nauvoo period to serve as "bishop of the Upper Ward, while Bishop Newel K. Whitney and Bishop Vinson Knight were assigned to the Middle and Lower Wards respectively." Died May 27, 1840, at his home in Nauvoo. (Additional information in *BE* 1:218-22; *ECH*—check index, p. 647.)

"He suffered persecution on sundry occasions. One day in July, 1833, a mob at Independence violently seized him and one Charles Allen, and dragged them to the public square. Here they were offered the alternatives of renouncing the Book of Mormon or going into exile. As American citizens they refused to comply with this un-American demand, but Bishop Partridge said he was willing to suffer for the Master. His voice was drowned in the tumult that followed. Some of the mob cried, 'Call upon your God to deliver you!' Others cursed. Finally, the two brethren were stripped and maltreated by the persecutors, but they suffered in silence and with dignity, as true martyrs." (Smith and Sjodahl, *DCC*, p. 191.)

David W. Patten is mentioned in 114:1; 124:19, 130.

Member of Council of Twelve Apostles 1835-38. Born Nov. 14, 1799 in New York, a son of Benenio Patten and Abigail Cole. Baptized June 15, 1832, and ordained an elder June 17. Served several missions in central part of United States. Ordained an apostle Feb. 15, 1835, under the hands of the Three Witnesses. Moved to Missouri, where he defended the Prophet Joseph Smith during period of apostasy there and in Kirtland, Ohio. Mortally wounded Oct. 25, 1838, in battle at Crooked River, Missouri. Died shortly thereafter and was buried at Far West October 27. In a revelation Jan. 19, 1841, over two years after the death of David Patten, the Lord referred to him in these words: "my servant David Patten . . . is with me at this time . . . I have taken [him] unto myself; behold, his priesthood no man taketh from him." (D&C 124:19, 130.) (Additional information in *BE* 1:76-80; *ECH,* pp. 152, 187-88, 572.)

"I have thought it more than mere coincidence that one of the first martyrs in this dispensation, David W. Patten, a member of the Twelve Apostles, lost his life near the valley of Adam-ondi-Ahman, that same valley in which Adam had gathered his posterity, which the Lord had revealed to the Prophet Joseph Smith was near Wight's Ferry, at a place called Spring Hill, Daviess county, Missouri. [Sec. 116.]" (Harold B. Lee, *CR*, April 1948, p. 53.)

"The Prophet went to see Brother Patten before he died, and he said of him: 'Brother David Patten was a very worthy man, beloved by all good men who knew him. He was one of the twelve apostles, and died as he had lived, a man of God, and strong in the faith of a glorious resurrection, in a world where mobs will have no power or place. One of his last expressions to his wife was—"Whatever you do else, O! do not deny the faith." ' " (Joseph Fielding Smith, *CHMR* 2:129.)

Ziba Peterson is mentioned in 32:3; 58:60.

Baptized April 11, 1830; an elder at the first conference of the Church. Called in October 1830 (D&C 32:3) to go to Lamanites with Parley P. Pratt. Sidney Rigdon was converted during this missionary trip. Later "silenced for wrongdoing," but reinstated Aug. 4, 1831, by unanimous vote after he had humbled himself and made confession. (Additional information in *ECH,* pp. 96, 113.)

"When the Prophet arrived in Missouri he received a revelation in which Ziba Peterson (he seldom used his first name) was rebuked and the Lord commanded that that which had been bestowed upon him should be taken away, and he should stand as a member of the Church. (*HC* 1:195; D&C 58:60.) In a letter from the First Presidency to the brethren in Zion, written in June, 1833, the following is recorded: 'We deliver Brother Ziba Peterson over to the buffetings of Satan, in the name of the Lord, that he may learn not to transgress the commandments of God.' (*HC* 1:367.) We have no further history of him as to his conduct or when he died." (Joseph Fielding Smith, *CHMR* 1:149.)

William W. Phelps is mentioned in 57:11; 58:40; 61:7, 9; 70:1.

Author of many Church hymns, including "Now Let Us Rejoice" and "Praise to the Man." Born Feb. 17, 1792, in New Jersey. Baptized in 1832 and joined the Saints in Kirtland. Accompanied Joseph Smith, Sidney Rigdon, and others on a mission to Missouri. In August 1831 saw, in open vision, the destroyer (Satan) in his power riding upon the waters of the Mississippi. The next morning, Joseph Smith had a revelation confirming the vision of W. W. Phelps. With others, later offered himself as ransom for Church during Missouri persecution. In Jackson County, Missouri, sold his possessions contrary to instructions and was disfellowshipped in 1838 and subsequently excommunicated. Wrote confession in June 1843 and was rebaptized. Moved to Utah in 1848 and helped to draft the Constitution for the State of Deseret. Died March 7, 1872. (Additional information in *ECH*—check index, p. 647.)

"William W. Phelps. . . . was born at Hanover, Morris County, N.J., February 17th, 1792. In the State of New York he had edited a newspaper and taken an active part in politics. In Missouri, whither he went in company with the Prophet Joseph, he founded *The Evening and Morning Star,* a monthly magazine devoted to the interests of the Church, and published by the Church. Its first number appeared at Independence, June, 1832. The printing office was destroyed by a mob in July, 1833, but in the following December another printing office was established at Kirtland, and the publication of the *Star* was resumed there. Phelps, in 1837, was appointed to act, with David and John Whitmer, as a President of the Church in Zion.

". . . At a meeting held in Far West, Missouri, Feb. 6, 1838, Wm. W. Phelps and his co-laborers in the presidency were rejected by the Saints in the Carter settlement, Missouri. Other branches of the Church subsequently voted the same way. During the sessions of the court of inquiry held at Richmond, Mo., in November, 1838, Wm. W. Phelps, who had become bitter in his feelings, was among those who testified against the Church leaders. He was finally excommunicated from the Church at a conference held at Quincy, Illinois, March 17, 1839, but early in 1841 he was received back into fellowship in the Church. . . ." (Smith and Sjodahl, *DCC*, p. 317.)

Orson Pratt is mentioned in 52:26; 75:14; 103:40; 124:129; 136:13.

Member of Council of Twelve Apostles 1835-81. Born Sept. 19, 1811, in New York, a son of Jared Pratt and Charity Dickenson, and a younger brother of Parley P. Pratt. Baptized Sept. 19, 1830, on the 19th anniversary of his birth. Received revelation (D&C 34) from the Prophet Joseph Smith Nov. 4, 1830. Ordained a high priest by Sidney Rigdon Feb. 2, 1832. Ordained an apostle Apr. 26, 1835, under the hands of the Three Witnesses at age 23. Excommunicated Aug. 20, 1842; rebaptized Jan. 20, 1843, and ordained to former office in the Council of the Twelve. In 1875, Brigham Young took him from his original position in the Council and placed him in the position he would have occupied had he first been a member of the Council in 1843. Served many missions in the United States and abroad. Edited many Church periodicals. Helped divide Book of Mormon and Doctrine and Covenants into verses and provided many cross-references. Led vanguard into the Salt Lake Valley in 1847. Debated polygamy question with the Rev. John P. Newman in August 1870. Sustained as Church Historian and General Church Recorder May 9, 1874. Died in Salt Lake City Oct. 3, 1881, as the last surviving member of the original Council of the Twelve. (Additional information in *BE* 1:87-91; *ECH;* see index, p. 645.)

"He was one of the greatest mathematicians of modern times and one of the clearest and most logical defenders of the Church and the mission of Joseph Smith that the Church has produced. His mathematical ability was a great asset to the Pioneers when they were crossing the plains and mountains from Winter Quarters to the Salt Lake Valley, and, with Erastus Snow, he blazed the way into the Salt Lake Valley, arriving on the 21st day of July, three days before the arrival of the main body of pioneers." (Joseph Fielding Smith, *CHMR* 1:155.)

Parley P. Pratt is mentioned in 32:1; 50:37; 52:26; 97:3; 103:30, 37; 124:129.

Member of Council of Twelve Apostles 1835-57. Born Apr. 12, 1807, in New York, third son of Jared Pratt and Charity Dickenson. Baptized Sept. 1, 1830, and ordained an elder the same day. Met Prophet Joseph Smith in spring of 1831 and was ordained high priest by him June 6, 1831. Taken prisoner at Far West; was with the Prophet at Richmond prison, which he detailed in a written account. Served many missions in eastern and southern parts of the country, England, Pacific islands, and South America. Published many books and articles for the Church, including *Autobiography of Parley Parker Pratt*. Author of several Church hymns, including "An Angel from on High," "Come O Thou King of Kings," and "Jesus, Once of Humble Birth." Led a company of pioneers across the plains. Assassinated May 13, 1857, near boundary line between Arkansas and Indian territory while serving a mission. (Additional information in *BE* 1:83-85; *ECH*—check index, pp. 647-48.)

"Parley P. Pratt was reared to hard work on a farm, and though his opportunities for acquiring an education were extremely limited, he was brought up in the strictest school of morals. Even in early youth he gave evidence of a profoundly religious nature, and while yet in his teens became identified with the Baptist church. In 1826 he left New York state and settled some thirty miles west of the town of Cleveland, in the state of Ohio, and laid the foundation of a wilderness home. The next year, 1827, he returned to Canaan, Columbia county, New York,—the county where much of his boyhood was spent, the home, too, of his parents—and there married Thankful Halsey, on the 9th of September, 1827. The same month the newly married couple returned to the wilderness home west of Cleveland. About eighteen months later Sidney Rigdon, who was connected with Alexander Campbell, Walter Scott and others in that aggressive reform movement among the Christian sects, which resulted in the founding of the sect of the 'Disciples' or 'Campbellites,' came into Mr. Pratt's neighborhood preaching the doctrines of faith, repentance and baptism. As his doctrine more nearly conformed to the scriptures than any other Mr. Pratt had heard, he accepted Sydney Rigdon's teachings, joined the 'Disciples,' and became a minister in that church. He determined to take up the ministry as his life's labor, sold his possessions and started first of all to call upon his relatives in New York. En route, however, he was moved upon by the spirit to stop off at Newark, in New York, while his wife continued her journey to her father's home. At Newark, Mr. Pratt first heard of and saw the Book of Mormon, and, without delay, hastened to Palmyra to investigate the story of its coming forth. At the home of the Smiths, near Manchester, he met with Hyrum, brother of the Prophet, and from him learned the particulars of the work. In company with Hyrum Smith he went to Fayette, where he met with Oliver Cowdery; and about the first of September he was baptized by him in Seneca Lake, and straightway was ordained an Elder of the Church. After these events he continued his journey to the home of his kindred in Columbia county, New York, where he baptized his brother Orson, then a youth of nineteen years. He returned to Fayette in time to attend the conference, where he met the Prophet Joseph, and received the appointment to the Lamanite mission as related in the text." (*HC* 1:119, footnote.)

Zera Pulsipher is mentioned in 124:138.

Charles C. Rich is mentioned in 124:132.

Willard Richards is mentioned in 118:6; 124:129; 135:2.

Second counselor to Brigham Young, 1847-54. Born June 24, 1804, in Massachusetts, a son of Joseph Richards and Rhoda Howe. Practiced medicine in Boston during summer of 1835, when he first heard of and saw the Book of Mormon. Before reading half a page, he declared, "God or the devil has had a hand in that book, for man never wrote it." Converted by the Book of Mormon and baptized Dec. 31, 1836, by Brigham Young. Ordained an elder Mar. 6, 1837, and ordained one of the Twelve Apostles Apr. 14, 1840, by Brigham Young in England. Made second counselor in First Presidency Dec. 27, 1847. Served several missions both in the United States and abroad. Present in Carthage jail at time of the deaths of Joseph and Hyrum Smith. Helped in publication of many Church tracts and periodicals; served as editor of *Deseret News.* During the Utah period, served in several civic positions as well as Church Historian and second counselor to Brigham Young. Died Mar. 11, 1854, at Salt Lake City. (Additional information in *BE* 1:53-56; *ECH*—check index, p. 649.)

Sidney Rigdon is mentioned in 36:2, 5; 41:8; 42:4; 52:3, 24, 41; 53:5; 58:50, 57-58; 60:17; 61:23, 30; 63:55, 65; 70:1; 71:1; 73:3; 76:11; 78:9; 82:11; 90:6, 21; 93:44, 51; 102:3; 103:29, 38; 104:20, 22; 115:1; 124:126.

First counselor to Joseph Smith from 1833-44. Born Feb. 19, 1793, in Pennsylvania, youngest son of William and Nancy Rigdon. A leader in the Campbellite movement. Converted through reading the Book of Mormon; baptized Nov. 14, 1830. Met the Prophet Joseph Smith for first time in December 1830. Served several missions for the Church and took charge of affairs in Kirtland while the Prophet participated in Zion's Camp. Ordained high priest in June 1831. Dedicated land of Zion in July 1831. Chosen as a counselor to Joseph Smith Mar. 18, 1833. During the Nauvoo period, elected as a member of the city council. Accused of being associated with the plans of John C. Bennett against Joseph Smith. At general conference in October 1843, was rejected by Joseph Smith as his counselor, but retained office through intervention of Hyrum Smith. Moved to Pittsburgh, Pa., where he was living at the time of the death of Joseph Smith. Returned to Nauvoo to claim the "guardianship" of the Church, but in a meeting Aug. 8, 1844, was rejected by those who recognized the Twelve Apostles as the head of the Church. Tried before high council Sept. 8, 1844, which resulted in his excommunication. Died July 14, 1876, in New York. (Additional information in *BE* 1:31-34; *ECH*—check index, p. 649.)

"Sidney Rigdon . . . became noted in Church history. . . . At the age of 25 years he joined a Baptist church. In 1819 he obtained a license as a minister, and a couple of years later he received a call to take charge of a church at Pittsburg, Pa. While engaged in this ministry, he became convinced that some of the doctrines of the Baptists were not Scriptural, and he resigned his position and joined his brother-in-law in the tanning business. At this time he became acquainted with Alexander Campbell, the reputed founder of the church known as 'Disciples,' or 'Campbellites,' and with one Mr. Walter Scott, and these three started that religious movement. . . .

"In the fall of 1830, Parley P. Pratt, Ziba Peterson, Oliver Cowdery, and Peter Whitmer, Jr., who were on their mission to the Lamanites, called at the house of Sidney Rigdon, and Parley P. Pratt, who knew him, presented him a copy of the Book of Mormon and related its story. He believed and was baptized, as were many members of his church in that vicinity. Sidney Rigdon and Edward Partridge shortly afterwards went to Fayette for the purpose of visiting the Prophet and learning something about the will of God concerning them.

"Sidney Rigdon accompanied the Prophet to Ohio, visited Missouri, suffered persecution at Hiram, Ohio, received wonderful manifestations in Kirtland, labored as counselor in the First Presidency, visited Canada and the Eastern States, shared prison at Liberty with the Prophet, went to Washington on behalf of the persecuted Saints, and assisted in building up the Church. Unfortunately, he did not endure to the end. . . .

"After the death of the Prophet he aspired to the leadership of the Church and refused to submit to the decision of the Apostles, which had been sustained by the people, and because he continued his agitation he was excommunicated." (Smith and Sjodahl, *DCC,* p. 181.)

"At the conference of the Church held in October, 1843, the matter of Sidney Rigdon's loyalty again came up. The Prophet expressed his dissatisfaction with Sidney Rigdon and said he had never magnified his office as a counselor since his escape from Missouri. Sidney Rigdon spoke in his own defense as did also Elder Almon B. Babbitt and William Law. On motion by William Marks, president of the Nauvoo Stake of Zion, seconded by Patriarch Hyrum Smith, Sidney Rigdon was permitted to retain his standing as a counselor to President Joseph Smith in the First Presidency. After this action was taken, the Prophet arose and said, 'I have thrown him off my shoulders, and you have again put him on me. You may carry him, but I will not.' " (Joseph Fielding Smith, *CHMR* 2:375.)

Burr Riggs is mentioned in 75:17.
Samuel Rolfe is mentioned in 124:142.
Shadrach Roundy is mentioned in 124:141.
Simonds Ryder is mentioned in 52:37.
Jacob Scott is mentioned in 52:28.
Lyman Sherman is mentioned in 108:1.
Henry G. Sherwood is mentioned in 124:81, 132.
Don C. Smith is mentioned in 124:133.
Eden Smith is mentioned in 75:36; 80:2.
Emma Smith is mentioned in 25:1; 132:51-52, 54.

First Relief Society president. Born July 10, 1804, in Pennsylvania, a daughter of Isaac Hale. First met the Prophet Joseph Smith in 1826; was married to him Jan. 18, 1827. Accepted religious experiences of her husband; was baptized by Oliver Cowdery in June 1830. Called an "elect lady" in a revelation to the Prophet (D&C 25) given July 1830, and instructed to prepare a collection of hymns for the Church. Chosen head of the "Female Relief Society of the Church" Mar. 17, 1842. After the death of the Prophet and expulsion of the Saints from Nauvoo in 1846, she chose to remain in Nauvoo, where she married Lewis C. Bidamon Dec. 23, 1847. Died in Nauvoo Apr. 30, 1879. (Additional information in *BE* 1:692-93; *ECH,* pp. 91, 123, 269, 308.)

"I have never seen a woman in my life, who could endure every species of fatigue and hardship, from month to month, and from year to year, with that unflinching courage, zeal, and patience, which she has ever done; for I know that which she has had to endure. . . . She has breasted the storms of persecution, and buffeted the rage of men and devils, which would have borne down almost any other woman." (Lucy Mack Smith, *History of Joseph Smith,* pp. 190-91.)

George A. Smith is mentioned in 124:129; 136:14.

First counselor to Brigham Young, 1868-75. Born June 26, 1817, in New York a son of John Smith and Clarissa Lyman. Cousin to Joseph the prophet. Baptized Sept. 10, 1832. Participated in Zion's Camp. Ordained a seventy Mar. 1, 1835. Junior member of the First Quorum of Seventy. Received endowments in Kirtland Temple in spring of 1836. Set apart as high councilor June 28, 1838, in Missouri. Served several missions, traveling thousands of miles. Had five wives during polygamy period. Took charge of much of the emigration from Council Bluffs. Talked at first meeting in Salt Lake

Valley. Held several positions in government during Utah Territory period. Became Church Historian Apr. 7, 1854, and was released from this position Oct. 8, 1870. Sustained as first counselor to President Brigham Young Oct. 6, 1868. Helped in establishment of colonies in southern Utah; St. George was named in his honor. Visited Jerusalem 1872-73. Died Sept. 1, 1875, at Salt Lake City. Brigham Young said he was a wise counselor and a great preacher. (Additional information in *BE* 1:37-42; *ECH*—check index, p. 650.)

Hyrum Smith is mentioned in 23:3; 52:8; 75:32; 94:13; 103:39; 115:1; 124:15, 124; 135:1, 6.

Second counselor to Joseph Smith, 1837-41; second Patriarch to the Church. Born Feb. 9, 1800, in Vermont, second son of Joseph Smith, Sr., and Lucy Mack. An early and strong believer in the religious experiences of his brother; was baptized in June 1829. Privileged to be one of the eight witnesses who viewed the plates from which the Book of Mormon was translated. Ordained a high priest Aug. 28, 1831. Called to be Assistant President of the High Priesthood Dec. 5, 1834. Appointed second counselor to Joseph Smith Nov. 7, 1837, upon rejection of Frederick G. Williams by the Church. On Jan. 19, 1841, was called by revelation to take office of Presiding Patriarch, replacing his deceased father; on Jan. 24, 1841, was made Assistant President and appointed a prophet, seer, and revelator. Imprisoned with the Prophet at Far West, at Liberty, and finally at Carthage, where he was killed June 27, 1844. On Jan. 19, 1841, the Lord said of Hyrum Smith, "I, the Lord, love him because of the integrity of his heart, and because he loveth that which is right before me." (D&C 124:15.) (Additional information in *BE* 1:52-53; *ECH*—check index, p. 650.)

"No mortal man who ever lived in this Church desired more to do good than did Hyrum Smith, the patriarch. I have it from the lips of my own sainted mother, that of all the men she was acquainted with in her girlhood days in Nauvoo, she admired Hyrum Smith the most for his absolute integrity and devotion to God, and his loyalty to the prophet of God." (Heber J. Grant, *CR*, October 1920, p. 84.)

Between Joseph and Hyrum there was a sacred bond of genuine friendship, unselfish and tender; a friendship of that pure quality of which there are but few instances on record. We may recall the beautiful story of David and Jonathan, or, that of Damon and Pythias; the friendship between Joseph and Hyrum was all that those names stand for, and, in addition, the sympathy engendered by natural affection, and made sacred by a common interest in the salvation of their fellow men. Hyrum watched tenderly over Joseph. He was a peacemaker. He was faithful to death, and shared the martyr wreath with his illustrious, younger brother.

"The following sentiment was expressed by the Prophet Joseph on the 11th of August, 1842:

" 'Brother Hyrum, what a faithful heart you have got! Oh, may the Eternal Jehovah crown eternal blessings upon your head, as a reward for the care you have had for my soul! O how many are the sorrows we have shared together; and again we find ourselves shackled with the unrelenting hand of oppression. Hyrum, thy name shall be written in the *Book of the Law of the Lord,* for those who come after thee to look upon, that they may pattern after thy works.' (*HC* 5:107-108.)

" . . . Like Abraham, Hyrum Smith was a Patriarch, and as such he was a great man; but he was greater still as 'the friend of God.' " (Smith and Sjodahl, *DCC,* p. 61.)

John Smith is mentioned in 102:3, 34.

Joseph Smith, Jr., is mentioned in 1:17, 29; 5:1, 2, 25; 9:1; 17:4, 5; 18:7; 19:13; 20:2; 25:5; 27:8; 28:2; 30:7; 31:4; 36:5; 41:7; 42:4; 43:12; 52:3, 24, 41; 55:2; 56:12; 58:58; 60:17; 61:23, 30; 63:41, 65; 64:5; 67:5, 14; 70:1; 71:1; 73:3; 76:11; 78:1, 9; 81:1; 82:11; 84:1, 3; 93:45, 47, 52; 102:1, 3; 103:21, 22, 35, 37, 40; 104:26, 43, 45-46; 105:27; 109:68; 124:1, 16; 127:12; 135:1, 3, 6; 136:37.

Prophet of the dispensation of the Fulness of Times. Born Dec. 23, 1805, in Vermont, a son of Joseph Smith, Sr., and Lucy Mack. Had first vision in the spring of 1820; visited by the Angel Moroni Sept. 21, 1823; translated the Book of Mormon; received the Aaronic Priesthood from John the Baptist May 15, 1829; received the Melchizedek Priesthood from Peter, James, and John; organized the Church April 6, 1830, serving as its First Elder and later as its President. Later had visions of the Savior, Moses, Elias, and Elijah. Receiver of most of the revelations in the Doctrine and Covenants. A prophet, seer, and revelator. Killed June 27, 1844. (Additional information in *BE* 1:1-8; *ECH,* see index pp. 650-51.)

"Joseph Smith did more for the salvation of men in this world than anyone else who ever lived in it, with the sole exception of our Lord and Savior—our Redeemer, Jesus Christ, the divine Son of God.

"Joseph was the instrument through whom the true Church and kingdom of God were again restored to earth. He brought forth the Book of Mormon, which he translated by the gift and power of God. He was the means of having it published in his own day on two continents. He sent the everlasting gospel, now restored, to the four quarters of the earth.

"He received numerous revelations from the Lord, which have been published in the Doctrine and Covenants, the Pearl of Great Price, and our Church history. He gathered thousands of Latter-day Saints from abroad to establish a great city at Nauvoo, Illinois, with shops and fertile farms, churches, schools, and a university. He projected the westward migration of the Latter-day Saints and the settlement of the Great Basin, a work carried out later by his legal successor, President Brigham Young.

"He lived great, and he died great, a martyr to the cause of Christ; and, like most of the Lord's anointed in ancient times, he sealed his mission and his testimony with his life's blood. (See D&C 135:3.)

"He left a name and a fame that will never die, and as the years roll on and the Church continues taking the gospel to every nation, kindred, tongue, and people, his name will be magnified even further, honored and blessed by the millions of faithful who come to know how truly great his calling really was. He was foreordained in heaven to this mighty work in latter days. He fulfilled his mission with honor and inspiration, a beacon to all who follow him, giving glory always to God on high, for whom he labored." (Mark E. Petersen, *Ensign,* November 1977, p. 11.)

"As to this man, Joseph Smith, let us say—

"Here is a man who was chosen before he was born, who was numbered with the noble and great in the councils of eternity before the foundations of this world were laid.

"Along with Adam and Enoch and Noah and Abraham, he sat in council with the Gods when the plans were made to create an earth whereon the hosts of our Father's children might dwell. Under the direction of the Holy One and of

Michael, who became the first man, he participated in the creative enterprises of the Father.

"In his premortal state he grew in light and knowledge and intelligence, attained a spiritual stature which few could equal, and was then foreordained to preside over the greatest of all gospel dispensations.

"Here is a man who was called of God as were the prophets of old. Born among mortals with the talents and spiritual capacity earned in preexistence, he was ready at the appointed time to perform the work to which he had been foreordained.

"In the spring of 1820 the Supreme Rulers of the universe rent the veil of darkness which for long ages had shrouded the earth. Choosing the time and the place and the person, they came down from their celestial home to a grove of trees near Palmyra, New York. Calling young Joseph by name, they then told him that pure and perfect religion was no longer found among men and that he would be the instrument in their hands of restoring the fulness of their everlasting gospel. . . .

"Here is a man who saw God and entertained angels. . . .

"Here is a man to whom the heavens were an open book, who received revelations, saw visions, and understood the deep and hidden mysteries of the kingdom by the power of the Holy Ghost. . . .

"Here is a man who has given to our present world more holy scripture than any single prophet who ever lived; indeed, he has preserved for us more of the mind and will and voice of the Lord than the total of the dozen most prolific prophetic penmen of the past.

"Here is a man who was persecuted, hounded, driven, and finally slain for the witness he bore and the testimony of Jesus that was his. . . .

"Here is a man who, like the Master, whose servant he was, cast out devils and healed the sick. . . .

"Here is a man whose greatness lies in the fact that he was a witness of that same Lord for whom his fellow prophets in days long past had laid down their lives. . . .

"Here is a man who was a prophet in the full and complete and literal sense of the word, as all who hearken to the voice of the Spirit shall know. . . .

"Here are the words of Deity, spoken to Joseph Smith, by

which all men can judge the state of their own spiritual development:

" 'The ends of the earth shall inquire after thy name, and fools shall have thee in derision, and hell shall rage against thee;

" 'While the pure in heart, and the wise, and the noble, and the virtuous, shall seek counsel, and authority, and blessings constantly from under thy hand.' (D&C 122:1-2.)

"All men may well ask themselves where they stand with reference to Joseph Smith and his divine mission. Do they inquire after his name and seek that salvation found only in the gospel of Christ as revealed to his latter-day prophet, or do they deride and despise the Lord's living oracles and say that God no longer speaks to men in the way he did anciently? The great question which all men in our day must answer—and that at the peril of their own salvation—is: Was Joseph Smith called of God?

"As for me and my house, we shall seek counsel and authority and blessing constantly from him and from those who now wear his prophetic mantle." (Bruce R. McConkie, *Ensign,* May 1976, pp. 94-97.)

"The story of Joseph's life is the story of a miracle. He was born in poverty. He was reared in adversity. He was driven from place to place, falsely accused, and illegally imprisoned. He was murdered at the age of thirty-eight. Yet in the brief space of twenty years preceding his death he accomplished what none other has accomplished in an entire lifetime. He translated and published the Book of Mormon, a volume of 522 pages which has since been retranslated into more than a score of languages and which is accepted by millions across the earth as the word of God. The revelations he received and other writings he produced are likewise scriptures to these millions. The total in book pages constitutes the equivalent of almost the entire Old Testament of the Bible, and it all came through one man in the space of a few years." (Gordon B. Hinckley, *Ensign,* May 1977, p. 65.)

Joseph Smith, Sr., is mentioned in 23:5; 90:20, 25; 102:3, 34; 124:19.

One of eight special witnesses of the Book of Mormon; served as first patriarch of the Church. Born July 12, 1771, in Massachusetts, the second son of Asael Smith and Mary Duty. On Jan. 24, 1796, married Lucy Mack by whom he had ten children. First person to receive Joseph's testimony of the Angel Moroni. Baptized Apr. 6, 1830, the day the Church was organized. Later served a mission and was instrumental in the conversion of his father, brothers, and sisters. Ordained to "High Priesthood" June 3, 1831. Ordained patriarch Dec. 18, 1833, and made an assistant counselor to Joseph Smith, Jr., in "the Presidency of the High Priesthood." Member of the first high council organized in Kirtland Feb. 17, 1834. Sustained as assistant counselor in the First Presidency Sept. 3, 1837. One of the founders of Nauvoo. Very benevolent, opening his house to all who were destitute. (See D&C 90:25.) Died Sept. 14, 1840. (Additional information in *BE* 1:181-82; *ECH*—check index, p. 651.)

"The Patriarch Joseph Smith, also a victim of Missouri persecution, died in Nauvoo, September 14, 1840. He was the first person to accept the Prophet's story. . . . During the persecutions in Kirtland he was made a prisoner by the apostate enemies of the Church, but gained his liberty and made his way to Far West in 1838. He was driven from Missouri by the exterminating order of Lilburn W. Boggs in the winter of 1838-9. He went to Quincy and later in the spring of 1839 to Commerce where he made his home. He was six feet two inches tall and weighed in perfect health about 200 pounds. His sufferings in Missouri and the exposure brought him to his grave. (*HC* 4:189-97.)" (Joseph Fielding Smith, *CHMR* 2:254.)

Samuel H. Smith is mentioned in 23:4; 52:30; 61:35; 66:8; 75:13; 102:3, 34; 124:141.

One of eight witnesses to the Book of Mormon; baptized May 25, 1829, the third person baptized in this dispensation. Born Mar. 13, 1808, in Vermont, the fourth son of Joseph Smith, Sr., and Lucy Mack. When shown part of the Book of Mormon that was translated, he prayed to the Lord and received a revelation sufficient to his being converted. One of six charter members of the Church on Apr. 6, 1830; ordained to the priesthood that same day. In a subsequent mission, left a copy of the Book of Mormon at the home of John P. Greene; it was reported that Heber C. Kimball and others were later converted by reading this copy. Ordained a high priest June 3, 1831, and subsequently served several missions. Was set apart to first high council of Kirtland Feb.

17, 1834. Became ill shortly after death of his brethren, Joseph and Hyrum, and died July 30, 1844. (Additional information in *BE* 1:278-82; *ECH*—check index, p. 652.)

"Samuel H. Smith had some wonderful experiences. After the engagement with a mob, known as the Crooked River battle, he went to Illinois, in company with about twenty others, through a wild part of the country. They were pursued by fifty well-armed men, who had orders to bring them back, dead or alive. Soon only four miles of prairie lay between them and their pursuers. Then a snowstorm came, with such a fury that they were completely hidden from the enemy, and escaped. Later on, their provisions gave out, and they subsisted on lynne buds and slippery elm bark. One evening the company appointed Samuel H. Smith their president, and prayed to the Lord for a revelation. That night the Spirit of the Lord came upon him, and he said: 'Thus saith the Lord; my servant Joseph is not injured, nor any of his brethren that are with him; but they will all be delivered out of the hands of their enemies; your families are all well, but anxious about you. Let your hearts be comforted, for I, the Lord, will provide food for you on the morrow.' This Revelation proved true in every detail. The next day they came upon an Indian camp, where they received a supply of good bread (*Historical Record,* p. 618). On his deathbed Joseph Smith, Sr., gave his son Samuel this blessing:

" 'Samuel, you have been a faithful and obedient son. By your faithfulness you have brought many into the Church. The Lord has seen your diligence, and you are blessed, in that He has never chastised you, but has called you home to rest; and there is a crown laid up for you, which shall grow brighter and brighter unto the perfect day.' " (Smith and Sjodahl, *DCC,* p. 121.)

Sylvester Smith is mentioned in 75:34; 102:3, 34.

Member of first high council chosen Feb. 17, 1834. Chosen and ordained one of the first Seven Presidents of the Seventy Feb. 28, 1835; released from this position Apr. 6, 1837, as he had previously been ordained a high priest. In August 1835, was appointed one of the clerks of the conference at which the revelations were accepted to be placed in the Doctrine and Covenants. In 1837, joined with Luke S. Johnson and others in opposing the Prophet. (Additional information in *ECH,* pp. 142, 152, 154, 167.)

"Sylvester Smith was a member of Zion's Camp, but it appears that his heart was not right at that time, for on one occasion he was in open rebellion and was severely rebuked. On the 28th of August, 1834, he appeared before the High Council in Kirtland to answer to a charge of violation of the laws of the Church, and more especially for having circulated false rumors about the conduct of the Prophet during the journey of Zion's Camp. The Council found that the charge had been proved, and ordered him to sign an acknowledgment of his error. He did so, though not in a spirit of humility. Later, however, he sent a communication to the *Messenger and Advocate* in which he vindicated the Prophet completely and humbly confessed his own fault. (*HC* 2:160.)" (Smith and Sjodahl, *DCC,* p. 439.)

William Smith is mentioned in 124:129.

Erastus Snow is mentioned in 136:12.

Daniel Stanton is mentioned in 75:33.

Northrop Sweet is mentioned in 33:1.

John Taylor is mentioned in 118:6; 124:129; 135:2.

Third President of the Church. Born Nov. 1, 1808, in England, a son of James and Agnes Taylor. Came to Canada in 1826. Baptized 1836 and ordained an elder shortly thereafter. Ordained a high priest in 1837. During apostasy of the Kirtland period, he stood firm in defending the Prophet Joseph Smith. Sustained by the Church as an apostle Oct. 5, 1838, and ordained Dec. 19, 1838, by Brigham Young. Served several missions at home and abroad and edited many Church periodicals, including *Times and Seasons.* Present in the Carthage jail at the time of the death of the Prophet, when he was severely injured. Served several missions, including England and France. Held several civic positions during the Utah period, including Speaker of the House of Representatives. Sustained as president of the Council of Twelve Apostles Oct. 6, 1877, and sustained President of the Church Oct. 10, 1880. During the persecution of polygamists, he spent much of his time in exile. Author of many hymns and poems. Died July 25, 1887 at Kaysville, Utah. (Additional information in *BE* 1:14-19; *ECH*—check index, p. 653.)

Ezra Thayre is mentioned in 33:1; 52:22; 56:5, 8; 75:31.

An early convert to the Church. With Northrop Sweet, received a revelation (D&C 33) from the Lord through Joseph Smith in October 1830, in which he was commanded to preach the gospel unto "a crooked and perverse generation."

"We have very little history of Ezra Thayre. For a number of years he faithfully performed his labors, although he had to be rebuked on at least one occasion. He was among the number first ordained to the office of High Priest at the conference of the Church in June 1831, and a few days later he was called to accompany Thomas B. Marsh on the journey to Missouri, where the Lord said the next conference of the Church was to be held. (D&C 52:22.) Later in the same month this commandment was revoked and Ezra Thayre was commanded to repent of his pride and of his selfishness, and obey the former commandment which the Lord had given him concerning the place on which he lived. Evidently, through his pride and selfishness he was not to be privileged to go to Missouri with the other brethren, and he was promised that this ban might be lifted providing he would turn from his evil ways. It appears that he was associated with the Colesville Branch while they were located in Ohio. He had paid his money, but had not divested himself of all his selfishness. The Lord informed him that if he did not repent he should receive his money 'and shall leave the place, and be cut off out of my church.' Evidently he repented and, at a conference held at Amherst, Ohio, January 25, 1832, he was appointed to travel with Thomas B. Marsh. (D&C 75:31.) He was a member of Zion's Camp and made the journey with that body to Missouri. On the return of that camp, he was chosen among those worthy to be ordained to the office of Seventy, February 28, 1835. (*HC* 2:185.)" (Joseph Fielding Smith, *CHMR* 1:152-53.)

Robert B. Thompson is mentioned in 124:12.

Joseph Wakefield is mentioned in 50:37; 52:35.

Micah B. Welton is mentioned in 75:36.

Harvey Whitlock is mentioned in 52:25.

David Whitmer is mentioned in 18:9, 37; 52:25.

One of Three Witnesses to the Book of Mormon. Born Jan. 7, 1805, in Pennsylvania. First heard of Mormonism in 1828 and became well acquainted with the Prophet during latter part of translation of the Book of Mormon (1829). He and his brothers received several revelations through the Prophet (D&C 14, 15, and 16). Baptized in June 1829 by Joseph Smith, and privileged shortly thereafter to see the plates of the Book of Mormon. One of charter members of the Church on Apr. 6, 1830. Ordained a high priest Oct. 25, 1831, by Oliver Cowdery, and soon thereafter moved to Jackson County, Missouri. Appointed president of the high council in Clay County July 3, 1834, and later sustained as president of the Saints in Missouri. Members withdrew the hand of fellowship from him in a conference held Feb. 4, 1838, and on Apr. 13, 1838, he was tried by a high council in Far West and was excommunicated. Continued to live in Missouri for the remainder of his life. Never denied his testimony of the Book of Mormon. Died Jan. 25, 1888. (Additional information in *BE* 1:263-71; *ECH*—check index, p. 654.)

"David Whitmer relates the following: 'Soon after this [the arrival of a letter from Oliver Cowdery] Joseph sent for me to come to Harmony to get him and Oliver, to bring them to my father's house. I did not know what to do. I was pressed with my work. I had some twenty acres to plow, so I concluded I would finish plowing and then go. I got up one morning to go to work as usual, and on going to the field, found between 5 and 7 acres of my ground had been plowed during the night. I do not know who did it, but it was done just as I would have done it myself, and the plow was left standing in the furrow.'

"This incident was related to Orson Pratt and Joseph F. Smith by David Whitmer, on the 7th of September, 1878, forty years after he had left the Church. It was to him a miraculous evidence, the force of which he never denied." (Smith and Sjodahl, *DCC*, p. 73.)

John Whitmer is mentioned in 69:2, 7; 70:1.

One of the eight witnesses to the Book of Mormon. Born Aug. 27, 1802, the third son of Peter Whitmer and Mary Musselman. Baptized in June 1829 by Oliver Cowdery. Served as scribe for Joseph Smith during translation of the Book of Mormon. Received revelation through the Prophet (D&C 15) and was present when the revelation concerning the sacrament was given (D&C 27). Called by revelation (D&C 30) in September 1830 to serve a mission. Chosen by revelation (D&C 47) Mar. 8, 1831, to serve as historian for the Church. Ordained a high priest June 3, 1831. Called in November 1831 by revelation (D&C 69) to accompany

Oliver Cowdery to Missouri. With others, offered himself as ransom for the Church during Missouri persecutions. Called July 3, 1834, to serve as one of the assistant presidents of the Church in Missouri, his brother David being called as president. Present at the Kirtland Temple dedication. Brought for trial before a Church group Nov. 7, 1837, but made confession. Excommunicated from the Church Mar. 10, 1838, and took with him the records he had kept as historian. Died July 11, 1878, at Far West, Missouri. (Additional information in *BE* 1:251-52; *ECH*—check index, p. 654.)

"He assisted Joseph as secretary; accompanied him to Colesville, where a Branch was organized; was Church historian; went with Oliver Cowdery to Jackson County, in 1831, to direct the publication of the *Book of Commandments,* and he was one of the Eight Witnesses to the Book of Mormon. But he did not remain faithful. He was excommunicated by the High Council at Far West, 1838, the charge being that he, together with David Whitmer and W. W. Phelps, had failed to account properly for $2,000 of the funds of the Church. He did not return to the Church, but he always maintained that his testimony concerning the Book of Mormon was true." (Smith and Sjodahl, *DCC,* p. 74.)

Peter Whitmer, Jr., is mentioned in 32:2.

One of eight witnesses to the Book of Mormon. Born Sept. 27, 1809, in New York, the fifth son of Peter Whitmer, Sr., and Mary Musselman. Zealous friend of the Prophet. Received a revelation in June 1829 (D&C 16). Baptized about that same time by Oliver Cowdery. One of the charter members of the Church on Apr. 6, 1830. Called in later revelations (D&C 30 and 32) to do missionary work. Ordained a high priest Oct. 25, 1831, by Oliver Cowdery. Died Sept. 27, 1836. (Additional information in *BE* 1:277; *ECH,* pp. 60, 66, 79, 96.)

"He was less than twenty years of age when he was baptized by Oliver Cowdery. In September, 1830, he was called by revelation (Sec. 30) to preach the Gospel, together with Oliver Cowdery, and the following month he was chosen by revelation to accompany Parley P. Pratt, Oliver Cowdery and Ziba Peterson on a mission to the Lamanites. (D&C 32.) A journey to Jackson County in those days was a difficult task . . . it is about the same distance as the Pioneers traveled from Winter Quarters to the Salt Lake Valley in 1847, and this was through a sparsely settled country. Peter Whitmer took an active part with the Saints in Missouri. . . . He suffered with the Saints in the persecutions and drivings in 1833, and found a temporary home in Clay County. Due to the persecutions and hardships, he took sick and died on a small farm about two miles from Liberty, Missouri, September 22, 1836, and was buried by the side of his brother Christian, who also fell a victim to mobocracy about ten months previous to the death of Peter Whitmer Jr." (Joseph Fielding Smith, *CHMR* 1:70.)

Newel K. Whitney is mentioned in 63:42; 64:26; 72:8; 78:9; 82:11; 84:112; 93:50; 96:2; 104:39-41; 117:1, 11.

Second Presiding Bishop of the Church. Born Feb. 5, 1796, in Vermont, a son of Samuel Whitney and Susanna Kimball. First met the Prophet in February 1831, after being baptized the previous November. Called by revelation (D&C 72) Dec. 4, 1831, to be a bishop to the Church in Kirtland. Presided at the trial of Sidney Rigdon in Aug. 1844. Sustained as First Bishop in the Church Oct. 7, 1844. Sustained as Presiding Bishop of the Church Apr. 6, 1847. Died Sept. 23, 1850, at Salt Lake City. (Additional information in *BE* 1:222-27; *ECH,* pp. 122, 322, 358, 402.)

"A natural business man, he made his own way in the world, and after figuring as a sutler during the war of 1812, and taking part in the battle of Plattsburgh, near Lake Champlain, he established himself as an Indian trader at Green Bay, Lake Michigan. He next settled in Ohio, where he made the acquaintance of Algernon Sidney Gilbert, a merchant of Painesville, whose partner he became in the successful firm of Gilbert and Whitney at Kirtland. In October, 1822, he married Elizabeth Ann Smith, a young lady from Connecticut, who is known in Church history as 'Mother Whitney.' When Oliver Cowdery and his fellow missionaries came to Kirtland, en route to Missouri, the Whitneys were Campbellites, members of Sidney Rigdon's flock, but upon hearing the fulness of the Gospel as preached by those Elders, they embraced it. In the Whitney family folk lore the incident of the Prophet's arrival at Kirtland is thus related: 'About the first of February, 1831, a sleigh containing four persons drove through the streets of Kirtland and drew up in front of the store of Gilbert and

Whitney. One of the men, a young and stalwart personage alighted, and springing up the steps walked into the store and to where the junior partner was standing. "Newel K. Whitney! Thou art the man!" he exclaimed, extending his hand cordially, as if to an old and familiar acquaintance. "You have the advantage of me," replied the merchant, as he mechanically took the proffered hand, "I could not call you by name as you have me." "I am Joseph the Prophet," said the stranger smiling. "You've prayed me here, now what do you want of me?" ' The Prophet, it is said, while in the East had seen the Whitneys, in vision, praying for his coming to Kirtland. 'Mother Whitney' also tells how on a certain night prior to the advent of Elder Cowdery and his companions, while she and her husband were praying to the Lord to know how they might obtain the gift of the Holy Ghost, which of all things they desired, they saw a vision as of a cloud of glory resting upon their house, and heard a voice from heaven saying, 'Prepare to receive the word of the Lord, for it is coming.' Shortly afterwards Oliver Cowdery and his associates came with the Book of Mormon, and with the message of the restored Gospel. Moreover, in further fulfilment of this vision, under the rooftree of the Whitneys the Prophet received a number of revelations contained in this volume." (*HC* 1:145-46, footnote.)

Lyman Wight is mentioned in 52:7, 12; 103:30, 38; 124:18, 62, 70.

Member of Council of Twelve Apostles 1841-49. Born May 9, 1796, in New York, a son of Levi Wight and Sarah Corbin. Baptized in 1830 by Oliver Cowdery, and ordained an elder shortly thereafter. Ordained a high priest at conference held in Kirtland in June 1831; during that conference, he testified he had seen a vision of the Savior. Called by revelation to go to Missouri in 1831. Valiant defender of the Saints during the Missouri persecution period. Joined Zion's Camp at Salt River June 8, 1834, walking from Michigan to Missouri. Ordained to high council of Missouri July 3, 1834. Received endowments in Kirtland during winter of 1835-36. Tried before high council court at Far West April 24, 1837, where he confessed. Chosen June 28, 1838, as second counselor to John Smith, who was serving as president of the stake at Adam-ondi-Ahman. Served in Jackson County prison with Joseph, Hyrum, and others, where they were offered human flesh for food. Appointed in April 1841 to fill vacancy among the Twelve Apostles caused by death of David W. Patten; ordained an apostle Apr. 8, 1841, by Joseph Smith. Upon the death of Joseph Smith, he rebelled against the authority of Brigham Young and went to Texas with a small group of Saints, where he remained until his death Mar. 31, 1858. Previously, at a meeting at the "Great Salt Lake City fort" on Dec. 3, 1848, fellowship in the Church was withdrawn from him. (Additional information in *BE* 1:93-96; *ECH*—check index, p. 654.)

"Lyman Wight was a peculiar character. At times his faith seemed strong enough to move mountains. After the Saints were driven out of Jackson County, into Clay County, volunteers were called for to go to Kirtland to report the situation to the Prophet. Several Elders excused themselves. Lyman Wight volunteered. Asked what the circumstances were in which his family would be placed, he told the Bishop that his wife had been placed by the side of a log in the woods, for shelter, and that she had a child three days old. They had provisions for three days. Under such circumstances he went on a mission to Kirtland, in company with Parley P. Pratt.

"On one occasion he was offered any office in the State he would name, if he would swear to a testimony against Joseph Smith. If you do not do it, the tempter added, you will be shot tomorrow at 8 o'clock. Wight replied, 'General, you are entirely mistaken in your man, both in regard to myself and Joseph Smith. Joseph Smith is not an enemy to mankind; he is not your enemy, and is as good a friend as you have got. Had it not been for him, you would have been in hell long ago, for I should have sent you there, and no other man than Joseph Smith could have prevented me, and you may thank him for your life. And now, if you will give me the boys I brought from Diahman yesterday, I will whip your whole army.' General Wilson said, 'Wight, you are a strange man; but if you will not accept my proposal, you will be shot tomorrow morning at eight.' Wight only made the characteristic reply that has become famous, 'Shoot and be damned.' " (Smith and Sjodahl, *DCC*, p. 311.)

Frederick G. Williams is mentioned in 64:21; 81:1; 90:6, 19; 92:1, 2; 93:41, 52; 102:3; 103:39; 104:27, 29.

Second counselor to Joseph Smith 1833-37. Born Oct. 28,

1787, in Connecticut, a son of William Wheeler Williams and Ruth Zodack. Baptized Oct. 18, 1830. By revelation (D&C 90:6), was ordained and set apart as second counselor in the First Presidency by Joseph Smith Mar. 18, 1833. Part of Zion's Camp. Participated in several short missions for the Church. Privileged to see an angel during dedication of Kirtland Temple, but shortly thereafter failed to carry out his responsibilities and was rejected as a counselor in the First Presidency at a conference held at Far West, Missouri, Nov. 7, 1837. Excommunicated Mar. 17, 1839, but at general conference in April 1840 at Nauvoo asked forgiveness and was rebaptized. Died at Quincy, Illinois, a faithful member of the Church, in October 1842. (Additional information in *BE* 1:51-52; *ECH*—check index, p. 654.)

"Elder Williams was a zealous worker during the first years of the Church's history in Ohio, but later became exceedingly rebellious and was rejected as a counselor in the First Presidency, at a conference held at Far West, Nov. 7, 1837. He was excommunicated March 17, 1839.

"In April, 1840, Elder Williams presented himself before the general conference assembly and confessed his sins, and stated his desire to return to the Church. Hyrum Smith presented his case and he was freely forgiven and was baptized." (Brooks, *LDS Reference Encyclopedia* 1:517-18.)

"His [Joseph Smith, Jun.] description of Frederick G. Williams is as follows: 'Brother Frederick G. Williams is one of those men in whom I place the greatest confidence and trust, for I have found him ever full of love and brotherly kindness. He is not a man of many words, but is ever winning, because of his constant mind. He shall ever have place in my heart, and is ever entitled to my confidence. He is perfectly honest and upright, and seeks with all his heart to magnify his Presidency in the Church of Christ, but fails in many instances, in consequence of a want of confidence in himself. God grant that he may overcome all evil. Blessed be Brother Frederick, for he shall never want a friend, and his generation after him shall flourish. The Lord hath appointed him an inheritance upon the land of Zion: yea, and his head shall blossom, and he shall be as an olive branch that is bowed down with fruit. Even so. Amen.' " (Joseph Fielding Smith, *CHMR* 1:471.)

Samuel Williams is mentioned in 124:137.

Calves Wilson is mentioned in 75:15.

Dunbar Wilson is mentioned in 124:132.

Wilford Woodruff is mentioned in 118:6; 124:129; 136:13.

Fourth president of the Church. Born Mar. 1, 1807, in Connecticut, a son of Aphek Woodruff and Beulah Thompson. Baptized Dec. 31, 1833. Proved to be a faithful and diligent servant of the Church during his entire lifetime. Ordained a priest in the fall of 1834, and went on his first mission. Notified on Aug. 9, 1838, in an official communication by Thomas B. Marsh, president of the Council of the Twelve, that he had been called by revelation "to bear the apostleship and occupy a place in the Council of the Twelve." Ordained an apostle Apr. 26, 1839, by Brigham Young. Served many missions for the Church, including missions to England and Canada. Sustained as Church Historian and General Church Recorder Oct. 7, 1853. Sustained as president of the Council of the Twelve Oct. 10, 1880. Sustained as President of the Church on April 7, 1889. Issued the Manifesto in September 1890, and it was sustained by the membership of the Church the following month. Died Sept. 2, 1898. (Additional information in *BE* 1:20-26; *ECH*—check index, p. 655.)

Brigham Young is mentioned in 124:127; 126:1.

Second President of the Church. Born June 1, 1801, in Vermont, a son of John Young and Abigail Howe. Baptized Apr. 14, 1832, and ordained an elder the same day. First met Prophet Joseph Smith in fall of 1832 at which time Brigham spoke in tongues, which the Prophet said was the pure Adamic language. Later that day the Prophet told others, "The time will come when Brother Brigham will preside over this Church." Participated in Zion's Camp. Called to be one of the members of the Council of the Twelve Apostles when it was organized Feb. 14, 1835. Always faithful to the Prophet and to the Church. Led the exodus of members of the Church from Missouri to Illinois, and later from Illinois to the Great Salt Lake Valley. Sustained as president of the Council of the Twelve Apr. 14, 1840. Accepted as leader of the Church Aug. 8, 1844, in his position as President of the Council of the Twelve Apostles. Sustained as President of the Church Dec. 27, 1847. Died Aug. 29, 1877. (Additional information in *BE* 1:8-14; *ECH*—check index, p. 655.)

Joseph Young is mentioned in 124:138.